Periodization Training for Sports

Second Edition

Tudor O. Bompa, PhD

Michael C. Carrera

**HUMAN
KINETICS**

Library of Congress Cataloging-in-Publication Data

Bompa, Tudor O.
  Periodization training for sports / Tudor O. Bompa, Michael Carrera.-- 2nd ed.
    p. cm.
  Includes bibliographical references and index.
  ISBN 0-7360-5559-2 (soft cover)
  1. Periodization training. 2. Weight training. I. Carrera, Michael, 1975- II. Title.
  GV546.B546 2005
  613.7'13--dc22
                                    2004028232
  ISBN-10: 0-7360-5559-2
  ISBN-13: 978-0-7360-5559-8

The Web addresses cited in this text were current as of 11/02/04 unless otherwise noted.

Acquistions Editor: Ed McNeely
Developmental Editor: Kase Johnstun
Assistant Editor: Cory Weber
Copyeditor: Patsy Fortney
Proofreader: Jim Burns
Indexer: Betty Frizzéll
Permission Manager: Carly Breeding
Graphic Designer: Nancy Rasmus
Photo Manager: Dan Wendt
Cover Designer: Keith Blomberg
Photographer (cover and interior): © Human Kinetics
Art Manager and Illustrator: Kareema McLendon
Printer: Versa Press

Human Kinetics books are available at special discounts for bulk purchase. Special editions or book excerpts can also be created to specification. For details, contact the Special Sales Manager at Human Kinetics.

Printed in the United States of America   10 9 8 7 6 5 4 3 2

Human Kinetics
Web site: www.HumanKinetics.com

United States: Human Kinetics
P.O. Box 5076
Champaign, IL 61825-5076
800-747-4457
e-mail: humank@hkusa.com

Canada: Human Kinetics
475 Devonshire Road Unit 100
Windsor, ON N8Y 2L5
800-465-7301 (in Canada only)
e-mail: orders@hkcanada.com

Europe: Human Kinetics
107 Bradford Road
Stanningley
Leeds LS28 6AT, United Kingdom
+44 (0) 113 255 5665
e-mail: hk@hkeurope.com

Australia: Human Kinetics
57A Price Avenue
Lower Mitcham, South Australia 5062
08 8277 1555
e-mail: liaw@hkaustralia.com

New Zealand: Human Kinetics
Division of Sports Distributors NZ Ltd.
P.O. Box 300 226 Albany
North Shore City
Auckland
0064 9 448 1207
e-mail: info@humankinetics.co.nz

To my grandchildren: Karina, Corey, and Leah-Claudia
—Tudor Bompa

To Sandra and Gabriel
—Michael Carrera

Contents

Part II Program Design

Part III Periodization of Strength

Preface

The market is saturated with strength training books, most of which are very traditional and have no distinction from other strength training books. Nearly all discuss some basic physiology, describe various exercises, and suggest a few training methods. Planning is rarely discussed, and periodization (the structuring of training into phases) is seldom mentioned simply because few authors understand its importance.

The purpose of any strength training method should be to prepare athletes for competition—the ideal test of their skills, knowledge, and psychological readiness. To achieve the best results, you need a planning-periodization program, or sport- and phase-specific variations in training.

This second edition of *Periodization Training for Sports* shows how to use periodization in structuring a strength training program for athletes in various sports. It includes energy system training and specifies which training methods are best for each training phase. The phases are planned according to the competition schedule, with each having a specific goal for developing power or muscular endurance. Ultimately, the entire training program is aimed at achieving peak performance for the most important competitions of the year.

Developing the sport-specific combination of strength and power before the competitive phase is a must, because these elements form the physiological foundation of athletic performance. The key element in the *Periodization Training for Sports* method is establishing a sequence of training phases for developing power and endurance.

A major objective of this book is to demonstrate that strength training is more than just lifting weights every day. You must also be mindful of the goals of specific training phases. This edition of *Periodization Training for Sports* offers a method for reaching your training objectives for competition through the use of planning-periodization. This method is a guide for structuring strength training phases and establishing goals that normally lead to improvements in performance. This edition of this book offers an in-depth look at structuring strength training programs according to the energy system requirements of the sport. This book also challenges many methods of training and devices currently being used in sport training.

Whatever your role in sport—strength coach, sport coach, instructor, personal trainer, athlete, or college student—you will benefit from this book by increasing your knowledge of periodization training and its physiological foundation. Once you apply this easy-to-understand concept, you will know that it is the best way to organize a strength training program for improving physiological adaptation, which ultimately produces better performance. Peak performance occurs because you plan for it!

As you read this book, you will recognize the superiority of *Periodization Training for Sports* over the methods you have used in the past. In applying this unique concept to your own needs, you will learn the following:

- The simple physiological concepts that enable the development of sport-specific strength

- The abilities required for achieving performance goals for each sport, such as maximum speed, power, and muscular endurance
- The role of strength training in overall development of the physiological abilities required for reaching the highest possible level
- The concept of planning-periodization and its specific application to strength training for your sport
- The concept of energy system training and its application to strength training for your sport
- Actual methods for dividing the annual plan into strength training phases, each with specific objectives
- A discussion of questionable novel training techniques and their true application in sport training
- How to develop several types of strength in a specific sequence to guarantee reaching the highest levels of power and muscular endurance in a particular year
- How to manipulate the load, force application, and number of repetitions during a workout, as well as the loading patterns in each phase, to create the specific physiological adaptations for reaching peak performance

Part I of the book (chapters 1 through 4) reviews the main theories influencing strength training and explains that power and muscular endurance are a combined physical quality. It also explains why certain athletic movements require a certain type of strength and why simply lifting weights will not benefit your performance. A brief history of the concept of periodization is also presented.

A successful strength training program depends on your level of knowledge in strength physiology. The information in chapter 2, "How Muscles Respond to Strength Training," is presented simply so that people from all backgrounds can understand it. New to the second edition, chapter 3, "The Training of Strength and the Application of the Energy Systems," uses practical examples to illustrate the integration of strength and the predominant energy system of various sports. The broader your knowledge in this area, the easier it will be to design programs that result in the transfer of strength training benefits to sport-specific skills. Part I ends with a brief explanation of training principles and how they apply to strength training.

Part II (chapters 5 through 7) begins with a discussion of the key elements in designing a strength training program. Both short- and long-term planning, focusing mainly on weekly and annual plans, and planning-periodization are explained in detail to help you comprehend this important concept in training.

In part III, chapters 8 through 13 discuss in detail all the phases that make up periodization. For each phase, the best training methods available for taking athletes to the highest level possible are presented. Throughout chapters 8 to 12 many novel training devices and methods are questioned for their use and application in sports training. Chapter 13 underscores the importance of recovery in strength training and contains information on facilitating a faster recovery after workouts.

In *Periodization Training for Sports*, you will find a more effective, more efficient method of training: outlines for an annual plan and models for maximizing peak performance.

Acknowledgments

Together we would like to express our sincerest thanks to the entire Human Kinetics team for their hard work and dedication in assembling this second edition of the book. Special thanks to Kase D. Johnstun, developmental editor, for his patience, advice, and understanding as we worked through implementing his many suggestions that resulted in a more logical and precise book. Finally, this book is dedicated to all the hard-working coaches, exercise physiologists, trainers, and health and fitness professionals who strive to bridge the gap between the art and the science of training.

Part I

Foundations of Strength Training

Strength, Muscular Endurance, and Power in Sports

Almost all physical activities incorporate the elements of force (or strength), quickness, duration, or range of motion, or some combination of these elements. Exercises to overcome resistance are called strength exercises. Speed exercises maximize quickness and high frequency. Exercises of long distance or duration, or many repetitions (reps), are endurance exercises. Flexibility exercises maximize range of motion, whereas coordination exercises involve complex movements.

Athletes vary in their talent to perform certain exercises. Inherited, or genetic, talent in the areas of strength, speed, and endurance plays an important role in athletes' ability to reach high levels of performance; these abilities are called *dominant motor* or *biomotor* abilities. *Motor* refers to movement, and the prefix *bio* indicates the biological importance of these abilities.

Success in training and competition is not determined solely by athletes' genetic potential, however. At times, athletes who strive for perfection in training with methodical planning-periodization and determination reach the podium or help their teams win major tournaments.

Although talent is extremely important, an athlete's ability to focus on training and relax in competition can represent the difference in achievement. To move beyond inherited talent, strength, or genetic potential, an athlete must focus on physiological adaptation in training.

Five Strength Training Programs

Athletes and coaches in various sports use five main programs for strength training: bodybuilding, high-intensity training, Olympic weightlifting, power training throughout the year, and periodization of strength. The choice of strength training program will of course depend on the physiological requirements of the sport. The periodization of strength program is undoubtedly the most influential training methodology.

■ *Bodybuilding* is a very creative sport in which the bodybuilder and trainer manipulate the sets, reps, and speed of training to elicit the highest level of exhaustion followed by a period of rest and regeneration. A high degree of water retention along with adaptations in the form of muscle protein production results in increased muscle size and strength.

Bodybuilders are chiefly concerned with increased muscle size. They perform sets of 6 to 12 reps to exhaustion. With few exceptions (possibly American football and some throwing events in track and field), increased muscle size is rarely beneficial to athletic performance. Because most athletic movements are explosive, the slow speed of contraction in bodybuilding has limited positive transfer to other sports. Athletic skills are performed quickly (from 100 to 180 milliseconds), but leg extensions in bodybuilding are three times slower, at 600 milliseconds (see table 1.1). Certain bodybuilding techniques such as supersets and drop sets are used during the hypertrophy phase of training in certain sports, in which the main objective is an increase in muscle size. However, because neuromuscular adaptations are not vital to bodybuilding, very high loads with long rest periods are not employed in bodybuilding. For this reason, bodybuilding is rarely used in strength training for sports.

Table 1.1   Duration of Contact Phase

Event	Duration in milliseconds
100-meter dash (contact phase)	100-200
Long jump (takeoff)	150-180
High jump (takeoff)	150-180
Vaulting in gymnastics (takeoff)	100-120
Leg extension (bodybuilding)	600

Reprinted, by permission, from Dietmar Schmidtbleicher, 1984, *Sportliches krafttraining* (Berlin: Jung, Haltong, und Bewegung bei Menschen).

■ *High-intensity training* (HIT) requires high training loads through the year with all working sets performed to at least positive failure. Firm believers in HIT claim that strength can be achieved in 20 to 30 minutes; they disregard the high-volume strength training used in events of long, continuous duration (mid- and long-distance swimming, rowing, canoeing, and cross-country skiing). HIT programs are not organized according to the competition schedule. For sports, strength is periodized according to the physiological needs of the sport in a given phase and the date for reaching peak performance. Athletes who train using HIT will often experience very quick gains in strength, but often tend to lose their strength and endurance as the competitive season progresses. Furthermore, without the proper planning of medium- and low-intensity days, the athlete cannot properly peak for the most important competition (s) of the competitive season.

■ *Olympic weightlifting* was an important influence in the early days of strength training. Even now, many coaches and trainers use traditional Olympic weightlifting moves such as the clean and jerk and power clean despite the fact that these moves rarely work the prime movers, the muscles primarily used in specific sport skills. Because exercises that train the prime movers should always be placed at the forefront of any strength training program, coaches should closely analyze the primary movements in their sport to decide whether Olympic weightlifting exercises would be beneficial. For example, American football linemen can benefit from the lifts, but rowers and swimmers, who often use Olympic lifts as part of their strength training regimens, probably do not.

Carefully assessing the needs of Olympic weightlifting techniques is essential, especially for young athletes or athletes with no strength training background, to avoid injuries. Even highly trained athletes have reported injuries caused by exaggerated use of Olympic weightlifting skills. Olympic weightlifting is a good way to improve overall body strength and power. Chronic overuse, however, can lead to injury and diminishing returns in strength gains.

- *Power training throughout the year* is characterized by the use of explosive bounding exercises, medicine ball throws, and strength training exercises throughout the year regardless of the yearly training cycle. Some coaches and trainers, especially in track and field and certain team sports, believe that power training should be performed from the first day of training through the major championship. They theorize that if power is the dominant ability, it has to be trained throughout the year except during the transition phase (off-season). They use exercises such as bounding and implements such as medicine balls and the shot. Certainly, athletic fitness does improve through the year. The key element, however, is the athlete's *rate* of improvement throughout the year, especially from year to year, not just *whether* the athlete improves. Strength training has been shown to lead to far better results than power training, especially when periodization of strength is used. Because power is a function of maximum strength, to improve power, one must improve maximum strength. Strength training results in faster power improvement and allows athletes to reach higher levels.

- *Periodization of strength* must be based on the specific physiological requirements of the sport and must result in the development of either *power* or *muscular endurance*. Furthermore, strength training must revolve around the needs of planning-periodization for that sport and employ training methods specific to a given training phase, with the goal of reaching peak performance at the time of major competitions. All periodization of strength programs begin with a general anatomical adaptation phase that prepares the body for other phases to follow. Depending on the requirements of the sport, one or two hypertrophy or muscle-building phases may be planned. The main goal of a periodization of strength training program is to bring the athlete to the highest possible level of maximum strength so that gains in strength will become gains in power or muscular endurance. The planning of the phases is unique to each sport and depends on the athlete's physical maturity, competition schedule, and peaking dates.

The concept of periodization of strength for sports has evolved from two basic needs: (1) the need to model strength training around the yearly plan and its training phases, and (2) the need to increase the rate of power development from year to year. The first athletic experiment using periodization of strength was done with Mihaela Penes, a gold medalist in the javelin throw at the 1964 Tokyo Olympic Games. The results were presented in 1965 in Bucharest and Moscow (Bompa, 1965a, 1965b). The original periodization of strength model was then altered to suit the needs of endurance-related sports that require muscular endurance (Bompa, 1977). Periodization of strength models for both strength-power and endurance sports are discussed in this book, including training methods. The basic periodization of strength model also appears in *Periodization: Theory and Methodology of Training* (Bompa, 1999).

In 1984, Stone and O'Bryant presented a theoretical model of strength training in which periodization of strength included four phases: hypertrophy, basic strength, strength and power, and peaking and maintenance. A comprehensive book on periodization, *Periodization of Strength: The New Wave in Strength Training* (Bompa, 1993a), was followed by *Periodization Breakthrough*

(Fleck and Kraemer, 1996), which again demonstrated that periodization of strength is the most scientifically justified method for optimizing strength and sport performance.

Sport-Specific Combinations of Strength, Speed, and Endurance

Strength, speed, and endurance are the important abilities for successful athletic performance. The *dominant* ability is the one from which the sport requires a higher contribution (for instance, endurance is the dominant ability in long-distance running). Most sports require peak performance in at least two abilities. The relationships among strength, speed, and endurance create crucial physical athletic qualities. A better understanding of these relationships will help both athletes and coaches understand power and muscular endurance and plan sport-specific strength training programs.

As illustrated in figure 1.1, combining strength and endurance creates *muscular endurance*, the ability to perform many repetitions against a given resistance for a prolonged period. *Power*, the ability to perform an explosive movement in the shortest time possible, results from the integration of maximum strength and maximum speed. The combination of endurance and speed is called *speed-endurance*. *Agility* is the product of a complex combination of speed, coordination, flexibility, and power as demonstrated in gymnastics, wrestling, American football, soccer, volleyball, baseball, boxing, diving, and figure skating. *Flexibility*, or the range of motion of a joint, is very important in training. Different sports require varying degrees of flexibility to promote injury prevention and also optimal sport performance. When agility and flexibility combine, the result is *mobility*, the ability to cover a playing area quickly with good timing and coordination. Agility, the basis for all biomotor abilities, is improved through adaptations in maximum strength.

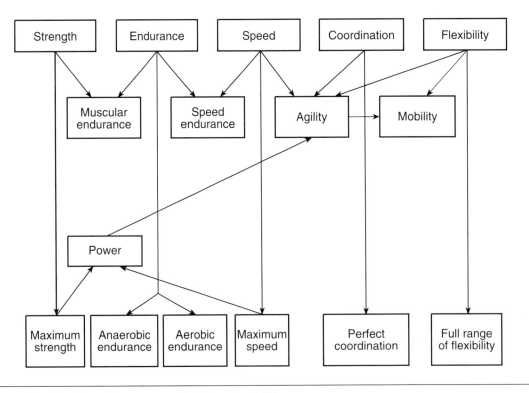

Figure 1.1 Interdependence among the biomotor abilities.

The sport-specific phase of specialized training that occurs during the initial years of training is crucial for all national-level and elite athletes who aim for precise training effects. Specific exercises during this period allow athletes to adapt to their specializations. For elite athletes, the relationship among strength, speed, and endurance depends on the sport and the athlete's needs.

Figure 1.2 illustrates three examples in which strength/force, speed, and endurance are dominant. In each case, when one biomotor ability dominates, the other two do not participate to a similar extent. This example, however, is pure theory and applies to few sports. In the vast majority of sports, each ability has a given input. Figure 1.3 shows the dominant composition of strength, speed, and endurance in several sports. Coaches and athletes can use figure 1.3 to determine the dominant biomotor abilities used in their sports.

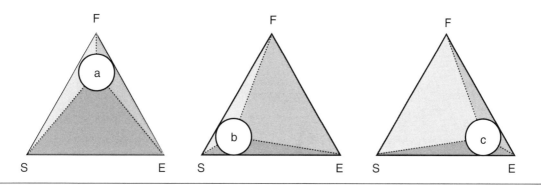

Figure 1.2 Relationships among the main biomotor abilities where *(a)* strength/force, *(b)* speed, and *(c)* endurance are dominant.

Each sport has its own specific physiological profile and characteristics. Understanding the energy systems and how they apply to sport training is vital for all coaches who design and implement sport-specific training programs. Although the purpose of this book is to discuss in specific terms the science, methodology, and objectives of strength training for sports, the physiological complexity of each sport also requires a very good understanding of the energy systems dominant in that sport, and how they relate to training.

Energy required for strength and aerobic training is produced in the body through the breakdown and conversion of food into a usable form of fuel known as ATP (adenosine triphosphate). Because ATP has to be constantly replenished and reused, the body relies on three main systems of energy replenishment to facilitate ongoing training: the anaerobic alactic (ATP-CP) system, the anaerobic lactic system, and the aerobic system. The three systems are not independent of each other but collaborate based on the physiological requirements of the sport. Sport-specific program development should always be focused on training the dominant energy system of the sport.

Specific development of a biomotor ability must be methodical. A developed dominant ability directly or indirectly affects the other abilities; the extent to which it does depends strictly on the resemblance between the methods employed and the specifics of the sport. So, development of a dominant biomotor ability may have a positive or, rarely, a negative transfer. When an athlete develops strength, he may experience a positive transfer to speed and endurance. On the other hand, a strength training program designed only to develop maximum strength may negatively affect the development of aerobic endurance. Similarly, a training program aimed exclusively at developing aerobic endurance may have a negative transfer to strength and speed. *Because strength is a crucial athletic ability, it always has to be trained with the other abilities.*

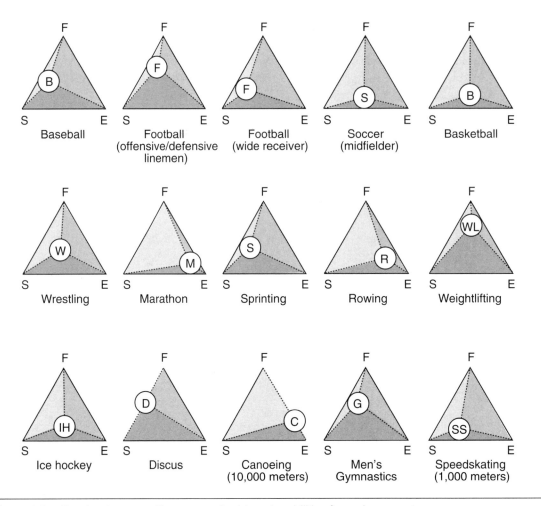

Figure 1.3   Dominant composition among the biomotor abilities for various sports.

Misleading, unfounded theories have suggested that strength training slows down athletes and affects the development of endurance and flexibility. Research discredits such theories (Atha, 1984; Dudley and Fleck, 1987; Hickson et al., 1988; MacDougall et al., 1987; Micheli, 1988; Nelson et al., 1990; Sale et al., 1990). A recent study that specifically looked at cross-country skiers found that maximum strength training alone not only improved maximum strength and the rate of force development of skiers but also had a positive transfer to work economy by increasing the time to exhaustion (Hoff, Gran, and Helgerud, 2002). Combined strength and endurance training does not affect improvement of aerobic power or muscular strength (i.e., no negative transfer results). Similarly, strength programs pose no risk to flexibility. Thus, endurance athletes in sports such as cycling, rowing, cross-country skiing, and canoeing can safely use strength and endurance training concurrently with their other training. The same is true for athletes in sports requiring strength and flexibility.

For speed sports, power represents a great source of speed improvement. A fast sprinter is also strong. High acceleration, fast limb movement, and high frequency are possible when strong muscles contract quickly and powerfully. In extreme situations, however, maximum loads may momentarily affect speed—for example, when speed training is scheduled after an exhausting training session with maximum loads. Fatigue at both the nervous system and muscular level will impede the neural drive and performance. For this reason, speed training should always be performed before strength training (see chapter 5).

Most actions and movements are more complex than previously discussed. Thus, strength in sports should be viewed as the mechanism required to perform skills and athletic actions. Athletes do not develop strength just for the sake of being strong. The goal of strength development is to meet the specific needs of a given sport, to develop specific strength or combinations of strength to increase athletic performance to the highest possible level.

Combining strength/force (F) and endurance (E) results in *muscular endurance* (M-E). Sports may require muscular endurance of long or short duration depending on the type of strength needed.

Before discussing this topic, a brief clarification of the terms *cyclic* and *acyclic* is necessary. *Cyclic* movements are repeated continuously, such as running, walking, swimming, rowing, skating, cross-country skiing, cycling, and canoeing. As soon as one cycle of the motor act is learned, the others can be repeated with the same succession. *Acyclic* movements, on the other hand, constantly change and are dissimilar to most others, such as in throwing events, gymnastics, wrestling, fencing, and many technical movements in team sports.

With the exception of sprinting, cyclic sports are endurance sports. Endurance is either dominant or makes an important contribution to performance. Acyclic sports are often speed or power sports. Many sports, however, are more complex and require speed, power, and endurance (for example, basketball, volleyball, soccer, ice hockey, wrestling, and boxing). Therefore, the following analysis may refer to certain skills of a given sport and not the sport as a whole.

Figure 1.4 analyzes various combinations of strength. The elements will be discussed in a clockwise direction starting with the F-E (strength-endurance) axis. Each strength combination has an arrow pointing to a certain part of the axis between two biomotor abilities. An arrow placed closer to F indicates that strength plays a dominant role in the sport or skill. An arrow placed closer to the midpoint of the axis indicates an equal or almost equal contribution of both biomotor abilities. The farther the arrow is from F, the less importance it has, suggesting that the other ability becomes more dominant. However, strength still plays a role in that sport.

The F-E axis refers to sports in which muscular endurance is the dominant strength combination (the inner arrow). Not all sports require equal parts of strength and endurance. For example, swimming events range from 50 to 1,500 meters. The 50-meter event is speed and power dominant; muscular endurance becomes more important as the distance increases.

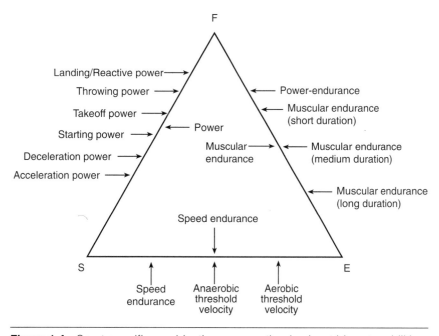

Figure 1.4 Sport-specific combinations among the dominant biomotor abilities.

Power-endurance (P-E) is on top of the F-E axis because of the importance of strength in activities such as rebounding in basketball, spiking in volleyball, jumping to catch the ball in Australian football and rugby, or jumping to head the ball in soccer. All of these actions are power-dominant movements. The same is true for some skills in tennis, boxing, wrestling, and the martial arts. To perform such actions successfully throughout a game or match, athletes have to train endurance as well as power because these actions are performed 100 to 200 or more times per game or match. Although a basketball player must jump high to rebound a ball, she must also duplicate such a jump 200 times per game. Consequently, both power and power-endurance have to be trained; however, the variables of volume and intensity are manipulated to adapt the body for repeat power performance.

Muscular endurance of short duration (M-E short) refers to the muscular endurance necessary for events ranging from 40 seconds to 2 minutes. In the 100-meter swimming event, the start is a power action, as are the first 20 strokes. From the midpoint of the race to the end, muscular endurance becomes at least equally as important as power. In the last 30 to 40 meters, the crucial element is the ability to duplicate the force of the arms' pull to maintain velocity and increase at the finish. For events such as 100 meters in swimming, 400 meters in running, 500 to 1,000 meters in speedskating, and 500 meters in canoeing, muscular endurance strongly contributes to the final result.

Muscular endurance of medium duration (M-E medium) is typical of cyclic sports two to five minutes long, such as 200- and 400-meter swimming, 3,000-meter speedskating, track-and-field mid-distance running, 1,000-meter canoeing, wrestling, the martial arts, figure skating, synchronized swimming, and cycling pursuit.

Muscular endurance of long duration (M-E long) requires the ability to apply force against a standard resistance for a longer period (over six minutes) as in rowing, cross-country skiing, road cycling, long-distance running, swimming, speedskating, and canoeing.

Speed-endurance refers to the ability to maintain or repeat a high-velocity action several times per game, as in American football, baseball, basketball, rugby, soccer, and power skating in ice hockey. Players in these sports need to train to develop their speed-endurance capacity.

The remaining two types of speed-endurance alter in combination and proportion of speed and endurance as distance increases. In the first case, sports require training velocity around the *anaerobic threshold* (4 millimoles of lactate or a heart rate of approximately 170 beats per minute). In the second case, training velocity must be around the *aerobic threshold* (2 to 3 millimoles of lactate or a heart rate of 125 to 140 beats per minute).

The F-S (*strength-speed*) axis refers mainly to strength-speed sports in which power is dominant.

Landing and reactive power is a major component of several sports, such as figure skating, gymnastics, and several team sports. Proper training can prevent injuries. Many athletes train only the takeoff part of a jump, with no concern for a controlled and balanced landing. The physical, or power, element plays an important role in proper landing technique, particularly for advanced athletes. Athletes must train eccentrically to be able to "stick" a landing, absorb the shock, and maintain good balance to continue the routine or perform another move immediately.

The power required to control a landing depends on the height of the jump, the athlete's body weight, and whether the landing is performed by absorbing the shock or with the joints flexed but stiff. Testing has revealed that for a shock-absorbing landing, athletes use a resistance force three to four times their body weight. Landing performed with stiff leg joints requires a force of six to eight times body weight. An athlete weighing 132 pounds (60 kilograms) requires 180 to 528 pounds (240 kilograms) to absorb the shock of landing. The same athlete requires 792 to 1,056 pounds (360 to 480 kilograms) to land with the leg joints stiff. When an athlete lands on one leg, as in figure skating, the force at the instant of landing is three to four times body weight for a shock-absorbing landing and five to seven times for landing with stiff leg joints.

Strength training can train landing power better, faster, and much more consistently than specific skill training can. Specific power training for landing can generate much higher tension in the muscles of the legs than performing an exercise with only body weight. Higher tension means improvements in landing power. In addition, through specific power training for landing, especially eccentric training, athletes can build a "power reserve" that is a force greater than the power required for a correct and controlled landing. The higher the power reserve is, the easier it is for the athlete to control the landing, and the safer the landing will be.

Reactive power is the ability to generate the force of jumping immediately following a landing (hence the word *reactive*). This kind of power is necessary in the martial arts, wrestling, and boxing and for quick changes in direction, as in American football, soccer, basketball, lacrosse, and tennis. The force needed for a reactive jump depends on the height of the jump and the athlete's body weight and leg power. Reactive jumps require a force equal to six to eight times body weight. Reactive jumps from a three-foot (one-meter) platform require a reactive force of 8 to 10 times body weight.

Throwing power refers to force applied against an implement, such as

Soccer players rely on a combination of reactive, takeoff, starting, accelerating, and decelerating powers to master the many techniques needed in game situations.

throwing a football, pitching a baseball, or throwing the javelin. The release speed is determined by the amount of muscular force exerted at the instant of release. First, athletes have to defeat the inertia of the implement, which is proportional to its mass (important only in throwing events). Then they must continuously accelerate through the range of motion so that they achieve maximum acceleration at the instant of release. The force and acceleration of release depend directly on the force and speed of contraction applied against the implement.

Takeoff power is crucial in events in which athletes attempt to project the body to the highest point, either to jump over a bar as in the high jump or to reach the best height to catch a ball or spike it. The height of a jump depends directly on the vertical force applied against the ground to defeat the pull of gravity. In most cases, the vertical force performed at takeoff is at least twice the athlete's weight. The higher the jump is, the more powerful the legs should be. Leg power is developed through periodized strength training as explained in chapters 6 and 10.

Starting power is necessary for sports that require high speed to cover a given distance in the shortest time possible. Athletes must be able to generate maximum force at the beginning of a muscular contraction to create a high initial speed. A fast start, either from a low position as in sprinting or from a tackling position in American football, depends on the reaction time and power the athlete can exert at that instant.

Acceleration power refers to the capacity to achieve high acceleration. Sprinting speed or acceleration depends on the power and quickness of muscle contractions to drive the arms and legs to the highest stride frequency, the shortest contact phase when the leg reaches the ground, and the highest propulsion when the leg pushes against the ground for a powerful forward drive. The capacity of athletes to accelerate depends on both arm and leg force. Specific strength training for high acceleration will benefit most team sport athletes from wide receivers in American football to wingers in rugby or strikers in soccer (see table 1.2).

Deceleration power is important in sports such as soccer, basketball, American football, and ice and field hockey. In these sports athletes run fast and constantly change direction quickly. Such athletes are exploders and accelerators as well as decelerators. The dynamics of these games change abruptly: Players running fast in one direction suddenly have to change direction with the least loss of speed, and then accelerate quickly in another direction.

Acceleration and deceleration both require a great deal of leg and shoulder power. The same muscles used for acceleration (quadriceps, hamstrings, and calves) are used for deceleration, except that they *contract eccentrically*. To enhance the ability to decelerate and move in another direction quickly, athletes must train decelerating power.

Role of Strength for Water Sports

For sports performed in or on water, such as swimming, synchronized swimming, water polo, rowing, kayaking, and canoeing, the body or the boat moves forward as a result of force. As force is performed against the water, the water exerts an equal and opposite force, known as drag, on the body or boat. As the boat or the swimmer moves through the water, the drag slows the forward motion or glide. To overcome drag, athletes must produce equal force to maintain speed and superior force to increase speed. The magnitude of the drag acting on a body moving through the water can be computed using the following equation (Hay, 1993):

$$F_D = C_D P A \frac{V^2}{2}$$

where F_D = drag force, C_D = coefficient of drag, P = fluid density, A = frontal area exposed to the flow, and V = body velocity relative to the water.

The coefficients of drag refer to the nature and shape of the body, including its orientation relative to the water flow. Long and slender vessels such as canoes, kayaks, or racing shells have a smaller C_D if the long axis of the boat is exactly parallel to the water flow.

A simplified version of the previous equation is as follows. This equation is not only easier to understand, but also easier to apply:

$$D \sim V^2$$

meaning that drag is proportional to the square of velocity.

In water sports, velocity increases when athletes apply force against the water. As force increases, the body moves faster. However, as velocity increases, drag increases proportionally to the square of velocity. The following example will better demonstrate this assertion. Assume that an athlete swims or rows at 2 meters (6.5 feet) per second. In this case:

$$D \sim V^2 = 2^2 = 4 \text{ kilograms (8.8 pounds)}$$

In other words, the athlete pulls with a force of 4 kilograms (8.8 pounds) per stroke. To be more competitive, the athlete has to swim or row at 3 meters (9.8 feet) per second. As such:

$$D \sim V^2 = 9 \text{ kilograms (19.8 pounds)}$$

Table 1.2   Sport-Specific Strength Development Required for Sports/Events

Sport/event	Types of strength required	Sport/event	Types of strength required
Athletics		**Football (Australian)**	Acceleration power, takeoff power, landing power, M-E short/medium
Sprinting	Reactive power, starting power, acceleration power, power-endurance	**Gymnastics**	Reactive power, takeoff power, landing power
Middle-distance running	Acceleration power, M-E medium	**Handball (European)**	Throwing power, acceleration power, deceleration power
Distance running	M-E long	**Ice hockey**	Acceleration power, deceleration power, power-endurance
Long jump	Acceleration power, takeoff power, reactive power	**Martial arts**	Starting power, reactive power, power-endurance
Triple jump	Acceleration power, reactive power, takeoff power	**Rhythmic sportive gymnastics**	Reactive power, takeoff power, M-E short
High jump	Takeoff power, reactive power	**Rowing**	M-E medium/long, starting power
Throws	Throwing power, reactive power	**Rugby**	Acceleration power, starting power, M-E medium
Baseball	Throwing power, acceleration power	**Sailing**	M-E long, power-endurance
Basketball	Takeoff power, power-endurance, acceleration power, deceleration power	**Shooting**	M-E long, power-endurance
Biathlon	M-E long	**Skiing**	
Boxing	Power-endurance, reactive power, M-E medium/long	Alpine	Reactive power, M-E short
		Nordic	M-E long, power-endurance
Canoeing/kayaking		**Soccer**	
500 meters	M-E short, acceleration power, starting power	Sweepers, full-backs	Reactive power, acceleration power, deceleration power
1,000 meters	M-E medium, acceleration power, starting power	Midfielders	Acceleration power, deceleration power, M-E medium
10,000 meters	M-E long	Forwards	Acceleration power, deceleration power, reactive power
Cricket	Throwing power, acceleration power	**Speedskating**	
Cycling		Sprinting	Starting power, acceleration power, M-E short
Track, 200 meters	Acceleration power, reactive power	Mid distance	M-E medium, power-endurance
4,000-meter pursuit	M-E medium, acceleration power	Long distance	M-E long
Road racing	M-E long	**Squash/handball**	Reactive power, power-endurance
Diving	Takeoff power, reactive power	**Swimming**	
Equestrian	M-E medium	Sprinting	Starting power, acceleration power, M-E short
Fencing	Reactive power, power-endurance	Mid distance	M-E medium, power-endurance
Field hockey	Acceleration power, deceleration power, M-E medium	Long distance	M-E long
Figure skating	Takeoff power, landing power, power-endurance	**Synchronized swimming**	M-E medium, power-endurance
Football (American)		**Tennis**	Power-endurance, reactive power, acceleration power, deceleration power
Linemen	Starting power, reactive power	**Volleyball**	Reactive power, power-endurance, throwing power
Linebackers, quarterbacks, running backs, inside receivers	Starting power, acceleration power, reactive power	**Water polo**	M-E medium, acceleration power, throwing power
Wide receivers, defensive backs, tailbacks	Acceleration power, reactive power, starting power	**Wrestling**	Power-endurance, reactive power, M-E medium

For an even higher velocity of 4 meters (13 feet) per second, drag will equal 16 kilograms (35 pounds). Obviously, to be able to pull with increased force, maximum strength must be increased. A body will not be able to generate increased velocity without increasing the force per stroke unit.

The training implications are obvious. Not only must maximum strength be increased, but the coach must ensure that athletes display the same force for all strokes throughout the duration of the race, because all water sports have a strong endurance component. This means that a maximum strength phase and an adequate muscular endurance phase must be incorporated in training, as suggested in chapter 11.

Muscle Response to Strength Training

Enhancing strength performance requires understanding the science behind strength training and learning how anatomy and physiology apply to human movement. Coaches and athletes who understand muscle contraction and the sliding filament theory realize why the speed of contraction is load related and why more force occurs at the beginning of a contraction than at the end. Coaches who understand muscle fiber types and recognize the role of genetic inheritance understand why some athletes are better than others at certain types of sporting activities (i.e., speed and power versus endurance). Unfortunately, many athletes and coaches avoid reading academic physiology texts or books filled with scientific terminology. Therefore, this book explains the scientific basis of strength training clearly and simply.

Understanding muscle adaptation and its dependence on load and training method(s) makes it easier to grasp why certain types of load, exercises, or training methods are preferred for some sports and not for others. Strength training success relies on knowing the types of strength that exist and how to develop them, as well as knowing what contractions are available and which are best for a given sport. This knowledge helps both coaches and athletes understand the concept of planning-periodization faster and easier, and improvement will soon follow.

Body Structure

The human body is constructed around a skeleton. The junction of two or more bones forms a joint held together by tough bands of connective tissue called ligaments. The skeletal frame is covered with 656 muscles, which account for approximately 40 percent of total body weight. Dense connective tissues called tendons attach both ends of the muscle to the bone. The tension in a muscle is directed to the bone through the tendon. The greater the tension is, the stronger the pull will be on the tendons and bone and, consequently, the more powerfully the limb will move. The periodized training that we propose in this book will consistently challenge the adaptation of the neuromuscular system as the load and type of training elicits physiological adaptations that generate more power and strength for sport performance. Our bodies are very plastic and adapt to the stimuli to which they are exposed. If the proper stimulus is applied, optimal physiological performance will ensue.

Muscle Structure

A muscle is a very complex structure that allows movements to occur. Muscles are composed of a number of sarcomeres that contain a specific arrangement of the contractile proteins *myosin* (thick filaments) and *actin* (thin filaments), whose actions are important in muscle contraction. A sarcomere is a unit of contraction in muscle fibers and is composed of the actin and myosin protein filaments. The ability of a muscle to contract and exert force is determined by its design, the cross-sectional area, the fiber length, and the number of fibers within the muscle. The number of fibers is genetically determined and is not affected by training; however, the other variables can be. For example, the number and thickness of myosin filaments is increased by training using maximum strength loads. Dedicated training increases the thickness of muscle filaments, increasing both muscle size and the force of contraction.

The body is made up of a number of different types of muscle fibers that live in groups and in essence report to a single *motor unit*. Our bodies are made up of thousands of motor units that house tens of thousands of muscle fibers. Each individual motor unit contains thousands of muscle fibers that sit dormant until they are called into action. Each motor unit rules over its family of fibers and directs their action by implementing the all-or-none law. When the motor unit is stimulated, the impulse sent to the muscle fibers within the motor unit either spreads completely, eliciting the action of all fibers in the family, or does not spread at all. Different motor units respond to different loads used in training. For instance, performing a bench press movement with 60 percent of 1-repetition maximum (1RM) will call up a certain family of motor units while the bigger motor units wait until a higher load is used. Because motor unit recruitment is load dependent, program design should reflect the activation and adaptation of the primary motor units and muscle fibers that dominate the sport. For instance, short sprints and field events such as the shot put require the use of heavy loads to facilitate the force development required to optimize speed and explosive performance.

Muscle fibers have different biochemical (metabolic) functions; some are physiologically better suited to work under anaerobic conditions, whereas others work better under aerobic conditions. Fibers that rely on and use oxygen to produce energy are called aerobic, type I, red, or *slow-twitch* fibers. Fibers that do not require oxygen are called anaerobic, type II, white, or *fast-twitch* fibers. Fast-twitch muscle fibers are further divided into IIA and IIB. Slow-twitch and fast-twitch fibers exist in relatively equal proportions within the body, and strength training is not thought to affect this 50–50 relationship to a great extent. Strength training, however, does affect fiber size, which generates a greater force production. Table 2.1 compares slow-twitch and fast-twitch fiber characteristics.

The fast-twitch motor unit's contraction is faster and more powerful than that of the slow-twitch motor unit. Successful athletes in speed and power sports are genetically equipped with a higher proportion of fast-twitch fibers, but they also fatigue faster. Athletes with more slow-twitch fibers are more successful in endurance sports because they are able to perform work of lower intensity for a longer time.

Table 2.1 Comparison of Fast-Twitch and Slow-Twitch Characteristics

Fast-twitch	Slow-twitch
White, Type II, anaerobic	*Red, Type I, aerobic*
• Fast to fatigue	• Slow to fatigue
• Large nerve cell—innervates from 300 to more than 500 muscle fibers	• Smaller nerve cell—innervates from 10 to 180 muscle fibers only
• Develops short, forceful contractions	• Develops long, continuous contractions
• Speed and power	• Endurance
• Recruited only during high-intensity work	• Recruited during low- and high-intensity work

Recruitment of muscle fibers follows the *size principle*, which states that motor units and muscle fibers are recruited from smallest to largest always beginning with the slow-twitch muscle fibers. If the load is of a moderate or low intensity, the slow-twitch muscle fibers are recruited and exercised as workhorses. If a heavy load is used, the slow-twitch fibers start the contraction, but it is quickly taken over by the activation of the fast-twitch muscle fibers.

Fiber type composition (i.e., the proportion of fast-twitch fibers within a muscle) plays an important role in strength sports. Muscles containing a high percentage of fast-twitch fibers are capable of quicker, more powerful contractions. Changing the proportion of fast-twitch and slow-twitch fibers within a muscle by training is critical for strength gains, yet the possibility remains controversial. Studies suggest, however, that a shift in fiber type from slow-twitch to fast-twitch may be possible as a result of prolonged high-intensity training. This means that the proportion of fast-twitch fibers increases at the expense of slow-twitch fibers (see figure 2.1) (Abernethy, Thayer, and Taylor, 1990; Jacobs et al., 1987).

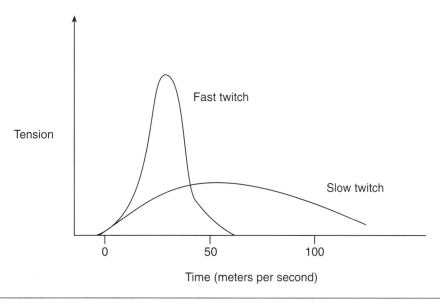

Figure 2.1 Twitch response of fast-twitch and slow-twitch fibers to the same intensity of stimulus. (Based on data from Costill, 1976; Komi and Bosco, 1978; Gollnick et al., 1972.)

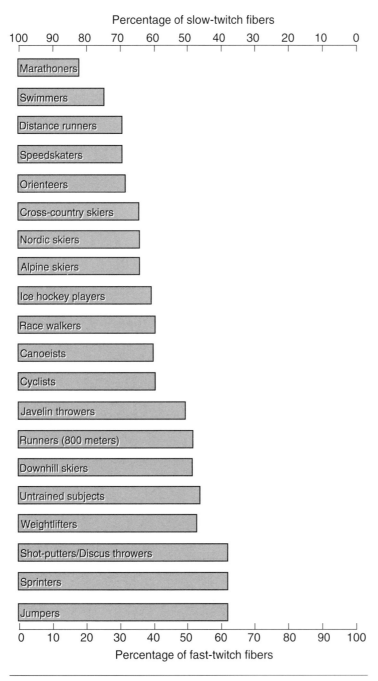

Figure 2.2 Fiber type distribution for male athletes. Note the dominance in slow-twitch fibers for athletes from aerobic dominant sports and in fast-twitch fibers for athletes from speed and power dominant sports. (Based on data from Costill, 1976; Gollnick et al., 1972.)

Differences in muscle fiber type distribution are visible among athletes involved in various sports. Figures 2.2 and 2.3 illustrate a general profile of fast- and slow-twitch fiber percentages for athletes in some sports. The drastic differences between sprinters and marathon runners clearly suggest that success in some sports is at least partially determined by muscle fiber composition.

The peak power generated by athletes is also related to fiber type distribution. The higher the distribution of fast-twitch fibers, the greater the power generated by the athlete. Similarly, the percentage of distribution of fast-twitch fibers in the muscles is also velocity related. The greater the velocity displayed by an athlete, the higher the percentage distribution of fast-twitch fibers. Such individuals make great sprinters and jumpers, and with this natural talent, they should be channeled into speed- and power-dominant sports. Attempting to make them distance runners would be a waste of talent. In such events, they would be only moderately successful, whereas they could be excellent sprinters or baseball or football players, to mention just a few speed- and power-related sports.

Mechanism of Muscular Contraction

Muscular contraction occurs from a series of events involving the protein filaments actin and myosin. The myosin filaments contain cross-bridges, tiny extensions that reach toward the actin filaments. Activation to contract stimulates the entire fiber, creating chemical changes that allow the actin filaments to join with the myosin cross-bridges. Binding myosin to actin

18

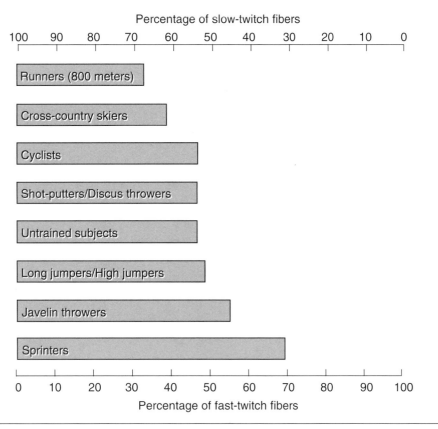

Figure 2.3 Fiber type distribution for female athletes.

by way of cross-bridges releases energy, causing the cross-bridges to swivel, pulling or sliding the myosin filament over the acting filament. This sliding motion causes the muscle to shorten (contract), producing force. Imagine a rowboat with the oars of the boat representing the myosin filaments and the water the actin filaments. As the oar hits the water, the boat is forcefully pulled forward. The greater the number of oars in the water and the greater the strength of the rowers, the greater the force production. The rowboat example is a visualization of how increasing both the number and thickness of the myosin filaments increases force production.

All sporting movements follow a system known as the *stretch–shortening cycle*, which is characterized by three main types of contractions: eccentric (lengthening), concentric (shortening), and isometric (static). A volleyball player who quickly squats only to jump and block a spike has completed a stretch–shortening cycle. Similarly, an athlete who lowers the barbell to his chest and rapidly explodes by extending his arms has completed a stretch–shortening cycle. To fully use the physiological assets of a stretch–shortening cycle, the muscle must quickly change from a lengthening to a shortening contraction (Schmidtbleicher, 1992).

The sliding filament theory described earlier provides an overview of how muscles work to produce force. The sliding filament theory involves a number of mechanisms that work to promote the effectiveness by which muscles contract. The release of stored elastic energy and reflex adaptation is vital to optimizing athletic performance. However, these adaptations only ensue when the proper stimulus is applied in training. For instance, an athlete's ability to use stored elastic energy to jump higher or propel the shot put farther is optimized with explosive type movements such as those used in plyometric training. However, the muscle components such as the series elastic components (which consists of tendons,

Baseball players integrate power training into their regimen to enhance hitting potential.

muscle fibers, and cross-bridges) are not able to effectively transfer energy to the movement unless the parallel elastic component (i.e., ligaments) and collagen structures (whose task is to provide stability and protection from injury) are strengthened. Anatomical adaptation must supercede power training if the body is to withstand the forces and impact the athlete must go through to optimize the muscles' elastic properties.

A reflex is an involuntary muscle contraction brought about by an external stimulus (Latash, 1998). Muscle spindles and the Golgi tendon organ are two main components of reflex control. Muscle spindles respond to the magnitude and rapidity of a muscle stretch (Brooks, Fahey, and White, 1996), whereas the Golgi tendon organ—found within the muscle–tendon junction (Latash, 1998)—responds to muscle tension. Athletic performance is increased when the inhibitory responses of both the muscle spindles and the Golgi tendon organ are enhanced. When a high degree of tension or stretch develops in the muscles, the muscle spindles and Golgi tendon organ involuntarily relax the muscle to protect it from harm and injury. The only way to inhibit the role of the reflexes is to adapt the body to withstand greater degrees of tension, which decreases the role of the reflexes. Maximum strength training that uses progressively heavier loads greater than 90 percent 1RM causes the neuromuscular system to withstand higher tensions by consistently recruiting a greater number of fast-twitch muscle fibers into action. The fast-twitch muscle fibers become equipped with a greater amount of protein, which aids in cross-bridge cycling and force production.

Muscular potential is optimized when all the intricate factors that affect the stretch–shortening cycle are called into action. Their influence can only be used to enhance performance when the neuromuscular system is strategically stimulated in the appropriate sequence. Periodization of strength bases the planning of phases according to the physiological makeup of the sport. Once the ergogenesis of the sport is outlined, the phases of training are planned in a stepwise approach to transfer positive neuromuscular adaptations to practical hands-on human performance. Understanding applied human physiology and a snapshot goal of each phase will help coaches and athletes integrate physiological principles into sport-specific training.

The musculoskeletal frame of the body is an arrangement of bones attached to one another by ligaments at the joints. The muscles crossing these joints provide the force for body movements. Skeletal muscles do not contract independently of one another. Rather, the movements performed around a joint are produced by several muscles, each with a different role.

Agonists, or *synergists*, are muscles that cooperate to perform a movement. *Antagonists* act in opposition to the agonists during movement. In most cases, especially in skilled and experienced athlctcs, the antagonists relax, allowing easy motion. Because athletic movements are directly influenced by the interaction between agonist and antagonist muscle groups, a jerky motion, or one rigidly performed, might result from an improper interaction between the two groups. The smoothness of a muscular contraction can be improved by focusing on relaxing the antagonists.

Prime movers are muscles primarily responsible for producing a comprehensive strength movement or technical skill. During a biceps curl, for example, the prime mover is the biceps muscle; the triceps acts as an antagonist and should be relaxed to facilitate smoother flexion.

Stabilizers, or *fixators*, are usually smaller muscles that contract isometrically to anchor a bone so the prime movers have a firm base from which to pull. The muscles of other limbs may come into play as well, acting as stabilizers so that the prime movers can perform their motion. For instance, during a "preacher curl," the shoulders, upper arms, and abdominal muscles contract isometrically to stabilize the shoulders, giving the biceps a stable base from which to pull.

The *line of pull* is an imaginary line that crosses the muscle longitudinally, between its two extreme heads. A muscle contraction achieves the highest physiological and mechanical efficiency when performed along the line of pull. For example, in elbow flexion, when the palm is up, the direct line of pull creates the highest efficiency. When the palm is down, contraction efficiency decreases because the tendon of the biceps muscle wraps around the bone radius. In this case, the line of pull is indirect, and a large portion of the contractile force is wasted. A similar situation occurs with the squat. If the feet are shoulder-width apart with the toes pointing forward, the quadriceps have a better line of pull than when the feet are far apart with the toes pointing diagonally forward. For maximum strength gains and optimal muscle efficiency, strength exercises must be performed along the line of pull.

Types of Strength and Their Training Significance

Training involves various types of strength, each having a certain significance for some sports and athletes.

General strength is the foundation of the entire strength training program. It must be the sole focus of the early training phase of anatomical adaptation. Anatomical adaptation is devoted to the development of the overall strength of the core and limbs. The development of a good base of aerobic endurance is also stressed in this phase along with muscle balance and injury prevention. Anatomical adaptation, as the name implies, prepares the body for the more difficult phases that follow. A low level of general strength may limit the overall progress of an athlete. It leaves the body susceptible to injury and potentially even asymmetrical shape or a decreased ability to build muscle strength.

Specific strength is the strength of only those muscles (mainly the prime movers) that are particular to the movements of a selected sport. As the term suggests, this type of strength is specific to each sport. Thus, any comparison between the strength levels of athletes involved in different sports is invalid. Specific strength training should be progressively incorporated toward the end of the preparatory phase for all advanced athletes.

Maximum strength refers to the highest force that can be performed by the neuromuscular system during a maximum contraction. It constitutes the heaviest load an athlete can lift in one attempt and is expressed as 100 percent of maximum or 1-repetition maximum (1RM). For training purposes, athletes must know their maximum strength for each exercise because it is the basis for calculating loads for every strength phase.

Power is the product of two abilities, strength and speed, and is considered to be the ability to apply maximum force in the shortest time.

Muscular endurance is defined as a muscle's ability to sustain work for a prolonged period. It is used largely in endurance-related sports and has a positive transfer to cardiorespiratory endurance.

Absolute strength refers to an athlete's ability to exert maximum force regardless of body weight. Absolute strength is required to reach very high levels in some sports (shot put and the heaviest weight categories in weightlifting and wrestling). Increases in absolute strength parallel gains in body weight in athletes following a systematic training program.

Relative strength represents the ratio between absolute strength and body weight. Relative strength is important in sports such as gymnastics or those in which athletes are divided into weight categories (wrestling, boxing). For instance, a gymnast may not be able to perform the iron cross on the rings unless the relative strength of the muscles involved is at least one to one. This means that the absolute strength must be at least sufficient to offset the athlete's body weight. Gains in body weight change this proportion—as body weight increases, relative strength decreases.

Strength reserve is the difference between absolute strength and the amount of strength required to perform a skill under competitive conditions. Strength gauge techniques used to measure rowers' maximum strength per stroke unit revealed values up to 233 pounds (106 kilograms); the mean strength per race was 123 pounds (56 kilograms) (Bompa, Hebbelinck, and Van Gheluwe, 1978). The same subjects were found to have absolute strength in power clean lifts of 198 pounds (90 kilograms). Subtracting the mean strength per race (123 pounds or 56 kilograms) from absolute strength (198 pounds or 90 kilograms) results in a strength reserve of 75 pounds (34 kilograms). The ratio of mean strength to absolute strength is 1 to 1.6. Similarly, other subjects were found to have a higher strength reserve with a ratio of 1 to 1.85. Needless to say, the latter subjects performed better in rowing races, leading to the conclusion that an athlete with a higher strength reserve is capable of reaching higher performance levels. Although the concept of strength reserve may not be meaningful to all sports, it is believed to be significant in sports such as swimming, canoeing, and rowing, as well as in jumping and throwing events.

Strength Training and Muscular Adaptation

Systematic strength training results in certain structural and physiological changes, or adaptations, in the body. The level of adaptation is evidenced by the size and definition of the muscles. The magnitude of these adaptations is directly proportional to the demands placed on the body by the volume (quantity), frequency, and intensity (load) of training. Training benefits an athlete only as long as it forces the body to adapt to the stress of physical work. In other words, if the body is presented with a demand greater than it is accustomed to, it adapts to the stressor by becoming stronger. When the load does not challenge the body's *adaptation threshold*, the training effect will be nil or at best minimal, and no adaptation will occur.

Different types of adaptation can occur. Periodization of strength offers a six-phase approach that follows the physiological rhythm of how muscles respond to strength training. Depending on the physiological makeup of the sport, a minimum of three of the six phases will be combined in sequence to form the periodization of strength. All periodization of strength models begin with phase 1. Four of the six possible phases are briefly discussed below. The remaining two phases—competition and transition—will be discussed in later chapters.

Phase 1: Anatomical Adaptation

The emphasis in the anatomical adaptation phase is "prehabilitation," with the hope of preventing the need for rehabilitation. The three main physiological objectives of this phase are to increase the oxidative capacity of the slow-twitch muscle fibers; strengthen the tendons, ligaments, and joints, which is plausible through a high volume of training; and increase the bone mineral content and proliferation of the connective tissue that surrounds the individual muscle fibers. Regardless of the sport, cardiovascular fitness is improved, muscular strength is adequately challenged, and neuromuscular coordination for strength movement patterns is tested and practiced. An increase in the cross-sectional area of muscle is not the focus but can occur during this phase. The anatomical adaptation phase is the foundation for the other phases of training. The name of the phase illustrates the fact that the main objective of strength training is not an immediate overload but rather a progressive adaptation of the athlete's anatomy.

Phase 2: Hypertrophy

One of the most visible signs of adaptation to strength training is the enlargement of muscle size, known as *hypertrophy*. Many of the principles used in hypertrophy training are similar to those used in bodybuilding. The two main physiological objectives of this phase are an increase in muscle cross-sectional area and an increased storage capacity for high-energy substrates and enzymes. The main difference between athletic hypertrophy and bodybuilding hypertrophy is the amount of load used in training. Bodybuilders train to exhaustion using relatively light to moderate loads, whereas athletes rely on heavier loads focusing on movement speed and rest between sets. Although hypertrophic changes occur in both fast-twitch and slow-twitch muscle fibers, more changes take place in the fast-twitch fibers. Hypertrophy training provides a strong physiological precept to nervous system training when it produces chronic changes.

When a muscle is forced to contract against a resistance, as happens in strength training, there is a sudden shift in blood flow to the working muscle. This transient increase in blood flow, known as short-term hypertrophy, temporarily increases the size and thickness of the muscle. Short-term hypertrophy is experienced during every strength training bout and usually lasts one to two hours following the training session. Although the benefits of a single bout of strength training are quickly lost, the additive benefits of multiple training sessions leads to a state of athletic hypertrophy.

Athletic hypertrophy results from structural changes at the muscle level. Because it is caused by an increase in either the number or size of the muscle filaments, its effects are enduring. This form of hypertrophy is desired for athletes using strength training to improve their athletic performance. This more challenging and effective form of hypertrophy is achieved

Football players rely on athletic hypertrophy to improve speed, agility, and power.

by using relatively heavy loads to stimulate and recruit the fast-twitch motor units to a degree that elicits structural changes such as increased numbers of cross-bridges and increased myosin protein size and number. In this manner, muscular adaptations will result in a stronger muscular engine prepared to receive and apply nervous system signals.

Phase 3: Maximum Strength

The development of maximum strength is probably the single most important variable in most sports. The ability to increase maximum strength depends on the diameter of the cross-sectional area of the muscles involved, the capacity to recruit fast-twitch muscle fibers, and the ability to synchronize or simultaneously call into action all the primary muscles that are involved in the movement (Howard et al., 1985). These changes represent both structural and neural flow changes that occur as a function of using very heavy loads in excess of 90 percent 1RM in training. Eccentric training with loads greater than 100 percent of 1RM can also be used to elicit these adaptive responses.

The popularity of maximum strength training is rooted in the positive increase in relative strength. Many sports such as volleyball, gymnastics, and boxing require greater force generation without a concomitant increase in body weight. In fact, an increase in maximum strength without an associated increase in body weight characterizes the maximum strength phase as central nervous system training (Schmidtbleicher, 1984). A novice athlete will benefit from traditional maximum strength training methods such as performing high loads with maximal rest between sets (three to five minutes). The more experienced athlete must continually stress and engage the nervous system by altering the loads, sets, and methods used in training.

The physiological benefits of sport performance lie in an athlete's ability to convert gains in strength and possibly muscular size to the particular sport. Building the foundation sets the stage, adding muscle generates force, and adapting the body to using heavy loads awakens the largest engines in the body (the fast-twitch motor units). Once the mind–muscle connection is linked, the physical requirements of the sport determine the next phase.

Phase 4: Conversion

Depending on the sport, following a maximum strength phase of training, the conversion to power, power endurance, or muscular endurance are the three fundamental options. Some sports require a combination of all three. Conversion to power or power endurance is accomplished by using relatively moderate to heavy loads (65 percent to 85 percent of 1RM) with the intention of moving the weight as quickly as possible. Although still engaging the nervous system, such methods as ballistic training or upper- or lower-body plyometric training improve an athlete's high-velocity strength or the ability to recruit and engage the high-powered fast-twitch motor units. A strong foundation of maximum strength is a must to maximize the rate of force production. In fact, slow-velocity training such as maximum strength training has been shown to transfer to gains in power as the athlete attempts to move the weight as quickly as possible (Behm and Sale, 1993).

Conversion to muscular endurance requires more than performing 15 to 20 reps per set. Depending on the demands of the sport, muscular endurance can be trained for short, medium, or long distances. Importantly, muscular endurance training that can require as many as 400 reps per set must be trained concomitantly with aerobic training. Similar physiological training objectives apply to aerobic training and muscular endurance training. Recall that the body replenishes energy for muscular contractions by a combined effort of three energy systems: the anaerobic alactic, the anaerobic lactic, and the aerobic systems. Conversion to muscular endurance training primarily requires the heightened adaptation of the aerobic training system and secondarily that of the anaerobic lactic system. The main objectives of aerobic training include improvements in physiological parameters such as changes in heart efficiency; biochemical parameters such as increased mitochondria and capillary density, which result in greater diffusion and use of oxygen; and metabolic parameters, which result in a greater use of fat as energy and an increased rate of removal of lactic acid. Because many medium- and long-endurance sports require resistance to be applied against water (e.g., rowing and swimming), the benefit of adapting the neuromuscular and cardiovascular system physiologically, biochemically, and metabolically is invaluable. To maximize performance in muscular endurance sports, maximum strength training must be followed by a combination of aerobic training and light-resistance strength training to prepare the body for the demands of the sport.

Once the mind–muscle connection has been adapted to maximum performance, it is time to put the gains to the test. Unfortunately, most athletes and coaches work hard and strategically as the competitive season approaches and cease to train once the season arises. Maintaining the strong and stable base that was formed during the precompetitive phases requires a continuation of training during the competitive season. Failure to plan at least two sessions dedicated to training the main systems involved in the sport will result in a decreased performance or early onset of fatigue as the season persists. Staying up is always easier than falling down and attempting to get on one's feet again. Periodization of strength is about planning phases to optimize physiological adaptation and planning to maintain the benefits for as long as the season lasts. When the season is over, serious athletes can take two to four weeks to regenerate their minds and bodies.

Stimulating the body for optimal performance takes time, planning, and persistency. Physiology is helpful in planning the program but an improvement in performance is achieved through the practical application of the many principles and methods of training inherent in the periodization of strength.

Strength and Energy Systems Training

Each sport has its own specific physiological profile and characteristics. Understanding the energy systems and how they apply to sport training is vital for all trainers who design and implement sport-specific programs. Although the scope of this book is to discuss in specific terms the science, methodology, and objectives of strength training for sports, the physiological complexity of each sport also requires a good understanding of the energy systems dominant in each sport, and how they relate to strength training. Trainers who separate strength training and its programming requirements from other physiological characteristics of their sport make a mistake that over time may affect their rate of success. This chapter illustrates how to integrate strength training and the specific energy systems needed by sports.

Energy Systems

Energy is the capacity to perform work. Work is the application of force, or the contracting of muscles to apply force against a resistance. Energy is required to perform physical work during training. The body derives energy from the muscle cell's conversion of foodstuff into a high-energy compound called adenosine triphosphate (ATP), which is stored in the muscle cell. ATP, as its name suggests, consists of one molecule of adenosine and three molecules of phosphate. Adenosine diphosphate (ADP), on the other hand, consists of one molecule of adenosine and two molecules of phosphate. In the process of creating energy, ATP is broken down to ADP + P (phosphate). To ensure a steady supply of ATP for a continuous supply of energy, ADP attaches itself to another phosphate molecule to reproduce ATP.

The energy required for muscular contraction when training with weights or performing aerobic exercise is released into the body by converting high-energy ATP into ADP + P. When this process occurs, energy is released and movement ensues. Because the body can store only a limited amount of ATP in the muscle cells, it must continually replenish ATP supplies to facilitate ongoing training.

The body can replenish ATP supplies by using any one of three energy systems, depending on the type of training: the anaerobic alactic (or ATP-CP) system, the anaerobic lactic system, or the aerobic system.

Anaerobic Alactic (ATP-CP) System

Muscles can store only a small amount of adenosine triphosphate (ATP). For this reason, energy depletes rapidly with strenuous training. For example, the ATP stored in muscle may only be able to fuel the first 6 to 10 reps of an exhausting 12- to 15-rep set. A burning sensation in the exercising muscles by the end of the 15th rep is an indication that both the ATP-CP and lactic acid systems were involved in the release of energy in the set. In response to the depletion of ATP in the muscle, creatine phosphate (CP), also called phosphocreatine, breaks down into creatine (C) and phosphate (P). Creatine phosphate, like ATP, is stored in the muscle cell. The transformation of CP into C and P does not release energy that is immediately usable for muscular contraction. Rather, the body uses this energy to resynthesize ADP + P into ATP, which is usable energy for muscle contractions.

Because CP is stored in limited amounts in the muscle cell, the ATP-CP system can only supply energy for a very brief time—up to 10 seconds. This system is the body's chief source of energy for extremely quick and explosive activities, such as the 100-meter dash, diving, weightlifting, and jumping and throwing events in track and field. Knowledge of this energy system has made creatine supplements very popular among strength, size, and power athletes who sprint, throw, play hockey, play soccer, or engage in bodybuilding.

Anaerobic Lactic System

The body reacts differently to longer bouts of intense exercise (lasting up to 40 seconds) such as the 200-meter and 400-meter dashes or weight training sets up to 40 to 50 reps, as found in the conversion of short to medium muscular endurance training. For the first 8 to 10 seconds, the anaerobic alactic system provides energy; after 10 seconds, the anaerobic lactic system kicks in. The anaerobic lactic system provides energy by breaking down a substance called glycogen (the storage form of glucose or sugar in the body) that is stored in muscle cells and in the liver, which releases energy to resynthesize ATP from ADP + P. The absence of oxygen during the breakdown of glycogen creates a by-product called lactic acid. When high-intensity training continues for a prolonged period of time, large quantities of lactic acid accumulate in the muscle, causing fatigue and eventually preventing the body from maintaining the level of intensity. Continuous use of glycogen during exercise eventually causes glycogen to be depleted and restoration to begin. Eating complex carbohydrates, fruits, and vegetables and getting plenty of rest are great ways to aid in the restoration of glycogen.

Aerobic System

The aerobic system requires 60 to 80 seconds to start producing energy for the resynthesis of ATP. Unlike the other systems, this system allows the resynthesis of ATP in the presence of oxygen, which can resynthesize energy through the breakdown of glycogen, fats, and proteins. The heart rate and the rate of breathing must increase sufficiently to transport the required amount of oxygen to the muscle cells. Glycogen is the source of energy used to resynthesize ATP in both the anaerobic lactic and aerobic systems. Unlike the anaerobic lactic system, the

Track athletes in events longer than the 800 meters primarily use the aerobic energy system to break down glycogen, fat, and protein to fuel the body.

aerobic system produces little or no lactic acid. An absence of lactic acid enables the body to continue to exercise.

The aerobic system is the primary energy source for events lasting between two minutes and three hours. Prolonged work beyond three hours may result in the breakdown of fats and proteins, substances that are needed to replenish ATP levels as the body's glycogen supply depletes. In all cases, the breakdown of glycogen, fats, or protein produces the by-products carbon dioxide and water, both of which are eliminated from the body through breathing and sweating. As a person's aerobic capacity improves, her ability to use fat for fuel also improves.

Bridging the Gap Between Theory and Practice

Training coaches without any real knowledge of energy systems often intuitively develop programs that train the dominant energy system of their sport. For instance, sprint coaches intuitively train their athletes with sprint distances even though they are unfamiliar with the benefits of such training on the anaerobic alactic energy system. However, energy system training should also take into consideration the recruitment of muscle fiber types. Improvement in energy system efficiency is dependent on the neuromuscular system's ability to withstand the development of tension and fatigue that results from chronic training. For instance, continual training of the anaerobic lactic system results in the fast-twitch muscle fibers being able to generate force in the presence of lactic acid accumulation. This is accomplished by an increase in motor unit recruitment patterns and the reuse of lactic acid by the slow-twitch muscle fibers. Designing a program that combines maximum strength training with 200- to 400-meter sprinting will maximize anaerobic metabolism.

The energy system tapped to produce energy during an athletic activity depends directly on the intensity and duration of the activity. The anaerobic alactic system primarily produces energy for all sports of short duration, up to 10 seconds, sports in which speed and power are the dominant abilities. Alactic-dominant sports include sprinting, throwing and jumping events in track and field, ski jumping, diving, vaulting in gymnastics, and Olympic weightlifting. Notice that the movements in these sports are of short duration, use high loads, and are explosive; in other words, they require maximum strength and power. Therefore, the anaerobic alactic energy system is used to recruit a high number of fast-twitch muscle fibers (maximum strength) and to increase the discharge rate of those fibers (maximum power).

The anaerobic lactic system, on the other hand, can be equated with high-intensity sporting activities of prolonged duration (70 seconds or slightly longer). The partial list of lactic-acid-dependent sports includes 200- to 400-meter running events in track and field, 50-meter swimming, track cycling, and 500-meter speedskating. Performance in these sports requires optimal adaptation in the anaerobic alactic system with suboptimal adaptation of the anaerobic lactic system. The optimization of efficiency in anaerobic metabolism is required for sports of slightly longer duration such as mid-distance events in track and field, 100- to 200-meter swimming, 500-meter canoeing and kayaking, 1,000-meter speedskating, most events in gymnastics, alpine skiing, rhythmic gymnastics, and pursuit in track cycling. The purpose of strength training for these sports is to develop power and power-endurance; the athlete has to be able not only to increase the discharge rate of the fast-twitch muscle fibers, but also to maintain the level of discharge for a longer period of time (from 10 to more than 60 seconds). Because power, power-endurance, and to some degree muscular endurance of short duration seem to be the dominant abilities for the previously listed sports, a strong foundation of maximum strength should be developed. Recall that gains in power, power-endurance, and muscular endurance of short duration are possible only as a result of increasing maximum strength.

As previously mentioned, the aerobic energy system is used to produce the energy for sports ranging from two minutes to over three hours. Many coaches have difficulty understanding how to train for events with such a wide range of duration. As a rule of thumb, the closer to two minutes the duration of an event is, the lower the aerobic contribution to overall performance will be. The opposite is also true: The longer the duration is, the more dominant the aerobic system will be. Many aerobic-dependent sports belong in this category: long, and to some degree mid-distance, events in track and field; swimming; speedskating, 1,000-meter kayaking and canoeing, wrestling, figure skating, synchronized swimming, rowing, cross-country skiing, cycling (road races), and triathlon. All of these sports will have a physiological benefit from training muscular endurance of both short and long duration.

Although most sports fall within a clear continuum of energy system contribution, special consideration must be applied to team sports, boxing, the martial arts, and racket sports. In these sports, all three energy systems are used according to the intensity, rhythm, and duration of the competition. Most of these sports use the anaerobic energy pathway during the active part of competition and rely on a strong aerobic base for quick recovery and regeneration between competitions. This sport category requires a high proportion of training dedicated to the improvement of maximum strength, power, and power-endurance without neglecting the importance of muscular endurance of short and medium duration. Figure 3.1 illustrates the relationships among the energy systems and the type of strength training suggested for the sports falling in each category.

	Anaerobic (aerobic independent)			Aerobic (aerobic dependent)			
Energy system	Alactic	Lactic acid		Aerobic			
Duration	0 10 s	40 s	70 s	2 min	6 min	25 min	1-2 h >6 h
Type of strength training needed	MxS P	MxS P, P-E	MxS P, P-E, M-ES	MxS P, P-E, M-EM	MxS P-E, M-EM, ME-L	MxS (<80%) M-EL	MxS (<80%) P-E, M-EL

Legend: MxS = maximum strength
P = power
P-E = power-endurance
M-ES = muscle-endurance of short duration
M-EM = muscle-endurance of medium duration
M-EL = muscle-endurance of long duration

Figure 3.1 Relationships between energy systems—duration in seconds (s), minutes (min), and hours (h)—and type of strength training for sports.

Figure 3.1 clearly shows the need for maximum strength training throughout the energy system continuum. Regardless of whether the sport is primarily anaerobic, aerobic, or an equal combination of both, the development of maximum strength is considered the foundation on which other dominant abilities are maximized. Increased muscle fiber density (laying down of protein filaments in muscle), motor unit recruitment patterns, and motor unit synchronization results in more muscle available to be used in sports requiring a high power output (anaerobic-dominant sports) and more muscle available to be used in endurance-based sports as the slow-twitch muscle fibers increase in size and diameter and provide a greater surface area for capillarization and mitochondrial density.

Every sport has its own physiological attributes and profile. In addition, the dominant bio-motor abilities and their distinctive combinations are unique to every sport. Consequently, effective training specialists intimately understand what separates one sport from another and successfully apply these physiological principles in the day-to-day training process. The following section on energy systems, how they relate to strength training, and how the six intensity zones can be used in most sport training will facilitate the application of these sport-specific characteristics in training.

Figures 3.1 and 3.2 demonstrate that many sports use the fuel produced by all three energy systems. *When a sport combines many energy systems, the training and physiology associated with the sport is more complex.* The six intensity zones illustrated in figure 3.2 are intended to point out the overall spectrum of energy systems training and their physiological and training characteristics. The heading of figure 3.2 illustrates the type of training for each intensity zone, the suggested duration of reps or drills, the suggested number of reps, the necessary rest interval to achieve the training goal, the lactic acid concentration following a rep or training session, and the percentage of maximum intensity necessary to stimulate a given energy system. Obviously, figure 3.2 is just a suggested guideline, an educated guess. However, the practical application of the six intensity zones must be planned according to athletes' potential, their work tolerance, and the specifics of a given training phase.

A brief analysis of each intensity zone will better illustrate certain details of each type of energy system training. The application of intensity zones to an athlete's training is more familiar to coaches of individual sports. The methodology used to apply the intensity zones to team sports, racket sports, the martial arts, and contact sports will determine the training efficiency and performance outcome.

Intensity zone	Type of training	Duration of a rep	Number of reps	Rest intervals	Lactic Acid concentration in mmols	Percentage of maximum intensity
1	Alactic system	4-12 s	10-30	2-5 min	1-2	>95
2	Lactic acid tolerance training	20-90 s	6-10	1-5 min	12-18	85-95
3	Maximum oxygen consumption training	3-5 min	8-12	2-3 min	6-12	80-85
4	Anaerobic threshold training	2-7 min	4-8	<5 min	4-6	65-80
5	Aerobic threshold training	10 min-2 h	1-6	2-3 min	2-3	60
6	Aerobic compensation	45 min-2 h	1-2	2-5 min	2-3	40-50

Figure 3.2 The physiological characteristics of training the energy systems via the six zones of intensity.

Intensity Zone 1

Anaerobic alactic system training is specific for all sports in which the anaerobic alactic energy system is dominant and in which the scope is to train speed and explosiveness. To benefit from training intensity zone 1, athletes must use very short (no longer than 12 seconds), fast or explosive reps or technical and tactical drills. To do so, they must plan intensities of over 95 percent of their maximum capacity, with a rest interval long enough for a complete fuel restoration (creatine phosphate).

The main scope of training is to increase maximum speed, fast propulsion off the starting blocks, quick reaction, and fast but short technical and tactical drills using ATP in the muscle and creatine phosphate (CP) as a fuel. Long recovery intervals between reps are essential to replace the muscles' CP supply.

If the rest interval is disregarded, as often happens in some team sports and contact sports, the restoration of CP will be incomplete, and as a result, anaerobic glycolysis will become a major source of energy. This in turn will produce high amounts of lactic acid that will force the athlete to either stop or slow down the speed of action. In the novice athlete, an aggressive increase in lactic acid buildup is often followed by muscle stiffness and discomfort. A rest interval of four to six minutes between sets is usually appropriate to allow full recovery. Light stretching or massage between sets can aid in the recovery process.

Intensity Zone 2

Lactic acid tolerance training increases athletes' ability to tolerate lactic acid buildup; it is useful for fast reps of 20 to 90/120 (120) seconds. Very high levels of lactic acid can result from high-intensity reps of 40 to 50 seconds. Lactic acid tolerance increases as a result of skeletal muscles' removal of lactic acid from the bloodstream. Recent studies have demonstrated that lactate transporters increase in number as a function of high-intensity training (Bonen, 2001). The ability to clear lactid acid from the bloodstream and transport it to slow-twitch muscle fibers for energy usage (Bonen et al., 1997) is an adaptive response that delays fatigue and inevitably improves performance.

Athletes who can tolerate the pain of acidosis (high lactic acid concentrations in the blood) can perform better longer. Therefore, the purpose of training intensity zone 2 is to adapt to the acidic effect of lactic acid buildup, to buffer the effects of lactic acid, to increase lactic acid removal from the working muscles, and to increase the physiological and psychological tolerance to the pain and agony of training and challenging competitions and games.

Training for intensity zone 2 can have two variations:

1. Organize high-intensity reps of longer duration (45 to 90 and up to 120 seconds) that would result in increased amounts (over 12 millimoles) of lactic acid. (A millimole, used as the measuring unit of lactic acid concentration in the blood, is one thousandth of a mole). To enable the athlete to repeat the same quality of work, long rest intervals (three to five minutes) are necessary to facilitate an almost complete removal of lactic acid. If the rest interval is not long enough, removal will be incomplete, and the acidosis will be severe. Under these conditions the athlete is forced to slow down the speed of a rep or drill below the intended level. Consequently, the athlete will not achieve the planned training effect, which is to increase the ability to tolerate the buildup of lactic acid

2. Organize a series of shorter reps or drills (20 to 45 seconds) with shorter rest intervals (30 seconds to 2 minutes), which will result in only the partial removal of lactic acid from the system. The physiological consequence of this type of training is that the athlete tolerates increased amounts of lactic acid, thus producing high levels of anaerobic power under the conditions of extreme acidosis. This method is often used as the competitive season approaches and the athlete's system is challenged to the maximum capacity. The first variation should be used first to prepare the body for the vigor of this variation.

Psychologically, the purpose of training intensity zone 2 is to push the athlete beyond the pain threshold. However, this type of training should not be used more than two, or at a maximum three, times per week because it exposes the athlete to critical levels of fatigue. Overdoing it may bring the athlete closer to the undesirable effect of overtraining and underproducing.

Intensity Zone 3

Maximum oxygen consumption training results in increased efficiency in oxygen transportation and usage. During training and competition both the central system including the heart and lungs and the peripheral system including the muscles, capillaries, and mitochondria are heavily taxed. Improved oxygen transportation to the muscle cell level, and especially increased efficiency in oxygen use, are important factors for improved performance in sports in which the aerobic system is dominant, or very important. Achieving this effect requires training periods of three to five minutes at 80 to 85 percent of maximum intensity (higher intensity for shorter reps and slightly lower intensity for longer reps).

The number of reps performed in a training session depends on the duration of the event: The longer the duration, the lower the number of reps. Therefore, an athlete may perform in a training session, say, 12 reps of three minutes each at 85 percent of 1RM, or six to eight reps at five minutes each at 80 percent of 1RM, with relatively similar training benefits. This zone of training is very popular in sports such as hockey that alter high-intensity movement with rest between shifts.

Intensity Zone 4

Anaerobic threshold training refers to an intensity of work in which the rate of lactic acid diffusion in the blood slightly exceeds the rate of removal (4 to 6 millimoles). The objective of intensity zone 4 is to increase the anaerobic threshold beyond 4 millimoles so that the athlete can maintain intensive work without accumulating excessive lactic acid buildup. During training an athlete may feel mild distress when working at a speed slightly faster than usual.

Shorter reps of one and a half to two minutes can use an intensity less than 80 percent of maximum, but with slightly longer rests between bouts (longer than five minutes). This type of training, as well as longer reps (five to seven 10-minute reps but at only 65 percent of maximum intensity) can stimulate the anaerobic metabolism without a significant rise of lactic acid production. Intensity zone 4 is often used in combination with intensity zone 2 as the athlete pushes the body to tolerate lactic acid buildup by training at the threshold of lactate accumulation. Remember that without a physiological challenge, overcompensation or an increase in physical performance beyond the preceding level of adaptation cannot occur

Intensity Zone 5

Aerobic threshold training is intended to increase athletes' aerobic capacity, which is so vital in many sports and events, especially those in which the oxygen supply represents a limiting factor for performance, such as medium- and long-duration running, swimming, and rowing events. Aerobic threshold training develops the functional efficiency of the cardiorespiratory system and the economical functioning of the metabolic system and increases the capacity to tolerate stress for long periods of time. Sufficient hydration is very important during training in this intensity zone. Insufficient hydration can reduce skin blood flow and the rate of sweating, which leads to a decreased rate of heat dissipation and hyperthermia (Coyle, 1999). This in turn can tremendously impair performance as cardiac output, stroke volume, and blood flow to the working muscles becomes impaired.

The purpose of aerobic threshold training is to increase aerobic capacity through the use of a high volume of work without interruption at a uniform pace. Interval training uses long reps (over 10 minutes) at intensities of moderate to medium-fast speed (lactic acid concentration of 2 to 3 millimoles and a heart rate of about 130 to 150 beats per minute).

The preparatory phase is the ideal time to improve the aerobic capacity of all athletes. Team sports, combative sports, and racket sports respond best when aerobic training is not planned in the form of traditional long easy distance runs. These sports require specific tactical drills, especially in the second part of the preparatory phase. Athletes involved in long-distance events, on the other hand, must use aerobic threshold training even during the competitive phase so that they continue to support the physiological environment that uses free fatty acids as a primary source of fuel.

Intensity Zone 6

Aerobic compensation training facilitates athletes' recovery following major competitions and high-intensity training sessions characteristic of intensity zones 2 and 3. Workouts using very light intensity (e.g., 40 to 50 percent of maximum intensity) must be planned, especially during the competitive phase, to eliminate the metabolites from the system and speed up the process of recovery and regeneration. This type of training should be used following important competitions and stressful workouts.

High-intensity endurance training is an important and necessary component of adaptation and performance enhancement. However, strenuous exercise often negatively affects the body before it can recover and become stronger. Active recovery such as cycling or running for 15 to 20 minutes at approximately 50 percent of maximum capacity can aid in recovery and regeneration. Strenuous endurance-type training followed by static rest such as lying down or sitting can delay the regeneration of the body's systems and the removal of the harmful by-products of training. Elevated levels of plasma free fatty acids, decreased levels of white blood cell counts, and low levels of immune system catalysts such as neutrophils and monocytes (Wigernaes et al., 2001) slow down healing. Active recovery has been shown to counteract the increase in free fatty acids, eliminate the drop in neutrophil and monocyte count, and override the drop in white blood cell count (Wigernaes et al., 2001). In other words, active recovery reignites immune system function following strenuous training, which in turn allows the body to regenerate at a quicker rate.

By the end of the training session, the difficult part of the workout is complete. Athletes willing to live with the sacrifice needed for improvement and adaptation should take 15 to 20 minutes at the end of the session to foster healing and regeneration. Not doing so will slow down the healing process and possibly negatively affect the next training session. Not taking the time to heal followed by continual work will imminently lead to overtraining and injury.

During very demanding weeks of training, intensity zone 6 may be used once or twice a week, sometimes combined with other intensities, but at the end of a workout.

The six intensity zones for training the energy systems are not applicable only to endurance-dominant sports. On the contrary, team, contact, and racket sports can greatly benefit from the development of sport-specific physical abilities by using this training methodology. All of these sports use the three energy systems in specific proportions. Therefore, the sport-specific proportions of the three energy systems have to be properly trained by using specific technical and tactical drills designed around the intensity and duration of the six intensity zones (see figure 3.2).

For instance, to train the anaerobic alactic system, athletes do not have to plan only short, maximum-velocity sprints. They can realize the same, yet more specific, benefits from using short, but very fast, specific technical or tactical drills. The closer the tactical and technical skills are to those used in the sport, the greater the adaptation will be.

A special consideration should be given to training intensity zone 5, which traditionally involves long-distance, low-pace jogging. Athletes will be more successful and react more positively if they use technical or tactical drills with lower intensity, but with the duration, number of reps, and rest intervals suggested in figure 3.2.

With intensity zone 6, aerobic compensation training, training is usually organized following a game or tournament, or a very demanding workout session. Low-intensity, longer-duration technical drills will have the desired compensation benefits, especially if the session is fun and incorporates psychological relaxation and physiotherapeutic techniques (e.g., massage, stretching, etc).

How to Integrate Strength and Energy Systems Training

After studying the six zones of training the energy systems, the question is how to integrate them with strength training programs that are specific for different sports. The examples of integrating energy systems training with strength training (discussed in the following sections) will focus mostly on two types of plans: the basic structure of yearly plans, and microcycles. The emphasis is on these two types of plans because they are the most important and practical of all the plans in the methodology of training.

Yearly Plan

Sports training is complex because every sport requires time to develop technical and tactical skills; speed; endurance; strength; power, agility, and quickness; and social and psychological relationships. The question is, how can we address these qualities and integrate all of these complex training elements to facilitate recovery and regeneration after competitions and between training sessions? Figures 3.3, 3.4, 3.5, 3.6, and 3.7 illustrate the application of strength and energy system training for variations of yearly plans and microcycles. It is important to notice how the dynamics of training the energy systems progresses from the preparatory phase to the competitive phase, so that best adaptation is reached prior to the start of the major competitions. Improvements are possible only if adaptation increases from year to year.

Figure 3.3 illustrates a yearly plan used by a college basketball team. In the top of the chart we refer to the months of the year and the specific training phases for a college basketball team. The periodization of strength and speed-endurance are presented in the following two lines. In the first case, the specific phases of the periodization of strength are suggested: anatomical adaptation; maximum strength; and then the conversion of maximum strength to sport-specific power, power-endurance, and agility or quickness.

The order of energy system zones in each training phase is intended to illustrate the emphasis of a given energy system. For instance, the anatomical adaptation phase in figure 3.3 suggests a higher volume of training for intensity zone 5 (aerobic threshold training) than for intensity zone 4. This approach is visible in each training phase for each example provided.

In the second case, for the periodization of speed-endurance, we'll use the intensity zone numbers to illustrate which energy system is trained in a given phase. The progression from aerobic-dominant types of training (intensity zones 4 and 5) to the lactic acid tolerance and anaerobic alactic system training (maximum speed) should follow the natural progression of the annual plan beginning with the preparatory phase and into the competitive phase. In each training phase we have prioritized the intensity zones; the first intensities are always the main training objective. Although during the early preparatory phase (July and early August) non-specific training methods can be used, from the second part of August on, sport-specific drills have to be a priority. The coach must design specific drills so that sport-specific intensities are trained in preparation for the competitive phase (intensity zones 1, 2, 3, and 4).

Periodization months	July	Aug	Sept	Oct	Nov	Dec	Jan	Feb	Mar	Apr	May	Jun
Training phases	Preparatory				Competitive						Transition	
Periodization of strength	AA	MxS		P, P-E, A/Q	Maint.: P, P-E, A/Q						Compensation	
Periodization of energy systems training zones (endurance and speed)	5, 4	3, 2, 1, 6		1, 2, 4, 6	1, 2, 4, 6						5	

Legend: AA = anatomical adaptation
A/Q = agility/quickness

Figure 3.3 Suggested guideline for integrating strength and energy systems training for an annual plan for a college basketball team. You may use this model to design annual plans for other team sports.

Unlike team sports (see figure 3.3), many individual sports in which endurance is dominant have one of the following:

1. A yearly plan with one peak (see figure 3.4). These include distance running, rowing, cross-country skiing, triathlon, road cycling, marathon canoeing, speedskating, and so forth. Because the calendar months are drastically different for summer and winter sports, the months are simply depicted with numbers 1 to 12.

Periodization months	1	2	3	4	5	6	7	8	9	10	11	12
Training phases	Preparatory			Preparatory				Competitive				T
Periodization of strength	AA	MxS (60-80%)	T	MxS (<80%), M-EL		Maint.: MxS (<80%), M-EL		Maint.: MxS (70-80%), M-EL				AA
Periodization of energy systems training (endurance and speed)	5, 4		5	4, 5, 3		3, 4, 2, 5, 6		3, 4, 2, 6				5

Note: The first transition phase (T) is one week long, whereas the second transition phase is four weeks long.

Figure 3.4 A suggested annual plan for endurance-dominant sports with one peak (one major competitive phase), where the integration of energy systems and strength training are periodized to facilitate best performance during the competitive phase (months 8-11, or May-August for the Northern hemisphere).

2. A yearly plan with two major peaks (see figure 3.5). These include sports with indoor and outdoor championships, such as track and field, or winter and summer championships, such as swimming. In some sports the second preparatory phase (preparatory 2) is shorter, such as in mid- and long-distance track-and-field events. Under these conditions, athletes must train the foundation of aerobic endurance during preparatory 1 and maintain it during the first phase of competition (competitive 1). Doing it differently would result in lower performance at the end of competitive 2, which is when major championships are scheduled.

Periodization months	Oct	Nov	Dec	Jan	Feb	Mar	Apr	May	Jun	Jul	Aug	Sep
Training phases	Preparatory			Competitive		T	Prep.	Competitive				T
Periodization of strength	AA	MxS (60- 90%)	M-E	Maint.: MxS (<80%), M-E		AA	MxS	Maint.: MxS (<80%), M-EL				AA
Periodization of energy systems training (speed and endurance)	5, 4		3, 2, 5, 4, 6	2, 3, 4, 6		5	3, 2, 5, 4, 6	2, 3, 4, 6				5

Figure 3.5 An example of an integrated annual plan for individual sports with two peaks. Please note how the energy systems and strength training are periodized to peak for the two competitive phases. NOTE: The duration of the first transition phase (T) is 2 weeks. A one-week transition may also be planned after MxS, in both Preparatory 1 and 2.

Intensity zone 1 (anaerobic alactic system training) is missing from the suggested training intensities for all the aerobic-dominant sports (see figures 3.4 and 3.5). Many North American training specialists might find this surprising because they consider speed training (or anaerobic alactic system training) essential for a good performance in these sports. For aerobic-dominant sports (road cycling, triathlon, distance running, cross-country skiing, and marathons and half marathons), the speed trained for 10 to 20 seconds is immaterial to the final performance.

The key element to success in aerobic dominant sports is not the high-velocity training typical of intensity zone 1 but rather the *mean velocity per race*, which is trained via intensity zones 3 through 5. In addition, training for intensity zone 1, which is often planned prior to major competitions, is far too stressful, both physiologically and psychologically. As a result, the athlete will enter the race with slightly depleted glycogen stores and an undesirable residual nervous system fatigue. Speed benefits, especially in the early part of the race, will increase more as a result of better strength training than by stressing intensity zone 1.

For mid-distance events, on the other hand, intensity zone 1, along with strength training, is essential for increasing maximum velocity. However, because the buildup of lactic acid is the major challenge in these events, intensity zone 2 has to be stressed, in obvious proportions, from the half of the first preparatory phase and onward.

Figure 3.6 illustrates a yearly plan for contact sports, such as the martial arts, boxing, and wrestling. Because the dates of competitions can differ between sports, the months of the year are numbered, rather than named. This is a tri-cycle yearly plan, meaning that there are three major competitions to train for. Certainly, such a plan is very condensed and relatively complicated as a result of the limited time available to establish the foundations of training (i.e., intensity zones 5 and 4). This is why, if possible, we try to make the first cycle longer, to spare more time for training fundamentals, including the improvement of technical skills.

Periodization months	1	2	3	4	5	6	7	8	9	10		11	12
Training phases	Preparatory			Competitive	T	Prep.		Comp.	T	Prep.		Comp.	T
Periodization of strength	AA	MxS	P, P-E, A/Q	Maint.: P, P-E, A/Q	AA	MxS	P, P-E, A/Q	Maint.: P, P-E, A/Q	AA	MxS	P, P-E, A/Q	Maint.: P, P-E, A/Q	AA
Periodization of energy systems training (endurance and speed)	4, 5	3, 2, 1, 6		1, 2, 3, 5	5	1, 2, 3, 6		1, 2, 6	5	3, 2, 1, 6		1, 2, 3, 6	6, 5

Figure 3.6 An illustration of integration of strength and energy systems training for contact sports.

Microcycle

The integration of strength and energy systems is a training necessity not only for yearly plans but also for microcycles. Two examples will illustrate the application of the concept of integration and alternation of energy systems and strength training. The first example, shown in figure 3.7, illustrates a five-day microcycle for racket sports, which is also applicable to contact sports.

Each of the training days shown in figure 3.7 has several training objectives, such as technical, tactical, and three types of strength training needed for these sports. All technical and tactical

Monday	Tuesday	Wednesday	Thursday	Friday	Saturday	Sunday
TA	TE	TE/TA	TE/TA	TA	Off	Off
2, 3	1, 2, 6	3, 5, 6	1, 2, 6	2, 3, 4	Off	Off
Strength P-E	Strength P, MxS	—	Strength P	Strength P-E	Off	Off

Legend: TE = technical training
          TA = tactical training

Figure 3.7 A suggested integration and alternation of energy systems and strength training for racket sports, contact sports, and the martial arts.

sessions should mostly use sport-specific drills according to the physiology of each intensity zone. In other words, training coaches would do well to elicit sport-specific adaptations by designing sport-specific drills for each intensity.

Consider intensity zone 3. Designing sport-specific drills for three to five minutes is more beneficial for athletes' sport-specific adaptation than asking them to run for three to five minutes with the required intensity. If the duration and the specific intensity are observed for the technical and tactical drills, especially from the second part of the preparatory phase on, the sport-specific adaptation is far superior to that realized from nonspecific types of training. Nonspecific training has to be planned mostly during the early part of the preparatory phase. As the competition approaches, sport-specific drills must be dominant.

Monday's training session involves tactical training and intensity zones 2 (lactic acid tolerance training) and 3 (maximum oxygen consumption training). (Intensity zone 1 is not recommended, even though the athletes are coming off of two days of rest.) Because this workout taxes the lactic acid and oxygen systems, the suggested strength training is power-endurance training. The main benefit of this strategy is that the lactic acid system is also taxed for power-endurance training, and as a result, the rate of posttraining recovery is the same. Matching intensity zones 2 and 3 with, say, maximum strength is a physiological design error because the rate of recovery and regeneration of each system is different.

Training priorities for Tuesday's training session are intensity zone 1 (anaerobic alactic), followed by intensity zone 2 (lactic acid tolerance), interposed with intensity zone 6. For faster regeneration between workouts, the latter type of training (aerobic compensation) can also be planned at the end of the workout. The strength training program planned for Tuesday is power and maximum strength, or a combination of both, which taxes the anaerobic alactic system, the same energy system used for intensity zone 1.

To alternate energy systems, and as a result, facilitate the speeded-up process of recovery and regeneration between training days of each system, the program for Wednesday is directed toward another energy system: aerobic. Planning intensity zone 6 at the end of the session is even more beneficial for faster recovery. Thursday's training has similar objectives as those for Tuesday, whereas the Friday program starts with drills taxing the lactic acid system and culminates in the second part of training with the aerobic system and the emphasis of sport-specific tactical drills.

At the end of Friday's training session we suggest power-endurance training, but with a higher number of reps (30 to 50 for two to three sets).

The example in figure 3.8 is created for aerobic-dominant sports, such as marathon running; road cycling; and long-distance events in swimming, running, and cross-country skiing.

Each of the six training days has specific training objectives. On Monday, for instance, the major training goal is aerobic endurance to stimulate central and peripheral adaptations. This

Monday	Tuesday	Wednesday	Thursday	Friday	Saturday	Sunday
Aerobic	Aerobic	Lactic acid/ Aerobic	Aerobic	Aerobic/ Lactic acid	Aerobic	Off
4, 5	3, 6	2, 6, 5	4, 5	4, 2, 6	5	Off
Strength M-EL	Strength MxS <80%	—	Strength M-EL	—	Strength P	Off

Figure 3.8 Integrated strength and metabolic training for an aerobic-dominant sport: late preparatory or competitive phase.

has to be a major concern for any athletes in these sports because the ability to transport and use oxygen and use free fatty acids as fuel is of primary concern during races. Such a goal is achieved by planning long reps, such as 6 reps of 10 minutes each; four reps of 20 minutes each; or long-duration (two reps at 45 minutes each), nonstop aerobic training (see figure 3.2). Strength training planned at the end of the workout has to address the same energy system, such as muscular endurance of long duration (exemplified in chapter 11).

On Tuesday the major objective is to improve maximum oxygen consumption via reps of three to five minutes each followed by compensation training (intensity zone 6). Although the type of strength training suggested for Tuesday (maximum strength below 80 percent) does not match the dominant energy system taxed in that day, this is needed to maintain the ability of the neuromuscular system to recruit higher numbers of fast-twitch muscle fibers. If this type of strength training is neglected (i.e., maximum strength is not maintained), the athlete will not achieve the force necessary to achieve performance objectives at the end of the competitive phase.

The program suggested for Wednesday is a difficult one. It starts with intensity zone 2 to train the body and mind to adapt, and as such, to tolerate the pain and stress of the lactic acid buildup using 20 to 90 reps of 120 seconds each. The benefit of this type of training is visible in the early part of a race when the runner is able to tolerate the lactic acid buildup. Intensity zone 6 is planned immediately after intensity zone 2 so that the body can compensate following such a physiological and psychological stress. After completing one 30-minute bout in intensity zone 6, the athlete can perform four 10-minute bouts in intensity zone 5, once again followed by 15 minutes of compensation training (intensity zone 6). Sometimes the recovery following a set is more important to adaptation than the set itself.

On Thursday we suggest once again stressing intensity zones 4 and 5 to improve the efficiency of the metabolic system, use free fatty acids as a fuel, and at the end, plan a muscular endurance of long duration strength training program. For Friday the plan is more complex. The main objective of this training session is to adapt the athlete to perform lactic acid system training (intensity zone 2) based on the residual fatigue that resulted from first performing anaerobic threshold training (intensity zone 4). Such a combination of training duplicates the physiological state the athlete encounters at the end of the race when he has to produce energy via the anaerobic system. The session will once again end with 30 minutes of compensation training (intensity zone 6). This microcycle ends with an easier aerobic training session (aerobic threshold training, or intensity zone 5), followed by 20 minutes of power training.

The number of strength training sessions suggested here might seem high. In actuality, the exercises have to be very specific and therefore as low as possible (i.e., between two and four). Athletes might finish such a strength training session in 15 to 20 minutes, which is not a long time considering the potential gains in specific adaptation.

Importance of Strength Training for Endurance Sports

Many athletes and training coaches have misconceptions about the use of strength, or endurance, training, regardless of whether the sport is speed or power dominant or aerobic endurance dominant. Following is a brief analysis of some of these misconceptions:

■ *Aerobic-endurance-dominant sports don't need strength training.* In many of these sports, such as running and cross-country skiing, the force of the propulsion phase (pushing off against the ground to project the body forward) is the essential element for an improved performance. The same is true for the arms' drive through the water in swimming; the force applied against the pedal in road cycling; or the force of the blade drive through the water in rowing, canoeing, and kayaking. Relying solely on specific training is far from sufficient to improve performance from year to year. Higher velocity is possible only as a result of superior force application against resistance (i.e., gravity, snow, terrain profile, and water).

A brief example from running will demonstrate the importance of strength training. (Figure 3.4 shows the periodized strength training necessary to improve the propulsion phase, and as a result, the mean velocity per race.) For improved propulsion, an athlete must increase the force applied against the ground. This is possible only if the athlete uses maximum strength, as indicated in figure 3.4. Two simple exercises, such as calf raises and knee lifts, will strengthen the major muscle groups including the gastrocnemius and soleus during the propulsion phase, and adapt the iliopsoas muscle group to lift the knee higher during running. As a result, a greater number of muscle fibers will be contracted during these actions, resulting in faster running.

A long-distance event requires much more than the improvement of force per stride using elements of maximum strength. Athletes must then convert this gain into muscular endurance of long duration so that the same force is applied for the entire duration of the race. Now the benefit is increased mean velocity per race, not just for the start. Let's assume that more muscle fibers will be recruited during the propulsion phase for an increased stride of 1 centimeter, or 3/8 of an inch. Considering that a runner performs 50,000 strides during a marathon, the actual gain per race is 500 meters (550 yards)! This, depending on the runner's performance time, could mean running the race faster by one and a half to two minutes!

■ *Uphill running develops leg strength and power.* Athletes who are asked why they are doing uphill running generally answer, "to improve leg strength and power." This has not been proven to be the case. For an exercise to qualify as a strength-power exercise, it has to be performed fast and explosively. In the case of running, the propulsion phase has to be around 200 milliseconds. The propulsion phase in uphill running is, at best, around 300 milliseconds.

Uphill running is performed in an interval training mode, meaning that the athlete runs uphill for 25 to 50 yards, or meters, in a set time, and jogs or walks back to the starting point. A rest interval of one to three minutes is taken between reps. Training demand depends on the distance of a rep, the time required to perform it, and the degree of the slope's inclination. A slope of more than 10 degrees is regarded as very challenging.

However, uphill running can have a major benefit for the cardiorespiratory system. When an athlete runs uphill, her heart rate can be around 160 to more than 170 beats per minute. This demonstrates that the heart is highly stimulated, and that uphill running strengthens the heart by increasing the stroke volume, or the force of the heart, to pump more blood to the working muscles. As such, the muscles are supplied with more nutrients and the oxygen needed to produce energy.

The best time to use uphill running as a training method to develop the cardiorespiratory system is from the second part of the preparatory phase onward, following the development of the aerobic foundation. Training can be organized according to the interval training methodology: several reps of selected distances, with a target time in mind, and a prescribed rest interval (i.e., eight 30-yard/meter reps at seven to eight seconds with a rest interval of two minutes). An uphill running workout can follow the specifics of energy system training, as follows:

1. Anaerobic alactic reps on a slope of less than 15 degrees performed as fast as realistically possible: 6 to 15 reps at five to eight seconds with a rest interval of two to three minutes.

2. Lactic acid reps on a slope of less than 10 degrees performed at a fast but steady pace: 6 to 10 reps at 15 to 30 seconds with a rest interval of one to two minutes.

■ *Long-distance aerobic training is necessary for the development of endurance for team, racket, and contact sports and the martial arts.* Although the methodology to develop motor abilities for sports has been improving constantly, some antiquated methods are still in use, especially in the area of developing endurance. All of these sports are speed- and power-dominant sports in which the role of aerobic endurance is less important, except for some team sports, such as soccer, lacrosse, rugby, and water polo. And yet, in sports such as American football, cricket, baseball, hockey, and basketball, long-distance jogging is still prescribed to develop aerobic endurance. During a game, for instance, an American football linebacker performs 40 to 60 reps of three to six seconds each with rests of one to three minutes. Running five miles will not improve his performance.

Athletes in these sports should be trained by using interval training methodology and specific speed- and power-endurance training such as jump squats followed by fifty 10- to 15-meter/yard maximum velocity sprints with rest intervals of two to three minutes. Athletes need four to six weeks of training, starting with fifteen 15-meter/yard sprints, to reach the required training level. Figure 3.9 illustrates a periodized program for specific endurance for the preparatory phase for athletes competing in this group of sports.

Preparatory Phase		
Aerobic/Anaerobic endurance	Alactic/Lactic acid endurance	Alactic/Lactic acid endurance
Long repetitions	Short repetitions	Position-specific repetitions
Non-specific training	Specific technical and tactical drills	Position-specific speed technical/tactical drills

Legend: Long repetitions = 3-600m/y repeated 4-8 (>10) times
Short repetitions = 50-200m repeated 8-14 times
Specific speed: According to the physiological requirement of the sport and the specifics of the position played (distance, type of speed required [i.e., changes of direction, stop-and-go, etc.], and the mean number of repetitions per game)

Figure 3.9 A suggested preparatory phase for speed- and power-dominant sports.

Long reps performed during the early part of the preparatory phase are nonspecific (see figure 3.9). From the second phase on, however, training has to be very specific; anaerobic alactic and lactic acid endurance will only improve through the use of specific technical and tactical drills. Training coaches should design specific drills for each intensity (duration, intensity, number of reps, and rest interval) so that their athletes will be trained according to the physiological needs of the sport and their player positions.

■ *Speed training must be accomplished via a game (racket sports, the martial arts, or other sport-specific method).* On the contrary, speed can also be developed using nonspecific training methods and techniques. In the case of team and racket sports, speed represents the ability to cover a given distance as fast as possible. For other sports, such as the martial arts and boxing, speed represents the ability to quickly deliver an offensive action, a punch, or to quickly react to the same kind of action delivered by the opponent. In both cases speed has a strength and power component. Equally true, in both cases an athlete will never be fast before being strong! Therefore, strength and power training can improve speed.

Preparatory Phase				
Periodization of strength/Power			Maximum speed	Sport-specific speed
AA	MxS	P, P-E	Maximum speed Maximum quickness Agility Integrate speed with MxS and Power training	Action-reaction Quick changes of direction/Stop-and-go agility Maximum velocity in different directions Integrate speed with MxS and Power training

Figure 3.10 Suggested periodization of sport-specific speed.

As illustrated by figure 3.10, the development of sport-specific speed is achieved through three major training phases:

1. Develop maximum strength and power via the periodization of strength.

2. Develop maximum velocity (different direction, changes of direction, and so on) with long rest intervals between reps (four to seven minutes, depending on the distance the athlete is repeating). Start with maximum velocity over short distance (15 to 20 meters/yards) and progressively increase the distance to 30, 40, and eventually 60 meters or yards. The critical element in the decision to increase the distance has to be dictated by the form the athlete maintains during a repetition. If the form (running technique) deteriorates toward the end of a repetition, it means the athlete lacks the necessary power to continue quality speed. Rigidity during running (contracted facial muscles, grimaces, or rigid and lifted shoulders) is another sign that the distance used is longer than the athlete can perform with good form and adequate power.

For the martial arts and contact sports the speed of delivering a hit or punch can be developed by using different training equipment, such as medicine balls, power balls, resistance provided by ankle and wrist weights, and so on. Such a program can also be periodized by starting with heavier weights and decreasing them as the competition phase approaches. In this way, maximum speed of delivering an offensive action is maximized.

3. Develop sport-specific speed according to the specifics of the sport and the position played. Now the athletes have to use game- and sport-specific technical and tactical drills, with specific distance, velocity, changes of direction, and rest intervals between reps. For the martial arts and contact sports, training should include offensive and defensive drills to train the athletes to act—and react—to match-specific situations. Agility drills specific for each sport are also helpful.

When integrated, strength training and energy system training can have a tremendous impact on an athlete's physiological adaptation to the sport. A subtle understanding of the major energy systems, phases of training, and of course the practical application of intensity zones will help training coaches design and implement sport-specific programs. As a rule of thumb, it is very important to design each training session with activities that stress the same energy system. This will force the body to train one system at a time and leave the other systems intact for other training days. Also, intensity zone training is best used in combination with sport-specific technical and tactical drills. In the early to middle preparatory phase, using traditional methods of training, anaerobic threshold or maximum oxygen consumption training is fine. As the competitive phase approaches, however, athletes must perform sport-specific drills that integrate the type of strength (e.g., power-endurance or muscular endurance) and energy system specific to the sport.

Principles of Strength Training for Sports

Training guidelines and principles fulfill important training goals for any student of strength training for sports. Proper application ensures superior organization with the fewest errors. The six basic laws of strength training (outlined in the following section) form the foundation from which all strength training programs should be formulated. The principles of training (appearing later in this chapter) outline the practical application of the laws in strength training programs. A house is only as strong as its foundation. The six basic laws of strength training work together to produce a strong, flexible, and stable athlete that can sustain the vigor of sport. This is achieved by developing the tendons, ligaments and bones; strengthening the core; and adapting the body to the movements of the sport. The laws apply to all athletes regardless of the physiological qualities of the sport. The principles of training promote a steady and specific increase in strength and other abilities by specifically adapting the program to the needs of the sport and, most importantly, to the physical capacity of the individual athlete. The laws and principles work hand in hand in the quest to develop superior programs of strength. These principles, together with the application of periodization of strength and the integration of strength training with the energy system training, are essential to any successful training program.

Six Basic Laws of Strength Training

Any strength training program should apply the six basic laws of training to ensure adaptation and keep athletes free of injury. This is especially important for young athletes.

Law 1: Develop Joint Flexibility

Most strength training exercises use the entire range of motion of major joints, especially the knees, ankles, and hips. Good joint flexibility prevents strain and pain around the knees, elbows, and other joints. Ankle flexibility (plantar flexion, or bringing the toes toward the calf) should be a major concern for all athletes, especially beginners. Good flexibility also prevents stress injuries. Athletes must start developing ankle flexibility during prepubescence and pubescence so that in the latter stages of athletic development they need only maintain it. Partner-assisted stretching and proprioceptive neuromuscular facilitation (PNF) are great methods for improving flexibility and relaxing the muscles after a stressful game or workout session.

Law 2: Develop Ligament and Tendon Strength

Muscle strength improves faster than tendon and ligament strength. Misuse and faulty use of the principle of specificity, or lack of a long-term vision, causes many training specialists and coaches to overlook the overall strengthening of ligaments. Yet most injuries are not at the muscle, but rather at the ligaments. Tendons and ligaments grow strong through anatomical adaptation. Without proper anatomical adaptation, vigorous strength training can injure the tendons and ligaments. Training tendons and ligaments causes them to enlarge in diameter, increasing their ability to withstand tension and tearing.

Made up of the fibrous protein collagen, ligaments play the important role of attaching articulating bones to each other across a joint. The collagen fibrils are arranged in varying degrees of folds to help resist an increase in load. The strength of a ligament directly depends on its cross-sectional area. Excessive force directed at a joint may rupture ligaments. During regular exercise or activity ligaments are easily elongated to allow movement in the joint to occur naturally. When a high load is applied such as in competition or training, the stiffness of the ligaments increase in order to restrict excessive motion in the joint. However if the load is too great, ligaments are not able to withstand the stress and an injury can occur. Obviously the best way to prevent injury is to avoid it or properly condition the body to handle the stress. Conditioning the ligaments with a cycle of loading and unloading as done in the anatomical adaptation phase of training adapts the structures to handle the stress and provide adequate time for regeneration. Progressively increasing the load used in training improves the visco-elastic properties of ligaments and allows them to better accomodate high tensile loads such as dynamic movements, plyometrics and maximum strength training.

The primary function of a tendon is to connect muscles to bone. Similarly important, tendons transmit force from muscle to bones so that movement can occur. Tendons also store elastic energy, which is so important in any ballistic movements, such as plyometrics. The stronger the tendon is, the greater is its capacity to store elastic energy. Sprinters and jumpers in track and field have very powerful tendons. Without these strong tendons they wouldn't be able to apply such great force against the bones to overcome the force of gravity.

Ligaments and tendons are trainable. Their material and structural properties change as a result of training, increasing their thickness, strength, and stiffness by up to 20 percent (Frank, 1996). Ligaments and tendons are also capable of healing, although they won't recover to their preinjury capability. Their mechanical properties are characterized as a load–deformation relation in response to tensile force (Woo et al., 1994).

Exercise, especially the type performed during the anatomical adaptation phase, can be considered an injury-prevention method. The abilities of tendons and ligaments to secure the anatomical integrity of joints (ligaments), and to transmit force (tendons), can decline if their strengthening is disrupted. Equally important to note, especially for steroids users, is that abusing this substance results in increasing the muscle force at the expense of the ligaments' and tendons' material properties (Woo et al., 1994). Increasing force without correspondingly strengthening ligaments and tendons results in the ligament and tendon injuries so many professional American football players experience.

Law 3: Develop Core Strength

The arms and legs are only as strong as the trunk. A poorly developed trunk is a weak support for hard-working limbs. Strength training programs should first strengthen the core muscles before focusing on the arms and legs.

Core muscles act as shock absorbers during jumps, rebounds, or plyometric exercises; stabilize the body; and represent a link, or transmitter, between the legs and arms. Weak core muscles fail in these essential roles, limiting the athlete's ability to perform. Most of these muscles seem to be dominated by slow-twitch muscle fibers because of their supporting role to the arms and legs. They contract constantly, but not necessarily dynamically, to create a solid base of support for the actions of other muscle groups of the body.

Many people complain of low back problems yet do little to correct them. The best protection against low back problems is well-developed back and abdominal muscles. Coaches and athletes must pay more attention to this area of the body.

Core strength training is currently being touted as a new theory with concomitant new exercises, some of which are useless and even dangerous. In this section we offer our point of view or school of thought regarding core training and the need to emphasize core training as a completely separate entity when designing a strength training program. As discussed below, it is our belief that focusing on the core does nothing to promote an increase in performance but only serves as a means of distracting the athlete from performing a host of exercises that are integral to sport performance, the prime movers of the sport.

The abdominal and back muscles surround the core area of the body with a tight and powerful support structure of muscle bundles running in different directions. Because many athletes have weak abdominal muscles in relation to their backs, general and specific abdominal muscle training is recommended. The rectus abdominis runs vertically and pulls the trunk forward when the legs are fixed, as in sit-ups, to maintain good posture. If the abdominal muscles are poorly developed, the hips tilt forward and lordosis, or a swayback, develops at the lumbar area of the spine.

The internal and external obliques help the rectus abdominis bend the trunk forward and perform all twisting, lateral bending, and trunk-rotating motions. They help an athlete recover from a fall in many sports and perform many actions in boxing, wrestling, and the martial arts. The anterior and lateral abdominal muscles perform delicate, precise trunk movements. These large muscles run vertically, diagonally, and horizontally.

Isolating the abdominal muscles requires an exercise that bends the spine but not the hips. Exercises that flex the hips are performed by the iliopsoas (a powerful hip flexor) and to a lesser extent by the abdominal muscles. Sit-ups are the most popular abdominal exercise. The best sit-up position is lying on the back with the calves resting on a chair or bench. This position isolates the abdominal muscles because the hips are already bent.

The back muscles, including the deep back muscles of the vertebral column, are responsible for many movements such as back extension and extending and rotating the trunk. The trunk acts as the transmitter and supporter of most arm and leg actions. The vertebral column also plays an essential role as a shock absorber during landing and takeoff actions.

Excessive, uneven stress on the spine or sudden movement while in an unfavorable position may lead to back problems. For athletes, back problems may be due to wear and tear caused by improper positioning or forward tilting of the body. Disc pressure varies according to body position relative to external stress. Stress on the spine increases during lifting in standing or seated positions or when the upper body swings, such as in upright rowing or elbow flexion. Sitting produces greater disc pressure than standing; the least stress occurs when the body is prone (such as during bench presses or pulls). In many exercises that use the back muscles, abdominal muscles contract isometrically, stabilizing the body.

The iliopsoas is an essential muscle for hip flexion and running. Though not large, it is the most powerful hip flexor, responsible for swinging the legs forward during running and jumping. Sports performed on the ground and ice require a well-developed iliopsoas. Exercises such as leg and knee lifts against resistance are keys to training this important muscle.

Activation Overflow   When an athlete performs a strength exercise, many muscles of the core area are activated and contract synergistically to stabilize the body, to act as a support so that a limb can perform the exercise. This synergistic contraction is called *activation overflow*, or *irradiation* (Enoka, 2002; Zijdewind and Kernell, 2001). The following examples will illustrate how this theory works:

- *Upright rowing* (standing with feet apart while arms, holding a barbell, are lowered in front of the thighs). As the arms flex to lift and lower the weight toward the chest, the abdominal and back muscles, including the erector spinae (core muscles), contract to stabilize the trunk so that the arms can perform the action smoothly. Without the support from the core muscles to stabilize the trunk, the prime movers would not be very effective in performing the task. However, while the exercise is performed, all the core muscles are activated, are contracted (activation overflow), and as a result, are strengthened. Because the level of muscle contraction is higher during this exercise than it is during most free-weight exercises for core strength, the core muscles are better developed.

- *Leg press and squatting.* During any leg actions against resistance, all the core area muscles are strongly activated to stabilize the trunk and use it as a support. This activation results in strengthening the muscles involved.

- *Spiking.* One of the most dynamic athletic skills, spiking in volleyball, could not be properly performed without the direct support of the core muscles. During spiking, the core muscles contract to stabilize the trunk so that the legs can perform an explosive takeoff as the arms hit the ball.

- During *running, jumping, throwing, quick feet/agility movement, and medicine ball exercises,*

The core muscles are key to spiking the volleyball, stabilizing the trunk, and enabling power to be converted from the legs to the arms.

the core muscles contract to fixate and stabilize the trunk so that the arms and legs can perform the athletic task.

Stability Ball Training Like everything in sport-specific training, the stability ball, also known as the exercise ball or balance ball, is not new. The stability ball first hit the scene back in the 1960s and has become a very popular device especially in rehabilitative settings. Since the 1990s stability balls have also become very popular in the sport and fitness fields. Their popularity in the fitness field is understandable, given that the field is all about variety and excitement.

Many of the exercises performed on the ball are effective for providing a good level of upper- and lower-body strength, flexibility, and of course, core strength. Some in the sporting world, however, overemphasize the benefits of these exercises for athletes, claiming that improvements in proprioception and balance translate to improvements in athletic performance. Balance is not a limiting factor for performance, and it is not in the same category as speed, reaction, strength, and endurance. Participation in the sport itself and practicing technical and tactical drills related to the sport is enough of a stimulus to adapt the body to the unstable environment of the sport. Selected exercises can be performed on the ball, but they should be limited to the anatomical adaptation or transition phases of training when general adaptation takes precedence over specific physiological adaptation.

Performing a maximum strength phase on a stability ball can be very detrimental to athletic performance. The ball limits the amount of weight the athlete can lift and thus reduces the activation of the fast-twitch muscle fibers. The only stability ball exercise we would recommend would be those for training the abdominal muscles. Other muscle groups can be trained more effectively with other means of training. The participation in the sport itself and practicing of technical and tactical drills related to the sport is enough of a stimulus to adapt the body to the unstable environment of the sport. Stability balls have a time and place in training. "Activation overflow" explains how the body adapts to training and how the major muscles involved in a movement in essence communicate to each other and offer their help. Our bodies are extremely plastic and adapt wonderfully to traditional methods of training. Most importantly to sports, an athlete's body performs better when it adapts better, thereby creating stability naturally.

Law 4: Develop the Stabilizers

Prime movers work more efficiently with strong stabilizer, or fixator, muscles. Stabilizers contract, primarily isometrically, to immobilize a limb so that another part of the body can act. For example, the shoulders are immobilized during elbow flexion, and the abdominal muscles serve as stabilizers when the arms throw a ball. In rowing, when the trunk muscles act as stabilizers, the trunk transmits leg power to the arms, which then drive the blade through the water. A weak stabilizer inhibits the contracting capacity of the prime movers.

Improperly developed stabilizers may hamper the activity of major muscles. When under chronic stress, the stabilizers spasm, restraining the prime movers and lessening athletic effectiveness. This is often seen in volleyball players who suffer injury as a result of inadequate muscle strength and balance in the shoulder muscles (Kugler et al., 1996). At the *shoulders*, supra- and infraspinatus muscles rotate the arm. The simplest, most effective exercise to strengthen these two muscles is to rotate the arm with a partner tightly holding the fist. The resistance provided by the partner stimulates the two muscles stabilizing the shoulder. At the *hips*, the piriformis muscle performs outward rotation. To strengthen this muscle, the athlete should stand with knees locked. While a partner provides resistance by holding one foot in place with both hands, the athlete performs inward and outward leg rotations. At the *knees*, the popliteus muscle rotates the calf. A simple exercise is for the athlete to sit on a table or desk with the knees flexed. A partner provides resistance by holding the foot as the athlete performs inward and outward rotations of the calf.

Stabilizers also contract isometrically, immobilizing one part of the limb and allowing the other to move. Stabilizers can also monitor the state of the long bones' interactions in joints and sense potential injury resulting from improper technique, inappropriate strength, or spasms produced by poor stress management. If one of these three conditions occurs, the stabilizers restrain the activity of the prime movers, avoiding strain and injuries.

Training coaches have recently been exaggerating the training of the stabilizer muscles, especially with the use of proprioception training, also known as balance training. A number of studies have demonstrated that proprioception training using balance boards helps provide stability to a formerly injured or instable ankle (Caraffa et al., 1996; Wester et al., 1996; Willems et al., 2002). The theory asserts that if balance board training helps promote greater stability through increasing the proprioception and strength of the stabilizer muscles of an unstable structure, it will further strengthen and prevent injury to an already stable structure. Although this may be true, the real question is how much time should be devoted to exercises intended to strengthen the stabilizer muscles. Completely disregarding the use of balance boards or proprioception training at this time would be premature. Certain studies show that proprioception training can decrease injury to the knee (Caraffa et al., 1996), whereas other studies disprove the benefits of proprioception training for injury prevention (Soderman et al., 2000). A recent review study in particular challenged the flaws in proprioception study design and implementation (Thacker et al., 2003).

Balance board training during the early part of the preparatory phase (the anatomical adaptation phase) can be helpful, but after that the board should be put away to allow time to train with methods that directly enhance the physical stature of the athlete and promote sport-specific strength, speed, and stamina. After all, even if exercises worked to improve an athlete's proprioception, the slow to intermediate nature of these exercises would never protect the joint from the fast and powerful movements that occur in sport (Ashton-Miller et al., 2001). Preparing the stabilizers for movement is important, and specifically training the movements of the sport with ideal sport-specific speed and power or endurance is vital to the performance and physical state of the athlete.

Law 5: Train Movements, Not Individual Muscles

Athletes should resist training muscles in isolation, as occurs in bodybuilding. The purpose of strength training in sports is to simulate sport skills, to involve in action the muscles specifically used in the intimate skills of a given sport. Athletic skills are multijoint movements occurring in a certain order, called a *kinetic chain* (movement chain). For instance, a takeoff to catch a ball has the following kinetic chain: hip extensions, then knee extensions, and finally ankle extensions, in which the feet apply force against the ground to lift the body. The body's use of multiple muscles to perform sport movements enhances the functional capabilities of the muscles involved because "each muscle has different force-length, force-velocity, and torque-velocity characteristics" (Enoka, 2002).

According to the principle of specificity, body position and limb angles should resemble those needed for the specific skills to be performed. When athletes train a movement, the muscles are integrated and strengthened to perform the action with more power. Therefore, athletes should not resort to weight training alone, but should broaden their training routines, incorporating medicine balls, rubber cords, shots, and plyometric equipment. Exercises performed with these instruments allow athletes to initiate skills more easily. Chapters 10 and 11 provide further examples of how these training instruments are used for better specific improvement.

From its very beginning, bodybuilding has promoted the concept of working muscles in isolation, a concept that has served this sport very well for generations. Isolation exercises do not apply to sports, however. Multijoint exercises in sport training have been used since track-and-field athletes introduced them in the early 1930s, prior to the 1936 Olympic Games. Most athletes still follow this tradition. Multijoint ~~exercises are~~ key to strength training efficiency.

Law 6: Don't Focus on What Is New, but on What Is Necessary

In the past few years the North American sport and fitness market has been invaded by many products that claim to improve athletic performance greatly. An understanding of biomechanics and exercise physiology, however, reveals that many of the products intended to improve strength, speed, and power actually inhibit them.

Balance training and overspeed training are two methods that have captured the minds of athletes, coaches, and trainers. Balance training is a safe method of training, but is widely overused in the sport training industry. Overspeed training and the many training devices that are used to enhance speed and power, however, are jeopardizing running technique and decreasing the rate of force development.

Seminars are often the preferred medium for promoting new ideas. In many instances the speaker shows new exercises and promises miraculous improvement. Not very often, however, do speakers address the issues of anatomical and neuromuscular adaptation, which are central to performance improvement and should be the foundation for all sport-specific programs.

Certainly, a good selection of exercises is very important; however, an exercise is essential only if it targets the prime movers or the main muscle groups used in performing an athletic skill—no more, no less. Whether the athlete uses a simple bench or a stability ball to perform bench presses is immaterial. The essential goal is to perform the exercise with a continuous acceleration through the range of motion.

At the beginning of a bench press, fast-twitch muscle fibers are recruited to defeat inertia and the heavy load of the barbell. As the athlete continues to press the barbell upward, he should attempt to generate the highest acceleration possible. Under these conditions the discharge rate of the same fast-twitch muscle fibers is increased. Maximum acceleration, therefore, must be achieved toward the end of the action to coincide with the instant of releasing a ball or other athletic implement during sports. If a high level of strength adaptation is required in the leg muscles, then athletes should squat, squat, and squat. The idea is to develop the greatest levels of strength and adaptation possible—in other words, to do what is necessary. Adding variety by implementing different exercises is fine as long as they target the same muscle group in the most specific way.

Principles of Strength Training

The purpose of any strength training program is a continual increase in the physical capacity of an athlete. Strength training principles offer methods of adapting the body to the various loads used in training and provide guidelines of how to individualize the program to the specific needs of the athlete and sport. Every strength training program should be built on principles.

Progressive Increase of Load

The legend of Milo of Croton in Greek mythology can best illustrate how to apply the principle of progressive increase of load in training. To become the world's strongest man, Milo started to lift and carry a calf every day beginning in his teenage years. As the calf grew heavier, Milo grew stronger. By the time the calf was a full-grown bull, Milo was the world's strongest man, thanks to long-term progression.

Physiologically, training gradually increases the body's functional efficiency, increasing its work capacity and resulting in performance improvement. The body reacts physiologically and psychologically to the increased training load. Similarly, nervous reaction and functions, neuromuscular coordination, and the psychological capacity to cope with stress also occur gradually. The entire process requires time and competent technical leadership.

Several sports have a consistent training load throughout the year, called a *standard load*. Most team sports maintain 6 to 12 hours of training per week for the entire year. Standard loading results in early improvements, followed by a plateau and then detraining during the competitive phase (see figure 4.1). This may cause decreased performance during the late competitive phase because the physiological basis of performance has decreased and prevents annual improvements. Only steadily increasing training load increments will produce superior adaptation and performance.

The *overload* principle is another traditional strength training approach. Early proponents of this principle claimed that strength and hypertrophy would increase only if muscles work at their maximum strength capacity against workloads greater than those normally encountered (Hellebrand and Houtz, 1956; Lange, 1919). Contemporary advocates suggest that the load in strength training should be increased throughout the program (Fox, Bowes, and Foss, 1989). As such, the curve of load increment rises constantly (see figure 4.2).

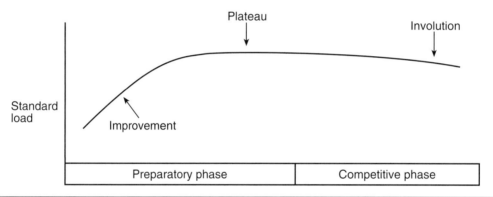

Figure 4.1 A standard load results in improvements only in the early part of the annual plan.

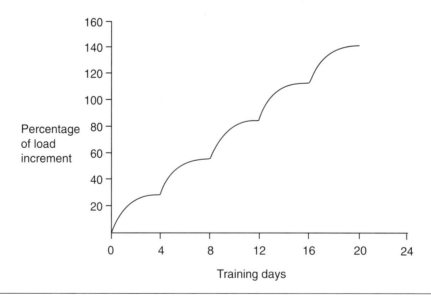

Figure 4.2 Load increments according to the overloading principle.

Proponents of overloading suggest two ways to increase strength: (1) brief maximum contractions resulting in high muscle activation and (2) submaximum contractions to exhaustion, inducing hypertrophy. The latter approach, popular among bodybuilders, is categorically impractical in athletics. Athletes cannot be expected to lift to exhaustion every day. Such physiological and psychological strain leads to fatigue, exhaustion, and overtraining. To be effective, a strength training program must follow the concept of periodization of strength, with specific goals for each phase leading up to the major competitions of the year.

The *step-type approach* is more effective than overloading. The athlete's ability to tolerate heavy loads improves as the result of adaptation to stressors applied in strength training (Councilman 1968; Harre 1982). The step-type method requires a training load increase followed by an unloading phase during which the body adapts, regenerates, and prepares for a new increase. The frequency of the increase in training load must be determined by each athlete's needs, rate of adaptation, and competitive calendar. An abrupt increase in training load may go beyond the athlete's capacity to adapt, affecting the physiological balance. The rate of the athlete's performance improvement determines training load increase. The faster the rate of performance improvement, the greater the training loads required for the athlete to keep up.

The step-type approach (see figure 4.3) does not mean increasing the load in each training session. A single training session is insufficient to cause visible body change. To achieve adaptation, the same training loads must be repeated several times. Often training sessions of the same type are planned for an entire week, followed by an increase the following week.

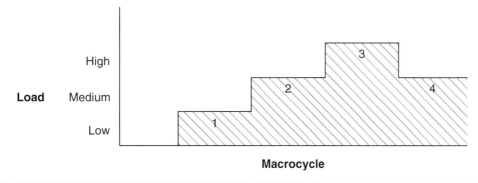

Figure 4.3 Illustration of a macrocycle. Each vertical line represents an increase in load, whereas the horizontal line represents the adaptation phase required by the new demand.

In figure 4.3, let's say each horizontal line represents a week, or a *microcycle*, of training and that the load is increased on Monday. This increase fatigues the body because it is not accustomed to such stress. The body adjusts by Wednesday, adapts to the load over the next two days, and by Friday the athlete feels stronger and capable of lifting heavier loads. Fatigue is followed by adaptation, then a physiological rebound or improvement. This new level is called a new *ceiling of adaptation*. By Monday the athlete is physiologically and psychologically comfortable.

The third step in figure 4.3 is followed by a lower step, or *unloading phase*. A reduction in overall demand allows the body to regenerate. During regeneration, the athlete partially recovers from the fatigue accumulated in the first three steps, replenishes energy stores, and psychologically relaxes. The body accumulates new reserves in anticipation of further increases in training load. Training performance usually improves following the regeneration phase.

The unloading phase represents the new lowest step for the next macrocycle. Because the body has adjusted to the previous loads, this new low step is of greater magnitude than the previous low, but is nearly equal to the medium one.

The shorter the adaptation phase is, the lower the height, or the amount of increase, the training load needs to be. A longer adaptation phase may permit a higher increase. Although training load increases in steps, the load curve for a training plan of longer duration has a wavy shape that represents the continuous increases and decreases in the training components (see figure 4.4).

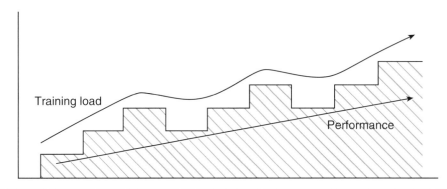

Figure 4.4 Curve of training load appears to be undulatory (wavy arrow), whereas performance improves continuously (straight arrow).

Although the step-loading method is applicable to every sport and athlete, two variations are possible, but they must be applied carefully and with discretion.

In *reverse step loading* (see figure 4.5), the load decreases rather than increases from step to step. Some Eastern European weightlifters maintain that this form of loading (planning the heaviest loads immediately following a cycle of low-intensity training) is more specific to their physiological needs. Reverse step loading has been used in weightlifting since the late 1960s, but has not been accepted in any other sport. The reason is simple: The goal of strength training for sports is progressive adaptation—gradually increasing the athlete's training capabilities. Performance improvements are possible only when training capabilities have increased. Reverse loading should be used only during the peaking cycle prior to competition (see chapter 12). Endurance improvements are much better achieved by step loading.

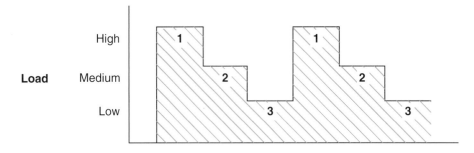

Figure 4.5 Reverse step loading.

The *flat step loading* pattern (see figure 4.6) is appropriate for advanced athletes with strong strength training backgrounds. High-demand training is performed at the same level for three cycles, followed by a low-load, recovery week. The load is then increased to medium during the third and other macrocycles as the athlete adapts. The high-demand cycles must be applied in concert with other types of training. As such, the three cycles have to be of high demand for all elements—technical, tactical, speed, and endurance training. When planning a lower-intensity cycle, all other elements must be of lower demand as well to facilitate relaxation and recovery.

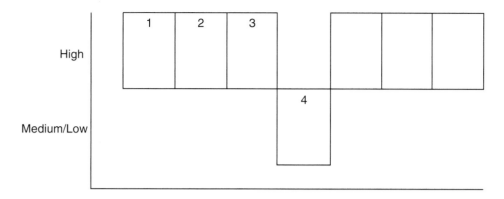

Figure 4.6 Flat step loading pattern.

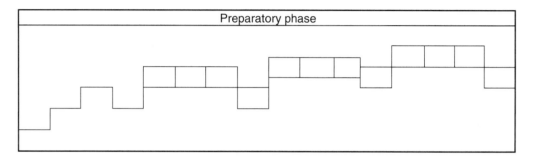

Figure 4.7 Suggested flat step loading pattern for the preparatory phase. Note that step loading is used at the beginning of the program since the load is progressively increased. After the first 5 weeks of progressive adaptation, flat step loading is used to ensure that training is very demanding and results in the specific adaptation necessary for performance improvement.

The dynamics of the loading pattern for a well-trained athlete are a function of the training phase and type of strength training sought. During the early part of the preparatory phase, the flat step loading pattern prevails, ensuring a better progression (see figure 4.7). The same loading pattern is suggested for athletes with one to two years' experience in strength training. For endurance sports, in which the development of muscular endurance is the focus of specific strength training, and for athletes competing at or beyond the national level, the flat step loading pattern also is suggested.

Variety

Contemporary training requires many hours of work from the athlete. The volume and intensity of training are continually increasing, and exercises are repeated numerous times. To reach high performance, the volume of training must surpass a threshold of 1,000 hours per year. Any athlete serious about training must dedicate four to six hours each week to strength training, in addition to technical, tactical, and energy system training.

Under these conditions, boredom and monotony can become obstacles to motivation and improvement. The best way to overcome these obstacles is to incorporate as much variety as possible into training routines. Instructors and coaches have to be well versed in the area of strength training and know as many exercises as possible to ensure such variety. In addition to improving training response, variety has a positive effect on the psychological well-being of athletes. The following suggestions will help enrich strength training programs:

- Alternate exercises designed for the prime movers whenever possible, especially if the new exercise or implement targets the same muscle group (prime movers). Variety is particularly helpful prior to and during the competitive phase.

- Vary the loading system using the principle of progressive increase of load in training.
- Vary the type of muscle contraction, especially between concentric and eccentric.
- Vary the speed of contraction (slow, medium, and fast), especially from the late preparatory phase onward.
- Vary the equipment (if possible) from free weights to heavy implements, isokinetics, and so on.

Variety in exercise selection keeps the athlete motivated and adaptation fresh. A problem arises when coaches and athletes feel the need to substitute an exercise or change the method solely for the sake of doing something new. The principle of variety should be used only if the change or substitution keeps the athlete on the path of adaptation. Also, when certain athletes reach a high level of competition and fitness, it is pertinent that certain exercises never leave their regime. Coaches can alter the load or the method used in training, but should always stick to the movements that best mimic the sport or best elicit the threshold of stimulation needed for maximum gains. For example, although lunges are also a great and effective exercise for leg development, they do not cause the same neuromuscular drive as squats. Squats are probably one of the single best exercises for lower-body maximum strength development and should never be replaced for the sake of boredom.

Coaches and athletes should remember that sports training is different from fitness training; fitness ideals don't always work in the sports training arena. Many strength training instructors preach that exercises should be altered every other week. This is beneficial when training clients who require constant variety and excitement, but it is not appropriate for athletes.

Alternation of strength exercises for sports can be done only if the new exercise is addressing the prime movers in that sport. Because adaptation is a physiological requirement for athletic improvement, the same type of training and muscle groups have to be targeted repeatedly to result in the highest degree of adaptation. Without constant increase in the adaptation of bodily systems, athletes will see no visible improvement in their performance. Yes, repeating the same type of exercise day in and day out is very boring. But so is constantly repeating the technical skills of running, swimming, cycling, and rowing, to name a few. Yet nobody is suggesting to runners, swimmers, cyclists, and rowers to alter their primary skill training because it is boring. Coaches should choose a number of exercises that have the same functional purpose, but add variety to training. They can spice up the training program, but should always keep the main focus in mind; the athletes' level of physiological adaptation.

Individualization

Contemporary training requires individualization. Each athlete must be treated according to individual ability, potential, and strength training background. Coaches are sometimes tempted to follow the training programs of successful athletes, disregarding their athlete's needs, experience, and abilities. Even worse, they sometimes insert such programs into the training schedules of junior athletes who are not ready, physiologically or psychologically, for such programs.

Before designing a training program, the coach should analyze the athlete's training potential. Athletes equal in performance do not necessarily have the same work capacity. Individual work abilities are determined by several biological and psychological factors and must be considered in specifying the amount of work, the load, and the type of strength training. Training background also determines work capacity. Work demand should be based on experience. Even when athletes exhibit great improvement, coaches must still be cautious in estimating training load. When assigning athletes of different backgrounds and experiences to the same training group, coaches should not ignore individual characteristics and potential.

Another factor to consider when planning a training program is the athlete's rate of recovery. When planning and evaluating the content and stress of training, coaches should remember to assess demanding factors outside of training. They should be aware of the athlete's lifestyle and emotional involvements. Schoolwork or other activities can affect the rate of recovery.

Gender differences also require consideration. The total body strength of women is 63.5 percent that of men. The upper-body strength of women is an average 55.8 percent that of men. The lower body strength of women, however, is much closer to that of men, averaging 71.9 percent (Laubach, 1976). Women tend to have lower hypertrophy levels than men have, mostly because their testosterone level is 10 times lower (Wright, 1980). Female athletes can follow the same training programs as male athletes without worrying about excessive bulky muscles. Women can apply the same loading pattern, use the same training methods, and follow similar methods of designing programs as men without concern.

A recent study looked at gender differences in strength and muscle thickness changes following upper- and lower-body resistance training. Twelve weeks of total body resistance training resulted in a greater increase in upper-body muscle thickness compared to the lower body in both men and women and similar time-course and proportionate increases in strength and muscle thickness for both men and woman (Evertsen et al., 1999).

Strength training, in other words, is as beneficial for women as it is for men. In fact, strength gains for women occur at the same or an even greater rate than those of men (Wilmore et al., 1978).

Strength training for women should be rigorously continuous, without long interruptions. Plyometric training should progress carefully over a longer period to allow adaptation to occur. Because women generally tend to be physically weaker than men, visible gains in performance will come from improved and increased strength training (Lephart et al., 2002). Further increases in strength will promote greater recovery and power capabilities from plyometric training. As for training the energy systems, the same training methods can be used, except for those that train the lactic acid systems because of issues of work tolerance.

A major issue regarding gender differences involves injury in sport. Female athletes often report a higher incidence of lower-body injuries, in particular to the knee joint. Studies have attempted to physiologically and anatomically explain the high proportion of injuries female athletes experience. When performing the kinematics and electromyographic activity of the one-legged squat, intercollegiate female athletes, as compared to their male counterparts, demonstrated more ankle dorsiflexion, ankle pronation, hip adduction, hip flexion, and external rotation and less trunk lateral flexion (Zeller et al., 2003). Furthermore, female athletes who participate in jumping and agility-type exercises tend to exhibit less muscular stiffness protection of the knee as compared to males (Wojitys et al., 2003). Involuntarily, females allow their knees to drift inward (knock knees), which places more stress on the knee joint and can aggravate or strain the anterior cruciate ligament. Although gender-specific planning is not entirely required, time should be dedicated to improving maximum strength, in particular the strength of the lower body, in female athletes. Increased strengthening of the quadriceps and hamstring at the end of the early preparatory phase can physiologically prepare the athlete for game-specific drills and power training, which places more stress on the knee joint and can lead to injury.

Specificity

To be effective and achieve greater adaptation, training must be designed to develop sport-specific strength. A strength training program and the selected training method(s) should consider the dominant energy system of the sport and the prime movers involved. Training specificity is also the most important mechanism for sport-specific neural adaptation.

The *dominant energy system* in the sport should be considered carefully. For instance, muscular endurance training is most appropriate for endurance sports such as rowing, long-distance swimming, canoeing, or speedskating (see chapters 6 and 11). The *specific muscle groups* involved (prime movers) and the movement patterns characteristic of the sport must also be considered. Exercises should mimic the sport's key movement patterns or dominant skills. They must also improve the power of the prime movers. Normally, gains in power transfer to skill improvement.

Specificity vs. a Methodical Approach   The principle of specificity sprang from the idea that the optimal strength training program must be specific. Mathews and Fox (1976) developed this theory into a principle of training. According to this principle, an exercise or type of training that is specific to the skills of a sport results in faster adaptation and yields faster performance improvement. Specificity should be applied only to advanced athletes during the competitive phase. These athletes perfect only the dominant strength in their selected sport.

Misuse of specificity results in asymmetrical and inharmonious body development and neglects the antagonist and stabilizer muscles. Misuse can also hamper the development of the prime movers and result in injuries. Overemphasizing specificity can result in narrow development of the muscles and one-sided, specialized muscle function. Compensation strength exercises should always be used in training, especially during the preparatory phase of the yearly plan. These exercises balance the force of agonist and antagonist muscles.

Although specificity is an important principle, its long-term application can result in stressful, boring programs, leading to overtraining, overuse injury, and sometimes burnout. Specificity is best applied at appropriate times in a program based on a methodical, long-term approach. Such a program should have three main phases: the general and multilateral phase, the specialized training-specific phase, and the high-performance phase (see figure 4.8).

During *general* and *multilateral* strength training, all muscle groups, ligaments, and tendons are developed in anticipation of future heavy loads and specific training. Such an approach would likely lead to an injury-free career. This phase may last two to four years depending on the athlete's age and abilities. Throughout this phase, the coach needs to be patient. Overall multilateral development is a basic requirement for reaching a highly specialized level of training.

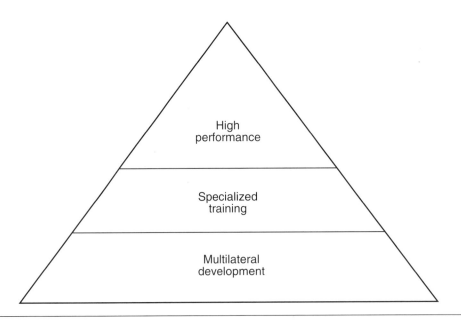

Figure 4.8   Suggested long-term approach to specificity of strength training.

After laying the foundation, the athlete begins the *specialized training specific phase*, which will continue throughout her career. This is not a strength training program that addresses the specific needs of the sport through all phases of a yearly training plan. Rather, this program includes periodization of strength, which always starts with a buildup or anatomical adaptation phase (see the discussion of periodization of strength in chapter 7). Depending on the age of the athlete, this phase can last two to three years.

The *high-performance phase* applies to athletes at the national and international levels. During this stage, specificity prevails from the latter part of the preparatory phase through the competitive phase of the yearly plan. This phase ends when the athlete stops competing.

Specificity of Exercises for Strength Training   Because mimicking the technical skill of a given sport in strength training can be difficult, coaches must try to imitate the *dynamic structure* of the skill as well as the *spatial orientation,* or the position of the body compared to the surrounding environment. Coaches should select exercises that place the body and limbs in positions similar to those used when performing a skill.

The angle between body parts or limbs influences how a muscle contracts and which parts of it contract. Effective training of the prime movers requires familiarity with this aspect. For example, sit-ups are popular abdominal exercises; however, body position changes the difficulty as well as the segment of the muscle (rectus abdominis) contracted maximally. Horizontal sit-ups involve mostly the upper part of the muscle. Inclined sit-ups primarily benefit the central section of the muscle because the movement is performed with an almost full range of motion. If the trunk is fixed and the legs are lifted, the role of the abdominal muscles decreases and the action is performed mostly by the hip flexors (iliopsoas muscle). The best position for activating the abdominal muscles is one that immobilizes the hips so the trunk moves by contracting the rectus abdominis muscle (inclined position, or with the legs resting on a chair, bench, or against a wall).

Similar concerns apply to the bench press. If the bench press is performed on a flat bench, the central parts of the pectoral muscles, the triceps, and parts of the deltoid muscle benefit. If the same exercise is performed on an inclined bench, the upper parts of the pectoral muscles contract fully. To stress the lower pectoral muscles, athletes should place their heads at the lower end of an incline bench. The grip used for the bench press also affects the muscles involved. A wide grip stresses mainly the exterior part of the pectoral muscles. A shoulder-width grip develops the inner part of the pectoral muscles. A narrow grip activates mostly the deeper part of the pectoral muscles and the triceps muscle.

To achieve maximum training specificity, an exercise has to imitate the angle of the skill performed. For instance, the arm extensions used by shot-putters and American football linemen use the triceps muscles. A bodybuilding exercise to develop the triceps is the elbow extension, which is performed either bent over or in an erect position with the elbow above the shoulder. Such exercises isolate the triceps from the other muscles involved in shot-putting or tackling (analytic method) and consequently are not very effective for these athletes. Incline bench presses at an angle of 30 to 35 degrees would be better because the angle is similar to that used in these sports. This exercise also works the other active muscles such as the pectoral muscles and deltoids.

Part II

Program Design

Manipulation of Training Variables

To create successful strength training programs, coaches and athletes manipulate two main training variables: volume and intensity. The volume and intensity of training change according to the competition schedule and the objective of training. Subsets of volume and intensity include load, which is generally expressed as a percentage of 1-repetition maximum (1RM); sets; repetitions; and rest intervals between sets. Manipulating these subsets will alter the volume and intensity of training and the desired training outcome.

Strength training programs must also include general and sport-specific exercises, as well as properly calculated rest intervals. As a rule of thumb, the early part of the yearly training program, which can include three to six months of preparatory training, should include a higher volume of training with minimal sport-specific exercises. As the competitive season approaches, intensity of training is stressed, volume is decreased, and sport-specific exercises become a major part of the training program.

Training Volume

Volume, or the quantity of work performed, incorporates the duration of training hours; the number of kilograms, pounds, or tonnes/short tons lifted per training session or phase of training; the number of exercises per training session; and the number of sets and reps per exercise or training session. Instructors, coaches, and athletes should keep records of the total pounds or kilograms lifted per session or training phase to help plan future training volumes.

Training volume varies based on the physical classification of the sport, strength training background, and the type of strength training performed. Athletes attempting

For tennis players with strength training backgrounds, their ability to endure continually higher training loads enables them to meet the strength requirements of their sport.

to develop muscular endurance or maximum strength use a high volume of training because of the many reps they perform and the high load. A medium training volume is typical for athletes in sports that require power because the load is low to medium and the rest interval is relatively long.

Overall training volume becomes more important as athletes approach high performance. There are no shortcuts. Athletic performance improves only by constant physiological adaptation to incrementally greater training volumes. As athletes adapt to higher volumes of training, they experience better recovery between sets and training sessions. This, in turn, results in more work per training session and per week and further increases in training volume.

Strength training volume depends on the athlete's biological makeup, the specifics of the sport, and the importance of strength in that sport. Mature athletes with strong strength training backgrounds can tolerate higher volumes.

A dramatic or abrupt increase in volume can be detrimental, irrespective of the athlete's sport or ability, resulting in fatigue, uneconomical muscular work, and possibly injury. A progressive plan with an appropriate method of monitoring load increments will avoid these detriments.

The *total volume* depends on several factors, the determinant being the importance of strength to the sport. For instance, international-class weightlifters often plan 33 short tons (30 tonnes) per training session and approximately 44,000 short tons (40,000 tonnes) per year. For other sports, the volume differs drastically (see table 5.1). Power and speed sports require a much higher volume than boxing does; in sports in which muscular endurance is dominant, such as rowing or canoeing, the volume of strength per year can be three to six times higher than that indicated in table 5.1.

Table 5.1 Suggested Guideline for Volume (in Tonnes) of Strength Training per Year

Sport/event	Volume/microcycle in training phases			Volume/year	
	Preparatory	Competitive	Transition	Minimum	Maximum
Shot put	24-40	8-12	4-6	900	1450
Football	30-40	10-12	6	900	1400
Baseball/cricket	20-30	8-10	2-4	850	1250
Jumps	20-30	8-10	2	800	1200
Rowing	30-40	10-12	4	900	1200
Kayaking/canoeing	20-40	10-12	4	900	1200
Wrestling	20-30	10	4	800	1200
Swimming	20	8-10	2-4	700	1200
Downhill skiing	18-36	6-10	2-4	700	1250
High jump	16-28	8-10	2-4	620	1000
Cycling	16-22	8-10	2-4	600	950
Triathlon	16-20	8-10	2-4	600	1000
Ice hockey	15-25	6-8	2-4	600	950
Speedskating	14-26	4-6	2-4	500	930
Lacrosse	14-22	4-8	2-4	500	900
Basketball	12-24	4-6	2	450	850
Javelin	12-24	4	2	450	800
Volleyball	12-20	4	2	450	600
Sprinting	10-18	4	2	400	600
Gymnastics	10-16	4	4	380	600
Rugby	10-20	4-6	4	320	600
Squash	8-12	4	4	350	550
Figure skating	8-12	2-4	2	350	550
Tennis	8-12	2-4	2	350	550
Boxing/martial arts	8-14	3	1	380	500
Golf	4-6	2	1	250	300

Training Intensity

In strength training, intensity is expressed as a percentage of load or 1-repetition maximum (1RM). Intensity, a function of the strength of the nervous stimuli employed in training, is determined by muscular effort and the degree to which the central nervous system (CNS) is called into action. Stimulus strength depends on the load, speed of movement, and variation of rest intervals between reps. Training load, expressed as intensity, refers to the mass or weight lifted. In isokinetic training, load is expressed as the force the athlete generates against the resistance provided by the machine. Strength training employs the following intensity zones and loads (see table 5.2).

Table 5.2 Intensity Values and Load Used in Strength Training

Intensity value	Load	Percent of 1RM	Type of contraction
1	Supermaximum	>105	Eccentric/Isometric
2	Maximum	90-100	Concentric
3	Heavy	80-90	Concentric
4	Medium	50-80	Concentric
5	Low	30-50	Concentric

A *supermaximum* load exceeds one's maximum strength (1RM). In most cases, loads between 100 and 125 percent of 1RM can be used by applying the eccentric method (yielding to the force of gravity). Athletes using supermaximum loads should have two spotters, one at each end of the barbell, to prevent accidents. Only athletes with a strong strength training background should use supermaximum loads. Most other athletes should be restricted to loads of no more than 100 percent of 1RM.

Maximum load is 90 to 100 percent of 1RM. *Heavy* is 80 to 90 percent of 1RM, *medium* is 50 to 80 percent of 1RM, and *low* is 30 to 50 percent of 1RM. Load should relate to the type of strength being developed and, more important, to the sport-specific combination resulting from the blending of strength with speed and strength with endurance. Details on training these sport-specific combinations are presented in the section on power training in chapter 10. Figure 5.1 gives general guidelines for the load to use in developing each of these combinations. The load will not be the same through all training phases. On the contrary, periodization will alter the load according to the goals of each training phase. Note that the load ranges from 20 percent to more than 105 percent of 1RM, and the corresponding intensities are shown in the next row. Below that are the sport-specific combinations and the suggested load for each.

Periodization incorporates the proper planning of all the performance abilities that are needed in the sport. For instance, training for a middle-distance runner addresses the training distance covered, sessions per week, and of course volume of work (e.g., sets and reps) performed in each strength training session.

The greater the number of reps and sets performed in a session, the greater the volume of work. Volume and intensity are very closely related and represent the quantity and quality of work. One is not more important than the other; both should be strategically manipulated when training for a desired effect.

As in most bodily systems, a dose response exists between the total volume of work and the level of adaptation. Beginner strength trainers or athletes will initially benefit from a low level

Percent of load	>105	100	90	80	70	60	50	40	30	20
Intensity	Super-maximum	Maximum	Heavy		Medium			Low		
Type of strength	Maximum strength				Power M-E					

Sport-specific strength combinations:

	>105	100	90	80	70	60	50	40	30	20
Landing/Reactive power	■	■	■							
Throwing power			■	■						
Takeoff power			■	■						
Starting power				■	■					
Deceleration power				■	■					
Acceleration power					■	■				
Power-endurance						■	■			
M-ES						■	■			
M-EM							■	■		
M-EL								■	■	

Figure 5.1 Relationship between the load and different types and combinations of strength.

of volume such as one to three sets, but will eventually plateau and require a greater level of stimulation for further adaptation. It is not surprising to have athletes perform the bench press for sets in excess of 10 to 12 sets or 50-plus reps depending on the desired physiological effect. Keep in mind that the term *intensity* as used in the sporting world is strictly a representation of a percentage of a load used in training. In other words, the only true way to increase intensity is to increase the load. For instance, an athlete who performs five reps to fatigue for the first set of a 90 percent 1RM lift and, following a four-minute rest, completes six reps to fatigue at the same load has not increased the intensity from set 1 to set 2. The volume has in fact increased from the first set to the second along with the stress inflicted in the muscle, but the load has remained at 90 percent. The intensity has not changed. Trainers or coaches must be careful not to correlate intensity with the muscular feeling that occurs following a set. As a general rule of thumb, the higher the number of sets performed, the lower the number of reps. For instance, a maximum strength phase may require an athlete to perform seven to nine sets at an interval of 85 to 95 percent of 1RM, but only three to five sets of 75 to 85 percent of 1RM during the hypertrophy phase of training.

Athlete training programs should always be individualized, and coaches or trainers should look for signs of fatigue. One of the biggest problems in the sports training world is the sacrifice of quality for quantity. Planning is never written in stone and should only be used as a guideline for program design. Session-by-session progress and setbacks should be noted and used in the revision of the training program. Coaches should watch for the point at which an athlete is no longer capable of performing the load for the desired number of reps. This is extremely critical, especially in the maximum strength phase of training when nervous system adaptations are the primary goal.

Table 5.3 shows a hypothetical training log of an athlete performing the bench press at MxS. The athlete decided to complete the program the coach designed and recorded the number of reps per set. Despite resting for a longer interval following the fourth set, the athlete was not able to complete the desired number of reps. The fifth set required a decrease in load to fulfill the repetition requirement. Because the goal was increased neural drive and motor unit recruitment, which is only achieved by using very heavy loads, the athlete in essence performed many wasted sets that will have a negative impact on the desired physiological effect. The athlete should have ended the exercise following the diminished performance of the fourth set.

Table 5.3 Bench Press Training: Comparison of Suggested Plan to Actual Program

Set	Suggested			Actual		
	Load (%)	Reps	Rest interval (min)	Load (%)	Reps	Rest interval (min)
1	80	6-8	3	80	8	3
2	84	5-7	4	84	6	4
3	87	4-5	4	87	4	6*
4**	87	4-5	4	87	3*	5*
5	90	2-3	4	87*	3*	5*
6	90	2-3	4	87*	3* (spot required to complete rep)	5*

*Differences from suggested program
**Exercise should have been terminated following 4th set

Number of Exercises

The key to an effective training program is adequate exercise selection. Establishing an optimum number of exercises is difficult, and some coaches, desiring to develop more muscle groups, select far too many. The resulting program is overloaded and fatiguing. The number and type of exercises must be selected according to the age and performance level of the athlete, the needs of the sport, and the phase of training.

Age and Performance Level

One of the main objectives of a training program for juniors or beginners is the development of a solid anatomical and physiological foundation. For strength training, the coach should select many exercises (9 to 12) that address the primary muscle groups. Such a program may last two to three years, depending on the athlete's present age and the expected age for achieving high performance.

The main training objective of advanced athletes is to reach the highest possible level of performance. Therefore, their strength programs, especially during the competitive phase, must be specific, with only a few exercises (three to six) directed at the prime movers.

Needs of the Sport

Strength training exercises, particularly for elite athletes, should meet the specific needs of the sport and address the prime movers dominant in that sport. For example, an elite high jumper may need to perform only three or four exercises to adequately strengthen all prime movers; an American football player or wrestler may have to perform six to nine exercises to accomplish the same goal. Therefore, the more prime movers used in a sport, the higher the number of exercises. However, well-selected multijoint exercises may serve to effectively lower the number of exercises.

Phase of Training

In a general strength training program, anatomical adaptation is desirable early in the preparatory phase. After the transition phase, a new yearly plan should start building the foundation for future training. For such a program to involve most muscle groups, the number of exercises has to be high (9 to 12), regardless of the specifics of the sport. As a program progresses, the number of exercises is reduced, culminating in the competitive phase when only three to five very specific exercises essential to the sport are performed. For instance, an American football, hockey, basketball, or volleyball player will perform perhaps 9 to 10 exercises during the preparatory phase and only 3 to 5 during the league season. By being selective, coaches can increase training efficiency and lower athletes' overall fatigue.

Strength training is done *in addition to technical and tactical training*. In short, an inverse relationship exists between the load used in training and the number of exercises per training session. A decrease in the number of exercises used in training indicates that the athlete is training for the specifics of the sport. As the number of exercises decreases, the number of sets per exercise increases. More work is placed on the specific prime movers of the sport to optimize the muscles' fitness, strength, and efficiency for competition. Once the competitive season begins, progressive adaptation is set aside and a low number of exercises and moderate set increments are used to foster the maintenance of physiological adaptation.

Even though the upper body is only minimally involved in some sports (e.g., soccer, many track-and-field events, cycling, etc.), many strength programs emphasize exercises for the upper body. In addition, many gym instructors, still influenced by bodybuilding theories, suggest far too many exercises for athletes. Athletes using high numbers of exercises decrease the number of sets targeted to each prime mover. When this happens, training adaptation, and therefore training effect, is very low. High training adaptation, and as a result, improvement of performance, is possible only when athletes perform higher numbers of sets for the chosen muscle group.

Order of Exercises

Exercises should alternate between limbs and muscle groups to ensure better recovery. If all parts of the body are exercised, the following order is suggested: legs, arms, abdomen; legs, arms, back; and so on. When selecting the number of exercises, training coaches should consider their involvement in performing the skills of the sport.

Strength training for sports has been unduly influenced by the training methodologies of bodybuilding and weightlifting. Many strength training books and articles, for example, propose exercising the small-muscle groups first and then the large-muscle groups. This results in fatiguing the small-muscle groups, which leaves athletes unable to train the large-muscle groups. Since the large-muscle groups are the prime movers in the sport, it is extremely important that the prime movers be trained in a nonfatigued state.

Another overused training method from the world of bodybuilding is the preexhaustion method. Using this method, trainees exhaust the prime movers with single-joint exercises such as leg extensions before executing multijoint exercises such as leg presses. Although this theory may be useful to bodybuilders, current research challenges its usefulness in sport (Augustsson et al., 2003). Sport trainers should avoid this method even during the hypertrophy phase of training. Multijoint exercises that have the major prime movers work together should be the main exercises in strength training programs for sports. Single-joint exercises can be used during the early preparatory phase such as in anatomical adaptation, but should be phased out in the later phases of training. Training for sport is all about optimizing muscle firing frequencies of strength, power, and endurance, not improving the aesthetic appeal of the athlete.

Sport strength training exercises should mimic the skills of the particular sport to maximize strengthening the prime movers and, in some cases, produce "motor memory," which consolidates the technical skills involved. Nervous system adaptations occur as a result of training with very heavy loads and constantly exposing the body to specific drills and exercise movements (Carroll, Riek, and Carson, 2001). Strength exercises that resemble the technical pattern repeat similar motions, giving the exercises a learning component. Imitation of technical skills also involves the chain of muscles in a pattern similar to their involvement in the sport. For instance, it makes sense for a volleyball player to perform half squats and toe raises together because spiking and blocking require the same moves. The chain of muscles involved is acting in the same sequence as in jumping. Thus, a volleyball player is not concerned with whether the small- or large-muscle groups are involved first, only with mimicking the motion and involving the chain of muscles in the same way as in spiking and blocking.

Two options are available for the order in which to perform the exercises prescribed by the coach. First, the athlete may follow the order of exercises in sequence from the top down (a "vertical" sequence), as listed on the daily program sheet. This method leads to better recovery for the muscle groups involved. By the time the first exercise is performed again, the muscles have recovered. Second, the athlete may perform all the sets for the first exercise and then move to the next exercise (a "horizontal" sequence). This sequence may cause local fatigue so great that by the time all the sets are performed for one exercise, hypertrophy may result instead of power or maximum strength. The vertical sequence is more beneficial because it allows a longer rest interval between sets and facilitates better regeneration. However, if hypertrophy is the training goal, the horizontal sequence will result in greater gains in lean muscle mass.

Number of Repetitions and Speed of Lifting

Both the number of reps and the speed of execution are functions of load. The higher the load, the fewer the reps and the more slowly they are performed. For development of maximum strength (85 to 105 percent of 1RM), the number of reps is very low (one to seven) (see figure 5.2). For exercises to develop power (50 to 80 percent of 1RM), the number of reps is moderate (5 to 10, performed dynamically). For muscular endurance of short duration, 10 to 30 reps will work. Muscular endurance of medium duration requires around 30 to 60 nonstop reps. Muscular endurance of long duration requires a high number of reps, sometimes up to one's limit, or more than 100 to 150.

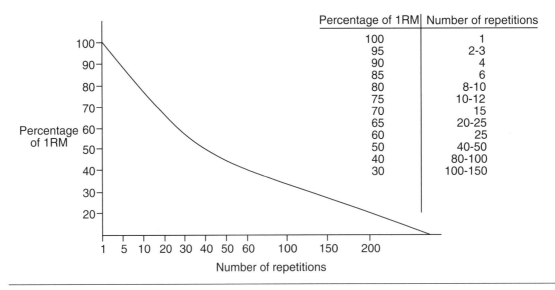

Percentage of 1RM	Number of repetitions
100	1
95	2-3
90	4
85	6
80	8-10
75	10-12
70	15
65	20-25
60	25
50	40-50
40	80-100
30	100-150

Figure 5.2 Curve of load vs. number of repetitions.

Figure 5.2 shows the relationship between load and repetition. Instructors who regard 20 reps to be adequate for enhancing muscular endurance may find the suggested number of reps shocking. However, 20 reps make an insignificant contribution to the overall performance of sports requiring muscular endurance of medium or long duration, such as rowing, kayaking, canoeing, long-distance swimming, speedskating, and cross-country skiing.

Speed is critical in strength training. For the best training effects, the speed of execution must be fast and explosive for some types of work; for others, it should be slow to medium. The key to proper execution of speed is the way athletes apply force against resistance. For instance, when an American football player, a thrower, or a sprinter lifts a heavy load of 90 percent of 1RM, the motion may look slow, but the force against the resistance is applied as fast as possible. Otherwise the athlete will not recruit and synchronize all the motor units necessary to defeat resistance. The fast-twitch muscle fibers are trained and recruited for the action only when the application of force is fast and vigorous. The speed of contraction plays a very important role in strength training. To achieve explosive force, the athlete must concentrate on activating the muscles quickly, even though the barbell is moving slowly. Only a high speed of contraction performed against a maximum load will rapidly recruit the fast-twitch fibers and result in increased maximum strength. Slow-velocity strength training (similar to maximum strength training) can improve high-velocity strength if the athlete attempts to move the weight as quickly as possible (Behm and Sale, 1993).

The speed of lifting is directly related to the time the muscle is under tension. Depending on the desired physiological response, the speed of movement should vary from phase to phase. Moderate speeds should be used during the anatomical adaptation phase of training; the athlete should spend approximately two to three seconds in the concentric portion of the lift, pause for one second for the transition from concentric to eccentric, and spend two to three seconds in the eccentric portion of the lift. The intended speed of contraction during the maximum strength phase should be as fast as possible, even though the actual speed is slow. Athletes should attempt an explosive concentric lift, followed by a two-second pause before slowly performing a three- to four-second eccentric contraction. The transition from an eccentric contraction to another concentric contraction is very important during the maximum strength phase. Because the goal of the phase is an increase in maximal force generation, the best way to optimize concentric strength is to remove any reflexive or elastic qualities that are developed during the eccentric phase of the lift by pausing two seconds before a further concentric lift.

Let's take the bench press as an example. When performing the bench press, the extending of the arms is the concentric portion of the lift, and returning the barbell to chest level and stretching the chest muscles is the eccentric portion of the lift. Generally speaking, an athlete will extend the arms during the lift and pause slightly at the top of the movement before slowly returning the bar to the starting position and lifting a second time. The eccentric portion of the lift has a physiological advantage over the concentric part in that, if properly executed, it can increase the force of the concentric lift that follows.

This eccentric system is the reason plyometric training is so popular in sports. In essence, plyometric training improves sport performance by heightening the physiological properties of the prime movers for quick and explosive actions. As an athlete eccentrically lowers the bar to the chest, neural mechanisms in the muscles are heightened and used during the concentric or lifting portion of the exercise if the transition from eccentric to concentric is made quickly, almost without a pause. An athlete attempting this type of lift demonstrates a sudden shake of the upper body and usually an increased arch in the low back as he moves from the moderate eccentric contraction to a quick and explosive transition to a concentric contraction. Thus, a true increase in pure force generation can be achieved by briefly pausing after the eccentric lift and making the upward motion of the bar a pure concentric lift without any positive influences from the eccentric contraction. This system of training, which can be used to help break an athlete through a strength plateau, should be used only during the maximum strength phase of training.

Time under tension, or lifting speed, is mostly popularized in hypertrophy training. Although varying lifting speed during the hypertrophy phase of training is extremely beneficial, we find its application by athletes in training at times difficult as they focus their attention on the lift. Manipulating both concentric and eccentric lifting speeds can be helpful when the goal is an increase in lean muscle mass. The main premise behind the theory of time under tension is that the greater the time the muscle fibers are contracted, the greater the protein breakdown and thus the higher the level of adaptation and muscle growth. When an athlete is training with loads directed toward the recruitment of fast-twitch type II muscles, the time under tension can have a very positive effect on hypertrophy of the trained muscle. However, athletes often have trouble remaining focused while concentrating on the number of reps along with the scheduled time for every rep. Coaches would do well to schedule the speed of lifting as slow, moderate, or fast, but manipulate concentric and especially eccentric repetition speed when attempting to maximize muscle fatigue and growth of lean muscle mass. Supersets, which combine two exercises for the same muscle group into one large set, can also provide good hypertrophy gains.

Number of Sets

A set is the number of reps per exercise followed by a rest interval. The number of sets depends on the number of exercises and the strength combination. The number of sets decreases as the number of exercises increases because athletes do not have the energy and work potential to perform many reps with a high number of sets. The strength combination being trained also influences the number of sets. For a rower, canoeist, or cross-country skier attempting to develop muscular endurance of long duration, the key element is the number of reps per set. Because the number of reps is high, athletes have difficulty performing more than three or four sets.

The number of sets also depends on the athlete's abilities and training potential, the number of muscle groups to be trained, and the training phase. A high jumper or diver in a specialized training program may use three to five exercises in six to eight sets per session. A higher number of exercises would require fewer sets, with obvious disadvantages. Consider a hypothetical high jumper who is using eight exercises involving several muscle groups of the legs, upper body, and arms. For each exercise or muscle group, the athlete performs work of 880 pounds (400 kilograms). Because the athlete can perform only four sets, the total amount of work per muscle group is 3,520 pounds (1,600 kilograms). When the number of exercises is reduced to four, the athlete can now perform, say, eight sets for a total of 7,040 pounds (3,200 kilograms) per muscle group. The athlete can double, even triple the total work per muscle group by decreasing the number of exercises and increasing the number of sets.

The training phase also dictates the number of sets per training session. During the preparatory (preseason) phase, in particular the anatomical adaptation phase, when most muscle groups are trained, more exercises are performed with fewer sets (see chapters 7). As the competitive phase approaches, training becomes more specific and the number of exercises decreases while the number of sets increases. Finally, during the competitive phase (season), when the purpose of training is to maintain a certain level of strength or a given strength combination, everything is reduced, including the number of sets, so that the athlete's energy is spent mostly for technical and tactical work. A well-trained athlete can perform 3, 8, 10, even 12 sets. Certainly, it makes sense to perform a higher number of sets. The more sets the athlete performs per muscle group, the more work the athlete can perform, ultimately leading to higher strength gains and improved performance.

Rest Interval

Energy is necessary for strength training. During training, an athlete uses the fuel of a given energy system according to the load employed and the duration of activity. During high-intensity strength training, energy stores can be taxed to a great extent and sometimes even completely exhausted. To complete the work, athletes must take a rest interval to replenish depleted fuel before performing another set.

The rest interval between sets or training sessions is as important as the training itself. The amount of time allowed between sets determines, to a great extent, how much energy can be recovered before the following set. Careful planning of the rest interval is critical in avoiding needless physiological and psychological stress during training.

The duration of the rest interval depends on several factors, including the combination of strength being developed, the load employed, the speed of the performance, the number of muscles involved, and the level of conditioning. In calculating the rest interval, athletes' body weight must also be considered because heavy athletes with larger muscles tend to regenerate at a slower rate than lighter athletes do. Rest interval is defined as the rest taken both between sets and between days of strength training.

Rest Intervals Between Sets

The rest interval is a function of the load employed in training, the type of strength being developed, and the rate or explosiveness of performing the task (see table 5.4).

Table 5.4   Suggested Guidelines for Rest Intervals Between Sets

Load percent	Speed of performance	Rest interval (minutes)	Applicability
>105 (eccentric)	Slow	4-5	Improve maximum strength and muscle tone
80-100	Slow to medium	3-5	Improve maximum strength and muscle tone
60-80	Slow to medium	2	Improve muscle hypertrophy
50-80	Fast	4-5	Improve power
30-50	Slow to medium	1-2	Improve M-E

During a rest interval, a high-energy compound of adenosine triphosphate (ATP) and creatine phosphate (CP) to be used as an energy source is replenished proportionate to the duration of the rest interval. When the rest interval is calculated properly, lactic acid accumulates more slowly, enabling the athlete to maintain the planned training program. If the rest interval is shorter than one minute, lactic acid concentration is high; when the rest interval is shorter than 30 seconds, lactate levels are so high that even well-trained athletes find them difficult to tolerate. A proper rest interval, on the other hand, facilitates the removal of lactic acid from the body. Some sports require athletes to tolerate lactic acid, such as short-distance running, swimming, rowing, canoeing, most team sports, boxing, and wrestling. Strength training for athletes in these sports should take into consideration the following:

- A 30-second complete rest restores approximately 50 percent of depleted ATP-CP.
- A one-minute rest interval for several sets of 15 to 20 reps is insufficient to restore the muscle's energy and enable performance of high muscular tension.

- Fatigue accumulated during maximum strength exercise followed by a short rest interval resulted in a decreased discharge rate of motor neurons, which affected speed. This was not the case following a three-minute rest interval (Bigland-Ritchie et al., 1983).
- A rest interval of three minutes or longer allows almost complete ATP-CP restoration.
- longer rest interval (i.e., over three minutes) resulted in a greater improvement of hamstring strength (Pincivero et al., 1997).

After an athlete works to exhaustion, a four-minute rest interval is insufficient to eliminate lactic acid from the working muscles or to replenish all the energy requirements such as glycogen.

One consequence of an inadequate rest interval between sets is an increased reliance on the lactic acid system for energy. The degree to which ATP-CP is replenished between sets depends on the duration of the rest interval. The shorter the rest interval, the less ATP-CP is restored and, consequently, the less energy is available for the next set. If the rest interval is too short, the lactic acid system provides the energy needed for subsequent sets. Reliance on this energy system results in increased lactic acid accumulation in the working muscles, leading to pain and fatigue and impairing the ability to train effectively. Also, during the rest interval, the heart pumps the highest volume of blood to the working muscles. A short rest interval diminishes the amount of blood sent to the working muscles. Athletes in this situation will not have the energy to complete the planned training session. A longer rest interval is required to combat excessive lactic acid accumulation.

A second consequence of an inadequate rest interval is local muscular and CNS fatigue. Most research findings point to the following possible causes and sites of fatigue:

- The nervous system transmits nerve impulses to muscle fibers through the *motor nerve*. A nerve impulse has certain degrees of force, speed, and frequency. The higher the force impulse, the stronger the muscle contraction, which gives athletes greater ability to lift heavier loads. The force of nerve impulses is greatly affected by fatigue, and as the level of fatigue increases, the force of contraction decreases. Thus, longer rest intervals (up to seven minutes) are necessary for CNS recovery during the maximum strength phase.

- The *neuromuscular junction* is the nerve attachment on the muscle fiber that relays the nerve impulses to the working muscle. Fatigue at this site is due largely to an increased release of chemical transmitters from the nerve endings (Tesch, 1980). Following a set, a two- to three-minute rest interval usually returns the electrical properties of the nerve to normal levels. After powerful contractions such as those typical of maximum strength training, however, a rest interval of longer than five minutes is needed for sufficient recovery to occur.

- The *contractile mechanisms* (actin and myosin) can also be a site of fatigue and performance breakdown. Acid accumulation decreases the peak tension, or the power of the muscle to contract maximally, and leads to a higher acidic concentration in the muscle, affecting its ability to react to the nerve impulses (Fox, Bowes, and Foss,1989; Sahlin, 1986). Depletion of muscle glycogen stores, which occurs during prolonged exercise (more than 30 minutes), also causes fatigue of the contracting muscle (Conlee, 1987; Karlsson and Saltin 1971; Sahlin, 1986). Other energy sources available to the muscle, including glycogen from the liver, cannot fully cover the energy demands of the working muscle.

- The CNS can also experience local muscle fatigue. During training, chemical disturbances occur inside the muscle that affect its potential to perform work (Bigland-Ritchie et al., 1983; Hennig and Lomo, 1987). When the effects of these chemical disturbances are signaled back to the CNS, the brain sends weaker nerve impulses to the working muscle, which decreases its working capacity in an attempt to protect the body. During an adequate rest interval of four to five minutes, the muscles are allowed to recover almost completely. The brain then senses no danger and sends more powerful nerve impulses to the muscles, resulting in better muscular performance.

Rest Intervals Between Strength Training Sessions

The rest interval between strength training sessions depends on the conditioning level and recovery ability of the athlete, the training phase, and the energy source used in training. Well-conditioned athletes always recover faster, especially as training progresses toward the competitive phase, when they are supposed to reach their highest physical potential.

Training coaches should consider the energy source taxed in training when determining the length and frequency of the rest interval between strength training sessions. Normally, strength training is planned following technical or tactical training. If athletes tax the same energy system and fuel (e.g., glycogen) during technical and strength training, the next training of this type must be planned for two days later because 48 hours are required for full restoration of glycogen (Fox et al., 1989; Piehl, 1974). Even with a carbohydrate-rich diet, glycogen levels will not return to normal in less than two days. If athletes perform only strength training, as some do on certain days during the preparatory phase, the restoration of glycogen occurs faster: 55 percent in 5 hours and almost 100 percent in 24 hours. This means that strength training can be planned more frequently.

Along with carbohydrate restoration, the amount of time required for nervous system and muscle protein recovery should also be taken into consideration when planning strength training sessions. Untrained subjects who partake in resistance training programs that include a combination of concentric and eccentric actions show muscle fiber breakdown (protein breakdown) that can persist as long as 48 hours after the bout of strength training (Gibala et al., 1995). The good news is that the concomitant net increase in the synthesis of muscle protein is greater than the breakdown.

Protein synthesis, or the rebuilding of muscle fibers, following a strength training session is further increased by the ingestion of protein-rich foods immediately following the session. Muscle protein recovery likely occurs at a faster rate in trained athletes.

Nervous system fatigue is also a very important factor to consider when planning strength training sessions. Scheduling high-intensity workouts on back-to-back days does not allow proper time for neural recovery. For instance, many athletes perform maximum strength training on Monday followed by plyometric training on Tuesday. Because both sessions tax similar neural pathways, recovery time between the two is inadequate and injury or signs of overtraining may occur. Numerous studies point to the fact that the high-intensity training typical of plyometric training can lead to decreased activity of both the Golgi tendon organs and muscle spindles, both systems being highly involved in nervous system training and adaptation. Time for proper recovery is a must for all bodily systems.

Plain and simple, scientific research overwhelmingly argues that recovery after a strength or aerobic training session must be adequate to allow time for all the body systems to regenerate and adapt to the stimulus before being introduced to a similar or more aggressive training session. In the circle of training, recovery plays as vital a role as the stimulus applied in training. Energy fuel must be restored, the nervous system must recover, and the net protein balance (synthesis minus breakdown) must remain positive for progressive increases in muscular strength, endurance, and size to occur.

Designing training programs solely according to the energy systems used can simplify the process. (Chapter 3 offers a more in-depth discussion of the role of the energy systems in training and the amount of time needed for recovery and regeneration following a training session.) Keep in mind that although our bodies are highly sophisticated, there are subtle similarities in most systems in terms of fatigue and recovery patterns.

Restoration of Phosphates

Lifting weights or performing high-level aerobic activity slowly fatigues the body and causes a shift from its normal physiological balance called *homeostasis*. The body has the highest efficiency in the homeostatic state. The body recovers and replenishes energy supplies to preexercise conditions through the restoration of phosphagen, phosphate compounds that occur in muscle. Following a fatiguing training session or set, the body recovers and returns to its homeostatic level. Phosphagen restoration reaches 70 percent in the first 30 seconds of recovery and 100 percent within three to five minutes. This explains why high-intensity resistance training such as lifting heavy weights for four to eight reps or sprinting for 50 meters requires a three to five-minute rest between sets.

Beginning a set without proper phosphate recovery will not allow optimal efficiency throughout the set. Therefore, in the maximum strength phase of training, athletes should rest for three to five minutes before performing further sets with the same muscle group. For maximum recovery after each set, athletes should use the vertical method of training when exercising at an intensity characteristic of the maximum strength phase. In other words, one set of each suggested exercise is completed before returning to the first exercise for the second set. This will allow ample time for phosphate recovery within the muscle.

Activity During Rest

Engaging in aerobic activity at approximately 20% $\dot{V}O_2$max while recovering between high intensity intermittent bouts of exercise positively impacts performance in subsequent bouts more so than stretching or passive rest. (Dorado et. al. 2004). To facilitate faster recovery between sets, athletes should perform relaxation exercises such as shaking the legs, arms, and shoulders, or light massage, which seem to speed up recovery. Using mental techniques to relax muscles can also be very beneficial.

During the rest interval, it is also important to perform "diversionary activities" such as pacing or stretching to involve the nonfatigued muscles in some light contractions (Asmussen and Mazin, 1978). Such physical activities have been reported to facilitate faster recovery of the prime movers. Local muscle fatigue is signaled to the CNS via sensory nerves. As a result, the brain sends inhibitory signals to the fatigued muscles, decreasing their work output during the rest interval. This causes the muscles to relax, which facilitates the restoration of the energy stores.

The purpose of stretching exercises is to artificially lengthen a muscle where the myosins and actins are overlapped. The sooner the muscles reach their anatomical length, the faster they start their recovery and regeneration process, eliminating the metabolites accumulated during training. Stretching exercises that address the muscles used should be planned after each set of a given exercise.

Loading Patterns

Athletes who perform too many sets at a lower load will experience hypertrophy training, not maximum strength. This may lead to fatigue that might impair maximum strength development. Even if athletes start with one or two sets of a submaximum load, they must increase to maximum load relatively quickly to obtain the most favorable conditions for maximum strength development.

In the pyramid pattern examples that follow, each program starts from its base and works toward the peak, or from the bottom to the top. Athletes should perform the suggested load for all the exercises selected for the workout before moving to the next load.

The *pyramid* is one of the most popular loading patterns. Its structure, shown in figure 5.3, implies that the load increases progressively to maximum while the number of reps decreases proportionately. The physiological advantage of using the pyramid is that it ensures the activation or recruitment of most if not all the motor units. To facilitate the highest level of strength adaptation, athletes should use a 10 to 15 percent loading pattern range. Any range greater than 15 percent will fatigue the athlete and not optimize strength gains.

The *double pyramid* consists of two pyramids, one inverted on top of the other. The number of reps decreases from the bottom up, then increases again in the second pyramid (see figure 5.4). Although the double pyramid has its merits, some cautions are necessary. Most proponents of this pattern suggest that the last sets, with loads of 85 and 80 percent, are meant to improve power. The assumption is that because the load is lower, the force can be applied faster. By the time these final sets are performed, however, both the CNS and the muscles involved may be exhausted, in which case these sets will not produce the expected benefits. On the contrary, because the fatigue may impair fast recruitment of the fast-twitch fibers, the actual outcome of the last sets of this loading pattern will be the development of muscle hypertrophy rather than power. Increases in power can only be obtained when an athlete is in a nonfatigued state, which generally occurs at the beginning of a session immediately following the warm-up.

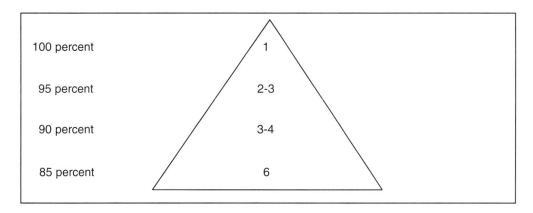

Figure 5.3 Pyramid loading pattern. The number of repetitions (inside the pyramid) refers to the number per set.

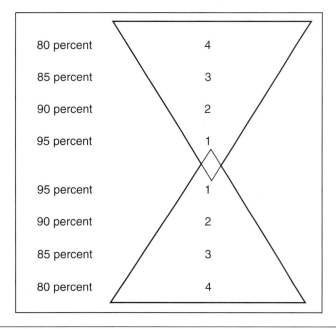

Figure 5.4 Double-pyramid loading pattern suggested by Grosser and Neumeier (1986).

If the intent is to enhance fast-twitch fiber recruitment, it must be done in the early part of the session. Coaches should not expect power enhancement at the end of a training day; fatigue may interfere. However, if both maximum strength and hypertrophy training are planned in the same training session, the double pyramid may be an acceptable solution.

The *skewed pyramid* (see figure 5.5) is proposed as an improved variant of the double pyramid. The load is constantly increased throughout the session, except during the last set, when it is lowered (80-85-90-95-80 percent). The intent of lowering that load in the last set is variation and motivation, because athletes will be asked to perform the lift as quickly as they can. As in the case of the double pyramid, fatigue may hamper a quick application of force, but this should not stop athletes from trying. Because only one set is performed and the number of reps is low (four to six), athletes will not experience exhaustion, so the single set will not trigger gains in hypertrophy.

The *flat pyramid* represents the best loading pattern for achieving optimal maximum strength benefits (see figure 5.6). In traditional pyramids, the load often varies from 70 to 100 percent. Load variations of such magnitude cross three levels of intensity: medium, heavy, and maximum. The load necessary to produce gains in maximum strength is between 85 and 100 percent; therefore, a traditional pyramid that uses a load of 70 to 100 percent may result in gains in both power and maximum strength. Although this may be of general benefit to athletes, it does not maximize gains in maximum strength.

The flat pyramid is the best option if the intent of the training is to develop maximum strength only. This type of loading pattern starts with a warm-up lift of, say, 60 percent, followed by an intermediary set at 80 percent, then stabilizes the load at 90 percent for the entire workout. If the instructor wishes to add variety at the end of training, a set of lower load may be used (figure 5.6 shows an example of 80 percent). The physiological advantage of the flat pyramid is that by using a load of only one intensity level, the best neuromuscular adaptation for maximum strength is achieved without "confusing" the body with several intensities.

Variations of the flat pyramid are certainly possible and necessary, as long as the load stays within the 85 to 100 percent intensity range required for gains in maximum strength. Varying the repetition count at different loads will stimulate an increase in strength without a constant

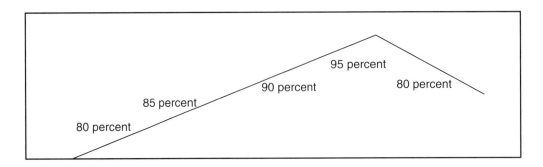

Figure 5.5 Suggested loading pattern for the "skewed pyramid."
Adapted, by permission, from T. Bompa, 1999, *Periodization training for sports* (Champaign, IL: Human Kinetics), 54.

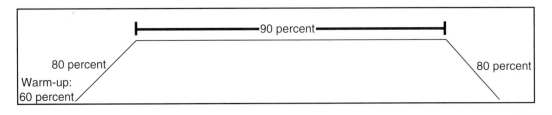

Figure 5.6 The flat pyramid represents the best loading pattern for the development of MxS.
Adapted, by permission, from T. Bompa, 1999, *Periodization training for sports* (Champaign, IL: Human Kinetics), 54.

increase in the load. Increasing the load without a visible sign of strength gains, however, will depreciate the value of the session and result in minimal gains in maximum strength. As a rule of thumb, athletes should attempt one rep more than they performed in their last set or session at a specific load to test whether a visible sign in strength has occurred. When the result is positive, they should continue with a progressive increase in load.

Training Program Design

All training programs must be planned, designed, and measured to assess whether the training objective has been achieved. The following steps will remove any confusion from the process of designing a program and assessing its significance to the athlete's level of development.

1. *Select the type of strength.* The type or sport-specific combination of strength that is relevant to the physiological demands of your sport is selected based on the concept of periodization which promotes a phase-specific program. This concept enables a coach or instructor to decide the percentage of 1RM to be used and the number of reps and sets. Details on training methods and progression are provided in chapters 8 through 12.

2. *Select the exercises to be used in training.* Instructors should select training exercises according to the specifics of the sport, the athletes' needs, and the phase of training. Each athletic skill is performed by prime movers, which can differ from sport to sport depending on the specific skill requirements. Therefore, instructors must first identify the prime movers and then select the strength exercises that best involve these muscles. At the same time, they must consider the athletes' needs. These may depend on their backgrounds and individual strengths and weaknesses. Because the weakest link in a chain always breaks first, compensation exercises should be selected to strengthen the weakest muscles.

The selection of exercises is also phase specific, as noted in chapter 7. Normally, during the anatomical adaptation phase, most muscle groups are employed to build a better and more multilateral foundation. As the competitive phase approaches, training becomes more specific and exercises are selected specifically to involve the prime movers.

3. *Test maximum strength.* Maximum strength is the highest load an athlete can lift in one attempt and is used by coaches to calculate their athletes' 1RM. A coach should know each athlete's maximum strength in at least the dominant exercises of the training program. Often the load and number of reps are chosen randomly, or by following the programs of other athletes, instead of using the objective data from each athlete. The athlete's individual data is valid only for a certain cycle of training, usually a macrocycle, because each athlete's degree of training and potential changes continuously.

Some coaches and instructors believe that testing for 1RM is dangerous, that lifting 100 percent can result in injury. It is not dangerous for trained athletes to lift 100 percent once every four weeks, or at the beginning of each macrocycle. Most injuries occur during training and competitions, not during testing. If we avoid challenging muscles to 100 percent, they can hardly adapt to apply their maximum potential in competition. It is important to remember, however, that a test for 1RM must follow a thorough, progressive warm-up.

4. *Develop the specific training program.* The previous steps give the coach a clear picture of the athlete's ability to tolerate work. The coach uses this information to determine the number of exercises, the percentage of 1RM to use, the number of reps, and the number of sets to prescribe for a macrocycle training program. The program cannot be the same for each macrocycle, however. Training demand must increase progressively so the athlete will adapt to a larger workload, which will be translated into an increase in strength. The training demand may be increased by increasing the load, decreasing the rest interval, increasing the number of reps, or increasing the number of sets. Coaches should test athletes to recalculate their 1RM

before each new macrocycle to ensure that progress in maximum strength is achieved and that the new load is related to the gains made in strength.

5. *Record the information.* The notation used in a training program chart to express the load, the number of reps, and the number of sets must be first understood before the information can be recorded. The load is notated as a percentage of 1RM, and athletes must be tested, especially during the preparatory phase at the beginning of each new macrocycle. By knowing an athlete's 1RM, the coach can select the percentage to be used in training according to the training goals of each phase.

The notation of load, number of reps, and number of sets is expressed as follows:

$$\frac{\text{Load}}{\text{no. of reps}} \text{ sets}$$

$$\frac{80}{10} 4$$

The numerator (80 percent) refers to the load, the denominator (10) represents the number of reps, and the multiplier (4) indicates the number of sets.

The advantage of suggesting the load as a percentage of 1RM is that when working with a larger group of athletes, such as a football team, the coach does not have to calculate the poundage for each player. By suggesting the load in percentage, the program is valid for each athlete. Individualization is therefore built in with this method. Each athlete uses his personal 1RM as the basis for calculating poundage, which may vary from player to player.

Any strength training program should be written on a sheet of paper or in the training journal. Table 5.5 illustrates an example format for a strength training program. The first column lists the number of the exercise to be performed in a given strength training session, from 1 to X. The second column shows the exercises. The third column specifies the load, number of reps, and number of sets. The last column indicates the rest interval to be taken following each set.

Table 5.5   Sample Chart for a Strength Training Program

Exercise no.	Exercise	Load, no. of reps, no. of sets	Rest interval (minutes)
1	Leg presses	$\frac{80}{6} 4$	3
2	Bench presses	$\frac{75}{8} 4$	3
3	Leg curls	$\frac{60}{10} 3$	2
4	Half squats	$\frac{80}{8} 4$	3
5	Abdominal curls	15×4	2
6	Deadlifts	$\frac{60}{8} 3$	2

Exercise Prescription

All athletic skills and actions are performed by muscles as a result of contraction. The 656 muscles distributed throughout the human body are capable of performing a great variety of movements. If athletes want to improve a skill or a physical performance, they must concentrate on training the muscles that perform the action, or the prime movers.

The process of prescribing exercises for a given muscle group (or groups) must be based on phase-specific considerations. During the anatomical adaptation phase, exercises must be selected that develop most muscle groups, both agonist and antagonist, to build a stronger base for the training phases to follow. As the competitive phase approaches, these exercises become very specialized, prescribed specifically for the prime movers.

For an adequate exercise prescription, consider the following steps:

1. Analyze how the skill is performed (direction, angle, and limb position).

2. Determine the prime movers responsible for the skill performance.

3. Select exercises that involve the prime movers based on their similarity to the direction and angle of contraction for the selected skill(s).

4. Once the exercises have been selected, have the athlete perform a high number of sets of the specific exercises to facilitate a high level of adaptation. As many as 10 to 12 sets are common for very sport-specific exercises.

Exercise prescription should be based on an understanding of how the muscles are producing a movement, not on exercises borrowed from weightlifting or bodybuilding. An exercise is good for a sport only if it follows the principle of specificity. It must involve the prime movers and the synergistic muscles used in performing the skills of the particular sport or event.

Coaches often turn to bodybuilding for exercise ideas without understanding the differences between sports and bodybuilding. One difference is in the type of method—analytic or composite—used to determine how an exercise achieves a specific training goal. Bodybuilders use the analytic method for high muscle definition. They analyze each muscle's individual action and movement, and then train each muscle in isolation to achieve the best size development.

In athletics, however, the composite method should be used because it involves all the muscles of a joint (or joints) necessary to produce an athletic skill, rather than an individual muscle. Exercises should involve the muscles and joints in a sequence similar to that used in the performance of a skill. For instance, to train the muscles involved in starting in sprinting, athletes should use reverse leg presses, lunges, and step-ups rather than knee extensions.

The analytic and composite methods differ in another important way. The analytic method results in only local adaptation with no cardiorespiratory benefits. In the composite method, however, by using large muscle groups of one to three joints, as in the reverse leg press, cardiorespiratory fitness improves as well, which is an important training goal for sports.

Specificity of Strength Exercises and the Need for Specific Adaptation

In many cases, athletes and coaches rate the success of a strength training program according to the amount of muscle the athlete builds (hypertrophy). With the exception of American football linemen, shot-putters, and heavyweight boxers and wrestlers, constant increase in muscle size is not a desirable effect for most athletes. Power and speed sports, or sports with quick, explosive action (e.g., baseball, football, hockey, most track-and-field events, volleyball) rely on *nervous system training*, which includes many power exercises and maximum loads (greater than 80 percent of 1RM) that result in *neural adaptation* (Enoka, 1996; Sale, 1986; Schmidtbleicher, 1992). Neural adaptation in strength training for most sports means increasing power and the speed of the contraction without increasing muscle mass.

Higher neural adaptation is achieved by carefully selecting training methods and exercises. Researchers and international-class coaches share similar views about what represents the specificity of strength training. These views are summarized as follows:

- Strength training methods must be specific to the speed of contraction used in the sport (Coyle et al., 1991; Kanehisa and Miyashita, 1983). This means that from the second half of the preparatory phase through the competitive phase, coaches should select methods that specifically increase the speed of contraction and, therefore, the level of power.

- Training methods and exercises must increase the contraction force in the intended direction of movement. This means selecting exercises according to the muscles used to perform the technical skill of a given sport (prime movers). Olympic weightlifting and bodybuilding exercises waste time, especially during the second part of the preparatory and competitive phases.

- Training methods must increase the activation and excitation of the prime movers. Selected exercises must be sport specific and activate the prime movers.

- Training methods must increase the discharge rate of motor neurons (Hortobagyi et al., 1996) or stimulate the muscles to perform an athletic action with power and high speed. Motor neurons innervate, stimulate, and arouse the muscles. The more specific the training method and exercises are, the better a muscle is trained to perform quick and powerful athletic movements.

- Motor unit recruitment and firing rate increase with higher loads and faster contractions (De Luca et al., 1982). Training methods that enhance maximum strength and power are the only ones that increase the firing rate of motor units and fast-twitch muscle fiber recruitment.

- Exercise action must be performed along the neural pathway used in the sport (Häkkinen, 1989). Exercises have to be selected so that contractions are performed in the same direction as the nerve stimulation that occurs during the performance of sport skills. If an exercise does not realistically simulate, or is not specific to, a technical skill, the muscle contraction is not along the neural pathway, resulting in a lower exercise efficiency in training.

- The sequence in which muscles are contracted during an exercise is crucial to the specifics of adaptation. Exercises, especially *multijoint exercises* (i.e., squats involving three joints), must simulate the sequence in which muscles contract while performing a specific technical skill.

- Neural adaptation resulting from specificity of strength training increases the number of active motor units. Well-selected training methods, such as maximum strength methods and power training, activate more motor units. As a result, an athlete can perform an exercise with higher speed of contraction and more power.

Maximum Muscle Efficiency in Relation to Limb Position

Strength training for sports is influenced by various theories, many of which are affecting the training methods coaches and athletes are choosing and the exercises they are selecting. For example, some theorize that a given grip is more effective than another in stimulating certain muscle groups, and that certain foot positions for squats are better than others.

To evaluate the maximum effectiveness of muscle contractions as related to limb position, data performed in 1998 and documented in *Serious Strength Training* (Bompa and Cornacchia, 1998) is presented below. Most studies that evaluate the effectiveness of muscle contraction use electromyography (EMG), which measures the electrical activity or excitability level of the muscles involved. The higher the electrical activity, the more effective the muscle contraction. In EMG studies, researchers can use the peak of the electrical activity (peak force) or, even better, calculate or integrate the full force under the curve. This improved method, called integrated electromyography, or iEMG, was used to compile the data in table 5.6 that evaluates muscle efficiency as affected by limb position.

The load used for the iEMG study was 80 percent of 1RM, which means maximum strength. Data were analyzed employing two one-way repeated-measures analyses of variance to determine which exercise yielded the greatest percentage of iEMG for each muscle. Table 5.6 shows which exercises produced the greatest amount of stimulation within each target muscle group. The findings are presented as percentages of maximum. Obviously, the exercise showing the highest percentage could be considered the best for the particular muscle group(s).

Table 5.6 iEMG Maximum Motor Unit Activation

Exercise	Percent iEMG	Exercise	Percent iEMG
Rectus Femoris (Quadriceps)		Lat pull-downs to the front	86
Safety squats (90-degree angle, shoulder-width stance)	88	Seated pulley rows	83
Seated leg extensions (toes straight)	86	**Biceps Brachii (Long Head)**	
		Biceps preacher curls (Olympic bar)	90
Half squats (90-degree angle, shoulder-width stance)	78	Incline seated dumbbell curls (alternate)	88
Leg presses (110-degree angle)	76	Standing biceps curls (Olympic bar/ narrow grip)	86
Smith machine squats (90-degree angle, shoulder-width stance)	60	Standing dumbbell curls (alternate)	84
Biceps Femoris (Hamstrings)		Concentration dumbbell curls	80
Standing leg curls	82	Standing biceps curls (Olympic bar/ wide grip)	63
Lying leg curls	71		
Seated leg curls	58	Standing E-Z biceps curls (wide grip)	61
Modified hamstring deadlifts	56		
Semitendinosus (Hamstrings)		**Anterior Deltoids**	
Seated leg curls	88	Seated front dumbbell presses	79
Standing leg curls	79	Standing front dumbbell raises	73
Lying leg curls	70	Seated front barbell presses	61
Modified hamstring deadlifts	63	**Medial Deltoids**	
Gastrocnemius (Calf Muscle)		Standing dumbbell side laterals	57
Donkey calf raises	80	Seated dumbbell side laterals	53
Standing one-legged calf raises	79	Cable side laterals	49
Standing two-legged calf raises	68	**Posterior Deltoids**	
Seated calf raises	61	Standing dumbbell bent laterals	85
Triceps Brachii (Outer Head)		Seated dumbbell bent laterals	83
Decline triceps extension (Olympic bar)	92	Standing cable bent laterals	77
Triceps pressdowns (angled bar)	90	**Pectoralis Major**	
		Decline dumbbell bench presses	93
Triceps dips between benches	87	Decline bench presses (Olympic bar)	90
One-arm cable triceps extensions (reverse grip)	85	Push-ups between benches	88
		Flat dumbbell bench presses	87
Overhead rope triceps extensions	84	Flat bench presses (Olympic bar)	85
Seated one-arm dumbbell triceps extensions (neutral grip)	82	Flat dumbbell flys	84
Narrow-grip bench presses (Olympic bar)	72	**Pectoralis Minor**	
		Incline dumbbell bench presses	91
Latissimus Dorsi		Incline bench presses (Olympic bar)	85
Bent-over barbell rows	93	Incline dumbbell flys	83
One-arm dumbbell rows (alternate)	91	Incline bench presses (Smith machine)	81
T-bar rows	89		

The Microcycle Short Term Plan

A successful strength training program should be part of a long-term training program and not only implemented during certain parts of the yearly plan. Also, strength training should not be performed just for the sake of it or because it improves performance. Although it does improve performance, it also enhances the overall training plan. Strength training helps protect athletes from injury, delays the onset of fatigue and enables the athlete to generate a high level of force that is required for optimal sport performance. It must meet the objectives of the training phase and coincide with the overall plan.

Because a training program is a methodical, scientific strategy for improving performance, it should be well organized and well designed. An effective training program also incorporates the principles of periodization of strength throughout the year.

The training program, whether short or long term, also reflects the coach's methodological knowledge and takes into account the athlete's background and physical potential. A good training plan is simple, objective, and flexible so that it can match the athlete's physiological adaptation and performance improvements. Planning theory is very complex, and this book discusses planning only as it pertains to strength training. Further information can be found in *Periodization: Theory and Methodology of Training* (Bompa, 1999). Information on the training session plan, the microcycle, the yearly plan, and the long-term plan for junior athletes will be discussed in this book. Refer to the "Periodization" sections of chapter 7 for more sport-specific information.

Before You Begin

The following methodological guidelines will ensure that each person's strength training needs are met safely and efficiently. Strength coaches should know an athlete's strengths and weaknesses, the type of strength the athlete needs for the major periodization plan, and the peaking strategy. Coaches should also consider the athlete's background in strength training when planning the strength training program.

Check the Equipment

Equipment varies from gym to gym, so athletes often must adjust to new machines and free weights. Before using any equipment, coaches and athletes should check it to ensure maximum safety; although many private clubs check equipment regularly, some do not. Strength training equipment must be maintained properly so that wear and rust do not endanger users. A thorough equipment check includes checking for loose belts and cracks and periodically lubricating cables, chains, and rods to ensure smooth operation.

Among the most popular equipment used for strength training are free weights and machines built by a variety of manufacturers. Athletes (or their coaches) should secure the collars before using free weights and, in the case of power racks, check to make sure the barbells are properly placed on the supports and the pins are secure. The weight key used for stacks should be locked in place by inserting and twisting it or by pressing it to the end.

Before prescribing equipment other than free weights and machines, strength coaches should question whether the equipment can duplicate the skills performed by the prime movers and permit constant acceleration through the range of motion. The first criterion pertains to training specificity, an important requirement during all training phases. The second criterion is crucial for speed and power sports, especially from the conversion phase through the competitive phase. If constant acceleration cannot be reproduced, there is no positive transfer from strength training to the sport's skills and performance.

Know and Use Spotting Techniques

Advanced strength trainers prefer free weights over machines. Training partners act as spotters, especially when maximum loads or the eccentric method are used. The eccentric method with free weights is impossible to perform and dangerous without spotters. Young and inexperienced athletes especially should be assisted by trained instructors and use power/squat racks.

Even experienced athletes should use spotters for high-risk movements (employing heavy loads) such as squats, military presses, cleans, and bench presses. Spotters can offer feedback on the technical accuracy of the lifts. To avoid problems, including injuries, spotters should observe the following guidelines:

- Before spotting, know the exercise, spotting technique, and number of reps to be performed.
- Check the equipment and, in the case of free weights, make sure that the weights are evenly distributed and the collars are properly secured.
- Assuming a ready position, feet shoulder-width apart, check the performer's grip on the barbell and, if necessary, help the performer lift the barbell from the rack.

During the performance, the spotter is ready to give a "liftoff" at the beginning of the lift, especially for maximum loads. Spotters should be attentive throughout the lift and stand close enough to provide help if necessary. They should count the number of reps to ensure a coordinated effort. When necessary, spotters can give motivation and feedback regarding performance.

Technical feedback is crucial in avoiding injuries (e.g., during the bench press, if one arm is higher, the weights might fall off the lower end of the barbell). If the lift is performed incorrectly, the spotter should stop the exercise. If the lifter fails in the attempt, the spotter should secure the barbell and help the lifter place it on the rack or supports.

Use Correct Form and Body Position

Proper lifting technique is an important factor in performance improvement and prevention of injury, especially for free weight exercises. Coaches should constantly stress the form or technique of lifting, especially during the early years of an athlete's involvement in strength training.

Athletes should keep a straight upper body and a flat back for all exercises, especially those involving lifting and carrying. They should avoid an overarched, hollow back or rounded back in all circumstances, paying particular attention with heavier loads. In both an overarched and rounded back, the spine, particularly the intervertebral discs, are under excessive strain. An athlete lifting a 110-pound (50-kilogram) weight with a rounded back yields an intervertebral stress some 65 percent higher than with a straight back (Hartmann and Tünnemann, 1988).

Head position determines back posture. Improper head position may cause undesirable muscle tension. An exaggerated, vigorous head extension (backward drop) increases tension in the back extensor muscles, causing a hollow back. A forward bend of the head causes a rounded back, stretching the back muscles and "shooting" the hips. The head follows rather than leads the hips. For these reasons, athletes and coaches should pay close attention to head position! The best position for half squats is with the upper body erect, the back straight, and the head upright, with the eyes looking forward or slightly upward.

The intervertebral discs of the spine can be cushioned by contracting the abdominal muscles, creating pressure against the training belt and compensating the back. In many lifting moves, the hips and abdominal muscles act as stabilizers, supporting the working muscles of the arms and legs.

Breathe Properly

Breathing technique is an important concern for anyone undertaking strength training, especially beginners. Some breath holding is normal during strength training, especially during heavy lifts. However, if the breath is held for the entire lift, blood pressure, intrathoracic pressure, and intra-abdominal pressure will increase because of the Valsalva maneuver, forcing expiration against a closed glottis (the space between the vocal cords). This may restrict the return of blood, causing veins to swell and the face to redden (MacDougall et al., 1985). The Valsalva maneuver (holding the breathe when performing a lifting movement), although seemingly hazardous, has a beneficial function. The intrathoracic and intra-abdominal pressure solidifies the trunk, which stabilizes the vertebral column and creates a strong support for the muscles to pull against.

The Valsalva maneuver is a reflex reaction to lifting heavy loads and should not be perceived negatively unless the breath is held for a long time, which can result in fainting. Because athletes rarely hold their breath for longer than two to three seconds in strength training, fainting almost never occurs. Nevertheless, coaches should take every precaution necessary to prevent the Valsalva maneuver, especially for beginners, by teaching athletes to breathe correctly and by encouraging young athletes to breathe naturally during strength training.

The natural pattern for breathing in strength training is to inhale just before and during the lowering or eccentric phase of the lift and exhale during the lifting or concentric phase. The exhalation is preceded by a very short Valsalva, releasing most of the air from the lungs at the very end of the lift. In any case, athletes should be instructed not to hold their breath for too long, especially during a maximum strength training session.

During isometric contractions, athletes should hold their breath for only a very short time or not at all. When the muscles contract, the natural tendency is to hold one's breath, but athletes should concentrate on breathing throughout the contraction. For jumping and throwing exercises, athletes should inhale before the action and exhale while performing it.

Purchase Strength Training Accessories

Belts, training gloves, and shoes are common strength training accessories. Strength training belts counteract weak abdominal muscles for all lower-body exercises and support the low back and abdominal muscles during a lift, creating an approximate balance between the low back and abdominal muscles. A belt should not be used as a substitute for strengthening these muscles. On the contrary, during the anatomical adaptation phase, and even during other phases of training, athletes should dedicate time to strengthening the back and abdominal muscles. Belts may be necessary during heavy lifts typical of maximum strength training. As a general rule, athletes should use weight belts only when lifting loads greater than 85 percent of 1RM. Muscle weaknesses can also be addressed through compensation work during the transition phase.

Although popular with fitness fans, gloves, which protect the palms from blisters, are rarely worn by dedicated athletes, who are content to let their functional calluses protect their palms.

Shoes for strength training have higher heels than normal athletic shoes. They provide good arch support and keep the feet and ankles tight. Elevated heels also have a mechanical advantage. For instance, to overcome the weight of a barbell during lifting, athletes tend to lean backward; a slight slip or fall onto the back at this time might be dangerous. Shoes with higher heels counteract this tendency by bringing the vertical projection of the center of gravity slightly forward. This prevents athletes from leaning backward during lifting and balances the weight of the barbell with the force and mass of the body.

Another advantage of strength training shoes is that they compensate for a lack of ankle flexibility during certain exercises. For better balance, half squats (and even deep squats) should be performed flat-footed; however, because many athletes lack good ankle flexibility, they tend to stay on the balls of their feet or toes when assuming this position. The higher heels on strength training shoes allow athletes to take a flat-footed and balanced position for these exercises.

Athletes with weak or vulnerable joints and beginning athletes often wrap or tape joints (wrists, elbows, ankles, or knees) to provide additional support. The wrapping should not be so tight that it affects blood circulation. If possible, athletes should loosen the wrap during the rest interval for comfort and to increase circulation.

Obtain Medical Clearance

Anyone desiring to participate in sports, especially those involving strength training, must obtain medical clearance. This is especially true for young athletes and beginners who may have undiagnosed heart conditions or cardiovascular disease. The strenuous nature of many sports and strength training activities may aggravate such health conditions. Strength training with heavy loads involves the Valsalva maneuver, which increases blood, chest, and abdominal pressure and can unduly stress an already weak heart and cardiovascular system. In addition, these increased pressures may limit or even restrict blood flow to and from the heart (Compton, Hill, and Sinclair, 1973).

Some children may experience other health problems such as growth plate or orthopedic abnormalities like degenerating arthritis. In these cases, strength training may result in increased skeletal and joint stress. Physicians should restrict young people with such problems from strenuous training in general, and strength training in particular, for their protection. Every concerned coach should require medical clearance for every athlete.

Training Session Plan

The training session is the main tool for organizing the daily workout program. To achieve better management and organization, the training session can be structured into four main segments. The first two (introduction and warm-up) prepare the athlete for the main part, in which the actual training takes place, and the last part (cool-down) returns the athlete to the normal physiological state.

Introduction

During the *introduction* to a training session, the coach or instructor shares with the athletes the training objectives for the day and how they are to be achieved. This is also the time when the coach organizes the athletes into groups and gives them necessary advice regarding the daily program.

Warm-Up

The specific purpose of the *warm-up* is to prepare athletes for the program to follow. During the warm-up, body temperature is raised, which appears to be one of the main factors in facilitating performance. The warm-up stimulates the activity of the central nervous system (CNS), which coordinates all of the systems of the body; speeds up motor reactions through faster transmission of nerve impulses; improves the biomechanical performance of the motor system; increases the contraction speed and peak power muscles can produce; and improves coordination (Enoka, 2002; Wade et al., 2000). Also, the elevation of body temperature warms up and stretches muscles, tendons, ligaments, and other tissues, which prevents or reduces ligament sprains and tendon and muscle strains. Similarly, warmed-up muscle tissue is able to accommodate higher-velocity stretches before the ligament–bone coupling experiences damage (Enoka, 2002).

The warm-up for strength training has two parts: the *general warm-up* and the *specific warm-up.* The general warm-up (10 to 20 minutes) involves light jogging, cycling, or step-ups, followed by calisthenics and stretching exercises to increase blood flow, which raises the body temperature. This prepares the muscles and tendons for the planned program. During the warm-up, athletes should also prepare mentally for the main part of the training session by visualizing the exercises and motivating themselves for the eventual strain of training.

The specific warm-up (three to five minutes) is a short transition to the working part of the session. By performing a few reps on the equipment to be used and employing much lighter loads than are planned for the day, athletes prepare themselves for a successful workout.

Main Part

The *main part* of the training session is dedicated to the actual training program, in which training objectives are accomplished, including strength training. In most sports, technical and tactical work are the main objectives of training, with strength development being a secondary priority. First-priority activities are thus performed immediately after the warm-up, followed by strength training.

The types of training to be performed in a given day depend on the phase of training as well as its objectives. Table 6.1 illustrates suggested options, where TE stands for technical training, TA for tactical training, MxS for maximum strength, P for power, P-E for power-endurance, SP for speed, END for endurance, and M-E for muscular endurance.

The training program must be based on scientific principles, with the dominant energy systems in a given sport representing the fundamental guideline. Before discussing certain combinations for both the training session and the microcycle (1 to 2 weeks of training depending on the training phase), coaches and athletes should remember the following:

Table 6.1   Suggested Options for Training Sessions

Sequences of types of training	1	2	3	4
	Warm-up	Warm-up	Warm-up	Warm-up
	TE	TA	TA	END
	SP	P-E	M-E	M-E
	MxS/P	M-E		

- In short-duration (less than 10 seconds), explosive types of sports, power tends to be the important element of strength. Skills of this type include sprinting, jumping, and throwing events in track and field; sprinting in cycling; tennis; ski jumping; free-style skiing; diving; pitching; batting; throwing in football; any takeoff and quick changes of direction in team sports; and quick limb actions in boxing, wrestling, and the martial arts.

- Speed-endurance (15 to 40 seconds) of fast actions interspersed with quick changes of direction and jumps tend to rely on power-endurance. These actions include 50 to 100 meters in swimming; 200 to 400 meters in track and field; 500 meters in speedskating; tennis; figure skating; and many game elements in team sports.

Softball pitchers benefit from strength training in short duration, maximizing their ability to use explosive bursts of power to propel the ball.

- Prolonged activities performed against any type of resistance (gravity, ground, water, snow, or ice) depend on power, power-endurance, and muscular endurance. These activities include rowing; swimming more than 100 meters; kayaking and canoeing; cross-country skiing; and certain elements of team, contact, and racket sports. Therefore, strength coaches must carefully analyze their sport and decide the proportions in which their athletes need to be exposed to power, power-endurance, and muscular endurance.

Many sports require technical and tactical training, maximum speed, speed-endurance, and aerobic endurance, all of which tax different energy systems. How can these components of training be combined without producing a high degree of fatigue, or without the adaptation of one element interfering with the improvement of the others? This can be done in one of two ways:

1. Combine these training components so athletes tax only one energy system per training session.

2. Alternate the energy systems in each microcycle so athletes train according to the prevailing energy system(s) in the particular sport.

Cool-Down

Whereas the warm-up serves as a transition from the normal biological state of daily activities to high-intensity training, the *cool-down* is a transition with the opposite effect: It brings the body back to its normal functions. During a cool-down of 10 to 20 minutes, athletes perform activities that facilitate faster regeneration and recovery from the strains of training. Athletes should not leave for showers immediately after the last exercise.

As a result of training, especially intensive work, athletes build up high amounts of lactic acid and their muscles are exhausted, tense, and rigid. To overcome this fatigue and speed up the recovery process, they should perform relaxation and stretching exercises. The removal of lactic acid from the blood and muscles is also necessary if the effect of fatigue is to be eliminated quickly. This is best achieved by performing 10 to 20 minutes of stretching and light but continuous aerobic activity that causes the body to continue perspiring (intensity zone 6). This will remove half of the lactic acid from the system, which helps athletes recover faster before the next training session.

Modeling and Programming Training Effects

Modeling is a scientific process used in many sciences, especially in mathematics, to create a theoretical model of a future environment. The more elements that the model incorporates of the environment it is meant to copy, the more effective the model will be. The purpose of model training for sports is to expose the athletes to technical, tactical, and physical environments similar to the environments of future competition, including the opposition they'll meet and the difficulties they'll encounter. Model training has the following phases:

1. Create a theoretical model (including the technical, tactical, physical, psychological, and social elements of the sporting environment).
2. Integrate the created model into the training sessions prior to the next competition.
3. If time permits, test the model against opponents of lesser athletic ability.
4. Modify the model based on the results of the test.
5. Retest the model against opponents of lesser athletic ability before applying the model in a competition.
6. Apply the model in the next official competition.

The following lists describe the training session models that tax the various energy systems used in sports.

Model Training Taxing the Anaerobic Alactic System

- Warm-up
- Technical training of short duration
- Maximum speed and agility training (4 to 12 seconds)
- Maximum strength training
- Power training

The order of activities in this model was established based on the physiological and mental needs of the athlete. Activities that require more nervous system concentration, mental focus, and thus a fresh mind must be trained first (i.e., technique, speed, or both). Maximum speed should be trained before maximum strength because gains in maximum strength and power have been found to be more effective when preceded by a few short but maximum-velocity sprints (Baroga, 1978; Ozolin, 1971). Changes in the CNS can also act as stimuli for gains in strength (Fox, Bowes, and Foss, 1989). Display of the muscles' maximum potential is often limited by the inhibiting influence of proprioceptors such as the Golgi tendon organs. The CNS itself also seems to inhibit the activation of all the motor units available in a muscle or muscle group. To partially overcome this, the coach should plan work of maximum intensity in some workouts, which would have stimulating effects on training either maximum strength or power.

One positive adaptation of strength and power training is an inhibition of the Golgi tendon organ that allows a greater amount of force to be generated. This particular training model is applicable to sports such as American football; baseball, softball, and cricket; sprinting, jumping, and throwing events in track and field; diving; racket sports; the martial arts; contact sports; and other sports in which the anaerobic alactic system is dominant. Although there are two strength training options, we suggest using only one type at a time. However, this does not exclude the possibility of using maximum strength in one day and power the next day.

The duration of a strength training session suggested in this model depends on the importance of strength in the sport and on the training phase. During the preparatory phase, a strength training session can last one to two hours; in the competitive phase it is much shorter (30 to a maximum of 45 minutes). The work is dedicated primarily to the maintenance of strength gained during the preparatory phase. Exceptions to this basic rule are made for throwers in track and field, linemen in American football, and wrestlers in the heavyweight category, who require more time for strength training (one to one and a half hours).

Model Training Taxing the Anaerobic Lactic System

- Warm-up
- Tactical training
- Power-endurance and agility of longer duration training
- Muscular endurance of short duration training

This second model is suggested for any sports in which the anaerobic lactic system is taxed (30 to 120 seconds). Thus, tactical training, especially prolonged but intensive drills, can be followed by a combination of strength training in which a certain degree of endurance is used: either power-endurance or muscular endurance of short duration. Most sports that use the anaerobic lactic energy system, such as team, racket, and contact sports and the martial arts, can benefit from applying this model once a week.

Model Training Taxing Aerobic Endurance

- Warm-up
- Tactical training
- Muscular endurance of medium duration training

Aerobic endurance includes endurance of medium duration which involves both the anaerobic lactic acid system and the aerobic system. Aerobic system training is generally of a longer duration and dedicated to training strictly the aerobic system with little adaptation to the anaerobic system. The preceding model combines tactical training of longer duration (3 to longer than

10 minutes) with muscular endurance of medium duration, both of which tax the anaerobic lactic system, but mostly the aerobic endurance or the ability of the athlete to delay the onset of fatigue. This model is good for specialized training sessions for team, racket, and contact sports and the martial arts, in which the scope of training is to stress the last part of the game or match.

Model Training Taxing the Aerobic System

- Warm-up
- Aerobic endurance training
- Muscular endurance of long duration training

Because there is a fine line between aerobic endurance training and strictly aerobic system training, your aerobic endurance will naturally improve when training the aerobic system. As such, the above model is most effective for sports in which aerobic endurance is either dominant or very important to achieving the expected athletic performance. These sports include distance running, triathlon, road cycling, cross-country skiing, rowing, canoeing, kayaking, mountain cycling, and marathon canoeing. For these sports, muscular endurance is trained at the end of the session because the fatigue that results may affect the athlete's ability to achieve the objectives of aerobic training.

Model Training to Develop Power and Agility Under the Conditions of Fatigue

- Warm-up
- Technical and tactical training taxing the aerobic system
- Power and agility training

Quite often the result of a competition is decided in the final minutes of the competition. To generate higher power and quickness, to display a high level of agility at the end of the competition, and as a result, to score more points, athletes must be trained for such conditions. The most efficient way to enhance these abilities is to train athletes under the conditions of fatigue similar to those they will encounter in the future. Training sessions with this objective strive to fatigue the athletes first, via aerobic conditions (intensity zones 3, 4, or even 5), followed by 20 to 30 minutes of high-intensity power and agility drills. These drills can be either specific or nonspecific.

Another option, especially for racket sports, the martial arts, boxing, and wrestling, is to use muscular endurance training for 20 to 30 minutes, followed by power and agility drills of high intensity.

Planning to Eat

Nutrition is a very common topic discussed in locker rooms and gyms across North America and abroad. How much protein to eat or what kind of supplements to take are common subjects of discussion during training sessions. This section is not intended to address in specific detail the nutritional requirements of athletes. However, pregame, in-game, and postgame (or exercise session) nutritional guidelines will be addressed.

Athletes' nutritional needs depend on their individual training programs and habitual nutrient intake. Most athletes consume a considerable amount of calories to satisfy their energy requirements and to promote recovery following a training session. Training of all types depletes glycogen stores and promotes muscle breakdown. What and when an athlete eats following a training session or game is as vital to recovery, regeneration, and physiological improvements as is rest and the use of active recovery techniques (see chapter 13).

Protein Intake

Protein, which is comprised of amino acids, is extremely important for building muscle tissue. Although optimal protein intake will vary from athlete to athlete, most athletes should consume 1.2 to 2 grams of protein per kilogram of body weight daily. This amount of protein should be consumed during the anatomical adaptation and conversion to power or power endurance phases of training. With the use of protein drinks and bars, many athletes eat more than the recommended amount of protein. If muscle hypertrophy is the goal, protein requirements can be extremely higher, at 2 to 3 grams per kilogram of body weight per day (Tipton and Wolfe, 2004).

Most of an athlete's ingested protein should come from a variety of sources including poultry, fish, beef, cheese, protein shakes, and the occasional protein bar. Eating as much as 2 to 3 grams (0.07 to 0.1 ounces) of protein should be considered when completing the hypertrophy and maximum strength phases of training, which include very high intensity strength training.

Postexercise Nutrition

A popular saying in the training world is, A workout is only as good as the recovery that follows. Proper nutrition immediately after the workout quickly shifts the body from a process of breakdown to one of regeneration. High-intensity training common in the many phases of strength, speed, and endurance training taxes the body's energy reserves, depleting glycogen stores and promoting the breakdown of muscle tissue. Immediately following a strength training session an athlete should consume at least 0.1 grams (0.004 ounces) of protein per kilogram of body weight for at least three hours after the session.

Following exercise, athletes are in a fasting state in which protein breakdown is greater than protein synthesis. This creates a negative balance. Ingesting a small amount of protein from food sources such as a cup of yogurt or protein shake shifts the body from a negative balance to a positive one; that is, protein synthesis becomes greater than protein breakdown. This positive net balance in protein synthesis can occur for up to 24 hours following the strength training bout (MacDougall et al., 1995) and speed up the rate of recovery. Although most trainees like to ingest a form of carbohydrate instead of protein following a strength training session, doing so slowly and only temporarily improves the rate of protein synthesis (Borsheim et al., 2004). We usually tell our athletes to prepare a 50- to 60-ounce protein shake mixed with a banana or strawberries and drink 10 to 15 ounces before the strength training workout and take sips of the shake throughout three to five hours or so following the session.

High-volume and high-intensity training often performed by endurance athletes not only promotes muscle breakdown but also depletes the high-energy glycogen stores. Following an endurance training bout, athletes should consume at least 1 gram of carbohydrates per kilogram (0.45 grams per pound) of body weight during the first three to five hours of recovery to maximize the resynthesis of muscle and liver glycogen. Fasting following a session will only further exhaust the body, delay compensation, and insufficiently prepare the athlete for the next training session, which might occur within the next 24 hours. Depending on the athlete's likes and dislikes, carbohydrates alone or a combination of carbohydrates and protein can be eaten immediately following a training session to start the resynthesis of glycogen. The rate of resynthesis will be the same with both variations as long as the total calories are kept constant.

Because protein-rich foods tend to satiate a person faster than carbohydrate-rich foods do, athletes should make sure to ingest high quantities of calories. Drinking a replacement shake that includes milk or water and some fruit during the first hour after a workout will spark the metabolism into storing glycogen. Athletes often find such a meal easier on the digestive system, which may not be in the mood for bulk foods. Subsequent meals should include a mixture of complex carbohydrates, protein, and fats.

Pregame Meal Tips

Athletes should eat a full meal three to four hours prior to the start of the game. Eating closer to the game could cause gastrointestinal problems. Use the following guidelines when putting together a pregame meal:

- The pregame meal should consist of at least 40 percent complex carbohydrates to fuel athletes for competition. They should stay away from simple carbohydrates such as fruits or processed foods. Soft drinks such as colas should not even be placed on the table. A small to medium bowl of pasta with tomato sauce, an 8-ounce (226-gram) piece of chicken or fish, and a side salad with a mixture of fresh vegetables would make a good pregame meal.

- Athletes who are beginning to feel hungry one to three hours before a game should not reach for fresh fruit, a chocolate bar, or a few candies. The sugar content of these items will offer a quick pick-me-up, but the energy level will drop quickly. These items, which are classified as high glycemic foods (see figure 6.1) leave the bloodstream almost as fast as they entered it and leave the athlete starving for energy. Lethargy is not a good feeling prior to a game. After the game, high glycemic foods can be consumed to enhance glycogen storage (Burkes, Collier, and Hargreaves, 1998).

- Athletes should avoid the consumption of alcohol 24 to 36 hours prior to the game and limit the consumption of caffeine on game day. Both caffeine and alcohol can dehydrate the body. Recently, caffeine has received unwarranted exposure as an ergogenic aid that has been overused by athletes (Graham, 2001). More studies are needed before the mechanisms by which caffeine can enhance performance are validated.

- Very fatty, greasy foods digest slowly and are hard on the digestive system. For this reason, fast foods should definitely be excluded from athletes' meal plans. Athletes should also be careful to eat foods that their bodies are accustomed to. The pregame meal is not the time to try out new recipes or uncommon foods.

Proper Hydration

Athletes must drink plenty of water before, during, and after the game. A well-hydrated body is better able to fight both muscular and cardiovascular fatigue. Water is always the preferred beverage even over sport drinks, although the palatability of these drinks may encourage fluid consumption. These drinks may not be necessary prior to the game but can be sipped throughout the game or competition. Athletes who compete in events or competitions lasting longer than 60 minutes can benefit from several sport drinks because they help replace lost electrolytes. Also, studies show that sipping approximately 150 milliliters of a sport drink in 20-minute intervals can help

During matches, hydration levels should be monitored to ensure the safety of athletes.

Food Item	Glycemic Index (GI)	Serving Size (g)	Glycemic Load (GL)
Apples, raw	34	120	5
Apple juice, unsweetened	41	250	11
Apricots	57	120	5
Apricots, dried	32	60	8
Banana, ripe	51	120	13
Cantaloupe	65	120	4
Cherries	22	120	3
Cranberry juice	68	250	24
Grapefruit	25	120	3
Grapes	46	120	8
Kiwi fruit	53	120	6
Mango	51	120	8
Orange	42	120	5
Orange juice	52	250	12
Peach	42	120	5
Pear	38	120	4
Pineapple	59	120	7
Plum	39	120	5
Prunes, pitted	29	60	10
Raisins	64	60	28
Strawberries, fresh	40	120	1
Strawberry jam	51	30	10
Tomato juice, no sugar added	38	250	4
Watermelon	72	120	4
Baked potato	85	150	26
White potato, cooked	50	150	14
French fries, frozen	75	150	22
Instant mashed potato	85	150	17
Sweet potato	61	150	17
Bagel, white, frozen	72	70	25
Baguette, white, plain	95	30	15
Rice noodles, dried, boiled	61	180	23
Rice pasta, brown, boiled	92	180	35
Cornflakes (Kellogg's)	92	30	24
Corn Pops (Kellogg's)	80	30	21

Figure 6.1 Glycemic food index.

decrease the reliance on muscle glycogen stores and thus prevent an earlier onset of fatigue (Davis et al., 1997, 1999). Some sport drinks on the market, however (Coombes and Hamilton, 2000), make claims that may not be validated by science; athletes would do well to shop wisely. High-intensity sports requiring short bursts of speed and power such as sprints, throws, and jumps tend not to benefit from the consumption of sport drinks (Powers et al., 1990). However, intermittent high-intensity activity typical of most team sports benefits from the consumption of sport drinks that offer a carbohydrate–electrolyte mixture (Welsh et al., 2002).

Dehydration usually results from intense training in moderate to hot environments. Athletes exercising intensely in the heat lose sweat at levels of 2 to 3 quarts (or liters) per hour. Hydration after exercise or training is important in posttraining recovery. When an athlete is in a state of dehydration, drinking water alone is not sufficient to return the body to the preexercise hydration state. Drinking water alone will trick the body into thinking it is overly hydrated and trigger the kidney to increase urine output, resulting in further fluid loss.

Studies show that the amount of urine produced a few hours after exercise is less when a higher concentration of sodium is ingested (Maughan et al., 1993). Sodium plays a major role in water balance; thus, drinking salt or sodium with the water will help keep the fluid in the body. The problem with many sport drinks is that they provide electrolyte mixtures in the form of sodium and potassium (sodium loss is much greater than potassium), but the quantity of sodium is very low in comparison to what is required. The obvious reason for this is that high-sodium drinks are unpalatable. Thus, although athletes may enjoy various sport drinks, coaches should motivate them to add a tablespoon or two of salt to every quart or liter of fluid consumed.

Following training, an athlete should drink a volume of fluid similar to or even greater than the amount lost via sweat. Because this varies among athletes, a relative amount can be calculated by weighing athletes before and after training or competition. As a rule of thumb, athletes should drink approximately 1.5 liters (or quarts) of fluids for every 2.2 pounds (kilogram) of weight lost. Proper hydration along with adequate nutritional supplements in the form of drinks or food begin the process of recovery and prepare the athlete for the vigor of training or competition that lies ahead.

Planning the Microcycle

The microcycle, or weekly training program, is probably the most important planning tool. Throughout the yearly plan, the nature and dynamics of microcycles change according to the phase of training, the training objectives, and the physiological and psychological demands of the athlete. A macrocycle, on the other hand, is a training plan of two to six weeks, or microcycles. Throughout these two types of plans, the load in strength training is increased depending on the type of cycle (e.g., developmental versus shock) and training phase.

Load Increments per Macrocycle

The work in each macrocycle follows a step-type progression (see figure 6.2). From an intensity standpoint, microcycles follow the principle of progressive increase of load in training.

As illustrated in figure 6.2, during the first three cycles, the load is progressively increased, followed by a regeneration cycle in which the load is decreased to facilitate recuperation and replenishment of energy before another macrocycle begins. Based on this model, table 6.2 suggests load increments using the notation given in chapter 4.

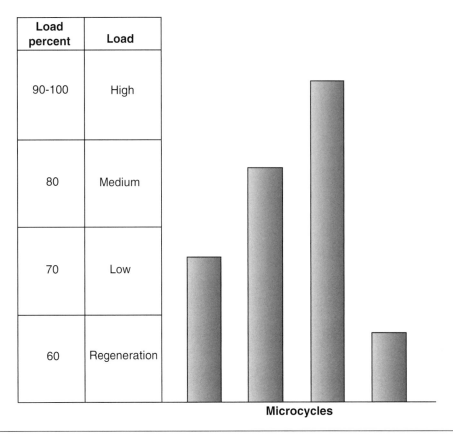

Load percent	Load
90-100	High
80	Medium
70	Low
60	Regeneration

Microcycles

Figure 6.2 Dynamics of increasing the training load over four microcycles.

Table 6.2 Load Increments for a Training Macrocycle

Training load	$\frac{70}{10}2\ \frac{80}{8}2\ \frac{85}{5}1$	$\frac{80}{9}2\ \frac{85}{5}2\ \frac{90}{3}2$	$\frac{85}{7}2\ \frac{90}{3}3\ \frac{95}{2}2$	$\frac{70}{10}4$
Step no.	1	2	3	4

As shown in figure 6.2, the work, or the total load in training, is increased in steps, with the highest increase occurring in step 3. To increase the work from step to step, the instructor or coach has two options: increase the load or increase the number of sets from five in step 1 to seven in step 3 (as in table 6.2).

Table 6.2 demonstrates using both of these options at the same time. This approach can be changed to suit the needs of different classifications of athletes. The approach in table 6.2 can be used for athletes with a good strength training background; young athletes will have difficulty tolerating a high number of sets. Young athletes should have a high number of exercises that will develop the entire muscular system and adapt the muscle attachments on the bones (tendons) to strength training. However, a high number of sets and exercises at the same time would be difficult to tolerate, so it is advisable to opt for a high number of exercises at the expense of the number of sets.

Step 4 represents a regeneration cycle in which both the load and the number of sets are lowered to reduce the fatigue resulting from the first three steps, to replenish the energy stores, and to promote psychological relaxation. The load suggested in each microcycle refers to the work *per day*, which can be repeated two to four times per week depending on the training goals.

Load Increments per Microcycle

The work, or the total load per microcycle, is increased mainly by increasing the number of days of strength training per week. Remember that in athletics, strength training is subordinate to technical and tactical training. Consequently, the load of strength training per week should be calculated keeping in mind the overall volume and intensity of training.

Before discussing strength training options per microcycle, it is important to mention that the total work per week is also planned according to the principle of progressive increase of load in training. Figures 6.3 through 6.5 illustrate three microcycles, each of which is suggested for each of the conventional steps referred to earlier.

In most cases, strength training is planned on the same days as other activities such as technical and tactical work. Similarly, in the training session, a coach may plan to work on the development of certain physical qualities such as speed, strength, or endurance. So what is the best approach to consider in planning strength training per microcycle?

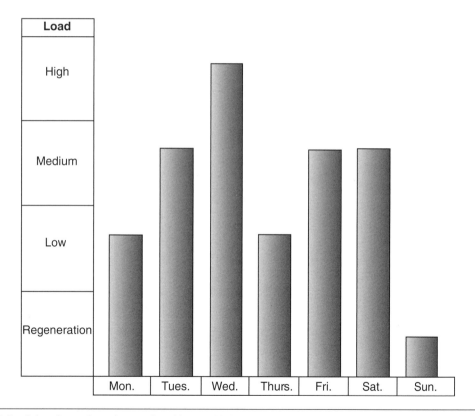

Figure 6.3 A low-intensity microcycle with one high-intensity training day and several medium- and low-intensity days. Sunday is a rest day.

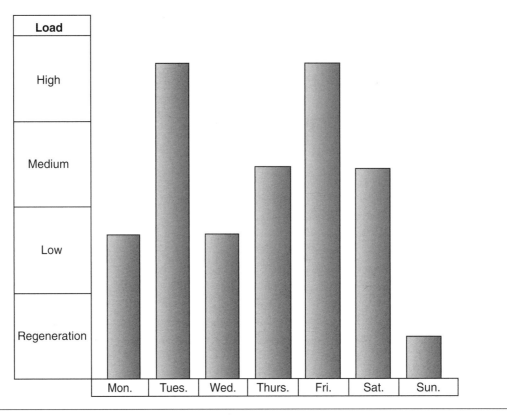

Figure 6.4 A medium-intensity microcycle.

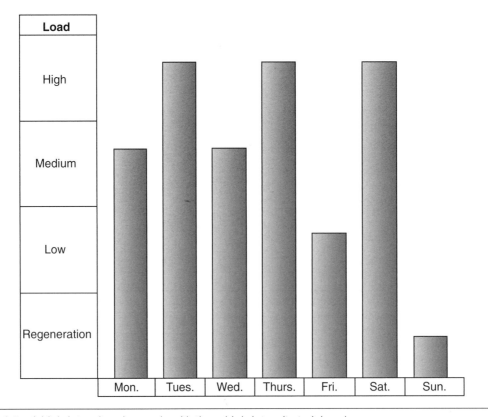

Figure 6.5 A high-intensity microcycle with three high-intensity training days.

Types of Strength and Restoration of Energy Systems

Some proponents suggest that strength training should be planned on "easy days." This makes some sense; however, from a physiological standpoint, this issue demands a more complex analysis.

To some extent, the majority of sports require training most, if not all, the motor abilities of speed, strength, and endurance. Each ability uses and is dependent on a particular energy system, and the rate of recovery and restoration of the fuel used differs for each system. The restoration of glycogen, the main fuel for strength training, takes between 24 and 48 hours. Glycogen restoration after continuous intensive work is achieved in approximately 48 hours, whereas after intermittent activity such as strength training, it is achieved in about 24 hours (Brooks, Brauner, and Cassens, 1973; Fox et al., 1989). Following maximum-intensity training in which the CNS is also taxed, up to 48 hours is needed for complete restoration. The rate of regeneration from aerobic activities is much faster, approximately eight hours. A quick restoration of energy stores also occurs as a result of so-called technical work, which is often of lower intensity. These types of training days can be considered "easy."

Let's assume that a coach plans intensive training sessions on Monday, Wednesday, and Friday and easy days on Tuesday and Thursday. Because there are 48 hours between the intensive days, and especially because an easy day occurs during those 48 hours, glycogen can reach full restoration before another planned intensive day. This can change drastically, however, if the coach schedules intensive strength training sessions on the easy days. In that case, the athletes are taxing the anaerobic energy system on the easy days as well as the intensive days, which taxes the glycogen every day. In this case the strength training becomes an obstacle to restoration. This complicates the energy expenditure–restoration ratio and can also bring athletes to a state of fatigue and even exhaustion. And it is only a short step from exhaustion to overtraining.

Consequently, strength training must be planned on the same days as technical and tactical or speed and power training—namely, the same days as the glycogen stores are taxed. This results in athletes depleting all of their glycogen stores, but the overall training program does not interfere with its restoration before the next high-intensity training is scheduled 48 hours later.

The following tables illustrate examples of strength training programs that are related to other athletic activities and the dominant energy systems. Table 6.3 suggests a microcycle for speed and power sports (American football, baseball, ice hockey, lacrosse) in which energy systems are alternated. Note that strength training is consistently planned on days when other types of activities tax the same energy system. For instance, drills for speed training, which tax the anaerobic alactic system, are followed by either power or power-endurance (P-E) training. Also note that two days of anaerobic activities (Monday and Tuesday) are followed by a day when aerobic training is taxed in the form of drills for tempo running (400 to 600 yards or meters at 60 percent of maximum speed, four to six reps) or longer-duration tactical drills.

Table 6.3 Strength Training Program for Speed- and Power-Dominant Sports

Mon.	Tues.	Wed.	Thurs.	Fri.	Sat.
Technical	Speed	Tempo running	Technical	Speed	Tempo running
MxS	Power/P-E	Tactical	MxS	Power/P-E	Tactical

Table 6.4 illustrates how the energy systems and the specifics of strength could be alternated for a sport in which aerobic endurance is dominant, such as rowing, kayaking, canoeing, cycling, triathlon, cross-country skiing, or swimming more than 400 meters. Each time aerobic endurance is trained, the only type of strength training proposed is muscular endurance (M-E). When anaerobic training is planned (Tuesday), it is followed by power-endurance, which taxes the same system (anaerobic lactic).

Table 6.4 Alternation of Energy Systems for Aerobic Endurance-Dominant Sports

Mon.	Tues.	Wed.	Thurs.	Fri.	Sat.
Aerobic endurance	Anaerobic endurance	Aerobic endurance	Mixed training	Aerobic endurance	Aerobic endurance
M-E	P-E	Compensation	P-E	M-E	Compensation

Note that two taxing days of training (Monday and Tuesday) are followed by a lighter aerobic training day for compensation and to supercompensate the glycogen stores depleted the day before. The same approach is used again in the second part of the cycle.

The alternation of energy systems and strength training could follow the model of table 6.5 for sports with high-complexity training (technical, tactical, and physical), such as all team sports, the martial arts, and racket sports. On Monday, all the proposed activities tax the anaerobic alactic system. Obviously, only two or three of the suggested training activities may be planned, which for strength training may mean either maximum strength or power.

Table 6.5 Sample Training Program for High-Complexity Sports

Mon.	Tues.	Wed.	Thurs.	Fri.	Sat.
Technical	Tactical	Technical	Technical/ Tactical	Technical/ Tactical	Technical/ Tactical
Speed	Specific endurance	Tactical	Anaerobic	Speed	Aerobic
MxS/Power	P-E	Compensation	MxS/Power	P-E	Compensation

On Tuesday, an anaerobic lactic day can be planned (tactical and specific endurance training). To tap the same energy system, the strength training program should consist of activities aimed at developing power-endurance. Wednesday is a compensation day of less demanding technical and tactical training. For the remaining three training days, two or three types of training activities, of which strength training is a part, must be selected.

During the competitive phase the approach used to maintain strength training depends strictly on the schedule of competitions. As such, we can suggest you design three microcycles, which take into account one or two competitions per week, along with a microcycle that includes a tournament per week.

Figure 6.6 illustrates different types of activities to plan between two competitions that fall at the ends of consecutive weeks. Because the days of competitions vary from sport to sport, we have selected to number the activities rather than specify the days of the week. The post-competition day is intended for recovery and regeneration, to remove the fatigue from the

Day	1	2	3	4	5	6	7	8
Types of activity	Competition	Day off Recovery/ Regeneration	Technical/ Tactical training Longer duration drills	Technical/ Tactical training Alactic/ Speed-Power-Agility training MxS (30 min.)	Technical/ Tactical training Lactic acid energy system Aerobic	Technical/ Tactical training Speed-Power-Agility training MxS (30 min.)	Model training (30-45 min.)	Competition

Loading pattern	High	Off	Low/ Medium	High	Medium	High	Low	High

Figure 6.6 Suggested strength training program for a microcycle falling between two competitions.

systems, and to ready the athlete to resume training the next day. As in other microcycles, the suggested training programs consider the physiological needs to alternate and tax mostly one energy system per day. As such, the maximum strength training is planned on the days when the anaerobic alactic system is taxed, and has the scope of strength maintenance. Certainly, the suggested maximum strength training is short and uses selected exercises specific to the sport the athlete is training for. It is very important that the intensity of training be subdivided in low, medium and high intensity days. Planning the training session accordingly will better help the athlete manage the demands or stress associated with training and competition.

Figure 6.7 illustrates a microcycle with two competitions per week. Under such conditions, the maintenance of strength is slightly different, one day of maximum strength and one for power, power-endurance, or muscular endurance. On day 5, the postcompetition day, we suggest activities that can stimulate recovery and regeneration, such as massage, stretching, sauna, and light intensity training. To best accommodate these activities, day 5 of training can be

Day	1	2	3	4	5	6	7	8
Types of activity	Competition	Day off Recovery/ Regeneration	Technical/ Tactical training Speed (alactic) Lactic acid energy system (model training) Power training (20 min.)	Competition	Recovery/ Regeneration Technical/ Tactical training	Technical/ Tactical training Speed (alactic) Maximum strength (30 min.)	Tactical training Model training (30-45 min.)	Competition

Loading pattern	High	Off	Medium	High	Low	High	Low	High

Figure 6.7 A suggested microcycle with two competitions per week. Although this plan is made for a microcycle with two competitions, in reality there are specified three. We used such an example so that you can better visualize the activities between days of competitions.

divided into two parts (for those athletes who can afford free time): recovery and regeneration in the morning and short, low-intensity technical and tactical training in the afternoon. On the precompetition days, athletes engage in tactical training similar to the activities they will meet the next day in competition.

Day	Mon.	Tues.	Wed.	Thurs.	Fri.	Sat.	Sun.
Types of activity	Day off Recovery/ Regeneration	Technical/ Tactical training Longer duration drills	Technical/ Tactical training Alactic/ Speed- Power- Agility training MxS (30 min.)	Technical/ Tactical training Model training	Competition	Competition	Competition
Loading pattern	Off	Medium	Medium/ High	Low	High	High	High

Figure 6.8 A suggested microcycle for a weekend tournament.

Figure 6.8 illustrates a microcycle for sports that use weekend tournaments, such as Friday, Saturday, and Sunday. Because such tournaments can be organized either a few weeks apart or repeated for several weeks in a row (i.e., high school and university competitions), the same structure can be used for one or more weeks. Coaches will want to make changes to the microcycle based on their athletes' specific conditions, level of fatigue, and classification, as well as on travel, whether they can organize daily training sessions, and so forth. On Thursday, coaches should organize a model tactical training to model the strategies their athletes will use for the duration of the tournament. Coaches who have time for a short training session during the tournament can use very low intensity activities, say, in the morning, to mimic the strategies their athletes will use in the afternoon or evening competition.

Integration of Microcycles Into Macrocycles

A microcycle shouldn't be an isolated entity; it should be integrated into the larger macrocycle. (See chapters 7 through 12 for more discussion on integrating different training phases and methods into a continuous training concept.) This integration should occur from the early part of the preparatory phase to the end of the competitive phase.

The integration of different types of microcycles into a macrocycle depends on the training phase, the classification of athletes, athletes' strength training backgrounds, and the type of macrocycle used. Two types of macrocycles are helpful during the preparatory phase: the developmental macrocycle and the shock macrocycle. These will subject athletes to a sudden increase in training volume and intensity and thereby challenge their level of adaptation. Step loading is useful in developmental macrocycles. Consisting of progressive increases in load, step loading is less stressful and therefore more applicable to the early part of strength training for the preparatory phase. The developmental macrocycle is advisable for entry-level and intermediate athletes, and for advanced athletes in the anatomical adaptation phase. The shock macrocycle is suggested for highly classified athletes with extensive strength training backgrounds. It is more challenging than step loading, but also results in higher levels of adaptation, and as a result, in greater improvement in the strength training capacity.

During the competitive phase the integration of microcycles into macrocycles depends directly on the schedule of competitions. Because competition schedules vary according to the sport, the integration of microcycles into macrocycles also varies. In individual sports, for instance, the first macrocycle (figure 6.9) consists of a postcompetition recovery and regeneration microcycle to eliminate fatigue before resuming normal training. This is followed by two developmental microcycles, which are followed by a precompetition peaking microcycle. The example from figure 6.9 can be shorter or longer depending on the time between major competitions. One developmental microcycle—or more than two—may be needed.

	Competitive Phase				
Type of microcycles	Post-competition: Recovery/ Regeneration	Developmental	Developmental	Pre-competition peaking	C
Number of strength training sessions per microcycle	1 (maximum), 2 (at the end of the microcycle)	2-4	2-4	1 (in the early days of the microcycle)	

Legend: C = competition

Figure 6.9 The integration of microcycles into a macrocycle for an individual sport.

Strength training can normally be performed during developmental microcycles to ensure that detraining doesn't affect the ability to reach peak performance at the end of the competitive phase, when championship competitions are scheduled. Highly classed athletes may benefit from shock microcycles, as illustrated in figure 6.10. The height of each block is intended to illustrate the demand in training. Because shock macrocycles are very challenging, coaches should plan a transition microcycle between them, in which the objective is to remove fatigue and apply recovery and regeneration strategies.

The structure of a macrocycle is different for team sports, in which each weekend represents an opportunity to compete, sometimes twice. As such, strength training has to be implemented according to the microcycles exemplified in this chapter, especially figures 6.6 through 6.8. Because team sports have such a high number of competitions, the scope of strength training programs has to be to maintain specific strength gains made during the preparatory phase. This avoids detraining. Moreover, thanks to the physiological benefits from maintaining high levels of specific strength, athletes' levels of athletic competency are maintained up to the time of championship games.

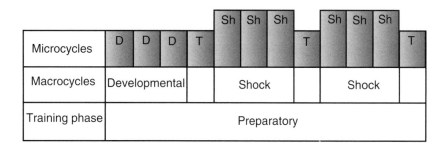

Figure 6.10 An illustration of the integration of developmental and shock microcycles.

Number of Strength Training Sessions per Microcycle

The number of strength training sessions per microcycle depends on the following:

- *Athletes' classification.* Young athletes should be introduced to strength training progressively. At first, they could be exposed to two short strength training sessions following technical or tactical work. Progressively over a period of two to four years, this could be increased to three or four sessions. Athletes competing at national or international competitions could take part in three or four strength training sessions per week, mainly during the preparatory phase.

- *Importance of strength in the chosen sport.* Based on the type of skills, energy system requirements, and dominant abilities in a given sport, strength training can have a lower or higher importance. In a sport in which aerobic endurance is clearly dominant, such as marathon running, strength is less important. On the other hand, in sports in which power is dominant, such as American football and throwing events, strength plays a dominant role. In the first example, one or two specific strength training sessions per week may suffice, whereas in the second example, training must occur at least four times per microcycle, especially during the preparatory/preseason phase.

- *Phase of training.* The number of strength training sessions depends on the phase of training: two to four during the preparatory phase and two or three during the competitive phase.

Athletes performing four strength training sessions per week will have to perform some on consecutive days. In such circumstances, coaches who are influenced by weightlifting or bodybuilding concepts apply the so-called split routine: They train different body parts separately each day to achieve faster recovery. Such a plan is unacceptable in athletics. Weightlifters and bodybuilders use the split routine because they train daily (international-class lifters often train two or three times a day). This routine allows them to recover between training sessions.

In sports, strength training is performed in addition to technical and tactical training. For maximum effectiveness, and for the most economical use of energy, strength training exercises must be selectively chosen to stress mainly the prime movers. To increase effectiveness, strength training exercises for sports should be reduced to the lowest level possible. This increases the number of sets and forces the prime movers to contract many times. The outcome is more power development for the required muscles. The following example will demonstrate this premise.

To make a ballplayer faster, a coach selects three exercises for leg power (knee extensors, knee flexors, and toe raises), one each for the abdominal muscles and back, and two for the arms and shoulders—seven exercises total. As anyone who understands physiology knows, you cannot be a fast runner without having strong knee extensors and flexors. Let's assume that this is the preparatory phase, and that the coach plans to have four strength training sessions per week consisting of four sets of eight reps, with a load of 220 pounds (100 kilograms) for 1 hour and 15 minutes. If the coach uses the split routine, the knee extensors and flexors will be trained as follows:

2 sessions per week × 4 sets × 8 reps × 220 pounds (100 kilograms) = 14,106 pounds (6,400 kilograms)

If, on the other hand, the coach decides that the split routine is not applicable to the athlete's needs, the result will be as follows:

4 sessions per week × 4 sets × 8 reps × 220 pounds (100 kilograms) = 28,212 pounds (12,800 kilograms)

The difference between these two options is 14,105 pounds (6,400 kilograms), which clearly shows that the split routine is impractical and inapplicable in strength training for sports.

The Yearly Training Plan

The yearly training plan is as important a tool for achieving long-range athletic goals as the microcycle is for achieving short-term athletic goals. It must be based on the concept of periodization of strength and employ its training principles as guiding precepts. An organized and well-planned yearly training plan is a requirement for maximizing strength improvements.

A primary objective of training is for the athlete to reach peak performance at a specific time, usually for the main competition of the year. For the athlete to achieve this high level of performance, the entire training program must be properly periodized and planned so that the development of skills and motor abilities proceeds logically and methodically throughout the year.

Periodization comprises two basic components. The first component, periodization of the yearly plan, addresses the various training phases throughout the year. The second component, periodization of strength, addresses structuring strength training to maximize its effectiveness in meeting the needs of the specific sport.

Periodization of the Yearly Plan

The first component of periodization consists of breaking down the yearly plan into shorter, more manageable training phases. Doing so enhances the organization of training and allows the coach to conduct the program systematically. In most sports, the yearly training cycle is divided into three main phases of training: preparatory (preseason), competitive (season), and transition (off-season). Each training phase is further subdivided into cycles, the most important being the microcycle. The duration of each training phase depends heavily on the competition schedule, as well as on the time needed to improve skills and to develop the dominant biomotor abilities. During the preparatory phase, the coach's primary objective is to develop the physiological foundations of the athletes, whereas during the competitive phase, it is to strive for perfection according to the specific demands of competition.

Figure 7.1 illustrates the periodization of the yearly plan into phases and cycles of training. This particular plan has only one competitive phase, so athletes have to peak only once during the year. Such a plan is called a *mono-cycle* or *single-peak* yearly plan. Not all sports have only one competitive phase. For example, track and field, swimming (in some countries), and several other sports have indoor and outdoor seasons or two major competitions for which athletes must peak. Such a plan is usually called a *bi-cycle* or *double-peak* yearly plan (see table 7.1).

	Yearly Plan					
Phases of training	Preparatory			Competitive		Transition
Sub-phases	General preparation		Specific preparation	Pre-competitive	Competitive	Transition
Macro-cycles						
Micro-cycles						

Figure 7.1 Periodization of a mono-cycle.

Table 7.1   Periodization of a Bi-Cycle

The Annual Plan					
Preparatory (I)	Competitive (I)	Transition (I)	Preparatory (II)	Competitive (II)	Transition (II)

Periodization of Strength

Coaches should be more concerned with deciding what kind of physiological response or training adaptation will lead to the greatest improvements than with deciding what drills or skills to work on in a given training session or phase. Once they have made the first decision, they will have an easier time selecting the appropriate type of work that will result in the desired development. Only by considering these overriding physiological factors will coaches be able to choose an approach that will result in the best training adaptation and ultimately lead to increases in physiological capacity and improved athletic performance. Such an innovative approach is facilitated by periodization. Recall from chapter 1 that the purpose of strength training for sports is not the development of strength for its own sake. Rather, the goal is to perfect either power, muscular endurance, or both according to the needs of each sport. The periodization of strength, with its specific sequence of training phases, is the best approach for achieving that goal, as this chapter will demonstrate. As illustrated in table 7.2, periodization

Table 7.2   Periodization of Strength for a Mono-Cycle

Preparatory			Competitive		Transition
Anatomical adaptation	MxS	Conversion to power/muscle-endurance	Maintenance of power/muscle-endurance	Cessation of strength training	Compensation training

of strength has six phases with specific strength training objectives. It is important to note that training phases are conventionally divided by a vertical bar, illustrating where one phase ends and another begins. However, changes of types of strength training from one phase to another is not as abrupt as implied in a chart. On the contrary, there is a smoother transition from one type of strength to another one (i.e. from maximum strength to power).

Phase 1: Anatomical Adaptation

Periodization of strength has become very popular worldwide, with the result that many training specialists and authors have discussed and written about this very efficient strength training concept. However, in their attempt to be different or to claim originality, some authors suggest a periodization of strength plan that starts with hypertrophy training. This might be acceptable in bodybuilding, but it is definitely not acceptable in strength training for sports. Except for some throwers and in some positions in American football, muscle size, or hypertrophy, is not a determining factor in high-performance athletics. On the contrary, athletes in most sports, such as basketball, soccer, and swimming, not to mention sports divided into weight-class categories, are extremely reluctant to increase nonfunctional muscle hypertrophy. Furthermore, as explained in chapter 9, to increase hypertrophy, athletes have to work each set to exhaustion, which at times may result in a high level of discomfort, or even in injuries. For this reason, the original model of periodization of strength starts with an anatomical adaptation phase.

Following a transition phase, during which athletes usually do very little strength training, it is scientifically and methodologically sound to start a strength program aimed at adapting the anatomy for the future strength program. The main objectives of this phase are to involve most muscle groups and to prepare the muscles, ligaments, tendons, and joints to endure the subsequent lengthy and strenuous training phases. Strength training programs should not focus on only the legs or arms; they should also focus on strengthening the core area—the abdominal muscles, the low back, and the spinal column musculature. These sets of muscles work together to ensure that the trunk supports the legs and arms during all movements and also act as shock-absorbing devices for many skills and exercises, especially landing and falling.

Additional objectives for anatomical adaptation are to balance strength between the flexors and extensors surrounding each joint; balance the two sides of the body, especially the shoulders and arms; perform compensation work for the antagonist muscles; and strengthen the stabilizer muscles (see "Exercise Prescription" in chapter 5).

In some cases, balanced development between agonist and antagonist muscles is impossible because some agonist muscles are larger and stronger than others. For instance, the knee extensors (quadriceps) are stronger than the knee flexors (hamstrings). The same is true for the ankle plantar flexors (gastrocnemius) and extensors (tibialis anterior). Because activities such as running and jumping are heavily used in most sports, the knee extensors and ankle plantar flexors are exposed to more training. Professionals in the field, however, must be aware of the agonist–antagonist ratios and attempt to maintain them through training. If they neglect to do so, and the agonists, the prime movers of given sport skills, are constantly trained, the imbalance will likely result in injuries (for example, rotator cuff injuries in baseball).

The transition and anatomical adaptation phases are ideal for balanced development of antagonist muscles because they occur at a time in the training cycle when there is no pressure from competition. Little information exists regarding the agonist–antagonist ratios, especially for the high-speed limb movements typical of sports. Table 7.3 provides some information on the subject, but for low, isokinetic speeds. This information should be used only as a guideline for maintaining these ratios, at least during the anatomical adaptation and transition phases.

Throughout the anatomical adaptation phase, the goal is to involve most, if not all, muscle groups in a multilateral-type program. Such a program should include a high number of exercises (9 to 12) performed comfortably without "pushing" the athlete. Remember, vigorous strength training always

Table 7.3 Agonist-Antagonist Ratios for Slow Concentric Isokinetic Movements

Joint	Strength training	Ratio
Ankle	Plantar flexion/dorsiflexion (gastrocnemius, soleus/tibialis anterior)	3:1
Ankle	Inversion/eversion (tibialis anterior/peroneals)	1:1
Knee	Extension/flexion (quadriceps/hamstrings)	3:2
Hip	Extension/flexion (spinal erectors, gluteus maximus, hamstrings/ iliopsoas, rectus abdominis, tensor fascia latae)	1:1
Shoulder	Flexion/extension (anterior deltoids/trapezius, posterior deltoids)	2:3
Shoulder	Internal rotation/external rotation (subscapularis/supraspinatus, infraspinatus, teres minor)	3:2
Elbow	Flexion/extension (biceps/triceps)	1:1
Lumbar spine	Flexion/extension (iliopsoas, abdominals/spinal erectors)	1:1

From Dan Wathen, 1994. In Baechle, T.R. (Ed.) *Essentials of Strength Training and Conditioning.* Champaign, IL: Human Kinetics.

develops the strength of the muscles faster than the strength of the muscle attachments (tendons) and joints (ligaments). Consequently, such programs can often result in injuries to these tissues.

When large-muscle groups are weak, the small muscles have to take over the strain of the work. As a result, the small-muscle groups may become injured more quickly. Other injuries occur because insufficiently trained muscles lack the force to control landings, absorb shock, and balance the body quickly to be ready to perform another action (not because of a lack of landing skills).

The duration of the anatomical adaptation phase depends on the length of the preparatory phase, the athletes' background in strength training, and the importance of strength in the given sport. A long preparatory phase allows more time for the planning of anatomical adaptation. Athletes who have a weak strength training background logically require a much longer anatomical adaptation phase. This fosters progressive adaptation to training loads and, at the same time, improves the ability of muscle tissue and muscle attachments to withstand the heavier loads of the following phases. Finally, compared to sports in which strength training is less important (such as marathon running), a well-planned and longer anatomical adaptation phase will influence the final performance and hopefully produce injury-free athletes. For young, inexperienced athletes, 8 to 10 weeks of anatomical adaptation training are necessary. Mature athletes with four to six years of strength training require no more than three or four weeks of this phase. For these athletes, an anatomical adaptation phase any longer than this will likely have no significant training effect.

Phase 2: Hypertrophy

In some sports an increase in muscle size is a very important asset. As described throughout the text, hypertrophy training, which is extremely popular in bodybuilding, is overly used in the sporting world. When applied to strength training for sports, hypertrophy training has to extend beyond the old definition of training to exhaustion. Hypertrophy training can be used as a primer for the maximum strength phase to follow by adapting the body to using progressively heavier loads.

We like to divide hypertrophy into two distinct phases: hypertrophy I and hypertrophy II. Hypertrophy I relies on using loads between 70 and 85 percent of 1RM with little rest (60 to 90 seconds maximum) between sets. Hypertrophy I prepares the fast-twitch muscle fibers for the hard work that is to follow during maximum strength training. Hypertrophy II is often used with athletes who require a distinct increase in muscle size and strength. This phase uses many bodybuilding techniques such as supersets and drop sets to increase the tension and protein synthesis within the musculature. The age, fitness level, and strength training experience of the athlete will determine the time and loads devoted to the training of hypertrophy I and II.

Phase 3: Maximum Strength

The main objective of this phase is to develop the highest level of force possible. This is possible only using very heavy loads in training (85 to 100 percent of 1RM). Most sports require either power (long jump), muscular endurance (800- to 1,500-meter swimming), or both (rowing, canoeing, wrestling, and team sports). Each of these types of strength is affected by the level of maximum strength. Without a high level of maximum strength, an athlete cannot reach high levels of power. Because power is the product of speed and maximum strength, it is logical to develop maximum strength first, then convert it to power.

The duration of this phase, from one to three months, is a function of the sport or event and the athletes' needs. A shot-putter or American football player may need a lengthy phase of three months, whereas an ice hockey player may need only one or two months to develop this type of strength. Because the load is normally increased in three steps, the duration of the maximum strength phase must be a multiple of 3. Based on these examples, a shot-putter or football lineman may need 9, 12, or 15 weeks of maximum strength training, but a hockey or soccer player may need only 6 to 9 weeks. The duration of this phase also depends on whether athletes follow a mono- or a bi-cycle yearly plan. For obvious reasons, young athletes may have a shorter maximum strength phase, with loads below maximum. A high number of sets with a low number of exercises are characteristic of this phase.

Phase 4: Conversion

The main purpose of the conversion phase is to convert or transform gains in maximum strength into competitive, sport-specific combinations of strength. Depending on the characteristics of the sport or event, maximum strength must be converted to a type of power, muscular endurance, or both. By applying an adequate training method for the type of strength sought and using training methods specific to the selected sport (for example, speed training), athletes gradually convert maximum strength into power. Throughout this phase, depending on the needs of the sport and the athlete, a certain level of maximum strength must be maintained. If not, power may decline slightly (detraining) toward the end of the competitive phase. This is certainly the case for professional American football and baseball players, because each of these sports has such a long season.

For sports in which power or muscular endurance is the dominant strength, the appropriate method must be dominant in training. When both power and muscular endurance are required, the training time and method(s) should adequately reflect the optimal ratio between these two abilities. For instance, for a wrestler, the ratio should be almost equal; for a canoeist in a 500-meter program, power should dominate; and for a rower, muscular endurance should dominate. For team sports, the martial arts, wrestling, boxing, and most other power-dominant sports, coaches should plan exercises that lead to the development of agility and quick reaction and movement times before or during the conversion phase. Only this type of approach will prepare the athletes for the sport-specific requirements of competition.

The duration of the conversion phase depends on the ability that must be developed. For conversion to power, four or five weeks of specific power training is sufficient. On the other hand, conversion to muscular endurance requires as many as six to eight weeks because the physiological and anatomical adaptation to such demanding work takes much longer.

Phase 5: Competitive

The tradition in many sports is to eliminate strength training when the competitive season starts. However, athletes who do not maintain strength training during the competitive phase will be exposed to a *detraining effect* with the following repercussions:

- Muscle fibers decrease to their pretraining size (Staron, Hagerman, and Hikida, 1981; Thorstensson, 1977).

- Loss of power as a result of decreases in motor recruitment becomes more visible. The body fails to recruit the same number of motor units as it once did, so there is a net decrease in the amount of force that can be generated (Edgerton, 1976; Hainaut and Duchatteau, 1989; Houmard, 1991).

- Speed decreases are followed by power decreases because muscle tension depends on the force and speed of stimuli and the firing rate.

Some detraining effects can be observed after just five or six days. Detraining becomes more evident after two weeks, when athletes do not perform skills requiring strength as proficiently as they did at the end of the conversion phase (Bompa, 1993a).

As the term suggests, the main objective of strength training for this phase is to maintain the standards achieved during the previous phases. Once again, the program followed during this phase is a function of the specific requirements of the sport. The ratios among maximum strength, power, and muscular endurance have to reflect such requirements. For instance, a shot-putter may plan two sessions to train maximum strength and two to train power, whereas a jumper may consider one and three, respectively. Similarly, a 100-meter swimmer may plan one session to train maximum strength, two to train power, and one to train muscular endurance, whereas a 1,500-meter swimmer may dedicate the entire strength program to perfecting muscular endurance. For team sports, ratios should be calculated according to the role of strength in the particular sport, and be position specific. For instance, a pitcher should perform maximum strength, power, and power-endurance equally, while also doing compensation work to avoid injuries of the rotator cuff. Distinctions should be made between linemen and wide receivers in American football and sweepers, midfielders, and forwards in soccer. Linemen should spend equal time on maximum strength and power, and wide receivers need only train for power; soccer players have to maintain both power and power-endurance.

Between two and four sessions a week must be dedicated to maintaining the required strength, depending on the athlete's level of performance and the role of strength in skill performance. Compared to the prepatory phase, the time allocated to the maintenance of strength is secondary in the maintenance phase. Therefore, the coach has to develop a very efficient and specific program. Two to a maximum of four exercises involving the prime movers may suffice to maintain previously reached strength levels. At the same time, the duration of each strength training session must be short, 30 to 60 minutes. The strength training program should end at least five days before the main competition of the year. The purpose of this *cessation phase* is to conserve energy for the competition.

Phase 6: Transition

Traditionally, the last phase of the yearly plan has been inappropriately called the "off-season," but in reality it represents a transition from one yearly plan to another. The main goal of this phase is to remove the fatigue acquired during the training year and replenish the exhausted energy stores by decreasing volume and especially intensity. Furthermore, during the months of training and competition, most athletes are exposed to numerous psychological and social stressors that drain their mental energies. During the transition phase, athletes have time to relax psychologically by being involved in various physical and social activities that are enjoyable.

The transition phase should last no longer than four to six weeks for serious athletes. A longer phase will result in detraining effects such as the loss of most training gains and a deterioration of most strength gains. Athletes and coaches should remember that strength is hard to gain and easy to lose.

Athletes who do not perform any strength training at all during the transition phase may experience decreased muscle size and considerable power loss (Wilmore and Costill, 1988). Because power and speed are interdependent, loss of speed will also occur. Some authors claim that the disuse of muscles also reduces the frequency of neuromuscular stimulation and the pattern of muscle fiber recruitment; thus, strength loss may be the result of not activating some muscle fibers.

Although physical activity is reduced by 30 to 40 percent during the transition phase, athletes should find the time to work on maintenance of strength training. Working on the antagonist, stabilizer, and other muscles that may not necessarily be involved in the performance of a skill can be beneficial. Similarly, compensation exercises should be planned for sports in which an imbalance may develop between parts or sides of the body, such as in pitching, throwing events, archery, soccer (work upper body), and cycling. The detraining that results from neglecting strength training in the off-season can be detrimental to athletes' rate of performance improvement in the following year.

Detraining

Improvement or maintenance of a desired level of strength is possible only if an adequate load or training intensity is administered continually. When strength training is decreased or ceased, as often happens during competitive or long transition phases, there is a disturbance in the biological state of the muscle cells and bodily organs. This results in a marked decrease in athletes' physiological well-being and work output (Fry, Morton, and Keast, 1991; Kuipers and Keizer, 1988).

Decreased or diminished training can leave athletes vulnerable to the "detraining syndrome" (Israel, 1972) or "exercise-dependency syndrome" (Kuipers and Keizer, 1988). The severity of strength loss depends on the time that elapses between training sessions. Many organic and cellular adaptation benefits may be degraded, including the protein content of myosin.

When training proceeds as planned, the body uses protein to build and repair damaged tissues. When the body is in a state of disuse, it begins to catabolize or break down protein because it is no longer needed for tissue repair (Appell, 1990; Edgerton, 1976). As this process of protein degradation continues, some of the gains made during training are reversed. Testosterone levels, which are important for strength gains, have also been shown to decrease as a result of detraining, which may diminish the amount of protein synthesis (Houmard, 1991).

A rise in psychological disturbances such as headaches, insomnia, a feeling of exhaustion, increased tension, increased mood disturbances, lack of appetite, and psychological depression are among the usual symptoms associated with total abstinence from training. Athletes may develop any one or a combination of these symptoms. In any case, these symptoms all have to do with lowered levels of testosterone and beta-endorphin, a neuroendocrine compound that is the main forerunner of euphoric postexercise feelings (Houmard, 1991).

Detraining symptoms are not pathological and can be reversed if training resumes shortly. If training is discontinued for a prolonged period, however, athletes may display symptoms for some time. This indicates the inability of the human body and its systems to adapt to the state of inactivity. The length of time needed for these symptoms to incubate varies from athlete to athlete, but they generally appear after two to three weeks of inactivity and vary in severity.

Coaches of athletes involved in speed- and power-dominant sports must be aware of the fact that when muscles are not stimulated with strength or power training activities, muscle fiber recruitment is disrupted (Wilmore and Cesti, 2004). This results in a deterioration of performance. Cesti reported that strength gained during a 12-week program decreased by 45 percent from the original strength as a result of strength training interruption.

The decrease in the muscle fiber cross-sectional area is quite apparent after several weeks of inactivity. But the fastest rate of muscle atrophy, especially the degradation of contractile protein, takes place in the first two weeks. These changes are the result of protein breakdown, as well as a reduction in the recruitment pattern of the working muscle. The increased levels of some chemicals (sodium and chlorine) in the muscle play a role in the breakdown of muscle fiber (Appell, 1990).

Muscle fiber degeneration is partly due to degeneration of the motor units, in which slow-twitch fibers are usually the first to lose their ability to produce force. Fast-twitch fibers are generally least affected by inactivity. This is not to say that atrophy does not occur in these fibers—it just takes a little longer than atrophy does in slow-twitch fibers. The rate of strength loss per day in inactive athletes can be roughly 3 to 4 percent in the first week (Appell, 1990). For some athletes, especially those in speed- and power-dominant sports, this can be a substantial loss.

Detraining also affects aerobic-dominant sports. Coyle and colleagues (1991) observed that strength training stoppage didn't affect the glycolitic enzyme activities, but did decrease by 60 percent the activities of oxidative enzymes. This demonstrates that anaerobic performance can be maintained longer than aerobic performance.

Speed tends to be the first ability affected by detraining because the breakdown of protein and the degeneration of motor units decreases the power capabilities of muscle contraction. Speed loss may also be due to the nervous system's sensitivity to detraining. Because the motor unit itself is the first thing to deteriorate, the reduction in nerve impulses in the muscle fiber make muscles contract and relax at very rapid rates. The strength and frequency of these impulses can also be affected by decreases in the total number of motor units recruited during a series of repeated contractions (Edgerton, 1976; Hainaut and Duchatteau, 1989; Houmard, 1991). As a result of diminished motor recruitment patterns, the loss in power becomes more pronounced. The body fails to recruit the number of motor units it once could, resulting in a net decrease in the amount of force generated.

Variations to the Periodization of Strength Model

The periodization of strength example presented earlier in this chapter (see table 7.2) was helpful for illustrating the basic concept, but it cannot serve as a model for every situation or every sport. Each individual or group of athletes requires specific treatment based on training background, the specific characteristics of the sports and events, and gender. This section will explain variations of periodization and offer follow-up illustrations of specific periodization models for sports and events.

Certain sports and certain positions in team sports require strength and heavy mass. For instance, it is advantageous for throwers in some track-and-field events, linemen in American football, and heavyweight wrestlers or boxers to be both heavy and powerful. These athletes would follow a unique periodization model with a phase of training planned to develop hypertrophy (see chapter 9). By developing hypertrophy first, strength potential seems to increase faster, especially if it is followed by maximum strength and power development phases. The latter are known to stimulate motor unit activation and to increase the recruitment of fast-twitch muscle fibers.

Table 7.4 shows a periodization model for heavy and powerful athletes such as throwers, linemen in American football, and heavyweight wrestlers and boxers. After the traditional anatomical adaptation (AA) phase, there is a phase of hypertrophy (Hyp.) of at least six weeks, followed by maximum strength training and conversion to power. During the maintenance phase, these athletes should dedicate equal time to preserving power and maximum strength. The yearly plan concludes with compensation training specific to the transition phase.

Because the preparatory phase of power sports can sometimes be very long (e.g., in U.S. and Canadian college football), the coach may decide to build even more muscle mass. Another model can be followed in situations (see table 7.5) in which phases of hypertrophy are alternated with phases of maximum strength. The numbers above each phase in table 7.5 and some of the following tables indicate the duration of that phase in weeks.

Although strength training patterns for female athletes are similar to those for males, during long prepatory phases, females need more individual variation, more frequent changes, and shorter maximum strength phases. Table 7.6 illustrates a periodization in which the preparatory phase is longer. This assumes either a summer sport (track, rugby, field hockey, some positions in football such as lineman) or a sport played during winter and early spring (volleyball).

For power-dominated sports, similar variations of power and maximum strength phases are necessary because gains in power are faster if muscles are trained at various speeds of contraction (Bührle, 1985; Bührle & Schmidtbleicher, 1981). In addition, both power and maximum strength training train the fast-twitch fibers, resulting in more effective recruitment of these fibers that are determinant in the production and display of maximum strength and power. This type of periodization is superior to the traditional "work to exhaustion" method proposed by coaches influenced by bodybuilding. Lots of pain does not result in power gain because it does not train the nervous system to improve synchronization and quick recruitment of fast-twitch fibers.

The alternation of maximum strength and power phases also changes the pattern of motor recruitment, which results in higher central nervous system stimulation, especially during the power phase or when the load for maximum strength is greater than 85 percent. For the development of maximum strength, maximum loads used with eccentric contraction and explosive power exercises, such as high-impact plyometrics, result in the recruitment of more fast-twitch

Table 7.4 Periodization Model for Athletes Requiring Hypertrophy

Preparatory			Competitive		Transition
Anatomical adaptation	Hypertrophy	MxS	Conversion to power	Maintenance: Power, MxS	Compensation

Table 7.5 Variation of Periodization for Development of Hypertrophy and MxS

Preparatory							Competitive		Transition
3 AA	7 Hyp.	6 MxS	3 Hyp.	3 MxS	3 Hyp.	3 MxS	3 Conversion to power	Maintenance: Power, MxS	Compensation

Table 7.6 Periodization Mode for Athletes Requiring Frequent Alternations of Training Phases

Preparatory						Competitive		Transition
7 AA	6 MxS	3 Power	6 MxS	3 Power	3 MxS	4 Conversion to power	16 Maintenance: Power	6 Compensation

fibers, which is the greatest benefit to the athletes. Maximum strength training results in motor unit recruitment patterns that stimulate high levels of force, and power training increases the frequency or speed at which the muscles carry out the work. Anyone who has witnessed the performance of a shot-putter, javelin thrower, or hammer thrower can appreciate the force and speed characteristics of the sport.

A central nervous system stimulus occurs only in the early stages of long phases of maximum strength training. If the same methods and loading pattern are maintained for longer than two months, especially for athletes with a strong strength training background, the pattern of fiber recruitment becomes standard, eventually reaching a plateau. No drastic improvements can be expected. The employment of submaximum loading will definitely not stimulate the fast-twitch muscle fibers or result in the development of maximum strength and power. Bodybuilding methods defeat their purpose in sports in which speed and power are dominant abilities. That explains why several of the tables in this chapter propose alternations of maximum strength and power phases. Also, the importance of maximum strength phases should not be underestimated because any deterioration in maximum strength would affect the ability to maintain power at the desired level throughout the competitive phase. Furthermore, we have seen greater results in maximum strength when eccentric training methods are used to break through strength plateaus. In sports in which athletes have to peak twice a year, such as swimming, and track and field, a bi-cycle yearly plan is optimal. Table 7.7 illustrates the periodization of strength plan for a double-peak (bi-cycle) yearly plan.

Some sports (such as wrestling, boxing, and the martial arts) have three main competitions, so athletes have to peak three times a year. The yearly plan for such sports is called a tri-cycle plan. Table 7.8 offers a periodization model for a tri-cycle plan.

For sports with a long preparatory phase, such as softball, American football, and track cycling, table 7.9 shows a periodization option with two peaks: an "artificial" peak and a real peak (the football season). This model was developed at the request of a football coach who

Table 7.7   Periodization Model for a Bi-Cycle

Oct	Nov	Dec	Jan	Feb	Mar	Apr	May	Jun	Jul	Aug	Sep
Prep. I			Comp. I		T	Prep. II		Comp. II		T	
AA	MxS		Conv. to power	Maint.	AA	MxS		Conv. to power	Maint.	Compen.	

Table 7.8   Periodization Model for a Tri-Cycle

Sep	Oct	Nov	Dec	Jan	Feb	Mar	Apr	May	Jun	Jul	Aug
Prep. I		Comp. I	T	Prep. II		Comp. II	T	Prep. III		Comp. III	T
AA	MxS	P/M-E	AA		MxS	P/M-E	AA	MxS	P/M-E		Compen.

Table 7.9   Double-Peak Periodization

Dec	Jan	Feb	Mar	Apr	May	Jun	Jul	Aug	Sep	Oct	Nov
Preparatory									Competitive		Transition
AA	MxS		Conv. to power	T	AA	MxS		Conv. to power	Maint.: Power/MxS		Compen.

Peak performance achieved at the end of April (artificial peak) and during the fall.

wanted to improve his players' maximum strength and power. This double-peak periodization model was very successful with both the football players and sprinters in cycling; all athletes increased their maximum strength and power to the highest levels ever. This new approach for a typical mono-cycle sport was based on the following reasons:

■ A very long preparatory phase with training methods that used heavy loading and had little variety was considered too stressful and thus had dubious physiological benefits.

■ A double-peak periodization has the advantage of planning two phases for maximum strength training and two for power training. (Linemen followed a slightly different approach, with hypertrophy training incorporated into the maximum phase.) The benefits were what the coach expected: increase in overall muscle mass, increase in maximum strength, and the highest level of power ever achieved by his players.

Periodization Models for Sports

To make this book more practical and more applicable, several sport-specific periodization models for strength are included. To illustrate the physiological implications for each sport, we have listed five factors before each periodization model is presented:

■ *Dominant energy system(s)* for the sport

■ *Ergogenesis*

■ *Energy supplier(s)*

■ *Limiting factor(s)* for performance from the strength training standpoint

■ *Training objective(s)*

For training purposes, the energy systems should be linked to the limiting factors for strength. Doing so will make it relatively easy to decide the strength training objectives. For instance, for sports in which the anaerobic alactic system is dominant, the limiting factor for performance is power. On the other hand, sports dominated by the anaerobic lactic or the aerobic system always require a certain component of muscular endurance. In this way, the coach can better train the athletes physiologically and, as a result, improve performance. For example, increments in power should never be expected if bodybuilding methods are applied. The phrase *limiting factors for performance* means that the desired performance will not be achieved unless those factors are developed at the highest possible level. A low level of development of the sport-specific combination of strength will limit or hinder the achievement of a good performance.

The following examples cannot cover all variations possible for each sport. To develop such a model, one would have to know the specific competition schedule. Thus, for sports such as track and field and swimming, the periodization models are designed around the main competitions in winter and summer.

Abbreviation Key for Multi-Sport Tables	
AA = Anatomical adaptation	M-EM = Muscle-endurance of medium duration
Comp. = Competitive	M-ES = Muscle-endurance of short duration
Compen. = Compensation	MxS = Maximum strength
Conv. = Conversion	P = Power
Hyp. = Hypertrophy	P-E = Power-endurance
L.A. = Lactic acid	Precomp. = Precompetitive
Maint. = Maintenance	Prep. = Peparatory
M-EL = Muscle-enduance of long duration	T = Transition

SPRINTING

A sprinter requires explosive speed and long, powerful strides. Endurance is not as important a consideration as acceleration because the sprinter needs to move quickly over a short distance.

- Dominant energy systems: anaerobic alactic; lactic
- Ergogenesis: 80% alactic; 20% lactic (Ergogenesis measures the percentage of each energy system's contribution to final performance)
- Energy supplier: creatine phosphate
- Limiting factors: reactive power; starting power; acceleration power; power endurance
- Training objectives: maximum strength; reactive power; starting power; acceleration power; power endurance

Model for Sprints

Dates	Oct	Nov	Dec	Jan	Feb	Mar	Apr	May	Jun	Jul	Aug	Sep
Periodization	Prep. I			Comp. I		T	Prep. II		Comp. II		Transition	
Period. of strength	5 AA	6 MxS	4 Conv. to P		10 Maint.: Improve P, Specific P	2 AA		5 MxS	4 Conv. to P	9 Maint.: Improve P, Specific P		6 Compen.
Period. of energy systems	L.A. O_2	L.A. Alactic O_2	Alactic			L.A. Alactic O_2		Alactic L.A.		Alactic Lactic acid	Games Play	

Note: The aerobic (O_2) training for a sprinter represents the cumulative effect of tempo training (repetitions of 600 m, 400 m, and 200 m).

THROWING EVENTS: SHOT PUT, DISCUS, HAMMER, AND JAVELIN

Training for throwing events in track and field requires great explosive power (based on improvement of maximum strength) and hypertrophy (especially for shot put and, to some degree, for discus). Dominant muscular strength in the legs, torso, and arms is required for generating maximum throwing power and acceleration through the range of motion, culminating with the release.

- Dominant energy system: anaerobic alactic
- Ergogenesis: 95% alactic; 5% lactic acid
- Energy supplier: creatine phosphate
- Limiting factors: throwing power; reactive power
- Training objectives: maximum strength; throwing power; reactive power

Model for Shot Put

Dates	Oct	Nov	Dec	Jan	Feb	Mar	Apr	May	Jun	Jul	Aug	Sep
Periodi-zation	Prep. I			Comp. I			T	Prep. II	Comp. II		T	
Period. of strength	3 AA	5 Hyp.	6 MxS Hyp.	3 Conv. to P	8 Maint.: MxS, Hyp., Improve P		2 AA	3 Hyp.	4 MxS Hyp.	2 Conv. to P	10 Maint.: MxS, Improve P	6 Compen.
Period. of energy systems	L.A. Alatic	L.A.	Alactic Lactic acid				L.A. Alactic	L.A.	Alactic Lactic acid		Games Play	

Note: Hypertrophy training follows AA and must be maintained in some places, but at a ratio of 3 MxS to 1 hypertrophy.

LONG-DISTANCE AND MARATHON RUNNING

High aerobic capacity is the essential physical attribute of distance runners. Equally important is the ability to maintain a steady pace so that the runner efficiently taxes the energy stores, where glycogen and free fatty acids are the fuels used to produce energy for the race. Fast pace at the finish is dependent on an athlete's capacity to produce energy anaerobically.

- Dominant energy system: aerobic
- Ergogenesis: 10K: 5% alactic; 15% lactic acid; 80% aerobic
  Marathon: 5% lactic acid; 95% aerobic
- Energy suppliers: glycogen; free fatty acids
- Limiting factor: requires muscular endurance of long duration
- Training objectives: muscular endurance; power endurance; maximum strength

Model for Long Distance/Marathon

Dates	Oct	Nov	Dec	Jan	Feb	Mar	Apr	May	Jun	Jul	Aug	Sep
Periodi-zation	Preparatory							Comp.			T	
Period. of strength	AA		12 	3 MxS	M-EM MxS		Conv. to M-EL	Maint.: Power, Muscle-endurance				
Period. of energy systems	O_2			O_2 Lactic acid		O_2 Lactic acid					O_2 Play	

Note: MxS = <80%

MIDDLE-DISTANCE RUNNING

Middle-distance runners are fast runners with strong starts, and they also are able to tolerate a large buildup of lactic acid during the race. The ability to respond quickly to changes in running pace is essential for good performance. High aerobic capacity and the ability to produce energy anaerobically at the end of the race are essential physical qualities for these athletes.

- Dominant energy systems: lactic acid; aerobic
- Ergogenesis: 20% alactic; 30% lactic; 50% aerobic
- Energy suppliers: creatine phosphate; glycogen
- Limiting factors: starting power; acceleration power; power endurance
- Training objectives: acceleration power; power endurance; maximum strength

Model for Middle-Distance Running

Dates	Oct	Nov	Dec	Jan	Feb	Mar	Apr	May	Jun	Jul	Aug	Sep
Periodization	Prep. I			Comp. I		T	Prep. II		Comp. II		T	
Period. of strength	4 AA	3 MxS	6 Conv. to P		8 Maint.: Power	2 AA	4 MxS	4 Conv. to M-EM	Maint.: Power		Compen.	
Period. of energy systems	O_2		O_2 Lactic acid Alactic			O_2		L.A. O_2 Alactic	Lactic acid O_2 Alactic		O_2 Play	

Note: The suggested order of energy system training also implies training priorities per training phase.

BASEBALL, SOFTBALL, AND CRICKET

Maximum power (displayed in the specific drills of batting and pitching), quickness, reaction, and high speed are among the dominant abilities for these three sports. Any restriction placed on training during long preparatory phases, especially in professional baseball, may reduce the amount of preparation time, and the long competition schedule can lead to fatigue or injury. Since power and maximum speed are greatly dependent on the ability to recruit the highest number of fast-twitch muscle fibers possible, maximum strength is the dominant ability in these athletes' quest for success. Maintaining power and maximum strength will help players succeed through the season.

- Dominant energy system: anaerobic alactic
- Ergogenesis: 95% alactic; 5% lactic acid
- Energy suppliers: creatine phosphate; glycogen
- Limiting factors: throwing power; acceleration power; reactive power
- Training objectives: maximum strength; throwing power; acceleration power

Model for an Elite Baseball Team

Dates	Dec	Jan	Feb	Mar	Apr	May	Jun	Jul	Aug	Sep	Oct	Nov
Periodization	Preparatory			Precomp.	Competitive							Transition
Period. of strength	4 AA	MxS	6	4 Conv. to P	Maintenance: Power, Power-Endurance							Compen.
Period. of energy systems	O_2 L.A.	L.A. Alactic O_2		Alactic Lactic acid								O_2 compen.

Notes: The aerobic (O_2) training represents the cumulative effect of tempo training and specific tactical drills of longer duration (2-5 minutes) performed nonstop.

The suggested order of energy systems training also implies training priorities per training phase.

Since the competition phase is very long, detraining of strength may occur. Therefore, players must maintain P and, as much as possible, MxS as well.

Model for an Amateur Baseball or Softball Team

Dates	Nov	Dec	Jan	Feb	Mar	Apr	May	Jun	Jul	Aug	Sep	Oct
Periodization	Preparatory						Competitive					Transition
Period. of strength	4 AA	MxS	6	3 P	3 MxS	3 P	3 MxS	4 Conv. to P	Maintenance: Power			Compen.
Period. of energy systems	O_2 L.A.	L.A Alactic O_2		Alactic Lactic acid								O_2 compen.

Notes: The aerobic (O_2) training represents the cumulative effect of tempo training and specific tactical drills of longer duration (2-5 minutes) performed nonstop.

Alternation of MxS with P phases for maximum gains in power.

BASKETBALL

Basketball requires players to be strong, agile, and capable of quick acceleration and deceleration and changes of direction. Proper strength and power training prepares a basketball player for the rigors of the season.

- Dominant energy systems: anaerobic alactic, lactic acid; aerobic
- Ergogenesis: 60% alactic; 20% lactic acid; 20% aerobic
- Energy suppliers: creatine phosphate; glycogen
- Limiting factors: takeoff power; acceleration power; power endurance
- Training objectives: maximum strength; takeoff power; acceleration power; power endurance

Model for a College Basketball Team

Dates	Jul	Aug	Sep	Oct	Nov	Dec	Jan	Feb	Mar	Apr	May	Jun
Periodi-zation	Preparatory				Competitive						Transition	
Period. of strength	AA $\quad$ 6	MxS $\quad$ 6		Conv. to P $\;$ 4	Maintenance: Power, Power-Endurance						Compen.	
Period. of energy systems	O_2 L.A.	L.A. Alactic O_2		Lactic acid Alactic O_2							O_2 compen.	

Model for an Elite Basketball Team

Dates	Aug	Sep	Oct	Nov	Dec	Jan	Feb	Mar	Apr	May	Jun	Jul
Periodi-zation	Preparatory			Competitive							Transition	
Period. of strength	AA $\quad$ 3	MxS $\quad$ 6	Conv. to P $\;$ 3	Maintenance: Power, Power-Endurance							Compen.	
Period. of energy systems	O_2 L.A.	L.A. Alactic O_2	Lactic acid Alactic O_2								O_2 compen.	

Notes: Aerobic training (O_2) represents the cumulative effect of tempo running during the AA phase and the specific drills for O_2 training during the other training phases (2-5 minutes nonstop).

The suggested order of energy systems training also implies training priorities per training phase.

SWIMMING

Sprinting

Sprinting swimmers use both their alactic and anaerobic energy systems during a race. They must be able to generate quick, powerful strokes to move efficiently through the water. The following model is a bi-cycle for a nationally ranked sprinter.

- Dominant energy systems: alactic; lactic; aerobic (for 100 meters)
- Ergogenesis: 25% alactic; 50% lactic acid; 25% aerobic (for 100 meters)
- Energy suppliers: creatine phosphate; glycogen
- Limiting factors: power; power endurance; muscular endurance of short duration
- Training objectives: power; muscular endurance of short duration; maximum strength

Model for a National-Class Sprinter in Swimming (Bi-Cycle)

Dates	Sep	Oct	Nov	Dec	Jan	Feb	Mar	Apr	May	Jun	Jul	Aug
Periodization	Preparatory I				Comp. I		T	Prep. II	Comp. II		Transition	
Period. of strength	4 AA	6 MxS	3 P	3 MxS	4 Conv. to P, P-E	7 Maint.: P, P-E, M-E	2 AA	3 MxS	6 Conv. to P, P-E, M-E	4 Maint.: P, P-E, M-E	7 Compen.	7
Period. of energy systems	O_2	L.A. O_2 Alactic	Lactic acid Alactic O_2 compen.				O_2	L.A. Alactic O_2	Lactic acid Alactic O_2 compen.		O_2 compen.	

Note: The order of energy system training per phase represents the priority of training for that phase as well.

Long Distance

Long-distance swimmers must train for muscular endurance. A long race taxes the aerobic energy system, but proper muscle-endurance training will give the swimmer an endurance edge. The following model assumes two competitive phases, one beginning in January and the other beginning in late spring.

- Dominant energy system: aerobic
- Ergogenesis: 10% alactic; 30% lactic acid; 60% aerobic
- Energy suppliers: glycogen; free fatty acids
- Limiting factors: muscular endurance of medium duration; muscular endurance of long duration
- Training objectives: muscular endurance of medium duration; muscular endurance of long duration; power endurance; maximum strength

Model for a National-Class Long-Distance Swimmer

Dates	Sep	Oct	Nov	Dec	Jan	Feb	Mar	Apr	May	Jun	Jul	Aug
Periodi-zation	Preparatory I				Comp. I		T Prep. II		Comp. II		Transition	
Period. of strength	5 AA	3 MxS	3 M-E	3 MxS	6 Conv. to M-EL	6 Maint.: M-E	4 AA	3 MxS	6 Conv. to M-EL	7 Maint.: M-E	6 Compen.	
Period. of energy systems	O_2	O_2 Lactic acid			O_2 Lactic acid		O_2		O_2 Lactic acid		O_2 compen.	

Master Athlete (Short Distances)

Power is the dominant training factor for a master athlete. The long preparatory phase is required for developing both power and maximum strength. Only one competitive phase is assumed, running from May through late August.

- Dominant energy systems: alactic; lactic acid; aerobic
- Ergogenesis: 25% alactic; 50% lactic acid; 25% aerobic
- Energy suppliers: creatine phosphate; glycogen
- Limiting factors: power; power endurance; muscular endurance of short duration
- Training objectives: power; power endurance; maximum strength

Model for a Master Athlete Short-Distance Swimmer

Dates	Oct	Nov	Dec	Jan	Feb	Mar	Apr	May	Jun	Jul	Aug	Sep
Periodi-zation	Preparatory							Competitive			Transition	
Period. of strength	13 AA			3 MxS	3 P	3 MxS	3 P	6 Conv. to P, P-E	10 Maintenance: Power, Power-Endurance		8 Compen.	
Period. of energy systems	O_2			Lactic acid O_2	Alactic Lactic acid O_2 compen.	Lactic acid Alactic O_2 compen.					O_2 compen.	

SWIMMING AND WATER SPORTS

WATER POLO

Water polo is a sport of high energy expenditure interspersed with fast acceleration and powerful shooting actions. Passing and shooting precision are essential skills to learn during the many hours of training.

- Dominant energy systems: lactic acid; aerobic
- Ergogenesis: 10% alactic; 30% lactic acid; 60% aerobic
- Energy supplier: glycogen
- Limiting factors: power; power endurance; acceleration power; shooting power
- Training objectives: power; power endurance; maximum strength; muscular endurance of medium duration

Model for Water Polo: National League

Dates	1	2	3	4	5	6	7	8	9	10	11	12
Periodization	Preparatory							Comp.			T	
Period. of strength	4 AA		6 MxS	3 T		6 MxS		8 Conv. to Power, P-E, M-EM	Maint.: MxS, P-E, M-EM			Compen.
Period. of energy systems	O_2 Lactic acid Alactic			O_2 Alactic Lactic acid			Lactic acid O_2 Alactic					O_2

Note: O_2 training implies also to use tactical drills of longer duration (2-4 minutes).

FOOTBALL

Linemen

Linemen must be able to react explosively when the ball is put into play, and they must withstand an opponent's strength. A hypertrophy phase is included to build bulk.

- Dominant energy systems: anaerobic alactic; lactic
- Ergogenesis: 70% alactic; 30% lactic acid
- Energy suppliers: creatine phosphate; glycogen
- Limiting factors: starting power; reactive power; power endurance
- Training objectives: maximum strength; hypertrophy; starting power; reactive power

Model for Linemen in College Football

Dates	Mar	Apr	May	Jun	Jul	Aug	Sep	Oct	Nov	Dec	Jan	Feb
Periodi-zation	Preparatory						Competitive					Transition
Period. of strength	4 AA	6 Hyp.	9 MxS			4 Conv. to P	Maintenance: MxS, Power					7 Compen.
Period. of energy systems	Lactic acid Alactic		Alactic Lactic acid									

Model for Linemen in Elite Football

Dates	Apr	May	Jun	Jul	Aug	Sep	Oct	Nov	Dec	Jan	Feb	Mar
Periodi-zation	Preparatory				Competitive							Transition
Period. of strength	4 AA	6 Hyp.	6 MxS		4 Conv. to P	Maintenance: MxS, Power						6 Compen.
Period. of energy systems	Lactic acid Alactic		Alactic Lactic acid									

Wide Receivers, Defensive Backs, Tailbacks

Unlike linemen, wide receivers, defensive backs, and tailbacks require speed and agility rather than muscular bulk.

- Dominant energy systems: anaerobic alactic; lactic
- Ergogenesis: 60% alactic; 30 % lactic acid; 10% aerobic (cumulative)
- Energy suppliers: creatine phosphate; glycogen
- Limiting factors: acceleration power; reactive power; starting power
- Training objectives: acceleration power; reactive power; starting power; maximum strength

Model for Wide Receivers, Defensive Backs, and Tailbacks in College Football

Dates	Mar	Apr	May	Jun	Jul	Aug	Sep	Oct	Nov	Dec	Jan	Feb
Periodization	Preparatory						Competitive				Transition	
Period. of strength	4 AA	3 MxS	3 P	3 MxS	3 P	3 MxS	4 Conv. to P	Maintenance: Power			Compen.	7
Period. of energy systems	Lactic acid O_2		Alactic Lactic acid O_2			Alactic Lactic acid					O_2 compen.	

Model for Wide Receivers, Defensive Backs, and Tailbacks in Pro Football

Dates	Apr	May	Jun	Jul	Aug	Sep	Oct	Nov	Dec	Jan	Feb	Mar
Periodization	Preparatory						Competitive				Transition	
Period. of strength	4 AA	3 MxS	2 P	3 MxS	2 P	3 MxS	4 Conv. to P	Maintenance: Power			Compen.	6
Period. of energy systems	Lactic acid O_2		Alactic Lactic acid O_2			Alactic Lactic acid					O_2 compen.	

CANOEING AND KAYAKING

500 and 1,000 meters

Flatwater sprints are all about speed and specific endurance. The racer must be able to quickly pull the paddle against the resistance of the water to move quickly to the finish line.

- Dominant energy systems: anaerobic alactic; lactic; aerobic
- Ergogenesis: 25% alactic; 35% lactic acid; 40% aerobic (particularly for the 1,000 m)
- Energy supplier: creatine phosphate; glycogen
- Limiting factors: starting power; maximum strength; power endurance
- Training objectives: starting power; power endurance; maximum strength; muscular endurance of short duration; muscular endurance of medium duration

Model for Canoeing/Kayaking (500 and 1,000 Meters)

Dates	Oct	Nov	Dec	Jan	Feb		Mar	Apr	May	Jun	Jul	Aug	Sep
Periodi-zation	Preparatory								Competitive			Transition	
Period. of strength	5 AA	6 MxS		4 P	1 T	3 MxS	3 P	3 MxS	8 Conv. to P	Maint.: Power	13	Compen.	6
Period. of energy systems	O_2			O_2 L.A.	O_2 Lactic acid Alactic		Alactic Lactic acid O_2					O_2 compen.	

Note: The order of energy systems training represents the order of priority in a given training phase.

Marathon

As opposed to sprints, marathon races require muscular endurance of long duration. In addition, a racer must have a well-developed aerobic energy system to endure the length of the race.

- Dominant energy system: aerobic
- Ergogenesis: 5% alactic; 10% lactic acid; 85% aerobic
- Energy suppliers: glycogen; free fatty acids
- Limiting factor: requires muscular endurance of long duration
- Training objectives: muscular endurance of long duration; power endurance; maximum strength

Model for Canoeing/Kayaking (Marathon)

Dates	Nov	Dec	Jan	Feb	Mar	Apr	May	Jun	Jul	Aug	Sep	Oct
Periodi-zation	Preparatory						Competitive				Transition	
Period. of strength	AA	6 MxS	6	P	3 MxS	3 Conv. to M-EL	9	Maintenance: Power			Compen.	
Period. of energy systems	O_2			O_2 Lactic acid							O_2	

128

SOCCER

The most popular sport in the world is a game of great technical and physical demand, in which power, speed, agility, and specific endurance determine the final result.

- Dominant energy systems: alactic; lactic acid; aerobic
- Ergogenesis: alactic 15%; lactic acid 15%; aerobic 70%
- Energy suppliers: creatine phosphate; glycogen
- Limiting factors: power; starting power; power endurance; acceleration power; deceleration power; reactive power
- Training objectives: power; power endurance; takeoff power; maximum strength

Model for Soccer: Amateur Team

Dates	Oct	Nov	Dec	Jan	Feb	Mar	Apr	May	Jun	Jul	Aug	Sep
Periodization	Preparatory						Competitive				T	
Period. of strength	AA	MxS		Power, MxS	4 / 2 T	Conv. to P, P-E	Maint.: Power, P-E, MxS				Compen.	
Period. of energy systems	O_2	O_2 Lactic acid		Lactic acid Alactic O_2	Alactic Lactic acid O_2		Lactic acid Alactic O_2				Compen.	

Notes: The aerobic energy system (O_2) can be trained via tempo training (60-600 m) and specific drills of 3-5 minutes nonstop.

The order of energy systems per phase also represents the priority of training in that training phase.

Model for Soccer: Professional Team

Dates	Aug	Sep	Oct	Nov	Dec	Jan	Feb	Mar	Apr	May	Jun	Jul
Periodization	Prep.		Comp.		T	Comp. II						T
Period. of strength	AA	2 / 6 MxS, Power, P-E	Maint.: Power, P-E, MxS									Compen.
Period. of energy systems	O_2 L.A. Alactic	Alactic L.A. O_2	Lactic acid Alactic O_2									

SKIING

Alpine Skiing

Alpine skiers must be able to react quickly to the course flags. Maximum strength development alternates with power development over the long preparation phase.

- Dominant energy systems: anaerobic alactic; lactic
- Ergogenesis: 40% alactic; 50% lactic acid; 10% aerobic
- Energy suppliers: creatine phosphate; glycogen
- Limiting factors: reactive power; power endurance; agility
- Training objectives: maximum strength; reactive power; power endurance

Model for Alpine Skiing

Dates	May	Jun	Jul	Aug	Sep	Oct	Nov	Dec	Jan	Feb	Mar	Apr
Periodization	Preparatory						Competitive				Transition	
Period. of strength	AA	5	MxS	6	P	3	MxS	3	P	3	MxS	Conv. to P	6	Maint.: Power		Compen.
Period. of energy systems	L.A. O_2	Alactic Lactic acid		Alactic Lactic acid			Lactic acid Alactic				Play Games	

Note: The aerobic training (O_2) is the cumulative effect of longer duration specific drills/strength training.

Skiing (Cross-Country and Biathlon)

Cross-country races require strong aerobic endurance. Maximum strength is converted to muscular endurance toward the end of the preparation phase, so the skier is primed to withstand the demands of a long race.

- Dominant energy system: aerobic
- Ergogenesis: 5% lactic acid; 95% aerobic
- Energy suppliers: glycogen; free fatty acids
- Limiting factor: requires muscular endurance of long duration
- Training objectives: muscular endurance of long duration; power endurance; maximum strength

Model for Nordic Skiing

Dates	May	Jun	Jul	Aug	Sep	Oct	Nov	Dec	Jan	Feb	Mar	Apr
Periodization	Preparatory							Competitive			Transition	
Period. of strength	AA	4	MxS	6	M-EL	9	MxS	3	Conv. to M-EL	11	Maint.: M-E		Compen.	
Period. of energy systems	O_2 L.A.	O_2 Lactic acid Alactic		O_2 Lactic acid		O_2 L.A. Alactic		O_2 Lactic acid					O_2

Note: The suggested order of energy systems training also implies training priorities per training phase.

RUGBY

Rugby is a game of high energy, power, and intricate skills performed in rhythm.

- Dominant energy systems: alactic; lactic acid; aerobic
- Ergogenesis: 10% alactic; 30% lactic acid; 60% aerobic
- Energy suppliers: creatine phosphate; glycogen
- Limiting factors: power; power endurance; acceleration power
- Training objectives: power; power endurance; maximum strength; muscular endurance of medium duration

Model for Rugby: Amateur Team

Dates	Sep	Oct	Nov	Dec	Jan	Feb	Mar	Apr	May	Jun	Jul	Aug
Periodi-zation	Preparatory						Competitive				T	
Period. of strength	AA	8	MxS	9	Conv. to power, P-E, MxS	8	Maintain.: Power, P-E, MxS				Compen.	
Period. of energy systems	O_2 Lactic acid		Alactic Lactic acid O_2		Lactic acid Alactic O_2						O_2	

Notes: O_2 training refers mostly to performing specific tactical drills of longer duration (3-5 minutes) performed nonstop. The suggested order of energy systems training also implies training priorities per training phase.

Model for Rugby: Professional Team

Dates	Jul	Aug	Sep	Oct	Nov	Dec	Jan	Feb	Mar	Apr	May	Jun
Periodi-zation	Preparatory			Competitive								T
Period. of strength	AA	3 MxS	6 Conv. to P, P-E, M-E, MxS	4 Maintain.: Power, P-E, MxS								Compen.
Period. of energy systems	O_2 L.A.	Alactic L.A. O_2	Lactic acid Alactic O_2									O_2

131

RACKET SPORTS (TENNIS, BADMINTON, SQUASH, RACQUETBALL)

Racket sports are characterized by very fast and reactive games in which precision, quick changes of direction, and reaction time determine success.

- Dominant energy systems: alactic; lactic acid
- Ergogenesis: 50% alactic; 30% lactic acid; 20% aerobic
- Energy suppliers: creatine phosphate; glycogen
- Limiting factors: power; reactive power; power endurance; agility
- Training objectives: power; power endurance; reactive power; maximum strength

Model for Tennis: Amateur Player

Dates	Oct	Nov	Dec	Jan	Feb	Mar	Apr	May	Jun	Jul	Aug	Sep
Periodi-zation	Preparatory					Competitive						T
Period. of strength	AA	8	MxS Power	9	5 Conv. to power, P-E, MxS	Maint.: Power, P-E, MxS						Compen.
Period. of energy systems	O_2 Lactic acid		Lactic acid Alactic O_2		Alactic Lactic acid O_2							O_2 compen.

Model for Tennis: Professional Player

Dates	1	2	3	4	5	6	7	8	9	10	11	12
Periodi-zation	Prep. I		Comp. I	T	Prep. II	Comp. II	T	Prep. III	Comp. III	T	Prep. IV	Comp. IV	T
Period. of strength	AA	MxS, Power, P-E	Maint.: Power, P-E	AA	MxS Power, P-E	Maint.: Power, P-E	AA	MxS, Power, P-E	Maint.: Power, P-E	AA	MxS, Power, P-E	Maint.: Power, P-E	AA
Period. of energy systems	O_2 L.A.	Alactic Lactic acid O_2		O_2 L.A.	Alactic Lactic acid O_2		O_2 L.A.	Alactic Lactic acid O_2		O_2 L.A.	Alactic Lactic acid O_2		O_2 compen.

Notes: This model assumes a program with four major tournaments.

Since dates for major tournaments vary, the months of the year are numbered rather than specifically named.

Aerobic (O_2) training means specific drills of longer duration performed nonstop (3-5 minutes).

The suggested order of energy systems training also implies the priority of training per training phase.

Model for Racket Sports (Handball, Squash, Badminton)

Dates	1		2	3	4	5	6	7		8	9	10	11	12
Periodization	Prep. I		Comp. I		T	Prep. II		Comp. II		T	Prep. III	Comp. III		T
Period. of strength	3 AA	3 MxS	4 Power	Maint.: Power, MxS	2 AA	6 MxS	4 Power	Maint.: Power, MxS		2 AA	3 MxS	3 Power	Maint.: Power, MxS	Compen.
Period. of energy systems	L.A. O$_2$ Alactic		Alactic Lactic acid O$_2$		L.A. O$_2$ Alactic	Alactic Lactic acid O$_2$		L.A. O$_2$ Alactic			Alactic Lactic acid O$_2$			O$_2$ compen.

Notes: The dates of competitions and tournaments vary in different geographical regions, so the months are numbered rather than specifically named.

This model is a tri-cycle.

The order of energy systems training also represents the priority of training in a given phase.

Aerobic training (O$_2$) can be done via tempo training and by performing specific drills of 3-5 minutes.

RACKET SPORTS

BOXING

Boxers must be able to react quickly and powerfully to an opponent's attack. Both aerobic energy and anaerobic energy are required during a bout.

- Dominant energy systems: anaerobic lactic; aerobic
- Ergogenesis: 10% alactic; 40% lactic acid; 50% aerobic
- Energy suppliers: creatine phosphate; glycogen
- Limiting factors: power endurance; reactive power; muscular endurance of medium duration; muscular endurance of long duration (professional boxers)
- Training objectives: power endurance; reactive power; maximum strength; muscular endurance of medium duration; muscular endurance of long duration

Model for Boxing

Dates	Sep	Oct	Nov	Dec	Jan	Feb	Mar	Apr	May	Jun	Jul	Aug
Periodi-zation	Prep. I	Spec. prep. I	M	T	Prep. II	Spec. prep. II	M	T	Prep. III	Spec. prep. III	M	Transition
Period. of strength	3 AA	3 MxS	3 Conv. to P	6 Maint.: Power, M-E	2 AA	3 MxS	3 Conv. to P	7 Maint.: Power, M-E	2 AA	3 MxS	3 Conv. to P	8 Maint.: Power, M-E	Compen.
Period. of energy systems	O_2 L.A.	Lactic acid Alactic O_2		O_2 Lactic acid		Alactic Lactic acid O_2		O_2	Alactic Lactic acid O_2			O_2 compen.

Notes: Spec. prep. = Specific preparatory for a match

M = Match

MxS at 60 to 80 percent of 1RM. For heavy weights use loads of 80 to 95 percent of 1RM.

O_2 training also means specific boxing drills of 2-5 minutes performed nonstop.

The suggested order of energy systems training also implies training priorities per training phase.

MARTIAL ARTS

Martial artists need flexibility, power, agility, and quick reflexes based on energy supplied by all three energy systems over the long preparatory phase.

- Dominant energy systems: alactic; lactic; aerobic
- Ergogenesis: 50% alactic; 30% lactic acid; 20% aerobic
- Energy suppliers: creatine phosphate; glycogen
- Limiting factors: starting power; power endurance; reactive power; muscular endurance of short duration
- Training objectives: starting power; reactive power; maximum strength; power endurance; muscular endurance of short duration

Model for the Martial Arts

Dates	Jun	Jul		Aug		Sep		Oct	Nov		Dec	Jan	Feb	Mar	Apr	May
Periodization	Preparatory											Competitive			Transition	
Period. of strength	4 AA	3 MxS	2 P	3 MxS	2 T	3 P	3 MxS	3 P	3 MxS		Conv. to P	6 Maint.: P			Compen.	7
Period. of energy systems	Lactic acid. O_2 Alactic		Alactic L.A. O_2		Lactic acid Alactic O_2						Alactic Lactic acid O_2				Play Games	

Notes: Aerobic (O_2) training can be done via specific drills of 3-5 minutes, nonstop.

The suggested order of energy systems training also implies training priority per training phase.

TRIATHLON

Triathlon, which requires proficiency in three athletic skills, is a great challenge to both physical and psychological endurance. Paramount to success in triathlon is the body's efficiency in using the main fuel-producing source: free fatty acids.

- Dominant energy system: aerobic
- Ergogenesis: 5% lactic acid, 95% aerobic
- Energy suppliers: glycogen; free fatty acids
- Limiting factor: requires muscular endurance of long duration
- Training objectives: muscular endurance of long duration; maximum strength

Model for Triathlon

Dates	Oct	Nov	Dec	Jan	Feb	Mar	Apr	May	Jun	Jul	Aug	Sep
Periodi-zation	Preparatory						Competitive					T
Period. of strength	8 AA	MxS	8	Conv. to M-EL, MxS			Maintenance: M-E					Compen.
Period. of energy systems	O_2	O_2 Lactic acid Alactic		O_2 Lactic acid			O_2 Lactic acid					O_2 compen.

Notes: The suggested order of energy systems training also implies training priorities per training phase.

Alactic training refers to MxS and not to speed training.

CYCLING: ROAD RACING

Road racing overwhelms the aerobic system. The only times in which cyclists tax the anaerobic energy system are at the finish of the race and during steep climbing. Cyclists must be prepared to work hard over a long distance, generating constant rotations per minute to maintain speed and power against the resistance of the pedals, environment, and terrain.

- Dominant energy system: aerobic
- Ergogenesis: 5% lactic acid; 95% aerobic
- Energy suppliers: glycogen; free fatty acids
- Limiting factors: muscular endurance of long duration; acceleration power; power endurance
- Training objectives: muscular endurance of long duration; power endurance; acceleration power; maximum strength

Model for Road Racing

Dates	Nov	Dec	Jan	Feb	Mar	Apr	May	Jun	Jul	Aug	Sep	Oct
Periodi-zation	Preparatory						Competitive				Transition	
Period. of strength	4 AA	6 MxS	6 M-EL	3 MxS		Conv. to M-EL	9 Maintenance: Power				Compen.	
Period. of energy systems	O_2				O_2 Lactic acid						O_2	

137

HOCKEY

Acceleration and quick changes of direction are important elements of ice hockey. Training should focus on refining skills and developing power and aerobic and anaerobic endurance.

- Dominant energy systems: alactic; lactic acid; aerobic
- Ergogenesis: 10% alactic; 40% lactic acid; 50% aerobic
- Energy suppliers: creatine phosphate; glycogen
- Limiting factors: acceleration power; deceleration power; power endurance
- Training objectives: maximum strength; acceleration power; deceleration power; power endurance

Model for Ice Hockey

Dates	Jun	Jul	Aug	Sep	Oct	Nov	Dec	Jan	Feb	Mar	Apr	May
Periodization	Preparatory				Competitive						Transition	
Period. of strength	4 AA	MxS 6	3 P	3 MxS	6 Conv. to P, P-E	Maintenance: P, P-E, MxS				23	Compen. 8	
Period. of energy systems	Lactic acid O$_2$ Alactic		Alactic Lactic acid O$_2$		Lactic acid Alactic O$_2$						O$_2$	

FIGURE SKATING

Figure skaters must develop powerful takeoff and landing (eccentric) strength to be able to complete the required jumps. Strong anaerobic and aerobic energy systems are also required, especially for long programs.

- Dominant energy systems: anaerobic lactic; aerobic
- Ergogenesis: 40% alactic; 40% lactic acid; 20% aerobic
- Energy suppliers: creatine phosphate; glycogen
- Limiting factors: takeoff power; landing power; reactive power; power endurance
- Training objectives: takeoff power; landing power; maximum strength

Model for Figure Skating

Dates	May	Jun	Jul	Aug	Sep	Oct	Nov	Dec	Jan	Feb	Mar	Apr
Periodization	Preparatory							Competitive			Transition	
Period. of strength	AA	11	MxS 3	P 3	MxS 3	P, P-E 4	MxS 3	Conv. to P, P-E 6	Maintenance	10	Compen.	7
Period. of energy systems	O_2 Lactic acid Alactic		Lactic acid Alactic O_2					Alactic Lactic acid O_2			Play Games	

Notes: The aerobic training (O_2) is performed via long duration and by performing specific drills, lines, and repetitions. The suggested order of energy systems training also implies training priorities per training phase.

GOLF

The power of the swing off the tee and the precision of putting on the green are paramount in this popular sport. Good aerobic endurance will help any player to cope with the fatigue of the game and therefore to improve concentration and effectiveness, especially during the last holes of the game.

- Dominant energy system: aerobic
- Ergogenesis: 100% aerobic
- Energy suppliers: creatine phosphate; glycogen
- Limiting factors: power; demands maximum mental concentration
- Training objectives: power; maximum strength; aerobic endurance

Model for Golf

Dates	Oct	Nov	Dec	Jan	Feb	Mar	Apr	May	Jun	Jul	Aug	Sep
Periodi-zation	Preparatory						Competitive					T
Period. of strength	4 AA	6 MxS	2 T	6 MxS, Power	2 T	8 Conv. to Power, MxS	Maint.: MxS, Power					Compen.
Period. of energy systems	Lactic acid O_2		Alactic Lactic acid O_2			Alactic O_2						O_2

VOLLEYBALL

A volleyball player must be able to react quickly and explosively off the ground to spike, block, or dive. Maximum strength, power, and specific endurance are required for carrying a player through the long competitive phase with power and confidence.

- Dominant energy systems: anaerobic alactic; lactic; aerobic
- Ergogenesis: 40% alactic; 20% lactic acid; 40% aerobic
- Energy suppliers: creatine phosphate; glycogen
- Limiting factors: reactive power; takeoff power; power endurance; muscular endurance of short duration
- Training objectives: power; power endurance; maximum strength; muscular endurance of short duration

Model for Volleyball

Dates	Jun	Jul	Aug	Sep	Oct	Nov	Dec	Jan	Feb	Mar	Apr	May
Periodization	Preparatory					Competitive					Transition	
Period. of strength	AA $\quad$ 6	MxS $\quad$ 6	P $\;$ 3	MxS $\quad$ 3	Conv. to P, P-E, M-E $\quad$ 7		Maint.: Power, P-E				Compen.	
Period. of energy systems	Lactic acid O_2	Alactic O_2 Lactic acid		Alactic Lactic acid O_2							O_2 compen.	

Notes: O_2 training means specific drills of long duration (3-5 minutes) performed nonstop.

The suggested order of energy systems training also implies training priorities per training phase.

WRESTLING

Technique and tactical skills as well as power, power endurance, and flexibility determine a wrestler's success.

- Dominant energy systems: alactic; lactic acid; aerobic
- Ergogenesis: 30% alactic; 30% lactic acid; 40% aerobic
- Energy suppliers: creatine phosphate; glycogen
- Limiting factors: power; power endurance
- Training objectives: power; power endurance; maximum strength; flexibility; muscular endurance of short duration

Model for Wrestling

Dates	1	2	3	4	5	6	7	8	9	10	11	12
Periodi-zation	Prep. I			Comp. I		T	Prep. II		Comp. II			T
Period. of strength	4 AA	MxS, Power, P-E	9	Maint.: Power, P-E, MxS		Compen.	4 AA	MxS, Power, P-E	6	Maint.: Power, P-E, MxS		Compen.
Period. of energy systems	L.A. O_2	Alactic Lactic acid O_2				Lactic acid O_2		Lactic acid Alactic O_2				O_2 compen.

Notes: This is a bi-cycle: national championships and an international competition.

O_2 training means specific drills of longer duration (2-3 minutes).

The suggested order of energy systems training also implies training priorities per training phase.

ROWING

Rowing requires aerobic endurance and the ability to generate powerful strokes against water resistance. Starting power and muscular endurance should also be highly developed.

- Dominant energy systems: lactic acid; aerobic
- Ergogenesis: 20% lactic acid; 80% aerobic
- Energy suppliers: creatine phosphate; glycogen
- Limiting factors: muscular endurance of medium duration; muscular endurance of long duration; starting power; maximum strength
- Training objectives: muscular endurance; power; maximum strength

Model for Rowing

Dates	Sep	Oct	Nov	Dec	Jan	Feb	Mar	Apr	May	Jun	Jul	Aug
Periodi-zation	Preparatory							Competitive			Transition	
Period. of strength	AA 6	MxS 9		P 3	MxS 3	P 3	MxS 3	Conv. to M-E 8	Maint.: M-E, Power 10		Compen. 7	
Period. of energy systems	O_2 Lactic acid			O_2 Alactic Lactic acid				O_2 Lactic acid Alactic			O_2	

Note: The suggested order of energy systems training also implies training priorities per training phase.

Periodization of Loading Pattern per Training Phase

Loading patterns in training are not standard or rigid. They are not applicable to every sport or every level. Just as loading patterns vary according to the sport or level of performance, they also change according to the type of strength being sought in a given training phase. To make this concept easier to understand and use, figures 7.2 through 7.8 show how it is applied in several sports. The examples illustrate the dynamics of loading patterns per training phase for a mono-cycle in amateur baseball and softball (figure 7.2), college basketball (figure 7.3), college football linemen (figure 7.4), an endurance-dominant sport such as canoeing (figure 7.5), and for a bi-cycle for sprinting in track and field (figure 7.6) and sprint and long-distance swimming (figures 7.7 and 7.8).

The charts indicate (from top to bottom) the number of weeks planned for a particular training phase, the type of training being sought in that phase, and the loading patterns (high, medium, and low). In some cases, the type of contraction being used (concentric, eccentric, or both) is also indicated. The two types of contraction are mainly useful for the maximum strength phase. Even if your chosen sport is not among the examples, once you understand the concept, you will be able to apply it to your own particular case. In addition, the examples are so varied that they are applicable through association.

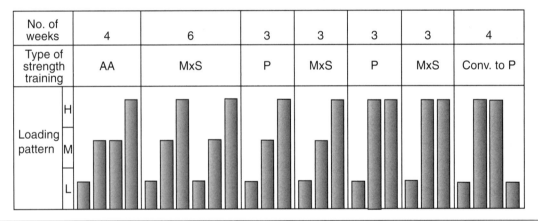

Figure 7.2 Variations of loading pattern for strength training phases for a baseball/softball/cricket team. Note that in some phases, the low and medium loading is at the upper levels, suggesting a more demanding training regimen. For similar reasons, and to maximize the level of power development, the last three training phases have two adjacent high loads followed by regeneration cycles (low loads).

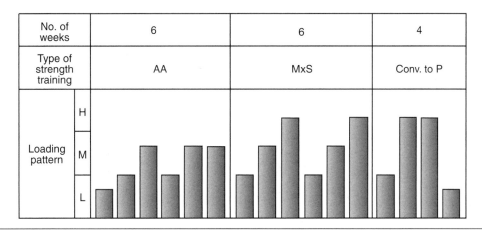

No. of weeks	6		6		4
Type of strength training	AA		MxS		Conv. to P
Loading pattern					

Figure 7.3 Suggested loading pattern for a college basketball team in which the preparatory phase is shorter and must be performed from early July through late October.

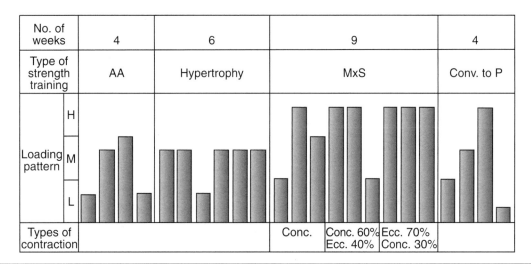

No. of weeks	4	6	9			4
Type of strength training	AA	Hypertrophy	MxS			Conv. to P
Loading pattern						
Types of contraction			Conc.	Conc. 60% Ecc. 40%	Ecc. 70% Conc. 30%	

Figure 7.4 Variations of loading pattern for periodization of strength for linemen in college football. A similar approach can be used for throwers in track and field and the heavyweight category in wrestling. Note that for the hypertrophy phase, the load is medium (60 to 80 percent of 1RM) but very demanding for 2 to 3 weeks in a row. For the maximum strength phase, the types of contraction—concentric or eccentric—and the percentage per week are also suggested.

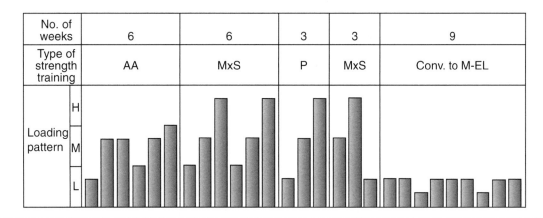

No. of weeks	6	6	3	3	9
Type of strength training	AA	MxS	P	MxS	Conv. to M-EL
Loading pattern					

Figure 7.5 Variations of loading pattern for marathon canoeing, a sport where muscular-endurance long is the dominant ability. A similar approach can be used for cycling, Nordic skiing, triathlon, and rowing. Note that for conversion to muscular-endurance long, the load is low (30 to 40 percent) but very demanding for 2 to 3 weeks in a row.

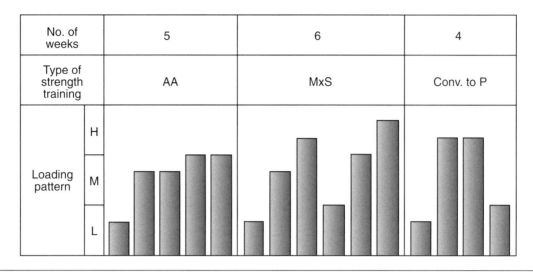

No. of weeks	5		6		4	
Type of strength training	AA		MxS		Conv. to P	

Figure 7.6 Variations of loading pattern for the first peak of a bi-cycle annual plan for sprinting in track and field.

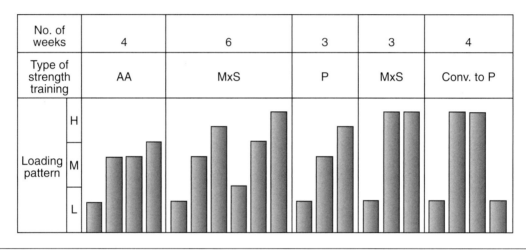

No. of weeks	4	6	3	3	4
Type of strength training	AA	MxS	P	MxS	Conv. to P

Figure 7.7 Variations of loading pattern for a sprinter in swimming (one peak of a bi-cycle annual plan). Note that training demand for the last two phases is high since the load is high for 2 adjacent weeks.

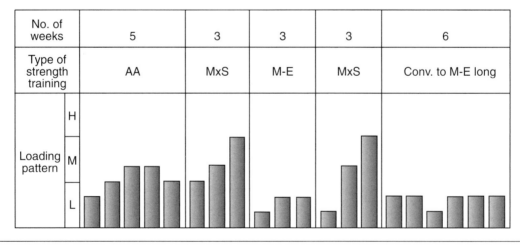

No. of weeks	5	3	3	3	6
Type of strength training	AA	MxS	M-E	MxS	Conv. to M-E long

Figure 7.8 Variations of loading pattern for swimming for a long-distance event. Note that the load for maximum strength should not exceed 80 percent of 1RM. Similarly, the load for muscular-endurance is low (30 to 40 percent) but the number of repetitions is very high (see chapter 11).

Periodization Effects on the Force–Time Curve

Because of the influence of bodybuilding, strength training programs often include a high number of reps (12 to 15) performed to exhaustion. Such programs mainly develop muscle size, not quickness of contraction. As illustrated in figure 7.9, the application of force in sports is performed very quickly, between 100 and 200 milliseconds. The only type of strength that stimulates such a quick application of force is maximum strength and power. The curve of force application of such strength components is less than 200 milliseconds, approaching 100 milliseconds.

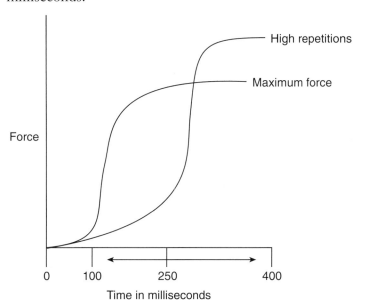

Figure 7.9 The force–time curve of two different weight training programs (from Schmidtbleicher, 1984).

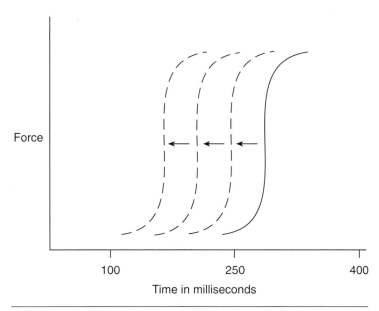

Figure 7.10 The purpose of strength training is to shift the force–time curve to the left.

The opposite is true if a variant of bodybuilding is employed. The total volume of strength training may be higher than maximum strength and power, but the force application is longer (more than 250 milliseconds) and thus is not specific to the needs of most sports. Because the application of force in training is very fast, the main purpose of training is to shift the force–time curve to the left, or as close as possible to the time of the force application (less than 200 milliseconds). Figure 7.10 illustrates the intent of training—namely, that through the use of maximum strength and power, the force–time curve can be shifted to the left.

This shift toward the sport-specific time of application of force is not achieved quickly. The whole point of periodization of strength is to use phase-specific strength training to shift the force–time curve to the left (i.e., decrease execution time) before the start of major competitions. This is when the quick application of strength is needed, as well as when athletes will benefit from gains in power.

As explained earlier, each training phase of the periodization of strength has certain objectives. By plotting the force–time curve for each training phase, both coaches and athletes will be able to see from another angle how training influences the force–time curve. Figure 7.11 shows the periodization of strength when a hypertrophy phase is also included. Certainly, only some sports may use this model, whereas many others will exclude hypertrophy from the yearly plan.

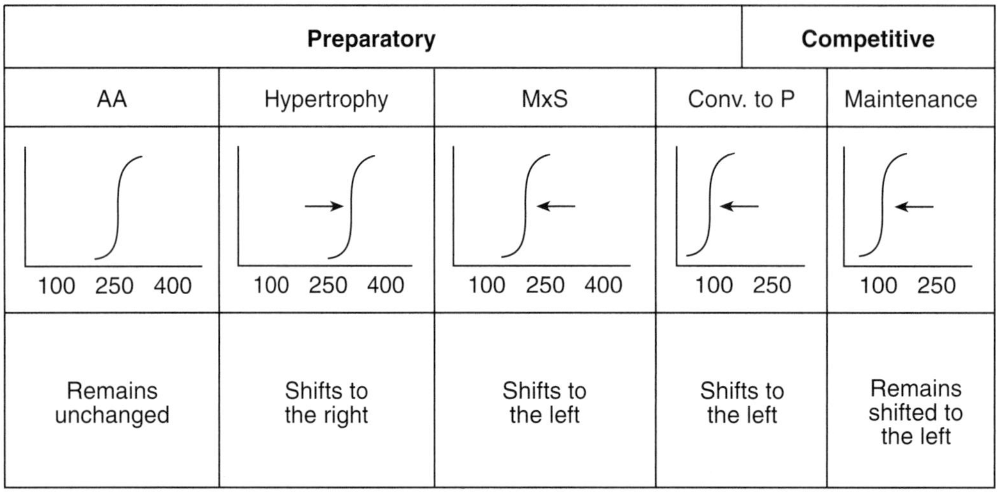

Preparatory				Competitive
AA	Hypertrophy	MxS	Conv. to P	Maintenance
100 250 400	100 250 400	100 250 400	100 250	100 250
Remains unchanged	Shifts to the right	Shifts to the left	Shifts to the left	Remains shifted to the left

Figure 7.11   Graphs showing how the specifics of training for each phase influence the force–time curve.

As figure 7.11 shows, the type of program performed during the anatomical adaptation phase has little effect on the force–time curve. At most, it may shift it slightly to the right (i.e., increase execution time). Typical hypertrophy training methods, however, increase the total volume of strength training performed, as illustrated by the height of the curve. The curve shifts to the right because the load is submaximum and each set is performed to exhaustion and thus not explosively. Such gains in muscle size do not translate into gains in the fast application of strength. The use of heavy loads from the maximum strength phase onward results in the explosiveness during the conversion of maximum strength to power shifting the curve to the left. As this type of strength training is continued during the maintenance phase, the curve should remain to the left.

A high level of power, or explosiveness, cannot be expected before the start of the competitive phase. Power is maximized only as a result of implementing the conversion phase; thus, high levels of power should not be expected during the hypertrophy and even during the maximum strength phases. As mentioned earlier, however, gains in maximum strength are vital if increments in power are expected from year to year, because power is a function of maximum strength. Periodization of strength is the best road to success for both muscular endurance and power development.

Part III

Periodization of Strength

Phase 1: Anatomical Adaptation

Strength training is an essential element in a coach's quest to produce good athletes. All athletes involved in competitive sports follow a yearly program intended to result in peak performance at the time of the main competition(s). Strength training is one of the key ingredients in building the physiological foundation for peak performance.

General athletic training must be planned and periodized in a way that ensures performance improvement from phase to phase and results in peak performance during the competitive season. The same is true of strength training. Like general athletic ability and skill, strength can be refined through various methods and phases of training to create a final product—sport-specific strength.

As was illustrated in table 7.2, strength training should occur throughout the yearly plan according to the concept of periodization of strength. As explained earlier, each sport requires a certain type of sport-specific combination of strength, which should represent the physiological base for performance. Athletes can transform strength into a sport-specific quality by applying periodization of strength and by using training methods specific to the needs of each strength training phase. Thus, training methods must change as the training phases change.

This and the next four chapters will discuss all available training methods as they relate to periodization of strength. Each training phase will be treated separately to show which method best suits that particular phase as well as the needs of athletes. The discussion will also focus on the positive and negative aspects of most methods and how to apply the methods, and suggest training programs using particular methods.

Circuit Training

During the early stages of strength training, especially with entry-level athletes, almost any strength training method or program will result in strength development to some degree. As the athlete develops a strength foundation, however, the coach should create a specific, periodized strength training program to maximize the athlete's natural abilities. Equally important for coaches to keep in mind is that each athlete has a unique rate of response, reaction, and adaptation to a given method, and therefore, a different rate of improvement. Strength training is a long-term proposition. Athletes do not reach their highest level after four to six weeks from the beginning of the strength training program, but rather during the competitive phase, which is months away from the anatomical adaptation phase.

The goal of the anatomical adaptation phase is to adapt the muscles, and especially their attachments to the bone, progressively to cope more easily with heavier loads during the following training phases. As such, the overall load in training must be increased without athletes experiencing much discomfort. The simplest method to consider for anatomical adaptation is *circuit training*, mainly because it provides an organized structure and alternates muscle groups.

Although circuit training can be used to develop the foundation of strength for the other training phases to come, it can also be used to develop nonspecific cardiorespiratory endurance by combining strength and endurance training. Some authors suggest that combining aerobic endurance with strength training during the same phase may seriously compromise the development of maximum strength and power. The claim is that strength training is incompatible with

Although many have argued against strength training and endurance training during the same phase, athletes involved in endurance sports like rowing that require power have no choice but to train both in the same phase.

long-distance aerobic training because fast-twitch fibers may adapt to behave like slow-twitch fibers. These studies scientifically validate the theory that planning a long and slow-duration aerobic activity (two hours or longer) for speed and power sports and combining maximum strength and hypertrophy training on the same day will negatively affect adaptation. Short-term adaptation will suffer.

However, athletes in sports in which both strength and aerobic endurance are dominant (rowing, kayaking, canoeing, and cross-country skiing) don't have a choice but to train both during the preparatory phase. The criticism of some of the previous claims is that most of this research was done just for a few weeks, whereas training is long term. Has the full adaptation to such training actually occurred? Some research suggests the opposite: that a certain compatibility exists between strength and endurance training performed at the same time (see chapter 1). The type of endurance training suggested in this text for the anatomical adaptation phase is very different from the long and slow-duration activities, as seen in the following examples.

Circuit training was first proposed by Morgan and Adamson (1959) of Leeds University as a method for developing general fitness. Their initial circuit training routine consisted of several stations arranged in a circle (hence the name *circuit training*) so as to work muscle groups alternately from station to station. As circuit training grew in popularity, other authors began to provide additional information. Perhaps the best book on the market is *Circuit Training for All Sports* (Scholich, 1992).

A wide variety of exercises and devices can be used in a circuit training routine, such as body weight, surgical tubing, medicine balls, light implements, dumbbells, barbells, and any strength training machines. A circuit may be of short (6 to 9 exercises), medium (9 to 12 exercises), or long (12 to 15 exercises) duration and may be repeated several times depending on the number of exercises involved. In deciding the number of circuits, the number of reps per station, and the load, coaches must consider the athlete's work tolerance and fitness level. Total workload during the anatomical adaptation phase should not be so high as to cause the athlete pain or high discomfort. Athletes should help determine the amount of work they can perform.

Circuit training is a useful, although not magic, method for developing the foundation of strength during the anatomical adaptation phase. Any other training method in which the muscle groups can be alternated can be equally beneficial. The key to any training method used during this phase is the number of exercises, number of reps and sets, and the rest interval. As shown in the following examples, the training methodology used for the anatomical adaptation phase has to be adapted to the physiological profile of the sport (e.g., speed or power vs. a sport in which endurance has a certain role) and the needs of the athlete. It must also develop most muscles used in that sport. In line with the overall purpose of the preparatory phase, and particularly the goal of anatomical adaptation, exercises should be selected to develop the core area of the body as well as the prime movers.

Circuit training exercises alternate muscle groups, which facilitates recovery. The rest interval between stations can be anywhere from 60 to 90 seconds, with one to three minutes between circuits. Because most gyms have many different apparatuses, workstations, and strength training machines, a wide variety of circuits can be created. This variety constantly challenges the athletes' skills and, at the same time, keeps them interested.

Circuit training should not be used as a testing device or to compare athletes. Athlete differences are due mainly to anthropometric differences. Because the speed of performance and the degree of flexion and extension can vary greatly, comparing athletes is unfair. On the contrary, achievements should only be compared with the individual athlete's past performance.

Program Design
for Circuit Training Method

Circuit training may be used from the first week of the anatomical adaptation phase. The coach should start by testing the athlete for 1RM to calculate the load for the prime movers, then select the workstations according to the equipment available. Athletes should follow a certain progression, depending on their classifications and training backgrounds. Younger athletes with little or no strength training background should start with exercises using their own body weight, or lower loads. Over time, they can progress to exercises using light implements and weights, then barbells and strength machines. Again, exercise during this phase must be selected to involve most muscle groups irrespective of the needs of the specific sport. However, the prime movers should also be targeted. After all, they are the *engines* behind the effective performance of sport-specific skills.

The circuits presented below (circuits A, B, and C), although far from exhausting all the possibilities available in a gym, are typical for entry-level, or junior, athletes. Athletes who are new to circuit training may want to split circuit B into two phases. As adaptation occurs, the athlete can begin adding exercises from phase II to the end of phase I until she can perform all eight exercises nonstop. Start with two groups of four as presented in Circuit B, and as the athlete adapts to the program, bring the fifth exercise into phase I and so forth. This keeps the athlete motivated to reach her goal and keeps her body open to new challenges and levels of adaptation.

Entry-level athletes should individualize the number of reps and sets by working up to the point of feeling slight discomfort or discomfort. *Slight discomfort* can be translated as uneasiness. *Discomfort*, on the other hand, refers to the threshold of pain at which the athlete has to stop the exercise. Working to discomfort actually challenges the athlete. Advanced athletes may work to high discomfort, which refers to surpassing the threshold of pain. As shown in some of the following examples, high discomfort is suggested only for the latter part of a circuit training for advanced athletes.

Circuit A (own body weight)

1. Half squats
2. Push-ups
3. Bent-knee sit-ups
4. Two-legged low hops on spot
5. Back extensions
6. Pull-ups
7. Burpees

Circuit B (own body weight; combination of two minicircuits)

Phase I

1. Half squats
2. Push-ups
3. Bent-knee sit-ups
4. Two-legged low hops on spot

Phase II

5. Back extensions
6. Pull-ups
7. Burpees
8. Abdominal rainbows

Circuit C (dumbbells and medicine ball)

1. Half squats
2. Medicine ball chest throws

3. Military presses
4. Bent-knee sit-ups (medicine ball held at chest level)
5. Medicine ball forward throws (between legs)
6. Lunges
7. Back arches, ball behind the neck
8. Upright rowing
9. Toe raises
10. Trunk rotations
11. Overhead backward medicine ball throws
12. Jump squats and medicine ball throws

Table 8.1 shows a circuit training program, including the duration of anatomical adaptation, the frequency of training sessions per week, and other parameters for both novice and experienced athletes. As shown in table 8.1, training parameters for experienced athletes are quite different from those for novices. A longer anatomical adaptation phase makes good sense for novice athletes because they need more time for adaptation and for creating a good base for the future. On the other hand, extending this phase much longer than five weeks will not result in visible gains for experienced athletes.

Table 8.1 Training Parameters for Circuit Training

Training parameters	Novice athletes	Experienced athletes
Duration of AA	8-10 weeks	3-5 weeks
Load (if weights are used)	30-40 percent	40-60 percent
No. of stations per circuit	9-12 (15)	6-9
No. of circuits per session	2-3	3-5
Total time of CT session	20-25 minutes	30-40 minutes
Rest interval between exercises	90 seconds	60 seconds
Rest interval between circuits	2-3 minutes	1-2 minutes
Frequency per week	2-3	3-4

Similar observations can be made regarding the number of stations per circuit. Because novice athletes have to address as many muscle groups as realistically possible, they use more stations and the circuits are longer. Advanced athletes, however, can reduce the number of stations to focus on exercises for the prime movers, compensation, and core exercises, resulting in shorter circuits.

The total physical demand per circuit must be increased progressively and individually. The example in figure 8.1 illustrates that the load and the pattern for increasing differs between novice and experienced athletes. Because novice athletes need longer and better adaptation, the load remains the same for two weeks. For experienced athletes, however, the load changes from cycle to cycle. The same is true regarding the load used in exercises performed against resistance: lower loads for entry-level athletes and slightly heavier loads for advanced athletes.

To better monitor improvements in training, as well as to calculate the load every three weeks, coaches should test their athletes' 1RM in weeks 1 and 4 and at the end of week 6.

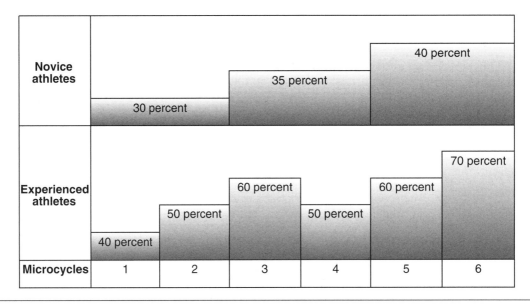

Figure 8.1 Suggested pattern for load increments during circuit training for novice and experienced athletes.

Figures 8.2 through 8.5 illustrate circuit training for several types of sports, for three and six weeks of anatomical adaptation training. A six-week cycle will give athletes time to build a stronger base, and offer the physiological benefits from longer and better adaptation. The suggested programs should be adapted to athletes' classifications and abilities.

Toward the end of the anatomical adaptation phase, the load reaches percentages that allow athletes to make an immediate transition to the maximum strength phase (see figure 8.2). This approach can be used for all athletes except those requiring increased muscle mass, such as throwers and American football linemen. For these athletes, a hypertrophy phase must be planned between the anatomical adaptation phase and the maximum strength phase.

The three-week anatomical adaptation program (see figure 8.3) is appropriate for athletes with a very short preparatory phase, especially those in racket and contact sports that have three or four major peaks per year. Because the anatomical adaptation phase is so short, the load in training is increased very quickly to ready the athletes for the maximum strength phase. Detraining in these sports is less of an issue because the transition phase is much shorter than those in most other sports.

Figure 8.4 illustrates an anatomical adaptation strength training program for team sports in which cardio fitness is important, such as soccer, basketball, rugby, lacrosse, water polo, or hockey.

Figure 8.5 illustrates circuit training for baseball and softball and racket sports. In these sports, certain specific exercises for trunk and hip rotation (abdominal rainbows, incline trunk rotations, and power ball side throws) are introduced as early as the anatomical adaptation phase for maximum adaptation.

No.	Exercise	Week 1	Week 2	Week 3	Week 4	Week 5	Week 6
1	Leg press	$\frac{40}{15}2$	$\frac{40}{15}3$	$\frac{50}{15}3$	$\frac{50}{15}2$	$\frac{60}{12}3$	$\frac{70}{8}3$
2	Push-ups	2×12	3×13	3×15	2×15	3×18	3×20
3	Bent-knee sit-ups	2×12	3×12	3×15	2×12	3×15	3×18
4	Upright rowing	$\frac{40}{12}2$	$\frac{40}{15}3$	$\frac{50}{15}3$	$\frac{50}{15}2$	$\frac{60}{12}3$	$\frac{70}{10}3$
5	Back arches (medicine ball)	2×10	2×12	3×12	2×12	3×12	3×15
6	Step-ups	2×30 sec.	3×30 sec.	3×45 sec.	2×45 sec.	3×45 sec.	3×60 sec.
7	Military press	$\frac{40}{12}2$	$\frac{40}{15}3$	$\frac{50}{15}3$	$\frac{50}{15}2$	$\frac{60}{12}3$	$\frac{70}{10}3$
8	Toe raises	$\frac{40}{15}2$	$\frac{50}{15}3$	$\frac{50}{20}3$	$\frac{50}{15}3$	$\frac{60}{20}3$	$\frac{70}{15}3$
9	Leg curls	$\frac{40}{12}2$	$\frac{40}{12}3$	$\frac{50}{15}3$	$\frac{50}{12}2$	$\frac{50}{12}3$	$\frac{60}{8}3$
10	Burpees	2×10	2×12	3×15	2×12	3×15	3×18

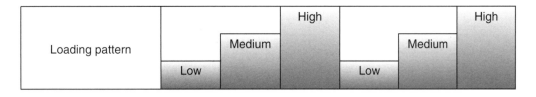

Loading pattern	Low	Medium	High	Low	Medium	High

Figure 8.2 An example of a standard strength training program for the anatomical adaptation phase. The rest interval between stations will be as long as necessary to reach a nearly full recovery.

No.	Exercise	Week 1	Week 2	Week 3	Rest interval
1	Skipping rope	3 min.	2 × 3 min.	4 × 2 min.	30 sec.
2	Bench press	$\frac{50}{15}2$	$\frac{60}{12}3$	$\frac{70}{12}3$	2 min.
3	Ab crunches	2 sets to slight discomfort	2-3 sets to dis-comfort	3-4 sets to high discomfort	1 min.
4	Half squats	$\frac{60}{15}3$	$\frac{70}{10}3$	$\frac{70}{12}3$	2-3 min.
5	Medicine ball (4 kg) chest throws	3 × 12	3 × 15	3 × 20	1-2 min.
6	Arm pulls/Front lat pull-downs	$\frac{50}{15}2$	$\frac{60}{12}2$	$\frac{70}{12}2$	2 min.
7	Toe raises	$\frac{60}{12}3$	$\frac{70}{10}3$	$\frac{70}{12}3$	1 min.
8	Incline/Horizontal trunk twists (in each direction)	2 × 10	2 × 12	3 × 12	2 min.
9	Low-impact plyometrics	2 × 8	3 × 3	3 × 10	2 min.

Loading pattern			
	Low	Medium	High

Figure 8.3 A suggested anatomical adaptation phase for sports with a short preparatory phase, such as racket sports, martial arts, and other contact sports. Note: Skipping rope aids in cardiorespiratory training.

No.	Exercise	Week 1	Week 2	Week 3	Week 4	Week 5	Week 6	Rest interval
1	Cardio	1 × 10 min.	1 × 10 min.	2 × 5 min.	2 × 5 min.	3 × 3 min.	4 × 2 min.	1 min.
2	Half squats	$\frac{40}{15}$ 2	$\frac{50}{12}$ 2	$\frac{60}{12}$ 3	$\frac{60}{12}$ 3	$\frac{70}{10}$ 2	$\frac{70}{10}$ 3	2-3 min.
3	Medicine ball (4 kg) back throw	2 × 15	2 × 15	2 × 20	2 × 20	3 × 15	3 × 15	1 min.
4	Ab crunches	2 sets to slight discomfort	2 sets to slight discomfort	3 sets to discomfort	3 sets to discomfort	3 sets to discomfort	3-4 sets to high discomfort	1-2 min.
5	Leg curls	$\frac{40}{10}$ 2	$\frac{40}{12}$ 2	$\frac{50}{12}$ 2	$\frac{50}{12}$ 2	$\frac{60}{12}$ 2	$\frac{60}{12}$ 2	2 min.
6	Incline press	$\frac{50}{12}$ 2	$\frac{50}{12}$ 3	$\frac{60}{12}$ 3	$\frac{60}{12}$ 3	$\frac{60}{15}$ 3	$\frac{70}{12}$ 3	2-3 min.
7	Toe raises	$\frac{60}{12}$ 2	$\frac{60}{12}$ 3	$\frac{70}{10}$ 3	$\frac{60}{12}$ 2	$\frac{70}{10}$ 3	$\frac{70}{12}$ 3	2 min.
8	Low-impact plyometrics	—	—	—	2 × 10	3 × 8	3 × 10	2-3 min.
9	Power ball (10 kg) side throws	2 × 12	2 × 15	2 × 15	3 × 10	3 × 12	3 × 15	2 min.
10	Cardio	1 × 5 min.	1 × 7 min.	1 × 7 min.	2 × 5 min.	3 × 3 min.	3 × 3 min.	1 min.

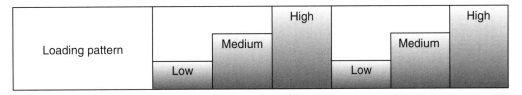

Figure 8.4 Circuit training for team sports in which cardiorespiratory endurance is an important component. Note: The cardio component in this example could include running, using a stair stepper, riding a bicycle ergometer, etc.

No.	Exercise	Week 1	Week 2	Week 3	Week 4	Week 5	Week 6	Rest interval
1	Side/Diagonal lunges (for each leg)	2×15	2×15	2×20	2×20	3×15	3×15	2 min.
2	Abs rainbow (for each side)	2 sets to slight discomfort	2 sets to slight discomfort	2 sets to discomfort	2 sets to discomfort	2-3 sets to high discomfort	2-3 sets to high discomfort	1-2 min.
3	Back extension	2 sets to slight discomfort	2 sets to slight discomfort	2 sets to discomfort	2 sets to discomfort	2-3 sets to high discomfort	2-3 sets to high discomfort	1-2 min.
4	Arm pulls/Front lat pull-downs	$\frac{50}{10}\,2$	$\frac{50}{12}\,2$	$\frac{60}{10}\,2$	$\frac{60}{12}\,2$	$\frac{70}{10}\,2$	$\frac{70}{12}\,2$	2 min.
5	Incline trunk twists (for each side)	2×10	2×10	2×12	2×12	3×12	3×12	1-2 min.
6	Bent-knee sit-ups	2 sets to slight discomfort	2 sets to slight discomfort	2-3 sets to discomfort	2-3 sets to discomfort	2-3 sets to high discomfort	2-3 sets to high discomfort	2 min.
7	Power ball (10 kg) side throws	2×12	2×12	2×15	2×15	3×15	3×15	1-2 min.
8	Toe raises	$\frac{60}{12}\,2$	$\frac{60}{12}\,2$	$\frac{60}{12}\,3$	$\frac{60}{12}\,3$	$\frac{70}{10}\,3$	$\frac{70}{12}\,3$	1-2 min.
9	Low-impact plyometrics	—	—	—	2×10	3×8	3×10	2-3 min.

Loading pattern			High			High
		Medium			Medium	
	Low			Low		

Figure 8.5 A suggested example of circuit training for baseball and softball and racket sports (such as tennis, squash, and racquetball) in which there are three specific exercises that target specific muscles for these sports.

Preventing Injuries in the Anatomical Adaptation Phase

Injury during sports training affects the future of many athletes. In the year 2000 in the United States alone, more than 150,000 soccer injuries occurred. Unfortunately, injuries are most common in team sports that attract young athletes. Many of these injuries could be avoided by introducing strength training with the purpose of promoting injury prevention. Continual education is extremely important, especially for coaches who work with young athletes whose bodies are in the process of maturing. Body weight strengthening exercises should be as much a part of the program as are technical and tactical skills of the sport.

In most young adult training programs, muscle strengthening is overemphasized and injury prevention is overlooked. Training ligament and tendons for the purpose of preventing injuries is often missing from a program simply because the anatomical adaptation phase is nonexistent. An improper periodization of strength, starting with a stressful hypertrophy phase, often results in higher incidents of injuries. Because the ligament–joint apparatus can become a limiting performance factor for many athletes, especially those with superficial strength training backgrounds, connective tissue adaptation should be the scope of every strength training program. Coaches should remember that muscle tissue adaptation takes a few days, whereas connective tissue adaptation (i.e., of ligaments and tendons) often takes several weeks or even months (McDonagh and Davies, 1984). This is why we are suggesting a longer AA phase for most athletes, that exercise prescription for the AA training has to focus not only on strengthening the muscles, but most importantly, to strengthen the connective tissues for the purpose of injury prevention. Recognizing this reality will serve coaches well during the maximum strength training phase, when the load is very challenging even for advanced athletes.

An important element in the quest to prevent injuries should be good flexibility exercises that are done religiously *at the end of the warm-up, during the rest interval performed after each exercise, and during the cool-down.* The joints emphasized have to be sport-specific, although shoulders, hips, knees, and ankles should also be considered. In addition, stretching the Achilles tendon (dorsiflexion, bringing the toes toward the bone tibia) will improve its range of motion.

Phase 2: Hypertrophy

Many people think that the larger a person is, the stronger that person is. This is not always the case. For example, a weightlifter may have a smaller body size yet be capable of lifting heavier loads than a larger, bulky-looking bodybuilder can lift. Rather than a large body, success in athletics requires a large, active, fat-free body mass. The greater the active body mass is, the greater the strength will be, because force depends on muscle density and diameter.

Bodybuilding hypertrophy and sport-specific hypertrophy differ in some important ways. In bodybuilding hypertrophy, the bodybuilder generally uses loads of 70 to 80 percent of 1RM for 9 to 12 reps. Some bodybuilders, however, attribute their success to low reps and high training loads, whereas others believe in performing as many reps as possible (usually in the 15- to 20-rep range). How can we know which method is correct, given that both types of bodybuilders are massively built and share similar records and numbers of wins?

Athletes and coaches of other sports must keep in mind that the purpose of bodybuilding is not optimal performance, but optimal symmetry. Although bodybuilders succeed in increasing muscle mass, the functionality of that muscle mass is questionable. Moreover, many bodybuilding routines, such as four- or five-day split routines or sometimes two workouts per day, do not allow for nervous system recovery and the recruitment of the fast-twitch muscle fibers that are integral to sport performance. Functionality—that is, improved performance—rather than increased muscle mass is the goal of athletics.

Sport-Specific Hypertrophy

The enlargement of muscle size (hypertrophy) for athletes in certain sports, such as throwers in track and field, linemen in America football, and heavyweight boxers and wrestlers, is best achieved by applying a sport-specific training methodology. Unlike bodybuilding, which focuses on enlarging overall musculature, hypertrophy training for sports focuses mainly on increasing the size of the specific prime movers by increasing the protein content of the striated muscles.

Symmetry is unrelated to sport and function is the main priority. Sport-specific hypertrophy is required in many sports but is achieved in different means than bodybuilding methods. Training for sport-specific hypertrophy requires heavy loads with minimal rest and high sets to increase the density (thickness) and amount of protein in the prime movers. Hypertrophy for sports must be chronic because an increase in muscle size cannot occur without an increase in strength. Moreover, many of the routines and methods used by bodybuilders such as four- or five-day split routines or sometimes two workouts per day do not allow for nervous system recovery and the recruitment of the fast-twitch muscle fibers that are integral to sport performance. Moreover, hypertrophy for sports stresses the use of compound, multijoint exercises that involve the prime movers with little concern for isolation exercises. Methods to maximize muscular exhaustion such as supersets and drop sets can be positively used to increase muscle strength and size.

Because improperly used bodybuilding techniques can be a handicap for most athletes, these techniques are used sparingly in sports training. Some athletes in a certain phase of strength development, for example, may benefit from bodybuilding methods. Because bodybuilding is relatively safe and employs moderately heavy loads, some novice athletes can use it, provided they do not work to exhaustion in each set. Also, athletes who want to move up a weight class in sports such as boxing, wrestling, and the martial arts may benefit from these techniques.

Program Design for Sport-Specific Hypertrophy Training

Like any other new training phase, hypertrophy training should begin with a test for 1RM. Athletes then start with a 70 to 80 percent load, or one that allows them to perform six reps. As they adapt to the load, they will progressively be capable of performing more reps. When they can perform 12 reps, the load is then increased to a level at which, again, they can perform only six reps. See table 9.1 for the training parameters of the hypertrophy phase.

Table 9.1 Training Parameters for the Hypertrophy Phase

Training Parameters	Work
Duration of hypertrophy phase	4-6 weeks
Load	70-80 percent
Number of exercises	6-9
Number of repetitions per set	6-12
Number of sets per session	4-6 (8)
Rest interval	3-5 minutes
Speed of execution	Slow to medium
Frequency per week	2-4

To achieve maximum training benefits, athletes must reach the highest number of reps possible in each set. This means reaching a degree of exhaustion that prevents them from doing the last rep, even when they are applying maximum contraction. Without performing each individual set to exhaustion, athletes will not achieve the expected level of muscle hypertrophy because the first reps do not produce the stimulus necessary to increase muscle mass. Thus, the key element in hypertrophy training is the cumulative effect of exhaustion in the total number of sets, not just exhaustion per set. This cumulative exhaustion stimulates the chemical reactions and protein metabolism in the body so that optimal muscle hypertrophy will be achieved.

Hypertrophy exercises should be performed at low to moderate speed to maximize the muscles' time under tension; however, athletes in sports in which speed or power is dominant are strongly advised against slow speed of execution, especially if the hypertrophy phase is longer than six weeks. The primary reason is that the neuromuscular system will adapt to a slow execution and, as a result, will not provide the stimulation for the recruitment of fast-twitch muscle fibers that is so crucial for speed- and power-dominant sports.

Unlike bodybuilding, hypertrophy training for athletics involves a lower number of exercises so as to involve mainly the prime movers and not all muscle groups. The benefit of such an approach is that more sets are performed per exercise (four to six or even as many as eight), thus stimulating better muscle hypertrophy for the prime movers.

Depending on the microcycle, the rest interval between sets can vary from three to five minutes. The closer the athlete gets to switching to a maximum strength phase of training, the longer the rest interval between sets must be. For instance, in a four- to six-week hypertrophy phase of training, the first one or two (or three) weeks can be used to stimulate maximum hypertrophy gains by using short rest periods (60 to 90 seconds between sets), and the last two or three weeks can use longer rest periods. Unlike other phases of training, hypertrophy training allows more room for changes in training methods.

During the rest interval of three to five minutes (which is longer than in bodybuilding), and at the end of the training session, athletes should stretch the muscles worked. Because of the many repetitions of contractions, the muscles shorten, which in turn produces premature inhibition of contraction of the antagonist muscles. This results in reduced muscle range of motion and decreased quickness of contraction, which affects the overall performance ability of the muscles involved. To overcome this effect, athletes should constantly stretch their muscles to artificially lengthen them to their biological length. In addition, a shortened muscle has a slower rate of regeneration because only the normal biological length facilitates active biochemical exchanges. These exchanges provide nutrients to the muscles and remove the metabolic wastes, facilitating better recovery between sets and after training sessions.

Figure 9.1 shows a sample six-week program developed for a heavyweight wrestler. The program suggested in each box was repeated four times a week. Table 9.2 shows a six-week hypertrophy training program for a female college basketball player who had a relatively large disproportion between height and weight. This phase was followed by a maximum strength and power phase, and the player was ready for the league games in early fall. At the end of the summer program, she had gained 14 pounds (6.3 kilograms) and had superior levels of maximum strength and power, factors that helped her visibly improve her game. Table 9.3 shows a sample hypertrophy program for an ice hockey player who wanted to gain muscle mass. Because the player had only three weeks available for training, the schedule was intensive, six days a week. The first eight exercises were performed on days 1, 3, and 5, and the next eight exercises were performed on days 2, 4, and 6.

No.	Exercise	Week 1	Week 2	Week 3	Week 4	Week 5	Week 6
1	Half squats	$\frac{60}{12}3$	$\frac{60}{12}4$	$\frac{70}{10}4$	$\frac{60}{12}3$	$\frac{75}{10}4$	$\frac{80}{8}4$
2	Seated rows	$\frac{60}{12}3$	$\frac{60}{12}4$	$\frac{70}{10}4$	$\frac{60}{12}3$	$\frac{75}{10}4$	$\frac{80}{8}4$
3	Twisted abdominals	3 × 15	3 × 18	4 × 12	4 × 12	4 × 15	4 × 18
4	Leg curls	$\frac{60}{10}3$	$\frac{60}{8}4$	$\frac{70}{8}3$	$\frac{60}{8}3$	$\frac{60}{8}4$	$\frac{70}{8}4$
5	Deadlifts	$\frac{60}{10}3$	$\frac{60}{8}4$	$\frac{70}{8}3$	$\frac{60}{8}3$	$\frac{60}{8}4$	$\frac{70}{8}4$
6	Bench press	$\frac{60}{12}3$	$\frac{60}{12}4$	$\frac{70}{10}4$	$\frac{60}{10}3$	$\frac{75}{10}4$	$\frac{80}{8}4$
7	Lateral deltoid raises	$\frac{60}{10}3$	$\frac{60}{8}4$	$\frac{70}{8}3$	$\frac{60}{8}3$	$\frac{60}{8}4$	$\frac{70}{8}4$
8	Shoulder shrugs	$\frac{60}{12}3$	$\frac{60}{12}4$	$\frac{70}{10}4$	$\frac{60}{12}3$	$\frac{75}{10}4$	$\frac{80}{10}4$
9	Toe raises	$\frac{60}{15}3$	$\frac{60}{15}4$	$\frac{70}{12}4$	$\frac{70}{10}3$	$\frac{75}{12}4$	$\frac{80}{10}4$
10	Lat pull-downs	$\frac{60}{12}3$	$\frac{60}{12}4$	$\frac{70}{10}4$	$\frac{60}{12}3$	$\frac{75}{10}4$	$\frac{80}{10}4$
11	Cleans	$\frac{60}{12}3$	$\frac{60}{12}4$	$\frac{70}{12}4$	$\frac{60}{12}3$	$\frac{75}{12}4$	$\frac{80}{10}4$

Loading pattern			High			High
	Low	Medium		Low	Medium	

Figure 9.1 Example loading pattern for a 6-week training program for the hypertrophy phase for a wrestler (heavyweight category).

Table 9.2 6-Week Hypertrophy Program for a Female College Basketball Player

Exercise	Dates					
	May 13-19	May 20-26	May 27-June 2	June 3-9	June 10-16	June 17-23
Leg presses	$\frac{60}{10}3$	$\frac{60}{12}3$	$\frac{60}{15}3$	$\frac{60}{10}3$	$\frac{60}{15}1\ \frac{70}{12}2$	$\frac{70}{12}3$
Abdominal curls	3 × 15	3 × 18	3 × 20	3 × 15	3 × 18	3 × 20
Incline bench presses	$\frac{60}{10}3$	$\frac{60}{12}3$	$\frac{60}{15}3$	$\frac{60}{10}3$	$\frac{60}{15}1\ \frac{70}{12}2$	$\frac{70}{12}3$
Leg curls	$\frac{60}{10}3$	$\frac{60}{12}3$	$\frac{60}{15}3$	$\frac{60}{10}3$	$\frac{60}{15}1\ \frac{70}{12}2$	$\frac{70}{12}3$
Shoulder shrugs	$\frac{60}{10}3$	$\frac{60}{12}3$	$\frac{60}{15}3$	$\frac{60}{10}3$	$\frac{60}{15}1\ \frac{70}{12}2$	$\frac{70}{12}3$
Toe raises	$\frac{60}{15}3$	$\frac{60}{15}1\ \frac{70}{12}2$	$\frac{70}{15}3$	$\frac{60}{15}3$	$\frac{70}{15}3$	$\frac{70}{18}3$
Lat pull-downs (front)	$\frac{60}{10}3$	$\frac{60}{12}3$	$\frac{60}{15}3$	$\frac{60}{10}3$	$\frac{60}{15}1\ \frac{70}{12}2$	$\frac{70}{12}3$
Preacher curls	$\frac{60}{10}3$	$\frac{60}{12}3$	$\frac{60}{15}3$	$\frac{60}{10}3$	$\frac{60}{15}1\ \frac{70}{12}2$	$\frac{70}{12}3$

Note: RI = 1 minute between sets.

Table 9.3 Hypertrophy Program for an Ice Hockey Player

Day	Week no. 1			Week no. 2			Week no. 3		
	1	3	5	1	3	5	1	3	5
Half squats	$\frac{60}{12}$ 3	$\frac{60}{12}$ 3	$\frac{60}{10}$ 4	$\frac{70}{10}$ 4	$\frac{70}{10}$ 4	$\frac{70}{10}$ 4	$\frac{80}{8}$ 4	$\frac{80}{10}$ 4	$\frac{80}{12}$ 4
Trunk seated rows	$\frac{60}{12}$ 3	$\frac{60}{12}$ 3	$\frac{60}{10}$ 4	$\frac{70}{10}$ 4	$\frac{70}{10}$ 4	$\frac{70}{10}$ 4	$\frac{80}{8}$ 4	$\frac{80}{10}$ 4	$\frac{80}{12}$ 4
Hip extensions	$\frac{60}{12}$ 3	$\frac{60}{12}$ 3	$\frac{60}{10}$ 4	$\frac{70}{10}$ 4	$\frac{70}{10}$ 5	$\frac{70}{10}$ 5	$\frac{80}{6-8}$ 5	$\frac{80}{8}$ 5	$\frac{80}{8}$ 5
Standing calf raises	$\frac{60}{12}$ 3	$\frac{70}{12}$ 3	$\frac{70}{12}$ 3	$\frac{70}{12}$ 4	$\frac{70}{10}$ 5	$\frac{70}{12}$ 5	$\frac{80}{8}$ 5	$\frac{80}{8}$ 5	$\frac{80}{8}$ 5
Deadlifts	$\frac{60}{10}$ 3	$\frac{60}{10}$ 4	$\frac{60}{12}$ 4	$\frac{70}{10}$ 4	$\frac{70}{8-10}$ 5	$\frac{70}{10}$ 5	$\frac{70}{6-8}$ 6	$\frac{70}{8}$ 6	$\frac{70}{8-10}$ 6
Twisted abdominals	3 × 15	3 × 15	3 × 15	4 × 12	4 × 12	4 × 12	5 × 10	5 × 10	5 × 12
Trunk extensions	3 × 15	3 × 17	3 × 17	4 × 15	4 × 15	5 × 12	5 × 15	5 × 15	5 × 15
Leg curls	$\frac{50}{8}$ 3	$\frac{50}{8}$ 3	$\frac{50}{10}$ 3	$\frac{60}{8}$ 3	$\frac{60}{8}$ 3	$\frac{60}{10}$ 3	$\frac{60}{8}$ 4	$\frac{60}{8}$ 4	$\frac{60}{10}$ 4

Day	Week no. 1			Week no. 2			Week no. 3		
	2	4	6	2	4	6	2	4	6
Shoulder shrugs	$\frac{60}{8-10}$ 3	$\frac{60}{10}$ 3	$\frac{60}{10}$ 3	$\frac{70}{10}$ 4	$\frac{70}{10}$ 4	$\frac{70}{10}$ 4	$\frac{80}{8}$ 4	$\frac{80}{10}$ 4	$\frac{80}{10}$ 4
Bench presses	$\frac{60}{8}$ 3	$\frac{60}{10}$ 3	$\frac{60}{10}$ 3	$\frac{60}{8}$ 3	$\frac{60}{10}$ 4	$\frac{60}{12}$ 4	$\frac{60}{12}$ 4	$\frac{70}{10}$ 4	$\frac{70}{12}$ 4
Preacher curls	$\frac{60}{8}$ 3	$\frac{60}{10}$ 3	$\frac{60}{12}$ 3	$\frac{60}{8}$ 3	$\frac{60}{10}$ 3	$\frac{60}{10}$ 4	$\frac{60}{12}$ 4	$\frac{60}{12}$ 4	$\frac{70}{10}$ 4
Lateral deltoid raises (elbow flexion)	$\frac{60}{8}$ 3	$\frac{60}{8}$ 4	$\frac{60}{8}$ 4	$\frac{70}{8}$ 4	$\frac{70}{8}$ 4	$\frac{70}{8-10}$ 5	$\frac{80}{6-8}$ 4	$\frac{80}{8}$ 5	$\frac{80}{8}$ 6
Triceps cable extensions	$\frac{60}{8}$ 3	$\frac{60}{8}$ 4	$\frac{60}{8}$ 4	$\frac{70}{8}$ 4	$\frac{70}{8}$ 4	$\frac{70}{8}$ 5	$\frac{80}{6}$ 4	$\frac{80}{8}$ 5	$\frac{80}{8}$ 6
Lat pull-downs (front)	$\frac{60}{12}$ 3	$\frac{60}{12}$ 3	$\frac{60}{12}$ 4	$\frac{70}{12}$ 4	$\frac{70}{12}$ 4	$\frac{70}{10}$ 5	$\frac{80}{6-8}$ 4	$\frac{80}{8}$ 4	$\frac{80}{8}$ 4
Seated military presses	$\frac{60}{12}$ 3	$\frac{60}{12}$ 3	$\frac{60}{12}$ 4	$\frac{70}{12}$ 4	$\frac{70}{12}$ 4	$\frac{70}{10}$ 5	$\frac{80}{6}$ 4	$\frac{80}{8}$ 4	$\frac{80}{8}$ 4
Seated rows	$\frac{60}{12}$ 3	$\frac{60}{12}$ 3	$\frac{60}{12}$ 4	$\frac{70}{12}$ 4	$\frac{70}{12}$ 4	$\frac{70}{10}$ 5	$\frac{80}{6}$ 4	$\frac{80}{8}$ 4	$\frac{80}{8}$ 4

Note: RI = 1 minute, except for standing calf raises, where it is 30 seconds.

Variations of Bodybuilding Hypertrophy

Hypertrophy training is intended for athletes for whom an increase in muscle size will help performance in their sport. Such athletes include football linemen and track and field athletes participating in shot put and discus events to name a few. Refer to chapter 7 for a detailed look at the periodization of strength model for your sport. To simplify hypertrophy training, we have broken it down into two phases: hypertrophy I and hypertrophy II. Hypertrophy I refers to sport-specific hypertrophy, whereas hypertrophy II uses various bodybuilding techniques to optimize muscle exhaustion and growth. Having discussed hypertrophy I at some length, we offer a more in-depth explanation of hypertrophy II methods in this section.

Athletes and coaches should be cautious when incorporating hypertrophy II methods into a training program. The physical maturity of the athlete and timing in the yearly training program must be taken into consideration. Hypertrophy II bodybuilding training methods work very well during the early preparatory season to help stimulate muscular fitness and the improvement of lean muscle mass. Sport-specific hypertrophy I techniques, on the other hand, should be implemented late in the preparatory season. Regardless of which method of hypertrophy is employed in training, multijoint exercises such as squats and leg presses, bench presses, back rows, chin-ups, dips, and core exercises should make up the majority of the program. Isolation exercises should be kept to a minimum.

Because reps to exhaustion represent the main element of success in bodybuilding, several variations of the original method were developed. They all have the same objective in that when exhaustion is reached, two or three more reps must be attained through hard work. The expected result is greater muscle growth, or increased hypertrophy.

Of the total number of variations (more than 20), the following are considered the most representative.

Split Routine In bodybuilding, athletes perform two or three exercises per muscle group. Because they address every muscle of the body, they may be in the gymnasium for at least half a day to finish the entire program. Even if athletes have the energy to do this, time constraints are an important limitation. The solution is to divide the total volume of work into parts and address one part of the body each day, hence the term *split routine*. This means that even if an athlete trains five or six times a week, an actual muscle group is worked only once or twice a week.

Assisted Repetitions As an athlete performs a set to temporary exhaustion of the neuromuscular system, a partner can assist by providing sufficient support to enable two or three more reps.

Resisted Repetitions In resisted repetitions, the athlete performs a set to temporary exhaustion. The partner then assists the athlete in performing two or three more reps concentrically while providing some resistance during the eccentric segment of contraction for each additional rep (hence the term *resisted repetitions*). As such, the eccentric part of the contraction is performed twice as long as the concentric part, which overloads the muscles involved beyond the standard level.

Athletes who perform resisted repetitions should be forewarned that the longer the active muscle fibers are held in tension, the higher the nervous tension and energy expenditure will be. If normal contraction time is two to four seconds, a repetition performed against resistance can be six to eight seconds long, consuming 20 to 40 percent more energy (Hartmann and Tünnemann, 1988). Because the muscles are held in tension longer, the muscles' metabolism is more strongly activated, which stimulates muscle growth beyond standard norms.

Supersets   In the superset, an athlete performs a set for the agonist muscles of a given joint, followed without a rest period by a set for the antagonist muscles (e.g., an elbow flexion followed immediately by an elbow extension).

Resisted repetitions and supersets should be performed only by experienced athletes with a lengthy training background because of the higher demands in training.

Variation   The athlete performs a set to exhaustion and, after 20 to 30 seconds, follows with another set for the same muscle group. Of course, because of exhaustion, the athlete may be unable to perform the same number of reps in the second set as he performed in the first.

Preexhaustion   This method is based on two premises. First, before large-muscle groups are contracted, the small muscles have to be preexhausted so that during the actual work, the entire load is taken only by the large-muscle groups. Second, before performing a set involving two or three joints (e.g., half squats), the muscles of a given joint have to be prefatigued and then further exhausted in the complete motion of all the other joints.

The preexhaustion method probably evolved from weightlifting and was then used in bodybuilding. Like the superset, preexhaustion is not yet proven and is still at the stage of speculation.

Bodybuilding workouts, even those using the split routine, are very exhausting; often 75 to 160 reps are performed in a single training session. Such high muscle loading requires a long recovery. Because of the type of work specific to bodybuilding, most if not all the ATP-CP and glycogen stores are exhausted after a demanding training session. Although the restoration of ATP-CP occurs very quickly, the exhausted liver glycogen requires 46 to 48 hours to replenish. Thus, heavy workouts to complete exhaustion should not be performed more than three times per microcycle (refer to the discussion of microcycle planning in chapter 6 for intensity variations).

Some may argue that athletes using the split routine train a group of muscles every second day, leaving 48 hours between the two training sessions, which is sufficient for the restoration of energy fuels. Although this may be true for local muscle stores, it ignores the fact that when glucose is exhausted, the body starts tapping the glycogen stores in the liver. If the liver source is tapped every day, 24 hours may be insufficient to restore glycogen. This may result in the overtraining phenomenon.

In addition to exhausting energy stores, constant training also puts wear and tear on the contractile proteins, exceeding their anabolism (the myosin's protein-building rate). A high protein supplement following a strenuous workout can help shift the body from a state of muscle breakdown to a state of synthesis (see chapter 7). The undesirable outcome of such overloading can be that the muscles involved no longer increase in size (i.e., there are no gains in hypertrophy). When this happens, coaches should reassess the application of the overloading principle and start using the step-type method as suggested by the principle of progressive increases of load in training. In addition, they should consider alternating the intensities each microcycle to facilitate regeneration, which is just as important as training. A workout is only as good as an athlete's ability to recover from it

As specified, the duration of the hypertrophy phase can be four to six weeks depending on the needs of the sport or event and the athlete. If both hypertrophy I and II training methods are used, hypertrophy II should be used early in the preparatory season. The total length of the preparatory phase is also important because the longer it is, the more time the athlete has to work on hypertrophy as well as maximum strength.

The end of the hypertrophy phase does not mean that an athlete who needs to build muscle mass must stop this training. As illustrated in table 9.4, hypertrophy training can be maintained and even further developed during the maximum strength phase. As such, depending on the needs of the athlete, the proportion between maximum strength training and hypertrophy training can be 3 to 1, 2 to 1, or even 1 to 1.

Table 9.4   Suggested Proportion Between Hypertrophy, Maximum Strength, and Power for Linemen

Preparatory				Competitive
3	4	6	5	
AA	Hypertrophy: 3-4 sessions	MxS: 2-3 sessions Hypertrophy: 1-2 sessions	Conv. to power: 2 sessions MxS: 1 session Hypertrophy: 1 session	Maintenance: Power, MxS, Hypertrophy

During the maintenance phase, only athletes such as shot-putters and linemen in American football should continue hypertrophy training, and then only during the first half. As the most important competitions approach, power and maximum strength training should prevail.

Bodybuilding books and magazines often refer to many other methods, some of which are said to "work miracles" for athletes. Coaches and athletes should take care to distinguish the fine line that separates fact from fantasy.

Phase 3: Maximum Strength

Nearly every sport requires strength, but what each sport really calls for is sport-specific strength. Maximum strength plays an important, if not the determinant, role in creating sport-specific strength. Although the role of maximum strength varies between sports, it mainly determines the length of the phase. The more important the role of maximum strength is (it is quite important for throwers in track and field and linemen in American football, for example), the longer the maximum strength phase will be (the opposite is true if the final performance is not particularly dependent on the maximum strength contribution, e.g., golf, table tennis). An athlete's ability to generate maximum strength depends to a great extent on the diameter or cross-sectional area of the muscle involved (more specifically, the diameter of the myosin filaments, including their cross-bridges); the capacity to recruit fast-twitch muscle fibers; and the ability to synchronize all the muscles involved in an action.

Muscle size depends greatly on the duration of the hypertrophy phase, but the increase in protein content in the form of cross-bridges and in particular the diameter of myosin filament depends on the volume and duration of the maximum strength phase. The capacity to recruit fast-twitch fibers depends on training content, in which maximum loads and explosive power should be dominant. This is the only type of strength training that activates the powerful fast-twitch motor units. Improving muscle synchronization depends strictly on learning, which requires many reps of the same exercise.

Strength improves as a result of creating high tension in the muscle, which is directly related to the training method employed. Maximum strength increases as a result of activating a large number of fast-twitch motor units. An athlete does not necessarily have to develop large muscles and high body weight to become significantly stronger.

The maximum strength phase helps triathletes to build lean muscle for peak performance.

Throughout maximum strength and power training, athletes learn to better synchronize the muscles involved and use loads that result in higher fast-twitch muscle fiber recruitment (loads greater than 85 percent). By using the methods for the maximum strength phase outlined in this chapter, especially the maximum load method, athletes will improve maximum strength with insignificant gains in muscle mass.

Of the three types of muscle contractions, eccentric contractions create the highest tension, followed by isometric and concentric. Concentric strength must be developed at the highest levels because most sport actions are concentric. Strength increases in one form of contraction will result in an increase in performance of the other contractions. Thus, the direct application of other forms of contractions such as isometric and especially eccentric will directly benefit athletic performance by supporting further improvements in concentric force.

Exercises used for the development of maximum strength are not performed under conditions of exhaustion as in bodybuilding. Because of the maximum activation of the central nervous system (CNS), including factors such as concentration and motivation, maximum strength training improves links with the CNS, thus improving muscle coordination and synchronization. High CNS activation (e.g., muscle synchronization) also results in adequate inhibition of the antagonist muscles. This means that when maximum force is applied, these muscles are coordinated in such a way that they do not contract to oppose the movement.

Little is known about the involvement of the CNS in maximum strength. Rising interest in the implications of the CNS in strength training suggests that the CNS acts as a stimulus for strength gains. The CNS normally inhibits the activation of all the motor units available for contraction. Under extreme circumstances, such as fear or life-and-death situations, the inhibition is removed and all the motor units are activated (Fox, Bowes, and Foss, 1989). One of the main objectives of maximum strength training is to learn to eliminate CNS inhibition. A reduction in CNS inhibition accompanied by an increase in strength results in the greatest improvement in performance potential.

Maximum Load Method (Isotonic)

In periodization of strength, the maximum load method of improving maximum strength is probably the most effective way to develop sport-specific strength, for the following reasons:

■ It increases motor unit activation, resulting in high recruitment of fast-twitch muscle fibers.

■ It represents the determinant factor in increasing power. As such, it has a high neural output for sports in which speed and power are dominant.

■ It is a critical element in improving muscular endurance, especially muscular endurance of short and medium duration.

■ It is important in sports in which relative strength is crucial, such as the martial arts, boxing, wrestling, jumping events, and most team sports because it results in a minimal increase in hypertrophy. (Relative strength is the relationship between body weight and maximum strength, meaning that the higher the relative strength is, the better the performance will be.)

■ It improves the coordination and synchronization of muscle groups during performance. The maximum load method has a learning component because, in physical actions, the muscles are involved in a certain sequence. The better the muscles involved in contraction are coordinated and synchronized and the more they learn to recruit fast-twitch muscle fibers, the better the performance is.

The maximum load method positively influences speed- and power-dominant sports by increasing the myosin diameter of the fast-twitch fibers and recruiting more fast-twitch fibers. This method can result in maximum strength gains that are up to three times greater than the proportional gain in muscle hypertrophy. Although large increases in muscle size are possible for athletes who are just starting to use the maximum load method, they are less visible in athletes with longer training backgrounds. The greatest gains in maximum strength occur as a result of better synchronization and increased recruitment of the fast-twitch muscle fibers.

The main factors responsible for hypertrophy are not fully understood, but researchers increasingly believe that increased muscle size is stimulated mainly by a disturbance in the equilibrium between the consumption and remanufacture of ATP known as the *ATP deficiency theory* (Hartmann and Tünnemann, 1988). During and immediately following maximum strength training, the protein content in the working muscles is low, if not exhausted, as a result of the depletion of ATP. As an athlete recovers between training sessions, the protein level exceeds the initial level, resulting in an increase in the size of the muscle fiber, especially if the athlete follows a protein-rich diet.

Loads of 80 to 90 percent seem to be the most effective. Equally important, though, is a long enough rest interval to facilitate the full restoration of ATP-CP. Higher loads of 85 to 100 percent, which permit only two to four reps, are of short duration and allow complete restoration of ATP. As such, the ATP deficiency and the depletion of structural protein are too low to activate the protein metabolism that stimulates hypertrophy. Consequently, maximum loads with long rest intervals result in an increase in maximum strength, and not in hypertrophy.

The maximum load method also increases testosterone level, which further explains improved maximum strength. Male athletes have better trainability than female athletes because of their higher levels of testosterone. During the maximum strength phase, the testosterone level increases only in the first eight weeks and then decreases, although it is still higher than at the start (Häkkinen, 1991). This is one reason for limiting the maximum strength phases to no longer than nine weeks. Apparently the level of testosterone in the blood also depends on the frequency of maximum load method sessions per day and week. Testosterone increases when the number of these sessions per week is low and decreases when maximum load training occurs twice a day. Such findings substantiate and further justify the suggestions made earlier regarding the frequency of high-intensity training sessions per microcycle.

Program Design for the Maximum Load Method

The maximum load method can be used only after a minimum of two years of general strength training (anatomical adaptation) using lighter loads. Strength gains can be expected even during long-term anatomical adaptation, mainly because of the motor learning that occurs as athletes learn to better use and coordinate the muscles involved in training.

Highly trained athletes with three to four years of maximum load training are so well adapted to such training that they are able to recruit some 85 percent of their fast-twitch fibers. The remaining 15 percent represents a "latent reserve" that is not easily tapped through training (Hartmann and Tünnemann, 1988). Once an athlete reaches such a level, further increases in maximum strength may be difficult to achieve. If further maximum strength development is necessary, alternate methods must be found to overcome this stagnation and continue improvement. New options include the following:

- Apply the principle of progressive increase of load in training. Every athlete who has done so has experienced improvements without the pain of exhaustion.

- Immediately begin a yearly plan for strength training based on the concept of periodization. By following this phase-specific training method, athletes will achieve the highest sport-specific strength at the time of the main competitions or league games.

- If an athlete has used periodization of training for two to four years and cannot overcome a plateau, alternate various stimulations of the neuromuscular system. Following anatomical adaptation and the first phase of maximum strength training, athletes should alternate three weeks of maximum strength training with three weeks of power training. Power training, with its explosiveness and fast application of force, will stimulate the CNS.

- For power sports, another option can be used for stimulation: Alternate three weeks of hypertrophy training with three weeks of maximum strength training. The additional hypertrophy phases will result in a slight enlargement in muscle size or an increase in "active muscle mass." This additional gain in hypertrophy will provide a new biological base for further improvement of maximum strength.

- Increase the ratio between concentric and eccentric types of contraction (see chapter 12). The additional eccentric training will produce a higher stimulation for maximum strength improvement because eccentric contraction creates higher tension in the muscle.

Among the most important elements of success for maximum load method training are the load used, the loading pattern, and the rhythm or speed of performing the contraction.

Load

Maximum strength is developed only by creating the highest tension possible in the muscle. Although lower loads engage slow-twitch muscle fibers, if most muscle fibers, especially fast-twitch fibers, are to be recruited in contraction, loads greater than 85 percent are necessary. Maximum loads with low reps result in significant CNS adaptation, better synchronization of the muscles involved, and an increased capacity to recruit fast-twitch fibers. That is why maximum strength and explosive power are also called nervous system training (Schmidtbleicher, 1984). If, as Goldberg and colleagues (1975) suggested, the stimulus for protein synthesis is the tension developed in the myofilaments, it is further proof that maximum strength training should be carried out only with maximum load.

To produce the highest maximum strength improvements, the prime movers must do the greatest amount of work. Coaches should plan training sessions with the highest number of sets the athlete can tolerate (8 to 12). Because this is possible only with a low number of exercises (no more than five), they should choose only exercises for the prime movers and resist the temptation to use higher numbers of exercises.

Ordering exercises to ensure better alternation of muscle groups will facilitate local muscle recovery between sets. Two approaches exist regarding the sequence of performing exercises to maximize muscle group involvement. Some prefer to perform one set of each exercise starting from the top (vertically). Others choose to perform all sets for the first exercise before moving on to the next (horizontally; see table 10.1). The vertical approach provides better recovery between sets and less fatigue. Minimizing fatigue is important because, in most sports, strength training is just one of the elements that lead to better performance. Thus, attention must be paid to how energy is spent, especially during the competitive phase. The overall fatigue experienced in training must also be considered. The horizontal approach is discouraged because it results in higher local fatigue and exhausts the muscles much faster. Working the muscles in a state of exhaustion results in hypertrophy rather than maximum strength. Maximum strength benefits only during the early sets; once exhaustion is reached, muscle mass benefits. When reviewing an athlete's progress and progression to the next platform of training, coaches should always decrease sets instead of decreasing intensity, depending on the athlete's gains in strength.

Table 10.1 Training Parameters for the Maximum Load Method

Training parameters	Work
Load	85-100 percent
Number of exercises	3-5
Number of repetitions per set	1-4
Number of sets per session	6-10 (12)
Rest interval	3-6 minutes
Frequency per week	2-3 (4)

Because a maximum load is used in maximum load training, the number of reps per set is low (one to four), and the suggested number of reps per exercise for a training session is between 15 and 80. The number of reps per exercise varies depending on the athlete's classification, training background, and training phase. To stimulate the necessary physiological and morphological CNS changes, a higher number of sets should always take precedence over a higher number of reps. Hartmann and Tünnemann (1988) proposed the following number of reps per exercise per training session for highly trained athletes:

- 100 to 95 percent: 15 to 25 reps
- 95 to 90 percent: 20 to 40 reps
- 90 to 80 percent: 35 to 85 reps
- 80 to 75 percent: 70 to 110 reps

The number of exercises dictates whether to use the lower or higher number of reps. Athletes performing four exercises should use the lower number; those performing two exercises, the higher number. If the number of reps is much lower than recommended, maximum strength benefits will seriously decline. These suggestions should reinforce the wisdom of selecting a low number of exercises. The lower the number of exercises, the more sets and reps can be performed and the greater the maximum strength improvement per muscle group.

The rest interval between sets is a function of the athlete's fitness level and should be calculated to ensure adequate recovery of the neuromuscular system. For the maximum load method, a three- to six-minute rest interval is necessary because maximum loads involve the CNS, which takes longer to recover. If the rest interval is much shorter, CNS participation in terms of maximum concentration, motivation, and the power of nerve impulses sent to the contracting muscles could plummet. Complete restoration of the required fuel for contraction (ATP-CP) may also be jeopardized.

Speed of Contraction

Speed of contraction plays an important role in maximum load training. Athletic movements are often performed fast and explosively. To maximize speed, the entire neuromuscular system must adapt to quickly recruiting fast-twitch fibers, a key factor in all sports dominated by speed and power. Even with the maximum loads typical of the maximum load method, the athlete's force application against resistance must be exerted as quickly as possible, even explosively.

To achieve explosive force, the athlete must maximize concentration and motivation before each set. The athlete must concentrate on activating the muscles quickly even though the barbell is moving slowly. Only a high speed of contraction performed against a maximum load will quickly recruit fast-twitch fibers, resulting in increased maximum strength. For maximum training benefits, athletes must mobilize all strength potentials in the shortest time possible and from the early part of the lift.

Considering the high demand placed on the neuromuscular system, maximum load training should occur no more than two or three times a week. Only elite athletes, particularly linemen in American football or shot-putters in track and field, should train four times a week. During the competitive phase, the frequency can be reduced to one or two maximum load sessions per week, often in combination with other strength components such as power.

Figure 10.1 shows the maximum strength phase of a strength training program for Olympic-class sprinters. To better exemplify the step method for load increment, the bottom of the chart graphically illustrates the step method loading pattern. This nine-week program was repeated twice a year because sprinters usually follow a bi-cycle yearly plan. Program weeks are numbered from 1 to 9. A testing session was planned in each of the low steps and was performed in the latter part of the week when the athlete had better recovered from the strain of a high step. Obviously, the goal of the test was to determine the new 100 percent (1RM) and then use it to calculate the load for the following three-week cycle. The discrepancy in the number of sets is a result of the fact that some exercises are a high priority and others are a lower priority. This way, most of the energy and attention are focused on the high-priority exercises.

The load is lower for leg curls than for most exercises simply because the knee flexors are often more prone to injury, not because this exercise represents a lower priority. In addition, the athlete had not reached a balanced development between knee extensors and flexors at that point. Notice that for the low step, the load is always decreased and the number of sets reduced. Figure 10.2 shows a six-week maximum strength program for a women's volleyball team (college level). In the program, force was applied aggressively, without jerking or snapping. During the rest interval, the limbs used were shaken to relax the muscles. Dumbbells were used for deadlifts. The program was repeated three times a week.

No.	Exercise	T	Week 1	Week 2	Week 3	T	Week 4	Week 5	Week 6	T	Week 7	Week 8	Week 9
1	Half squats	✓	$\frac{70}{8}_1$ $\frac{80}{6}_2$	$\frac{80}{6}_2$ $\frac{85}{5}_3$ $\frac{90}{3}_1$	$\frac{85}{5}_2$ $\frac{90}{3}_3$ $\frac{95}{2}_1$	✓	$\frac{80}{6}_2$ $\frac{85}{4}_1$	$\frac{85}{5}_2$ $\frac{90}{3}_3$ $\frac{95}{2}_1$	$\frac{90}{3}_2$ $\frac{95}{2}_2$ $\frac{100}{1}_2$	✓	$\frac{80}{6}_3$	$\frac{85}{5}_1$ $\frac{90}{3}_3$ $\frac{95}{2}_2$	$\frac{90}{3}_2$ $\frac{95}{2}_3$ $\frac{100}{1}_2$
2	Arm pulls	✓	$\frac{70}{8}_1$ $\frac{80}{6}_2$	$\frac{80}{6}_2$ $\frac{85}{5}_3$ $\frac{90}{3}_1$	$\frac{85}{5}_2$ $\frac{90}{3}_3$ $\frac{95}{2}_1$	✓	$\frac{80}{6}_2$ $\frac{85}{4}_1$	$\frac{85}{5}_2$ $\frac{90}{3}_3$ $\frac{95}{2}_1$	$\frac{90}{3}_2$ $\frac{95}{2}_2$ $\frac{100}{1}_2$	✓	$\frac{80}{6}_3$	$\frac{85}{5}_1$ $\frac{90}{3}_3$ $\frac{95}{2}_2$	$\frac{90}{3}_2$ $\frac{95}{2}_3$ $\frac{100}{1}_2$
3	Leg curls	✓	$\frac{60}{12}_1$ $\frac{70}{10}_2$	$\frac{60}{12}_1$ $\frac{70}{10}_2$ $\frac{80}{6}_2$	$\frac{70}{8}_2$ $\frac{80}{6}_3$ $\frac{85}{4}_2$	✓	$\frac{70}{8}_3$	$\frac{70}{8}_1$ $\frac{80}{6}_2$ $\frac{85}{5}_3$	$\frac{80}{6}_1$ $\frac{85}{5}_2$ $\frac{90}{3}_2$	✓	$\frac{80}{5}_3$	$\frac{80}{6}_1$ $\frac{85}{5}_3$ $\frac{90}{3}_2$	$\frac{85}{5}_2$ $\frac{90}{3}_2$ $\frac{95}{2}_2$
4	Reverse leg press	✓	$\frac{70}{8}_2$ $\frac{80}{6}_2$	$\frac{80}{6}_2$ $\frac{85}{5}_3$ $\frac{90}{3}_1$	$\frac{85}{5}_2$ $\frac{90}{3}_3$ $\frac{95}{2}_1$	✓	$\frac{80}{6}_2$ $\frac{85}{4}_1$	$\frac{85}{5}_2$ $\frac{90}{3}_3$ $\frac{95}{2}_1$	$\frac{90}{3}_2$ $\frac{95}{2}_2$ $\frac{100}{1}_2$	✓	$\frac{80}{6}_3$	$\frac{85}{5}_1$ $\frac{90}{3}_3$ $\frac{95}{2}_2$	$\frac{90}{3}_2$ $\frac{95}{2}_3$ $\frac{100}{1}_2$
5	Bench press	✓	$\frac{70}{8}_2$ $\frac{80}{6}_2$	$\frac{80}{6}_2$ $\frac{85}{5}_3$ $\frac{90}{3}_1$	$\frac{85}{5}_2$ $\frac{90}{3}_3$ $\frac{95}{2}_1$	✓	$\frac{80}{6}_2$ $\frac{85}{4}_1$	$\frac{85}{5}_2$ $\frac{90}{3}_3$ $\frac{95}{2}_1$	$\frac{90}{3}_2$ $\frac{95}{2}_2$ $\frac{100}{1}_2$	✓	$\frac{80}{6}_3$	$\frac{85}{5}_1$ $\frac{90}{3}_3$ $\frac{95}{2}_2$	$\frac{90}{3}_2$ $\frac{95}{2}_3$ $\frac{100}{1}_2$
6	Power cleans	–	$\frac{60}{10}_1$ $\frac{70}{8}_2$	$\frac{60}{8}_1$ $\frac{70}{6}_2$ $\frac{80}{4}_1$	$\frac{70}{6}_1$ $\frac{80}{4}_2$	–	$\frac{70}{6}_3$	$\frac{70}{6}_1$ $\frac{80}{4}_2$	$\frac{80}{4}_4$	–	$\frac{70}{6}_3$	$\frac{70}{6}_1$ $\frac{80}{4}_3$	$\frac{80}{4}_4$
	Loading pattern		Low	Medium	High		Low	Medium	High		Low	Medium	High

Figure 10.1 Example of a maximum load method program for an Olympic-class sprinter.

177

No.	Exercise	Dates					
		May 13-19	May 20-26	May 27-June 2	June 3-9	June 10-16	June 17-23
1	Squats/Leg press	$\frac{70}{8}_3$	$\frac{70}{8}_1\,\frac{80}{6}_2$	$\frac{80}{8}_1\quad\frac{90}{3}_2$	$\frac{70}{10}_3$	$\frac{80}{8}_1\,\frac{90}{3}_2$	$\frac{90}{3}_1\,\frac{95}{2}_2$
2	Sit-ups	3 × 15	3 × 18	3 × 20	3 × 15	3 × 18	3 × 20
3	Military press	$\frac{70}{8}_3$	$\frac{70}{8}_1\,\frac{80}{6}_2$	$\frac{80}{8}_1\quad\frac{90}{3}_2$	$\frac{70}{10}_3$	$\frac{80}{8}_1\,\frac{90}{3}_2$	$\frac{90}{3}_1\,\frac{95}{2}_2$
4	Leg curls	$\frac{50}{12}_1\,\frac{60}{10}_2$	$\frac{60}{10}_3$	$\frac{60}{10}_2\quad\frac{70}{8}_1$	$\frac{60}{10}_3$	$\frac{60}{12}_1\,\frac{70}{10}_2$	$\frac{70}{10}_3$
5	Toe raises	$\frac{70}{8}_3$	$\frac{70}{8}_1\,\frac{80}{6}_2$	$\frac{80}{8}_1\quad\frac{90}{3}_2$	$\frac{70}{10}_3$	$\frac{80}{8}_1\,\frac{90}{3}_2$	$\frac{90}{3}_1\,\frac{95}{2}_2$
6	Front lat pull-downs	$\frac{70}{8}_3$	$\frac{70}{8}_1\,\frac{80}{6}_2$	$\frac{80}{8}_1\quad\frac{90}{3}_2$	$\frac{70}{10}_3$	$\frac{80}{8}_1\,\frac{90}{3}_2$	$\frac{90}{3}_1\,\frac{95}{2}_2$
7	Simple deadlifts	$\frac{50}{12}_1\,\frac{60}{10}_2$	$\frac{60}{10}_3$	$\frac{60}{10}_2\quad\frac{70}{8}_1$	$\frac{60}{10}_3$	$\frac{60}{12}_1\,\frac{70}{10}_2$	$\frac{70}{10}_3$

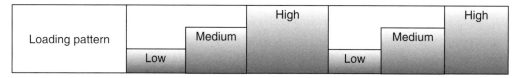

Loading pattern: Low, Medium, High, Low, Medium, High

Note: Rest interval between sets is 3 to 4 minutes.

Figure 10.2 Six-week maximum strength phase for a college women's volleyball team.

Isometric Method

The isometric training method was known and used for some time before Hettinger and Müler (1953) and again Hettinger (1966) scientifically justified the merits of static contractions in the development of maximum strength. This method climaxed in the 1960s and then faded in popularity. Although static contraction has little functional effect for muscular endurance, it is still useful for the development of maximum strength and can be used by throwers in their strength training efforts. Static conditions can be realized through two techniques: (1) attempting to lift a weight heavier than one's potential and (2) applying force (push or pull) against an immobile object.

An isometric contraction produces high tension in the muscle, making this method most useful during the maximum strength phase. With disputed merits, it can also be used in the maintenance phase to preserve maximum strength. Even if, as some enthusiasts claim, isometric training can increase maximum strength by 10 to 15 percent more than other methods, it has clear limitations in the development of power and muscular endurance.

As isometric force is applied against a given resistance, the tension in the muscle builds progressively, reaching maximum in about two or three seconds and, toward the end, decreasing in a much shorter time (one or two seconds). Because training benefits are angle specific, each group of muscles must be trained at a different angle. For instance, if the range of motion of a joint is 180 degrees, to achieve benefit throughout this range, angles of 15, 45, 75, 105, 135, and 165 degrees must be used. Only then does the tension cover the entire range of motion. Reservations can also be expressed regarding the transfer of angle-specific strength gains into dynamic or explosive athletic actions, which often involve muscles throughout the entire range of motion.

The isometric method has both advantages and disadvantages. Isometric exercises can be performed with simple apparatuses or equipment and can result in rapid increases in strength, especially for beginners. A partner is not needed. This method can be used to rehabilitate injured muscles. Because no joint motion occurs, "the athlete may continue training even with a joint or bone injury" (Hartmann and Tünnemann, 1988). This can certainly reduce the risk of muscular atrophy. Isometric training produces negligible increase in muscle hypertrophy. This can be an advantage for athletes in sports dominated by relative strength. The duration of a training session is short (20 to 30 minutes). Well-trained athletes may be able to contract most if not all the motor units. Fatigue experienced at the end of a training session may be no higher than that for the maximum load method.

Isometric training has disadvantages, too. Because strength development is angle specific, contractions must be performed at different angles (every 30 degrees) to cover the entire range of motion. Maximum strength gains cannot be applied readily to dynamic contractions. There is no learning component of the technical skills involved in the selected sport or muscle memory. Because isometric contraction is static, it does not develop flexibility, so training may affect muscle elasticity. Moreover, an oxygen debt is acquired during work because isometric contractions are performed in a state of apnea (breath holding). Athletes must compensate for this by breathing at a higher rate during the rest interval. Gains in maximum strength may be lost as quickly as they are gained. Although isometric training may add to overall gains in maximum strength, it does not shift the force–time curve to the left, a disadvantage that must not be ignored. Finally, isometric contractions have little, if any, cardiorespiratory benefit. In fact, blood circulation may be restrained during a contraction, hampering the supply of nutrients. Athletes with heart and circulation problems are strongly discouraged from engaging in isometric training.

Program Design for the Isometric Method

Achieving maximum gains with isometric training requires exercises as similar as possible to the technical skill. The isometric method should be used primarily by advanced athletes in combination with other maximum strength methods. See table 10.2 for training parameters.

Table 10.2 Training Parameters for Isometric Training

Training parameters	Work
Load	80-100 percent
Number of exercises	4-6
Duration of contraction per set	6-12 seconds
Duration of contraction per session	60-90 seconds
Number of sets per session	6-9
Rest interval	60-90 seconds
Frequency per week	2-3

Isometric contraction can be performed with all limbs using angles from completely open to fully bent. The following issues should be considered:

- Isometric training is most effective when contraction is near maximum (80 to 100 percent).
- The duration of the contraction can be between 6 and 12 seconds, a total of 60 to 90 seconds per muscle per training session.

- The training load is intensified by increasing the number of exercises and sets, not by increasing the duration of contractions.

- During the 60- to 90-second rest interval, relaxation and breathing exercises are recommended. The latter is a compensatory necessity because static contraction is performed in a state of apnea. In addition, the intrathoracic pressure is elevated, which restricts circulation and thus oxygen supply.

- For a more effective program, static contractions should be alternated with isotonic contractions, especially for sports that require speed and power.

- A more effective variant of the isometric method is the functional isometric contraction, which involves free weights. This variant combines isotonic with isometric exercises: The athlete lifts an object to a certain angle and then holds for six to eight seconds. While working through the entire range of motion, the athlete may stop two to four times, which combines the isotonic and isometric methods. This variant has a better physiological benefit, hence the term *functional*, especially for muscular endurance of short duration.

Tetanus Training Method

The tetanus training method is suggested for use during the hypertrophy and maximum strength phases of training. The aim of tetanus training is the development of maximum tension in the muscle. Tetanus training can be performed with loads between 70 and 100 percent of 1RM. Because this training method requires a slow contraction speed dispersed with bouts of isometric contractions, it should be used during the late part of the hypertrophy phase or the early part of the maximum strength phase.

As discussed earlier, the main objective of maximum strength training is the increased recruitment and synchronization of the fast-twitch muscle fibers. This occurs by using relatively heavy loads that stimulate an increase in the size, thickness, and number of myosin filaments. Traditional strength training methods average three to six minutes of rest between sets to facilitate complete regeneration of the CNS and strengthen the subsequent twitch response. The periodization of tetanus training requires the use of heavy loads, a low number of exercises similar to traditional maximum strength training (with the exception of a shorter rest period between sets), and the need for complete neuromuscular exhaustion. The tetanus training guidelines outlined in this section can also be used during the hypertrophy phase of training to elicit muscular exhaustion and promote protein synthesis.

Physiologically speaking, a tetanus response represents a summation of twitch responses. Motor unit force is determined by the rate at which the CNS sends action potentials from the motor neuron to the muscle fibers. The greater the rate, the greater the magnitude of motor unit force. Research measures a state of tetanus by electrically stimulating a muscle so that it is possible to quantify and qualify the twitch response. When a muscle is electrically stimulated, motor units are called into action, forming an irregular force profile referred to as "unfused tetanus." An action potential causes an additive effect of twitch responses overlapping one another, which produces a total force that is greater than an individual twitch response. As the frequency of the action potentials increases, tetanus changes from an irregular force to profile to a "fused tetanus" or plateau profile (Enoka, 2002). The peak force of a fused tetanus represents the maximum force that a motor unit can exert. Fast-twitch motor units display the greatest force ratios of time and magnitude of peak force (Enoka, 2002). Figure 10.3 illustrates the difference between an unfused tetanus and a fused tetanus. Notice that a fused tetanus displays a higher force production.

Practically speaking, transferring the results of intricate laboratory research into practical sport settings is difficult. Athletes are not hooked up to electrical stimulation machines ready to be charged with maximum tetanus. Obviously, the goal of maximum strength training is to

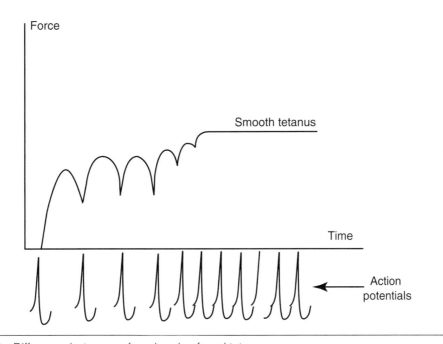

Figure 10.3 Difference between a fused and unfused tetanus.

Adapted, by permission, from ML Latash, 1998, *Neurophysiological basis of movement* (Champaign, IL: Human Kinetics), 31.

create a period of tetanus in which the motor units of the prime movers are maximally activated to produce the greatest possible force. This is really the only way to physiologically produce maximum power output. At its best, the tetanus training discussed here can be used to elicit a high level of motor unit recruitment and force production. We are attempting to bridge the gap between the laboratory and the sporting field. Athletes we have trained have successfully used this technique. It should be used during the late preparatory and competitive phases of the yearly plan as a method to elicit or maintain maximum force production.

Program Design for Tetanus Training Method

To induce a tetanus state for the benefit of improved performance, coaches should consider the following methods:

- *Isometric contraction.* One to three sets of four to six seconds, at about 80 percent of maximum isometric contraction, specifically addressed to the prime movers. The number of exercises should be as low as possible. This preliminary isometric tension increases the effect of the dynamic work by 20 percent (Verhoshansky, 1997).

- *Isometric–dynamic.* One isometric contraction immediately followed by a dynamic contraction for the same muscle groups. One or two sets of three or four reps: four to six seconds for isometric contractions and two to four reps for dynamic contraction with a load of 70 to 80 percent. Athletes should stress the concentric contraction to recruit as many fast-twitch fibers as possible and increase the discharge rate of the same muscle fibers. The action of the prime movers should be involved.

- *Dynamic–explosive.* Two or three sets of four or five throws of the heaviest implements (i.e., power balls) immediately followed by lighter balls (either power or medicine balls).

- *Complex drill.* For better exemplification we'll use a half squat exercise (for sprinters, jumpers, throwers, spikers in volleyball, and those in the martial arts). One or two sets in this sequence: (1) slow eccentric contraction, (2) isometric contraction for two to four seconds in the deepest part of the squat, and (3) concentric contraction with maximum acceleration and takeoff.

- *Complex drill followed by a 10- to 15-meter sprint.* This drill is similar to the complex drill, except that, immediately following the takeoff, the athlete does a very short sprint.
- *Complex drill followed by three to five plyometrics (reactive jumps).*

The best combinations are those that use an explosive movement at the end of the exercise such as a takeoff jump.

The benefit of tetanus training is that athletes reach an optimal state of arousal or precompetitive state, in which both physiologically and psychologically they are highly stimulated for the competition to come. From the neuromuscular point of view the athlete is in a tension mode, in which many muscle fibers are in intense contraction and are accompanied by the storage of elastic energy. All of the previously described techniques increase speed, reactivity, explosive strength, and especially the discharge rate of fast-twitch muscle fibers.

Figures 10.4 and 10.5 illustrate two examples of the periodization of tetanus training. Tetanus training is suggested for the prime movers only. Because this training method can be quite stressful mentally and physically, only athletes with a good background in strength training should use it. The duration of tetanus training should be approximately three to six weeks, depending on the athlete's background. Tetanus training should follow a maximum strength phase in which concentric–eccentric contraction has been used; however, it can be implemented

Periodization of Tetanus Training

Training phase	Preparatory			
Number of weeks	3-6	6	1	3-6
Periodization of strength	AA	MxS	T	MxS
Type of contraction	Concentric-eccentric	Concentric-eccentric	AA	Tetanus*

* Tetanus training is suggested for the prime movers only.

Figure 10.4 Periodization of strength leading to tetanus training.

No.	Exercise	Type of contraction	Week 1	Week 2	Week 3	Week 4	Week 5	Week 6	Rest Interval
1	Bench press	Tetanus	2 at 85%	3 at 90%	4 at 90%	2 at 85%	3 at 95%	4 at 95%	5 min.
2	Squats	Tetanus	2 at 85%	3 at 90%	4 at 90%	2 at 85%	3 at 95%	4 at 95%	5 min.
3	Ab crunches	Concentric-eccentric	2 to discomfort	2 to discomfort	2 to high discomfort	2 to discomfort	3 to high discomfort	3 to high discomfort	1-2 min.
4	Toe raises	Tetanus	2 at 85%	3 at 90%	4 at 90%	2 at 85%	3 at 95%	4 at 95%	5 min.
5	Leg curls	Concentric-eccentric	$\frac{60}{12}2$	$\frac{70}{10}2$	$\frac{70}{10}2$	$\frac{70}{10}2$	$\frac{80}{8}2$	$\frac{80}{10}2$	2 min.
6	Power cleans	Concentric-eccentric	$\frac{70}{7}2$	$\frac{70}{7}2$	$\frac{80}{6}2$	$\frac{80}{8}3$	$\frac{85}{4}3$	$\frac{85}{5}3$	4-5 min.

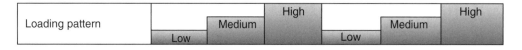

Loading pattern				
	Low	Medium	High	
			Low	Medium	High

Figure 10.5 An example of tetanus training for a shot-putter. Note: Exercising to "discomfort" means to stop when you feel the threshold of pain. Exercising to "high discomfort" means to pass the threshold of pain.

at the end of a hypertrophy I or II phase of training. One or two training sessions per week with at least 48 hours of rest between bouts are suggested. Shot-put, discus, and hammer throw athletes; heavyweight wrestlers; linemen in American football; and athletes in other sports in which maximum strength is essential to increase athletic performance can benefit from bouts of tetanus training.

Eccentric Method

Any strength exercise performed with free weights or most isokinetic equipment employs concentric and eccentric contractions. During the concentric phase, force is produced while the muscle shortens; during the eccentric phase, force is produced as the muscle lengthens.

Practice has demonstrated that the eccentric phase always seems to be easier than the concentric phase. In a bench press, the return of the barbell to the starting point (the eccentric part of the lift) always seems easier than the lift itself. Thus, one could logically conclude that because an athlete can work with heavier loads during the eccentric contraction, strength is certainly improved to higher levels by using the eccentric method alone.

Researchers have concluded that eccentric training creates higher tension in the muscles than isometric or isotonic contractions do. Furthermore, because higher muscle tension normally means higher strength development (Goldberg et al., 1975), eccentric training could logically be considered a superior training method.

Komi and Buskirk (1972) demonstrated the superiority of the eccentric method over the isokinetic method. Other researchers have found that gains in maximum strength appear to result mostly from changes in neural activation rather than hypertrophic response (Dudley and Fleck, 1987). This means that maximum strength improvements do not result from gains in muscle mass, but rather from specific neural adaptations such as an increase in fast-twitch muscle fiber recruitment, increased strength with little or no hypertrophy, and modifications in the neural commands used to control the movement. The CNS commands the eccentric contraction differently. This occurs mostly as grading, or ranking, the amount of muscle activation necessary to complete a task (Enoka, 1996). The amount of muscle activation and the number of fibers involved are proportional to the training load. The neural command for eccentric contraction is unique in that it decides (1) which motor units should be activated, (2) how much they have to be activated, (3) when they should be activated, and (4) how the activity should be distributed within a group of muscles (Abbruzzese et al., 1994).

Because muscles resist fatigue during eccentric contraction, activity can be longer than for concentric contraction (Tesch et al., 1978), possibly because of the altered recruitment order of motor units. The load in eccentric training is much higher than the load in the maximum concentric contraction; therefore, the speed of performance is quite slow. Because such a slow rate of contraction does not result in higher neural activation, it stimulates protein synthesis at a higher rate, resulting in muscle hypertrophy. However, if the eccentric contraction is performed faster, the muscle force is higher than it would be in the concentric method (Åstrand and Rodahl, 1985). This can create a major difficulty in training, especially if free weights are employed. Two spotters are needed to help the athlete lift the barbell for the concentric phase because the load for eccentric training is higher than 1RM. The spotters should also ensure that as the bar is lowered, the athlete does not drop it onto the chest, causing injury. The need for such careful assistance as the bar is being slowly lowered makes performing the exercise quickly impossible. Unless one has access to special isokinetic equipment, or can stop the barbell before it reaches the chest (security pins or keys), fast eccentric contraction is difficult and unsafe.

Athletes may experience muscle soreness during the first few days of eccentric training. This is to be expected because higher tension provokes some muscle damage. As athletes adapt, the muscle soreness will disappear (7 to 10 days). Short-term discomfort can be avoided by increasing the load in steps.

As expected, the eccentric method shifts the force–time curve to the left. Heavy loads that generate high tension in the muscles improve strength because they result in a high recruitment of the powerful fast-twitch motor units. Strength gains are even greater if the force is exerted faster.

Program Design for the Eccentric Method

Only athletes with three to five years of strength training should use the eccentric training method because it employs the heaviest loads (110 to 160 percent of 1RM). The eccentric method can be used alone in a training session or a short training phase, or can be combined with other methods, especially the maximum load method. Eccentric contractions should not be used excessively. Every time an athlete uses maximum or supermaximum loads, maximal mental concentration is required, which can be psychologically wearing. Athletes should use the eccentric method carefully no more than twice a week, or in combination with power training.

To achieve maximum training benefits, athletes should use the maximum load method for as long as practically possible. Once they reach a plateau at which they are achieving little or no improvement, the coach should turn to the eccentric method. Coaches should remember to balance the antagonist muscles by exposing them to the same methods, but not necessarily the same number of sets. To avoid injury, athletes using this method should have two spotters. Active recovery techniques will eliminate discomfort, reduce soreness, and encourage faster regeneration (for additional information, see chapter 13).

Table 10.3 presents training parameters for the eccentric method. The range of the load is presented as the percentage of maximum strength capacity for the concentric contraction and suggests a resistance between 110 and 160 percent. Less experienced athletes should use lower loads. The most effective load for highly trained athletes is around 130 to 140 percent. The speed of execution is slow because the load is supermaximum. Such loads should be used only after at least two seasons of maximum strength training in which the eccentric contraction method is also employed. The suggested number of sets per exercise should be used as a guideline for experienced athletes. This number should be lowered for other athletes according to their training potential. The same applies to the number of sets

Table 10.3 Training Parameters for the Eccentric Method

Training parameters	Work
Load	110-160 percent
Number of exercises	3-5
Number of repetitions per set	1-4
Number of sets per exercise	4-6 (8)
Number of sets per session	20-36
Rest interval	3-6 minutes
Speed of execution	Slow
Frequency per week	1

per training session, which also depends on the number of exercises. The rest interval is an important element in the capacity to perform highly demanding work. If athletes do not recover well enough between sets to complete the next set at the same level, the rest interval must be increased slightly.

The athlete's motivation and concentration capacity are important factors in eccentric training. Because eccentric contractions use such heavy loads, athletes must be highly motivated and able to concentrate. By being mentally and psychologically prepared, they will be capable of performing eccentric contractions effectively. The eccentric method is rarely performed in isolation from the other maximum strength methods. Even during the maximum strength phase, the eccentric method is used with the maximum load method; therefore, only one eccentric training session per week is suggested. For elite athletes, the frequency may eventually be increased during the third step in the pattern to increase the load in training. See table 10.4 for a sample six-week program designed for a college football team. Figure 10.6 shows the last three weeks of a six-week program developed for an international-class shot-putter. A three-week conversion to power phase followed, then a week of unloading prior to an important competition.

Table 10.4 Progression and Proportions Between Concentric and Eccentric Contractions

Week	1	2	3	4	5	6
Types of training and frequency per week	Concentric 3×	Concentric 4×	Concentric 3× Eccentric 1×	Concentric 1× Eccentric 2×	Concentric 2× Eccentric 2×	Concentric 2× Eccentric 2×

No.	Exercise	Week 4	Week 5	Week 6
1	Squats (eccentric)	$\frac{120}{6}$ 4	$\frac{130}{4}$ 4	$\frac{140}{3\text{-}4}$ 4
2	Incline bench press (eccentric)	$\frac{120}{6}$ 4	$\frac{130}{4}$ 4	$\frac{140}{3\text{-}4}$ 4
3	Deadlifts (concentric)	$\frac{75}{8}$ 3	$\frac{75}{8}$ 3	$\frac{75}{8}$ 3
4	Toe raises (concentric)	$\frac{90}{3}$ 3	$\frac{90}{4}$ 3	$\frac{90}{5}$ 3
5	Jump squats (takeoff=concentric, landing=eccentric)	$\frac{70}{5\text{-}6}$ 3	$\frac{70}{6}$ 3	$\frac{70}{6}$ 3

Loading pattern	Low/Medium	High	High

Figure 10.6 The last 3 weeks of a 6-week program developed for an international-class shot-putter.

Maxex Training

The previous methods for developing maximum strength should not be applied rigidly or in isolation, especially for sports in which speed and power are dominant. For all team sports; sprinting, jumping, and throwing events in track and field; the martial arts; boxing; wrestling; alpine skiing; ski-jumping; fencing; diving; figure skating; and sprint events in swimming maximum strength methods can be combined with plyometrics. Maximum tension exercises can be combined with exercises requiring explosiveness. This new method, which combines maximum force with exercises for explosiveness, is called *maxex training*.

The variations of training methods proposed need not be performed year-round. They can be planned at the end of the preparatory phase or, in the case of several maximum strength phases, during the last phase. A maximum strength phase is still necessary before any power training because power is a function of maximum strength. The incorporation of power training during the maximum strength phase enhances speed and explosiveness to ready athletes for the competitive phase. Combining maximum strength with power must be done carefully and conservatively. Although many combinations are possible, training has to be simple so athletes can focus on the main task of the workout or training phase. The more variations coaches use, the more they may confuse their athletes and disrupt the way their bodies adapt.

The concept of maxex training relies on science, manipulating two physiological concepts to produce speed and explosiveness and improve athletic performance. The first part of the maxex routine is performed against a heavier load, which stimulates a high recruitment of fast-twitch muscle fibers. The follow-up explosive/quickness movements increase the firing rate of the fast-twitch muscle fibers, preparing the athlete for the quick, explosive actions required for all speed and power sports during the competitive phase.

Maxex training applies to the upper body as well. In sports like basketball, baseball, ice hockey, football, lacrosse, the martial arts, boxing, wrestling, kayaking, squash, European handball, water polo, wrestling, and throwing events in track and field, strong arms and shoulders are essential. Without exhausting all options, drop jumps, jumping squats, drop push-ups, and medicine ball throws are exercises that can be applied to the above sports for maxex training.

During the MxS phase, athletes can combine MxS methods with some of the given variations or with plyometrics (either low or medium impact). Table 10.5 suggests such combinations for an athlete who plans three strength training sessions per week.

Table 10.5 Possible Combination of MxS With Maxex Training

Monday	Tuesday	Wednesday	Thursday	Friday	Saturday
TE/TA		TE/TA		TE/TA	
15 minutes Maxex		15 minutes Maxex		15 minutes Maxex	
45 minutes MxS		60 minutes MxS		45-60 minutes MxS	

Notes: TE = Technical training
TA = Tactical training

Phase 4: Conversion

Today almost every athlete uses some sort of strength training program to improve performance. However, most strength programs fail to transform the strength gains made during the maximum strength training phase into sport-, or event-specific strength such as power, speed, and agility. Without converting maximum strength into speed, power, agility, and muscular endurance, athletes cannot maximize their athletic potential for the benefit of increasing sports performance. Periodization of strength is designed to effect such transformations during the conversion phase so that peak performance will be achieved during the main competitions.

For athletic purposes, any increase in power must be the result of improvements in either strength, speed, or a combination of the two. An athlete can be very strong, with a large muscle mass, yet be unable to display power because of an inability to contract already strong muscles in a very short time. To overcome this deficiency, the athlete must undergo power training that will result in improving the rate of force production.

The advantage of explosive, high-velocity power training is that it "trains" the central nervous system (CNS). Increases in performance can be based on neural changes that help the individual muscles achieve greater performance capability (Sale, 1986). This is accomplished by shortening the time of motor unit recruitment, especially of fast-twitch fibers, and increasing the tolerance of the motor neurons to increased innervation frequencies (Häkkinen, 1986; Häkkinen and Komi, 1983).

Power training exercises activate and increase the discharge rate of fast-twitch muscle fibers as quickly as possible to encourage better CNS adaptation. Training practice and research has shown that muscle adaptation requires considerable time and progresses from year to year. Adaptation, especially in well-trained athletes, shows itself in the form of higher and better synchronization of motor units and their firing patterns. Another physiological adaptation phenomenon, so critical in the display of power, is that muscles discharge a greater number of muscle fibers in a very short time.

Neuromuscular adaptation to power training also results in improved intramuscular coordination, or better linkage between the excitatory and inhibitory reactions of a muscle to many stimuli. As a result of such adaptation, the CNS "learns" when and when not to send a nerve impulse that signals the muscle to contract and perform a movement.

A further indication of adaptation to power training is evidenced by better intermuscular coordination or the ability of the agonist and antagonist muscles to cooperate to perform a movement effectively. Improved intermuscular coordination enhances the ability to contract some muscles and relax others (i.e., to relax the antagonist muscles), which results in improvements in the speed of contraction of the prime movers, the agonist muscles.

The human body can adapt to any environment and therefore any type of training. If an athlete is trained with bodybuilding methods, which is often the case in North America, the neuromuscular system adapts to them. As a result, the athlete should not be expected to display fast, explosive power because the neuromuscular system was not trained for it. Because they focus on slow contraction rate, bodybuilding methods increase muscle size (hypertrophy) but do not increase power, speed, agility, or quickness.

To develop sport-specific power, a training program must be specifically designed to achieve that objective. Such a program has to be specific to the sport or event and use exercises that simulate the dominant skills as closely as possible. Because power training addresses muscles specifically, intramuscular coordination becomes more efficient and the skill becomes more precise, smoother, and quicker.

During the conversion phase, athletes should use most of their energy for technical and tactical training and much less for power training. Coaches must plan training with the lowest possible number of exercises that closely relate to the skill. Such programs must be efficient, with two or three exercises performed dynamically over several sets for maximum return. Time and energy should not be wasted on anything else.

The conversion program must be performed quickly and explosively to recruit the highest number of motor units at the highest rate of contraction (increased discharge rate). The entire program should have only one goal: moving the force–time curve as far to the left as possible (refer to figure 7.9) so that the muscles contract explosively. Coaches should select only the training methods that fulfill the requirements of power development—that is, that enhance quickness, facilitate explosive application of force, and increase the reactivity of the muscles involved.

The methods presented in this chapter can be performed separately or in combination. When they are combined, the total work per session must be divided among them.

Power Training

Power is the main ingredient for all the sports in which the rate of producing, and especially of displaying, force, speed, and agility is high. Sports known as speed- and power-dominant sports include sprinting, jumping, throwing events in track and field, team sports, racket sports, gymnastics, diving, and the martial arts. For performance to improve, the level of power must improve. Power, therefore, is the main ingredient necessary to produce a fast, quick, and agile athlete.

People use different terms for power, including *dynamic strength* and the aberrant and confusing terms *strength-speed* and *speed-strength*. However, if we are committed to employing science in sports training, the correct term should be borrowed from physics and physiology, both of which use the term *power*. It is defined as

- "the rate of producing force,
- the product of force and velocity (P = F × V, or force times velocity),
- the amount of work done per time unit, or
- the rate at which muscles can produce work." (Enoka 2002)

Power is measured in watts.

Physiological Strategy to Increase Power

Some sport practitioners and authors still maintain the philosophy that athletes who want to increase power should do power drills; athletes who want to be fast should do short reps with high speed; and athletes who want to be quick and agile should do agility drills. This training philosophy contradicts the fundamental physiological principle that a given type of work results in a proportional adaptation. An athlete who maintains the same type of work for longer periods of time will experience a plateau, stagnation of improvement, or even a slight detraining, resulting in performance deterioration. To reverse this trend, and to ensure that power is consistently improved for the benefit of increased performance during the competitive phase, athletes must constantly stimulate the neuromuscular system to increase the recruitment of fast-twitch muscle fibers. This can be done by applying the training methods proposed by the concept of periodization of strength.

Research shows that an increase in peak power is more modest with lighter loads and greatest with heavier loads. Greatest increases in power are obtained from higher force and not from higher-velocity training (Aagard et al., 1994; Enoka, 2002). Furthermore, the peak power a muscle can produce is directly dependent on gains in maximum strength (Fitts and Widrick, 1996). The same is true for speed. Maximum velocity will not increase unless power is first increased. Trainers have known this since the 1950s. These findings validate and add more substance to the theory of periodization of strength, allowing us to draw the conclusion that speed, agility, and quickness will never increase unless maximum strength is trained first, and then converted to power.

We propose the following two training phases to maximize power, speed, agility, and quickness (Bompa, 1993a, 2005):

1. Increase the recruitment of fast-twitch muscle fibers.
2. Increase the discharge rate of the same fast-twitch muscle fibers.

During the first phase (see figure 11.1), the scope of training is to recruit the highest number of fast-twitch fibers. This usually occurs during the maximum strength phase, in which athletes use loads of over 80 percent of 1RM. These training loads result in the constant stimulation of the neuromuscular system, which then recruits high numbers of fast-twitch muscle fibers. To avoid detraining and a loss in strength, maximum strength training sessions should be planned during the competitive phase of the yearly plan.

The power exerted during athletic actions depends on the number of active motor units, the number of fast-twitch fibers recruited into the action, and the rate at which those

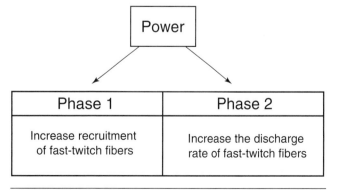

Figure 11.1 The physiological strategy used to increase power, speed, and agility.

fibers are discharged, producing a high force–frequency relation (Enoka, 2002). The increase in the discharge rate of fast-twitch fibers is achieved by training with lighter loads, around 30 to 35 percent of 1RM (Enoka, 2002; Moritani, 1992; Van Cutsem, Duchateau, and Hainaut, 1998), using any types of lighter implements, such as shots from track and field, power balls, and medicine balls; plyometrics; or specific drills for speed, agility, and quickness. Such exercises, performed with maximum power, speed, and quick application of force against the resistance provided by the implements and the pull of gravity, facilitate the accessing and activation of the high-threshold motor units. High-velocity exercises are a necessity during the second phase to increase the discharge rate of the fast-twitch fibers.

Clearly, then, the main scope of strength training for sports is to continually increase maximum strength so that 30 percent of 1RM is always higher, for the maximum benefit of increasing peak performance.

Heavy Loads Versus Light Loads in Power Enhancement

Trainers and athletes often debate the merits of using either heavy loads or light loads to improve power performance. The fact is that both have roles at different points in training. That is the beauty of periodization: All training methods have a place in the various phases of training.

The speed at which an athlete can perform concentric (shortening) movements such as pushing a barbell up from the chest in a bench press depends on the load the athlete is using. As the load is increased, the velocity of the shortening activity decreases. However, the opposite is true for eccentric or lengthening movements. When performing an eccentric contraction, the force production is greater when the movement is performed at a high velocity. This explains the positive transfer of plyometric-type exercises to the enhancement of power performance. The intrinsic elastic properties of muscles favor the absorption and reuse of stored elastic energy, which is optimized when a muscle is lengthened as quickly as possible. Both heavy loads and light loads are necessary in training to fully use the full spectrum of velocity and force production.

Low-velocity strength training (characteristic of the maximum strength phase) enhances intramuscular coordination, the coordination between muscles and muscle groups. Intramuscular coordination is enhanced as a result of both motor unit recruitment, synchronization, and the firing rates of motor units. In essence, low-velocity training using high resistance leads primarily to improvements in muscular strength. High-velocity training (characteristic of traditional power training), which involves training with lighter resistances at higher velocities, increases the rate of force development. This obviously includes a speed component. An interesting study concluded that the intent to produce ballistic contractions, and not the speed of movement, was responsible for a high-velocity training effect (Behm and Sale, 1993). However, because heavy loads do not allow for a sport-specific speed of movement, the transition from maximum strength training to sport-specific speed is vital to sports that require accelerated movements. A long jumper who spends hours squatting will develop a high level of strength. The ability to transfer that strength into jump-specific movements that synchronize the use of all prime movers can only be achieved by performing plyometric drills.

The degree of emphasis on heavy loads versus light loads ultimately depends on the type of sport. The periodization of strength program is characterized by a maximum strength phase (heavy load) followed by a conversion phase (light load). A combination of both as presented in the periodization model works best. To explore this issue, a study compared the training of three groups. Group 1 performed heavy squat training, group 2 performed plyometric training with a light load, and group 3 combined both squat and plyometric drills. Because the largest gain in indexes of power occurred in group 3, the authors concluded that optimal training benefits are acquired by combining heavy load training with explosive movements (Adams, Worlay, and Throgmartin, 1987).

Agility Training

Agility training is one of the most misunderstood elements of sports training. Many trainers and specialists measure agility as the ability to do many agility drills, or the ability to change direction quickly. In reality, *agility is power*. Without high levels of power, no one would ever be agile or quick. Agility, therefore, is the ability to accelerate quickly (which is concentric strength); to decelerate (eccentric strength), as in "stop and go"; or to change direction or perform the cuts so important in many sports, especially in team and racket sports. Without a consistent activation and increased recruitment of fast-twitch fibers, agility will not have the expected rate of improvement. Athletes who repeatedly perform agility drills, therefore, will ultimately reach a plateau and stagnate in their performance of any skills in which agility is a determinant factor. For these reasons, the periodization of agility is based on the physiological strategy suggested in figure 11.1.

The periodization model illustrated in figure 11.2 will result in the greatest improvement in agility (Bompa, 2005). At the top of the chart are the traditional training phases of the yearly plan and the specific phases of the periodization of strength, explained in the previous chapters. During the anatomical adaptation phase, in which the foundation of strength and general conditioning is the scope, repeating agility drills won't result in any visible improvements because the neuromuscular system is not yet trained to recruit fast-twitch fibers. As the improvement of maximum strength, and the recruitment of fast-twitch fibers, becomes the scope of training (during the maximum strength phase), agility training can be initiated in the form of repeating known drills and learning new ones. As the neuromuscular system improves its ability to recruit higher numbers of fast-twitch fibers, especially toward the end of the maximum strength phase, the velocity or quickness of performing agility drills improves. This is maximized toward the end of the conversion phase and the competitive phase, when the discharge rate of fast-twitch fibers increases as a result of increasing the velocity of agility drills and applying force against lighter implements or against the force of gravity. From this phase of training on, and throughout the maintenance phase, agility is maximized and contributes to performance improvement.

Training phases	Preparatory			Competitive	Transition
Periodization of strength	AA	MxS	Conversion to power	Maintain MxS and Power	Compensation training
Periodization of agility	No agility drills	Learning phase: repeat known, and learn new agility drills	Increase velocity of agility drills	Increase velocity of agility drills	No agility drills. Agility is not a scope of training
Benefits to the effectiveness of agility	Low		Good to High	Maximum effectiveness	Low

Figure 11.2 The periodization of agility.

Finally, many trainers still consider agility and quickness, or quick feet, separate physical qualities. This is visible in many seminars and books published on these topics. When the neuromuscular system is trained according to the physiological strategy suggested in figure 11.1, the final physiological product is an increased discharge rate of the fast-twitch fibers. As a result of high adaptation to the previous types of training, athletes are powerful, run faster, and perform any type of drill with quickness. The human body doesn't care whether we use two different terms to describe the same neuromuscular quality. The body is capable of performing powerful actions, moving limbs fast, or changing directions fast, regardless of whether we have different names for these actions.

During the preparatory phase of the yearly plan, athletes can improve agility and quickness by using other implements or types of training such as power balls, medicine balls, and plyometric exercises. For best training organization and periodization, plyometric exercises are organized into five intensity categories. These intensities and the weight of power and medicine balls can also be periodized (see figure 11.3).

Training phases	Preparatory				Competitive
Periodization of strength	AA	MxS	Conversion to power, MxS		Maintenance: MxS, Power
Periodization of PB/MB (weight of the implement)	Medium	Heavy	Medium	Medium-Light	Medium-Light
Periodization of plyometrics	5	5, 4	3	3, 2	3, 2, 1	3-2 (1)

Note: Power balls (PB) have a weight between 2-35 lbs (1-15 kg). Light weights are between 2-10 lbs (1-4 kg); medium weights are between 12-20 lbs (5-8 kg), and heavy weights are between 20-35 lbs (8-15 kg). Medicine balls (MB) have a weight between 2-15 lbs (1-6 kg).

Figure 11.3 Periodization of power/medicine balls and plyometrics.

To illustrate the periodization of power and medicine ball training and plyometrics, figure 11.3 shows the activities and intensities of the preparatory phase. During the anatomical adaptation phase, which emphasizes the foundation of strength, medium loads are used for the implements, and low intensity (5) is used for plyometrics. Core strength exercises and exercises strengthening the limbs are strongly suggested. During the maximum strength phase the loads used for power ball and medicine ball are high to activate a higher number of motor units into the action. At the same time the intensity of plyometric exercises increases so that the reactivity of the neuromuscular system is heightened. Finally, during the conversion phase, the loads decrease for power ball and medicine ball to maximize the benefits of quickness of force application while the intensity of plyometrics is highest. In this way the eccentric contractions or lengthening of the muscles are pushed to a maximum, which results in higher force production. Under these conditions the discharge rate of the fast-twitch muscle fibers increases to ensure that peak performance is reached at the time of the major competition.

Isotonic Method

Attempting to move a weight as rapidly and forcefully as possible through the entire range of motion is one of the classical methods of power training. Free weights, or other equipment that can be moved quickly, are good means of developing power. The weight of the equipment used for the isotonic method represents the *external resistance*. The force necessary to defeat the inertia of a barbell or to move it is considered the *internal strength*. The more internal strength exceeds external resistance, the faster the acceleration will be. If an athlete has to apply 95 percent of 1RM to lift a barbell, she will be incapable of generating any acceleration. If the same athlete works on maximum strength for one or two years, her strength will have increased so much that lifting the same weight will require only 30 to 40 percent of 1RM. The athlete will then be capable of moving the barbell explosively, generating the acceleration necessary to increase power. This explains why the periodization of strength requires a maximum strength phase prior to power training. No visible increments of power are possible without clear gains in maximum strength.

A high level of maximum strength is also necessary for the early part of a lift or throw. Any barbell or implement (such as a ball) has a certain inertia, which is its mass or weight. The most difficult part of lifting a barbell or throwing an implement explosively is the early part. To overcome the inertia, a high level of tension has to be built in the muscle. Consequently, the higher the maximum strength, the easier it is to overcome the inertia and the more explosive the start of the movement will be. As an athlete continues to apply force against the barbell or implement, he creates acceleration. As more acceleration is developed, less force is necessary to maintain it.

To increase acceleration continuously, limb speed must be increased constantly. This is possible only if the athlete can quickly contract the muscle, which is why athletes involved in speed- and power-dominant sports need to power train during the conversion phase. Without power training, an athlete will never be able to jump higher, run faster, throw farther, or deliver a quick punch. For improvements to occur, more than just maximum strength is needed. Athletes must also have the capacity to use maximum strength at a very high rate, which can only be achieved through power training methods.

Program Design for the Isotonic Method

During the maximum strength phase, the athlete is accustomed to maximum or supermaximum loads. Therefore, using loads between 30 and 80 percent of 1RM will help develop sport-specific power, and at the same time meet the challenge to create high acceleration that is required for power performance.

For most sports involving cyclic motions, such as sprinting, team sports, and the martial arts, the load for the isotonic method can be 30 percent or higher (up to 50 percent). For sports involving acyclic motions such as throwing, weightlifting, and line play in American football, the load can be higher (50 to 80 percent) because these athletes have a much higher mass and maximum strength to start with and must defeat a higher external resistance. (See table 11.1 for a summary of training parameters.) Researchers have examined the optimal training load for developing dynamic athletic performance. In a comparison of heavy load training (80 to 90 percent of 1RM), plyometric training such as depth jumps, and bounding and explosive weight training (30 percent of 1RM at high speed) similar to the isotonic method, the explosive weight training group achieved the best overall results in enhancing power performance (Wilson et al., 1993).

Table 11.1 Training Parameters for the Isotonic Method

Training parameters	Work
Load: Cyclic	30-50 percent
Acyclic	50-80 percent
Number of exercises	2-4 (5)
Number of repetitions per set	4-10
Number of sets per session	3-6
Rest interval	2-6 minutes
Speed of execution	Dynamic/fast
Frequency per week	2-3

Because the key element for power training is not how many reps you perform, but rather the ability to activate the highest number of fast-twitch fibers, a low number of reps (4 to 10) is suggested. Athletes should not overlook safety. When a limb extends, it should not be snapped. Exercises should be performed as smoothly as possible without jerking the barbell or implement.

For sports that require power performed in an explosive manner, such as throwing, jumping, diving, cricket, batting, pitching, or line play in American football, reps do not necessarily have to be nonstop. They can be performed with some rest between them so the athlete can concentrate maximally to achieve the most dynamic move. The athlete can perform one to four reps at a time, as long as they are performed explosively for maximum fast-twitch muscle fiber recruitment and increased discharge rate. When the athlete can no longer perform explosively, he should stop even if he has not completed the set. Continuing the reps without explosiveness trains power-endurance (discussed at the end of this chapter) rather than isotonic power. Only maximum concentration and explosive action will result in the greatest fast-twitch fiber recruitment and discharge rate, and these are possible only when an athlete is relatively fresh.

During the rest interval, regardless of whether the athlete is working on isotonic power or power-endurance, the athlete should try to relax the muscles previously involved. Relaxing during the rest interval enhances the resynthesis of ATP, resupplying the working muscles with the necessary fuel.

Exercises for power training must be very sport specific to mimic the skills. Bench presses and power cleans, although traditional power training exercises, have no built-in magic! Power cleans are useful for throwers or linebackers, but not necessarily for athletes in tennis, soccer, or racket sports. These athletes could better use jumping squats while holding heavier dumbbells (15 percent in each hand).

Selecting the lowest number of exercises (two to a maximum of five) allows the athlete to perform the highest number of sets realistically possible (three to six) for maximum benefit of the prime movers. When deciding the number of sets and exercises, coaches should remember that power training is performed in conjunction with technical and tactical training, and only a certain amount of energy is left for it.

A key element in developing power in the isotonic method is the speed of exertion. For maximum power improvement, exertion speed must be as high as possible. Fast application of force against an implement or weight throughout the range of motion is essential and must start from the early part of the movement. To be able to displace the barbell or implement immediately and dynamically, the athlete must apply maximum concentration to the task.

Table 11.2 shows a sample power training program for a college-level female basketball player with four years of strength training.

Table 11.2 3-Week Power Training Program for a Female College Basketball Player

Exercise	Week 1	Week 2	Week 3
Jump squats	$\frac{60}{8}$ 3	$\frac{70}{6}$ 4	$\frac{70}{8}$ 4
Bent-over row	$\frac{70}{8}$ 3	$\frac{70}{8}$ 3	$\frac{70}{10}$ 3
Military presses	$\frac{60}{6}$ 3	$\frac{60}{8}$ 3	$\frac{70}{8}$ 3
V-sits	3 × 15	3 × 15	4 × 15
Power cleans	$\frac{50}{6}$ 3	$\frac{60}{6}$ 3	$\frac{60}{8}$ 3

Ballistic Method

Muscle energy can be applied in different forms and against different resistances. When the resistance is greater than the internal force of the athlete, no motion occurs (isometric). If the resistance is slightly less than the maximum capacity of the athlete, the barbell or strength training equipment will move slowly (isotonic). If, however, the athlete's internal force clearly exceeds the external resistance (e.g., with a medicine ball), a dynamic motion occurs (ballistic).

For power training purposes, an athlete's internal or muscle force can also be applied against implements such as the shots used in track and field, medicine balls, heavy barbells, and rubber cords (surgical tubing). The resulting motion occurs explosively because the force of the athlete far exceeds the resistance of these instruments. The method of employing such instruments to enhance power is called the ballistic method.

During a ballistic action, the athlete's energy is dynamically exerted against the resistance from the beginning to the end of the motion. As a result, the implement is projected a distance proportional to the power applied against it. Throughout the motion, the athlete must be able to develop considerable strength to accelerate the equipment or implement continuously, culminating in the release. To project the implement the maximum possible distance, the highest acceleration must be achieved at the instant of release.

The fast, ballistic application of force is possible as a result of quick recruitment of fast-twitch muscle fibers and effective intermuscular coordination of the agonist and antagonist muscles. After years of practice, an athlete can contract the agonist muscles forcefully while the antagonist muscles reach a high level of relaxation. This superior intermuscular coordination maximizes the force capabilities of the agonist muscles because the antagonist muscles exert no opposition to their quick contraction.

Program Design for the Ballistic Method

Ballistic exercises can be planned at the end of a training session or following the warm-up, depending on training objectives. If technical and tactical work has been planned on a given day, the development and improvement of power becomes a secondary goal. However, for sprinting, field events in track and field, and the martial arts, in which speed and power are dominant, power work can often be planned immediately after the warm-up, especially in the late preparatory phase. Table 11.3 summarizes the training parameters for a ballistic program.

Power training of an explosive nature is enhanced when the athlete is physiologically fresh. A well-rested CNS can send more powerful nerve impulses to the working muscles for quick contractions. The opposite is true when the CNS and muscles are exhausted and inhibition is dominant; this prevents the effective involvement of the fast-twitch muscle fibers. When the athlete performs

Table 11.3 Training Parameters for the Ballistic Method

Training parameters	Work
Load	Standard
Number of exercises	2-5
Number of repetitions per set	10-20
Number of sets per session	3-5
Rest interval	2-3 minutes
Speed of execution	Explosive
Frequency per week	2-4

intensive work prior to explosive power training, her energy supplies (ATP-CP) are exhausted. If energy is not available, quality work is impossible because fast-twitch fibers fatigue easily and will hardly be activated. Consequently, the movements will be performed without vigor.

Speed of performance is paramount when using the ballistic method. Each rep should start dynamically with the athlete attempting to increase the speed constantly as the release or end of the motion approaches. This enables a higher number of fast-twitch motor units to become involved. The critical element is not the number of reps and sets. To increase power, the athlete does not have to perform many reps. The determining factor is speed of performance, which dictates the speed of muscle contraction. Therefore, exercises should be performed only as long as quickness is possible. *Repetitions must discontinue the moment speed declines.* The speed and explosiveness of an exercise are guaranteed only as long as high numbers of fast-twitch fibers are involved. When they fatigue, speed decreases. Continuing an activity after speed declines is futile because at this point the slow-twitch fibers might be called into action, an unwanted situation for athletes seeking power development. The plasticity of the CNS can be favorable or work against the objective of training. It is extremely important that adaptation lead to the improvement of sport performance.

The ballistic training load is dictated by the standard weight of the implements. Medicine balls weigh from 2 to 6 kilograms (4.4 to 13 pounds), whereas heavy balls weigh between 10 and 32 kilograms (22 and 70 pounds).

As in other power-related methods, the number of ballistic exercises must be as low as possible so that the athlete can perform a high number of sets to achieve maximum power benefits. Again, exercises should closely mimic technical skills. If this is impossible, the coach should select exercises that involve the prime movers.

For any explosive power method, the rest interval should be as long as necessary to reach almost full recovery so the athlete can repeat the same quality of work in each set. Because most ballistic exercises require one or more partner(s), a short interval between each repetition is dictated by necessity. For instance, a shot has to be fetched, a position taken, and a few preparatory swings made before the shot is heaved back to the first athlete. By that time, some 15 to 20 seconds have elapsed in which the athlete can rest. For this reason, the number of reps is higher in ballistic training than in other power training methods.

The frequency per week of using the ballistic method depends on the training phase. In the late preparatory phase, it should be low (one or two sessions); during the conversion phase, it should be higher (two to four). The sport or event must also be considered. The frequency will be higher for speed- and power-dominant sports than for sports in which power is of secondary importance. Table 11.4 shows a sample of a program that combines ballistic and maximum acceleration exercises. This program has been used successfully with American football, baseball, lacrosse, soccer, and hockey players.

Table 11.4 Ballistic Method Combined With Maximum Acceleration

Exercise	Week 1	Week 2	Week 3
Medicine ball chest throws	2 × 10	3 × 12	3 × 15
Jump squats and medicine ball chest throws	2 × 8	3 × 10	3 × 15
Medicine ball overhead backward throws	2 × 10	3 × 12	3 × 15
Medicine ball side throws (for each side)	2 × 12	3 × 15	3 × 20
Medicine ball forward overhead throws	2 × 10	3 × 10	3 × 12
Two-handed shot throws from chest followed by 15-meter/yard sprint	4×	6×	6×
Push-ups followed by 15-meter/yard sprint	4×	6×	8×

Power-Resisting Method

This method represents a three-way combination of the isotonic, isometric, and ballistic methods. The following description of an exercise will help explain this method. An athlete lies down to perform a sit-up, with his toes held against the ground by a partner. The coach stands behind the athlete. The athlete begins the sit-up. When he reaches approximately a quarter of the hip flexion (135 to 140 degrees), the coach places his palms on the athlete's chest or shoulders, stopping the movement. At this point, the athlete is in a maximum static contraction, trying to defeat the resisting power of the coach by recruiting most or all of the motor units possible. After three or four seconds, the coach removes his hands and the maximum static contraction is converted into a dynamic ballistic motion for the rest of the sit-up. The athlete slowly returns to the starting position and rests for 10 to 30 seconds before performing another rep.

The most important parts of this method are the maximum isometric contraction and the ensuing ballistic action. The ballistic-type motion, with its quick muscle contraction, results in power development. The actions used in this method are similar to those of a catapult machine. The initial isotonic action must be performed slowly. Following the stop, the maximum isometric contraction represents a high pretension (the loading phase) of the muscles involved. As the chest or shoulders are released, the trunk is catapulted forward (the ballistic phase).

Similar power-resisting exercises can be performed for other parts of the body, such as the following:

- Pull-ups in which the athlete performs an early elbow flexion, at which point the coach or partner stops the action for a few seconds; a dynamic action then follows.
- Dips.
- Jumping squats with no weights.
- Half squats with weights.
- Bench presses.
- Trunk rotations with a medicine ball held sideways in the hands. The athlete performs a backward rotation, and as the rotation comes forward, the athlete is stopped for two to four seconds; the ballistic action that follows culminates with the release of the ball.

Any other movements that duplicate the previous phases of action can be categorized under the ballistic method, with similar effects on power development.

Another type of power stimulation can be achieved through isotonic weight training by alternating the loads. The athlete first performs two to four reps with a load of 80 to 90 percent, followed immediately by a similar number of reps performed with a low-resistance load of 30 to 50 percent. The heavy-load reps represent a neuromuscular stimulation for the low-resistance reps, allowing the athlete to perform the last reps more dynamically.

A large variety of exercises, from bench pulls to bench presses, can be used with this method. A note of caution regarding motions involving knee and arm extensions: Snapping or jerking actions (forced, snapped extensions) should be avoided because they can result in joint damage.

Program Design for the Power-Resisting Method

The load for the power-resisting method is related to the exercise performed. For the isometric phase, the contraction should last three or four seconds, or the duration necessary to reach maximum tension. For exercises in which the resistance is provided by a barbell, the load should be 80 to 90 percent for the stimulating phase and 30 to 50 percent for the explosive phase. Exercises should match the direction of prime mover contraction. For maximum power benefit, the number of exercises should be low (two to four) so the athlete can perform a large number of sets (three to five).

Power-resisting training can be performed separately or combined with other power training methods. The latter is preferable because other power training methods may be more beneficial for certain sports or athletes. Table 11.5 summarizes the training parameters for the power-resisting method.

Table 11.5 Training Parameters for the Power-Resisting Method

Training parameters	Work
Load	Exercise related
Number of exercises	2-4
Number of repetitions per set	4-8
Number of sets per session	3-5
Rest interval	2-4 minutes
Speed of execution	Explosive
Frequency per week	1-2

Plyometric Method

Since ancient times, athletes have explored a multitude of methods designed to enable them to run faster, jump higher, and throw an object farther. To achieve such goals, power is essential. Strength gains can be transformed into power only by applying specific power training. Perhaps one of the most successful power training methods is the plyometric method.

Also known as the stretch–shortening cycle, or myostatic stretch reflex, plyometrics refers to exercises in which the muscle is loaded in an eccentric (lengthening) contraction, followed immediately by a concentric (shortening) contraction. Research has demonstrated that a muscle stretched before a contraction will contract more forcefully and rapidly (Bosco and Komi, 1980; Schmidtbleicher, 1984). For example, by lowering the center of gravity to perform a takeoff or swing a golf club, the athlete stretches the muscle, resulting in a more forceful contraction.

Plyometric action relies on the stretch reflex found in the belly of the individual muscle. The main purpose of the stretch reflex is to monitor the degree of muscle stretch and prevent overstretching. When an athlete jumps, a great amount of force is required to propel the body upward. The body must be able to flex and extend quickly to leave the ground. A plyometric exercise relies on this quick body action to attain the power required for the movement.

Plyometric movement is based on the reflex contraction of the muscle fibers resulting from the rapid loading of these same fibers. When excessive stretching and tearing become a possibility, the stretch receptors send proprioceptive nerve impulses to the spinal cord. Then the impulses rebound back at the stretch receptors. Through this rebounding action, a braking effect prevents the muscle fiber from stretching farther, releasing a powerful muscle contraction.

Plyometric exercises work within complex neural mechanisms. Neural adaptations take place in the body's nervous system to enhance both strength and power in athletic training (Sale, 1986; Schmidtbleicher, 1992). Neural adaptations can increase the force of a muscle without increasing its size (Dons et al., 1979; Komi and Bosco, 1978; Sale, 1986; Tesch et al., 1983). Improving the ways that the CNS controls the body's athletic movements is one of the goals of plyometric training.

Plyometric training causes muscular and neural changes that facilitate and enhance the performance of more rapid and powerful movements. The CNS controls muscle force by changing the activity of the muscle's motor units; if a greater force generation is required, a greater number of motor units are recruited. One of the benefits of plyometric training is the increased activation of the fast-twitch motor units. An increase in electromyographic recording (EMG) following a training program would indicate one of three things: A greater number of motor units have been recruited, more motor units are firing at higher rates, or some combination of the first two reactions have occurred (Sale, 1992).

The contractile elements of the muscles are the muscle fibers; however, certain noncontractile parts of the muscles create what is known as the *series elastic component*. Stretching the series elastic component during muscle contraction produces elastic potential energy similar to that of a loaded spring. This energy augments the energy generated by the muscle fibers. This action is visible in plyometric movements. When the muscle is stretched rapidly, the series elastic component is also stretched and stores a portion of the load force in the form of elastic potential energy. The recovery of the stored elastic energy occurs during the concentric, or overcoming, phase of muscle contraction triggered by the myostatic reflex.

The inclusion of plyometric training enhances an athlete's ability to perform more rapid and powerful movements—key skills used on the basketball court.

In plyometric training a muscle will contract more forcefully and quickly from a prestretched position. The more rapid the prestretch is, the more forceful the concentric contraction will be. Correct technique is essential. The athlete must land in a prestretched position (legs and arms bent). The shortening contraction should occur immediately after completion of the prestretch phase. The transition from the prestretch phase should be smooth, continuous, and as swift as possible.

Plyometric training results in the following:

- The quick mobilization of greater innervation activities.
- The recruitment of most, if not all, motor units and their corresponding muscle fibers.
- An increase in the firing rate of the motor neurons.
- The transformation of muscle strength into explosive power.
- Development of the nervous system so it will react with maximum speed to the lengthening of the muscle; this will develop the ability to shorten (contract) rapidly with maximum force.
- Fatigue induced by repeated reactive training that affects eccentric and concentric work capacity. Fatigue is characterized by increased contact time (Gollhofer et al., 1987).

- Improvements in explosive force with only slight increases in thigh girths and with selective increases in mean cross-sectional area of fast-twitch fibers (Häkkinen and Komi, 1983). This is indicative of performance enhancement at the neuromuscular level.

- Golgi tendon organ inhibition, which could lead to greater stretch loads, increased muscle spindle firing, and greater energy storage, all of which contribute to an enhanced power output (Schmidtbleicher, 1992).

A good strength training background of several years will help an athlete progress faster through plyometric training. Prior experience is also an important factor in preventing injury. In terms of establishing a good base of strength and developing shock-absorbing qualities, the benefits of introducing children to plyometric exercises should not be dismissed; however, these exercises must be performed over several years, and the principle of progression must be respected. The key element of this approach is *patience*.

A healthy training progression for children would be to first expose them to low-impact plyometrics over several years, say, between the ages of 14 and 16. After this initial period, they can be introduced to more demanding reactive jumps. Throughout these years of long-term progression, teachers and coaches should teach young athletes the correct plyometric techniques using the "hop" and "step" from the triple jump as the ABCs of plyometric training.

Several points of controversy surround plyometric exercises. One is the amount of strength that should be developed before doing plyometrics. Some authors consider the ability to perform half squats with a load twice the body weight a safe guide. Others address the type of training surface, what equipment to use, and whether additional weights such as heavy vests and ankle and waist belts should be worn when performing these exercises.

Where injury is a concern, exercises should be performed on a soft surface, either outdoors on grass or soft ground or indoors on a padded floor. Although this precaution may be appropriate for beginners, a soft surface can dampen the stretch reflex; only a hard surface can enhance the reactivity of the neuromuscular system. Thus, athletes with an extensive background in sports, strength training, or both, should use a hard surface.

Finally, weighted ankle and waist belts should not be used during plyometric drills. These weights tend to decrease the reactive ability of the nerve–muscle coupling and obstruct the reactivity of the neuromuscular system. Furthermore, although such overloading may result in increased strength, it certainly slows the speed of reaction and the rebounding effect.

Mechanical Characteristics of Plyometrics

Plyometric action relies mechanically on the stretch reflex found in the belly of each muscle. The main purpose of the stretch reflex is to monitor the degree of muscle stretch and thereby prevent overstretching and possible tearing of any muscle fiber. When an athlete is jumping off the ground, a large amount of force is required to propel the entire body mass upward. To leave the ground, the body must be able to flex and extend the limbs very quickly. A plyometric exercise relies on this quick body action to attain the power required for the movement.

Mechanically, when the takeoff leg is planted, athletes must lower their center of gravity, creating a downward velocity. This "amortization phase" is an important component of any jumping activity because athletes prepare for takeoff in a different direction during this phase. A long amortization phase, also called the shock-absorbing phase, is responsible for a loss of power. For example, long jumpers who do not plant the takeoff leg properly will lose both the upward and horizontal velocity required to propel them forward. Athletes who perform jumping actions must work toward a shorter and quicker amortization phase. The shorter this phase is, the more powerful the concentric muscle contraction will be when the muscle has previously been stretched during the eccentric contraction or amortization phase (Bosco and Komi, 1980).

This action is possible because of the recovery and use of all the energy that has been stored in the elastic components of the muscle during any stretching action.

All jumping motion can be improved by analyzing each biomechanical component of the jump. An example of this is improvement in a high jumper's technique. High-jump performance can be enhanced by eliminating the deep knee bend phase and shortening the time interval between the eccentric and concentric contractions. Eliminating a deep flexion results in the more efficient use of the elastic qualities of the muscle.

First jumpers need to lower their center of gravity, creating a downward velocity. They must then produce forces to counter the downward motion (amortization phase) to prepare for the upward thrusting phase. Remember that force equals mass times acceleration ($F = m \times a$). Greater force is required to decelerate the body more quickly and result in a shorter amortization phase. From this, a second equation can be derived:

$$\text{Average force of amortization} = \text{body mass} \times \text{change in velocity/time of amortization}$$

This equation shows that if athletes want to decrease the time of amortization, they must generate a greater average force. If they are unable to do so, a longer, less efficient amortization phase will result, with a loss of horizontal velocity because of the weakened concentric contraction.

The equation also points out the importance of maintaining a low level of body fat and a high power-to-weight ratio. An increase in body mass requires an even greater average force of amortization. A greater downward velocity at impact requires an increase in the average force produced during the amortization phase. For example, when long or high jumpers lower their center of gravity before takeoff, they reduce the impact of the forces.

The entire body must be used efficiently to maximize jumping ability. The upward acceleration of the free limbs (e.g., the arms) after the amortization phase acts to increase the vertical forces placed on the takeoff leg. For example, triple jumpers must be able to apply peak force as many as six times their body weight to compensate for the inability to lower their center of gravity during the more upward hopping phase. Long jumpers, on the other hand, can manipulate their bodies more easily just before takeoff. Jumpers will achieve effective takeoff only if they can apply large forces on impact and produce a shorter, quicker amortization phase.

Training for the takeoff phase of the jump is difficult because few conventional exercises apply. Many jumpers use traditional weight training (e.g., squats) to train for the takeoff phase of their jumps. This type of weight training places a large load on the leg extensors, which over time will provide an adequate strength training base. The main problem with using only weight training, however, is that a heavy squat lift is unlikely to be fast enough to use the elastic qualities of the muscles.

Bounding exercises, on the other hand, can successfully simulate an effective takeoff and improve overall jumping ability. Bounding has similar force–time characteristics as the takeoff. It also allows athletes to practice resisting heavy loads on the takeoff leg and to exert force in a short time interval. Bounding exercises also involve multijoint movement and facilitate the development of the required muscle elasticity.

Program Design for the Plyometric Method

To design a plyometric program properly, coaches and trainers must be aware that the exercises vary in level of intensity and are classified in different groups for better progression. The level of intensity is directly proportional to the height or length of an exercise. High-intensity plyometric exercises such as reactive or drop jumps result in higher tension in the muscle, which recruits more neuromuscular units to perform the action or to resist the pull of gravitational force.

Plyometric exercises can be categorized into two major groups that reflect their degree of impact on the neuromuscular system. Low-impact exercises include skipping; rope jumps; jumps with low and short steps, hops, and jumps; jumps over a rope or low bench 10 to 15 inches (25 to 35 centimeters) high; throws of a 5- to 9-pound (2- to 4-kilogram) medicine ball; tubing; and throwing light implements (e.g., a baseball). High-impact exercises include standing long and triple jumps; jumps with higher and longer steps, hops, and jumps; jumps over a rope or high bench 15 inches (35 centimeters) or higher; jumps on, over, and off boxes 15 inches (35 centimeters) or higher; throws of an 11- to 13-pound (5- to 6-kilogram) medicine ball; throwing heavy implements; drop jumps and reactive jumps; and "shock" muscle tension induced by machines.

From a more practical viewpoint, plyometric exercises can be divided into five levels of intensity (see table 11.6). This classification can be used to plan better alternation of training demand throughout the week. In table 11.6, the suggested number of reps and sets is for advanced athletes. Coaches should resist the temptation to apply these numbers to beginners or athletes with an insufficient foundation in sports or strength training.

Table 11.6 Five Levels of Intensity of Plyometric Exercises

Intensity level	Type of exercises	Intensity of exercises	No. of reps and sets	No. of reps per training session	Rest interval
1	Shock tension, high reactive jumps >60 centimeters (>24 inches)/(200)	Maximum	5-8 × 10-20	120-150	8-10 minutes
2	Drop jumps 80-120 centimeters (32-48 inches)	Very high	5-15 × 5-15	75-150	5-7 minutes
3	Bounding exercises: Two legs One leg	Submaximum	3-25 × 5-15	50-250	3-5 minutes
4	Low reactive jumps 20-50 centimeters (8-20 inches)	Moderate	10-25 × 10-25	150-250	3-5 minutes
5	Low-impact jumps/throws: On spot Implements	Low	10-30 × 10-15	50-300	2-3 minutes

Any plan to incorporate plyometric exercises into a training program should consider the following factors:

- The age and physical development of the athlete
- The skills and techniques involved in plyometric exercises
- The principal performance factors of the sport
- The energy requirements of the sport
- The particular training phase of the yearly plan
- The need to respect methodical progression over a long period (two to four years), progressing from low-impact (levels 5 and 4 in table 11.6), to simple bounding (level 3), and then to high-impact exercises (levels 2 and 1)

Although plyometric exercises are fun, they demand a high level of concentration and are deceptively vigorous and taxing. The lack of discipline to wait for the right moment for each exercise can result in athletes performing high-impact exercises before they are ready. The injuries or physiological discomforts that result are not the fault of the plyometric exercises. Rather, they are the result of the coach's or instructor's lack of knowledge and application. The five levels of intensity will help coaches design a plan that includes appropriate exercises that follow a consistent, steady, and orderly progression and incorporates appropriate rest intervals.

Progression through the five levels of intensity is long term. The two to four years spent incorporating low-impact exercises into the training programs of young athletes are necessary for the progressive adaptation of ligaments, tendons, and bones. They also allow for the gradual preparation of the shock-absorbing sections of the body, such as the hips and spine.

Table 11.7 illustrates a long-term comprehensive progression of strength and power training including plyometric training. Coaches should observe the age suggested for the introduction of plyometrics, as well as the precept that high-impact plyometrics should only be introduced after four years of training. This is the time required to learn proper technique and to allow for progressive anatomical adaptation. From this point on, high-impact plyometrics can be part of an athlete's normal training regimen.

Table 11.7 Long-Term Strength Development and the Progression of Plyometric Training

Age groups	Forms of training	Method	Volume	Intensity	Means of training
Prepuberty (12-13 years)	General exercises only Games	Muscular endurance	Low Medium	Very low	Light resistance exercises Light implements Power ball/Medicine ball
Beginners (13-15 years)	General strength Event-oriented exercises	M-E	Low Medium	Low	Dumbbells Tubing Power ball Selected machines
Intermediate (15-17 years)	General strength Event-oriented exercises	Bodybuilding M-E Power	Low Medium High	Low Medium	All the above Free weights
Advanced (>17 years)	Event-oriented exercises Specific strength	Bodybuilding M-E Power MxS Low-impact plyometrics	Medium High Maximum	Medium High	Free weights Special strength equipment
High performance	Specific strength	All the above Eccentric Plyometrics Low impact High impact	As above	Medium High Supermaximum	As above

The intensity in plyometric exercises—the amount of tension created in the muscle—depends on the height from which the exercise is performed. Although the height is determined strictly by the individual qualities of the athlete, the following general principle applies: The stronger the muscular system, the greater the energy required to stretch it to obtain an elastic effect in the shortening phase. Thus, what is optimal height for one athlete may not generate enough stimulation for another. Therefore, the following information should be treated only as a guideline.

According to Verkhoshanski (1969), to facilitate athlete gains in dynamic strength (power), the optimal height for depth (reactive) jumps for speed training should be between 30 and 43 inches (75 and 110 centimeters). Bosco and Komi (1980) reported similar findings. The latter authors concluded that above 43 inches (110 centimeters) the mechanics of the action are changed; the time and energy it takes to cushion the force of the drop on the ground defeats the purpose of plyometric training. Other authors tried exceptional heights. Zanon (1977) employed the following heights for elite long jumpers: 8.2 feet (2.5 meters) for men and 7 feet (2.1 meters) for women. The landing from boxes of these heights was immediately followed by a long jump for distance!

As far as the number of reps is concerned, plyometric drills fall into two categories: single-response and multiple-response. The former consist of a single action such as a high-reactive jump, shock tension (level 1 in table 11.6), or a drop jump (level 2), in which the main purpose is to induce the highest level of tension in the muscles. The objective of such exercises is to develop maximum strength and power. Repetitive exercises such as bounding (level 3) and low-reactive (level 4) and low-impact (level 5) jumps result in the development of power and power-endurance. As suggested in table 11.6, the number of reps can be between 3 and 30, with the number of sets ranging from 5 to 25 depending on the goal of training, the type of exercise, and the athlete's background and physical potential.

Often, especially for multiple-response exercises, it is more convenient and practical to equate the number of reps with a distance, for example, five sets of 50 meters rather than five sets of 25 reps. This eliminates the need to count the number of reps constantly.

An important factor for high-quality training is adequate physiological recuperation between exercises. Often athletes and coaches either pay too little attention to the duration of the rest interval or are simply caught up in the traditions of a given sport, which often dictate that the only rest interval required is the time needed to move from one station to another. This amount of time is inadequate, especially considering the physiological characteristics of plyometric training.

Fatigue consists of local fatigue and CNS fatigue. Local fatigue results from depletion of the energy stored in the muscle (ATP-CP) (the fuel necessary to perform explosive movements) and the production of lactic acid from reps longer than 15 seconds. During training, athletes also fatigue the CNS, the system that signals to the working muscle to perform a given amount of quality work. Plyometric training is performed as a result of these nerve impulses, which have a certain speed, power, and frequency. Any high-quality training requires that the speed of contraction, its power, and its frequency be at the highest level possible.

When the rest interval is short (one to two minutes), the athlete experiences local and CNS fatigue. The working muscle is unable to remove lactic acid and has insufficient time to replenish the energy necessary to perform the next reps with the same intensity. Similarly, a fatigued CNS is unable to send the powerful nerve impulses necessary to ensure that the prescribed load is performed for the same number of reps and sets before exhaustion sets in. Because exhaustion is often just a short step away from injury, coaches and athletes should pay utmost attention to the rest interval.

As suggested in table 11.6, the rest interval is a function of the load and type of plyometric training performed—the higher the intensity of the exercise is, the longer the rest interval should be. Consequently, for maximum-intensity exercises (high-reactive jumps), the rest interval between sets should be 8 to 10 minutes or even longer. The suggested rest interval for intensity level 2 is five to seven minutes; for levels 3 and 4, it should be between three and five minutes, and for low-impact activities (level 5), it should be around two to three minutes.

The type of plyometric training that an athlete performs must be specific to the individual sport. For example, athletes who require a greater degree of horizontal power should engage in more bounding and hopping drills, whereas vertical jump exercises are appropriate for athletes whose sports require vertical power. Coaches should also consider the training environment. Many studies have demonstrated that reflexes can be altered or modified using specific training modes (Enoka, 1994; Schmidtbleicher, 1992). Plyometrics is one form of training that induces particular adaptations in various reflexive actions. However, for the reflexive learning process to be reproduced in the competitive realm, the athlete must be in the same psychological and physiological state as when the reflex adaptation was induced. Thus, the training environment should be a near perfect replica of the competitive environment.

Power-Endurance Method

Sports such as sprints in track and field, swimming, and wrestling, and positions such as running back or pitcher, require a high degree of power applied several times repetitively. Sprinting, including sprinting in all team sports requiring explosive running (American football, basketball, baseball, ice hockey, rugby, soccer, and Australian football), is often misjudged. When sprinters cover the classic 100 meters in 10 to 12 seconds, they have trained to perform powerful leg actions throughout the entire race, not just at the start and for the following six to eight strides. In a 100-meter race, athletes take 48 to 54 strides, depending on stride length; thus each leg makes 24 to 27 contacts with the ground. In each ground contact, the force applied is approximately twice the athlete's body weight!

Consequently, athletes who compete in these sports need to perform powerful actions over and over. In American football, rugby, and Australian football, athletes are often required to repeat a strenuous activity after only a few seconds of game interruption. The same athletic performances are required in the martial arts, boxing, wrestling, and racket sports. To do this successfully, these athletes need a high power output and the ability to repeat it 20 to 30 (and up to 60 times) times dynamically and as explosively as possible.

The equation for training power-endurance is as follows:

$$HV \times HI$$

Hockey players must perform powerful leg actions throughout the game, increasing the need to train using the power endurance method.

or high volume (HV) of reps performed explosively, fast, and quickly (high intensity, or HI), using exercises as close to the pattern of technical skills as possible.

Athletes with a high level of power-endurance will have the capacity to avoid a decrease in stride frequency and velocity at the end of a race or a longer sprint.

Program Design for the Power-Endurance Method

Power and power-endurance are the determinant abilities in several sports, and maximum strength is a determinant factor in both abilities. This section describes the training methodology for developing power-endurance in an explosive manner.

Power-endurance requires 30 to a maximum of 50 percent of maximum strength repeated rhythmically and explosively. Such a load requires dynamic reps executed explosively 20 to 30 (up to 60) times nonstop. Such an important training requirement can be achieved progressively, starting with a lower number of reps (12 to 15) and increasing them to 30 to 60 over four to six weeks, which is the duration of the conversion phase for such sports.

Early in the conversion phase, the fast-twitch muscle fibers are trained to instantaneously display the highest possible level of power. Parallel with that, athletes should increase the quickness of performance for the purpose of increasing the discharge rate of the fast-twitch muscles as much as possible. Now, for power-endurance purposes, the fast-twitch fibers are trained to cope with the fatigue and the buildup of lactic acid induced by performing many reps dynamically. Training is now aimed at developing the endurance component of speed, or specific power moves, typical for some of the sports mentioned earlier, which is accomplished by progressively increasing the number of reps and sets. This requires athletes to exert maximum willpower to overcome fatigue and to reach optimum mental concentration before performing each set.

This six-week progression can be reduced to four weeks. However, a program that is shorter than that is totally insufficient to achieve the physiological goal of power-endurance.

To perform a high number of sets for each prime mover, the number of exercises must be as low as possible (two to four, rarely five). At the same time, each rep in a set of 20 to 40 reps has to be performed explosively, and the rest interval has to be three to five minutes long to allow for CNS recovery.

During this type of work, athletes will experience a high level of lactic acid buildup. This is why the number of reps has to be high so that the athlete learns to tolerate the lactic acid buildup and perform successfully under this condition. Without this training, the athlete will not perform successfully during competition.

Speed of performance must be dynamic and explosive. Unless this rule is strictly observed, power or power-endurance training will build muscle mass rather than power; the outcome will be hypertrophy rather than power-endurance! Athletes often require a few weeks before they can perform 20 to 30 (60) reps explosively nonstop. In the meantime, they should stop when they become incapable of performing a rep dynamically because at that point power-endurance is no longer being trained. A summary of training parameters for power-endurance is listed in table 11.8. Figure 11.4 shows a sample four-week training program for a racket-sport athlete.

Pulling Devices and Elastic Cords

The sport-specific training industry is growing at a rapid pace. Along with the introduction of theories and methods of training, many products have entered this market over the past 10 years. Although many coaches and trainers endorse the use of speed- and power-enhancing products such as pulling devices and elastic cords, we believe that many of these products can be detrimental to training. In this section we discuss a few controversial training methods.

Table 11.8 Training Parameters for Power-Endurance

Training parameters	Work
Load	30-50 percent
Number of exercises	2-5
Number of repetitions per set	15-30
Number of sets per session	2-4
Rest interval	3-5 minutes
Speed of execution	Very dynamic
Frequency per week	2-3

No.	Exercise	Week 1	Week 2	Week 3	Week 4	Rest Interval
1	Jumping half-squats	$\frac{50}{15}2$	$\frac{50}{20}2$	$\frac{50}{20}2$	$\frac{50}{25}3$	4-5 min.
2	Power ball (2-3 kg) side throws (each arm alternatively)	2×30	2×40	3×45	3×50	2-4 min.
3	Power ball overhead-forward throw	3×15	3×20	2×30	3×30	2 min.
4	Deceleration drill	12 reps	15 reps	20 reps	20 reps	3 min.
Loading pattern		Medium	High	Medium	High	

Figure 11.4 Suggested power-endurance for racket sports.

Over the past 10 to 15 years a series of pulling devices have entered the fitness and sport-specific industry for the purpose of increasing speed and power performance. It is speculated that using elastic cords or cables to pull oneself forward will stimulate the neuromuscular system more than natural sprinting and thus increase maximum speed. Some of these devices, such as sleds or harnesses, have a limited benefit; others, such as elastic cords, may actually work against the natural mechanics of sprinting and decrease speed as a result.

Maximum acceleration is generated not by artificially pulling the body forward, but by *pushing* it forward. In high-velocity running the body is propelled forward by the power applied against the ground during the propulsion phase (the push-off in ice hockey or the pulling-pushing against the water resistance in water polo). The more powerful the propulsion is, the shorter the duration of the contact phase will be. As such, the athlete is able to run faster.

One of the first researchers to measure the duration of the contact phase was Schmidtbleicher (1984). He found that the best sprinters have a short contact phase of between 100 and 200 milliseconds. The duration of foot contact with the ground for mediocre sprinters is well over 200 milliseconds. Therefore, high velocity is the result of a powerful and fast force applied against the ground (in the propulsion phase). A pulling force produced by artificial means will not have the same effect.

As a cable or elastic band pulls a player forward, velocity is decreased rather than increased. The artificial forward pull places the landing leg in an unknown, disturbed neuromuscular function. As the foot touches the ground, the proprioceptors detect that the leg is being pulled over the landing phase far too quickly compared to normal running, destabilizing the steadying and running mechanics. The proprioceptors send information about this new condition to the CNS telling it to monitor the status of the neuromuscular system (Enoka, 2002). These neural actions work to correct the disturbing factors and stabilize the leg before it can once again perform a strong propulsion action. The few milliseconds necessary to relay these neural signals and stabilize the body is just long enough to prolong the duration of the contact phase. A longer contact phase means a decrease in sprinting velocity.

The force of propulsion is also affected by the forward pull of an artificial pulling device. As the coach or partner pulls the athlete forward, the propulsion leg does not have enough time to powerfully apply force against the ground. Consequently, a strong propulsion phase is quite impossible. As the force of propulsion decreases, the duration of the contact phase increases and the player's velocity decreases.

This artificial pull also changes the mechanics of running. During stabilization of the landing leg, the trunk leans backward slightly, moving the center of gravity to behind the support leg. This is a typical position for deceleration, not for acceleration—not a favorable position for a strong forward push. As a neuromuscular reaction to the backward lean of the trunk, the forward driving leg is lifted over the horizontal line, lengthening the duration of this leg's action and slowing running velocity.

Elastic Bands (and Cords) and Power Development   Elastic bands, and especially elastic cords, have been used in sports training since the 1950s, first in Romania, and then in other countries, arriving in the United States by the late 1970s.

The first problem with the use of elastic bands and cords is the risk of injury. As the elastic cord is stretched, resistance increases. As resistance increases, the speed of contraction decreases, and the strain in the joint increases. This strain may overstretch the ligaments, resulting in a joint injury over time.

The second problem with the use of these elastic devices is their inability to develop power. Any action performed with the scope of developing power has to continuously increase acceleration throughout the range of motion, with maximum speed achieved at the instant of release (of the ball or javelin). Without constant acceleration, the discharge rate of the fast-twitch muscle fibers is low, and the development of power quite impossible.

Elastic cords may have some role in training muscular endurance. Athletes can perform many reps against the cord's resistance, without jerking. Such a training program can be organized in a form of interval training with long durations and a high number of reps.

Elastic Cords and Speed Development   Swimmers have been using elastic cords in their training to increase their maximum speed. One end of the cord is hooked around the waist of the swimmer while the other end is attached to the opposite end of the pool. The swimmer stretches the cord to its limit and then allows the cord to pull him forward. As the cord is pulling the swimmer forward, he has to swim as fast as possible. When the artificial pulling stops, unfortunately so does the speed. The velocity is not produced by the athlete, but rather by the elastic property of the cord. This does not affect the swimmer's ability to achieve maximum speed.

Sport-Specific Application of Power Training

Power must be developed to meet the needs of a given sport, event, or team position. To further illustrate the need for the sport-specific application of power, definitive examples are presented in this section. Many elements of the previously described power training methods are also applicable.

Landing and Reactive Power

In several sports, not only is landing an important skill, but it is often followed by the performance of another skill (e.g., another jump in figure skating or a quick move in another direction, as in tennis or many team sports). Thus, the athlete must have the power to control the landing as well as the reactive power to perform another move quickly.

The power needed to control and absorb the shock of landing is related to the height of the jump. Landings such as drop or depth jumps from 32 to 40 inches (80 to 100 centimeters) often load the ankle joints with six to eight times the athlete's body weight. To absorb the shock from a figure skating jump, a power of five to eight times one's body weight is required. Muscles must be trained for shock-absorbing power to reduce impact forces at the instant of landing.

Landing involves an eccentric contraction. Without proper training, the result will be an incorrect landing and exposure to injury because higher tension is produced with the same amount of muscle fiber activity, and the elastic tissue of the tendons is placed under greater stress. To overcome this, eccentric contraction as well as plyometrics should be applied in training.

Schmidtbleicher (1992) specified that at the instant of ground contact, athletes experience an *inhibitory effect*. He noted that well-trained athletes cope with impact forces much better than poorly trained athletes do, and that drop jump training reduced inhibitory effects. He concluded that the inhibitory mechanisms represent a protective system, especially for novice athletes, that shields them against injury.

To enhance landing and reactive power, concentric and eccentric contractions should be a part of training. Eccentric strength training and plyometrics, primarily drop jumps, that mimic the desired landing skill are important. Drop or reactive jumps are performed from a raised platform (box, bench, or chair), with the athlete landing in a flexed position (knees slightly bent) to absorb the shock. The athlete lands on the balls of the feet without touching the heels to the ground.

During the dropping phase, the muscles adopt a reflex or ready-to-work position, which enhances the tension and the elastic properties of the muscles. At landing, especially if the athlete is quickly preparing for another action, energy is stored in the elastic elements of the muscle. At the ensuing takeoff or quick move in another direction, this readily available energy releases a stretching reflex that recruits more fast-twitch fibers than under normal strength training conditions. This enables the athlete to perform another quick and explosive action immediately. Practitioners should understand that these reflexes (including the muscle spindle reflex) are trainable, and that drop or reactive jumps can be improved as a result of a well-periodized training.

Specific exercises for developing landing and reactive power are illustrated in the following sections. These example combinations are not meant to be an exhaustive list, but to inspire coaches to devise their own versions.

Throwing Power

For a pitcher in baseball, a quarterback in American football, or a thrower in track and field, throwing power is generated mostly by fast-twitch muscle fibers. The larger the diameter of the individual fiber, the faster it contracts. Similarly, the more fibers involved in a simultaneous contraction, the greater the power for delivery of an implement.

Throwers and athletes in sports such as fencing, boxing, and baseball must be able to develop considerable power to accelerate the implement or the equipment they use. These athletes often have to overcome the inertia of an implement or piece of equipment with the greatest possible speed from the beginning of the movement, increasing acceleration throughout the movement, especially before the release. To achieve this, internal strength must exceed the resistance of the implement. The more one exceeds the weight of the implement, the higher the acceleration will be. A well-planned maximum strength and power training phase is required for sports that use throwing power. The greater the difference is between the maximum strength of the athlete and the resistance of the implement, the higher the acceleration will be.

Specific power training for throwing events and movements must concentrate on the maximum application of force and use the isotonic and ballistic methods. For the isotonic method, the reps (4 to 10) need not be performed nonstop and at a high rate. For maximum benefit of explosive contraction in which the greatest number of fast-twitch fibers are recruited at once, athletes should perform one rep at a time while achieving the highest mental concentration before each of them.

Takeoff Power

In many sports (jumping events in track and field, ski jumping, volleyball, basketball, soccer, figure skating, and diving), good performance is possible only if the athlete is capable of an explosive takeoff. In many cases, takeoff occurs following a short-distance, high-velocity run, during which the muscles prestretch and store energy. At takeoff, this energy is used as an acceleration thrust, producing a powerful jump.

The depth of the crouch needed at the instant of joint flexion depends on leg power. The deeper the crouch is, the greater the force required from the leg extensors is. The crouch is a mechanical necessity, though, because it puts the muscles in a state of stretch, giving them a greater distance to accelerate, culminating in a takeoff. The depth of the crouch must be proportional to the power of the legs. If the flexion is too great, the extension (or shortening phase) will be performed slowly, and as a result, the jump will be low.

Many jumpers use traditional weight training (e.g., squats) to train for the takeoff phase. This type of weight training places a large load on the leg extensors and, over time, will provide an adequate strength training base. The main problem with using only weight training is that a heavy squat lift is unlikely to be fast enough to make use of the elastic qualities of the muscles. The single-leg takeoff, however, uses multijoint movements, all happening simultaneously.

Plyometric and bounding exercises can be used to simulate an effective takeoff and improve the athlete's overall jumping ability. Bounding has the potential to possess force–time characteristics similar to those of the takeoff. In addition, it allows the athlete to practice resisting heavy loads on the takeoff leg and exert force in a short time interval. Bounding exercises also involve multijoint movements and provide the opportunity to develop the required muscle elasticity.

Starting Power

Starting power is an essential and often determinant ability in sports in which the initial speed of action dictates the final outcome (boxing, karate, fencing, the start in sprinting, or the beginning of an aggressive acceleration from standing in team sports). The athlete's ability to recruit the highest possible number of fast-twitch fibers to start the motion explosively is the fundamental physiological characteristic necessary for successful performance.

In sprinting, starting is performed with the muscles in the prestretched position (both knees bent), from which they can generate greater power than when relaxed or shortened. In this position, the elastic elements of the muscles store kinetic energy that acts like a spring at the sound of the gun. The power used by national-class athletes is very high at the start: 290 pounds (132 kilograms) for the front leg and 225 pounds (102 kilograms) for the back leg. The higher the starting power is, the more explosive and faster the start will be.

In boxing and the martial arts, a quick and powerful start of an offensive skill prevents an opponent from using an effective defensive action. The elastic, reactive component of muscle is of vital importance for delivering quick action and powerful starts. The more specific the power training during the conversion phase, the better a muscle's stretch reflex and the greater the power of the fast-twitch fibers.

The stretching and reactive components of the muscle that are key to starting a motion quickly and powerfully are trainable through isotonic, ballistic, and especially maxex and plyometric exercises. They can be performed in a set of repetitive motions or separately. In the latter case, exercises in a set are performed one at a time so the athlete has enough time to reach maximum mental concentration to perform them as explosively as possible. These conditions make it possible to recruit a high number of fast-twitch fibers, and consequently, the athlete can perform the action with the greatest power available.

Acceleration Power

In sprinting, swimming, cycling, rowing, and most team sports, the athlete's ability to accelerate to develop high speed is crucial for improving performance. Power is an essential attribute for every sport that requires high acceleration. Without power, an athlete cannot perform the powerful push against the ground that is needed for the propulsion phase in running or to overcome water resistance in sports performed in water.

In sprinting, for instance, the force applied against the ground is two to three times that of the athlete's body weight. In rowing, the oarsperson must use a constant blade pressure of 88 to 132 pounds (40 to 60 kilograms) per stroke to maintain high acceleration. In all sports requiring acceleration power, the forceful actions involved must be performed repetitively and very rapidly. The greater the difference between maximum strength and, in the previous instances, water resistance or the power applied against the ground, the higher the acceleration.

To achieve high acceleration, the development of maximum strength is essential. A key physiological requirement for the ability to display power is a relatively large diameter of the contracting muscle filaments. These filaments, primarily the protein-rich myosin cross-bridges, can increase their size or hypertrophy only through maximum strength training methods. Because this is achieved during the maximum strength phase, the gains have to be converted to power through specific power training methods. The isotonic, ballistic, power-resisting, and plyometric methods can assist athletes in successfully applying the series of muscle impulses that will activate a great number of fast-twitch fibers. When this is achieved, acceleration power reaches the desired high levels.

These methods can be done using either a low number of reps (6 to 10) performed explosively and with high frequency, or individually, one rep at a time. In the first case, the goal is repeated displays of power; in the second case, the goal is to apply the highest amount of power in a single attempt. In sports in which acceleration power is required, athletes must be capable of performing powerful actions with high frequency, so both methods must be used. By applying periodization of strength, athletes increase the likelihood of achieving these effects as well as reaching peak acceleration power before major competitions.

Deceleration Power

In several sports, especially tennis and team sports, deceleration is as important as acceleration. To overtake an opponent or make oneself available to receive a pass, a team sport player must accelerate and run as quickly as possible. In sports such as soccer, basketball, lacrosse, and ice hockey, they also need to decelerate, decreasing speed very quickly to stop, and then quickly change running direction or jump to rebound an oncoming ball. Often an athlete who can decelerate fast can create a tactical advantage. Performing a quick deceleration can require leg power up to twice one's body weight.

Deceleration is performed through eccentric contraction of the leg muscles. This is facilitated by placing the feet ahead of the center of gravity and leaving the upper body behind it. Strong legs and good biomechanics enable athletes to decelerate quickly. Muscles developed to decelerate quickly from a fast sprint rely on their elastic properties to amortize and reduce impact forces. The ability to amortize these forces requires power and degrees of leg flexion similar to those needed for absorbing shock while landing.

To train the muscles to decelerate quickly, athletes must employ several training methods such as eccentric contraction and plyometrics. For eccentric contraction, the maximum strength method (eccentric) must be applied with progression from medium to supermaximum loads. For plyometrics, after a few years of normal progression from low- to high-impact exercises, drop (depth) and reactive jumps should be used. Athletes will successfully develop the needed deceleration power by following the methodology described for these methods.

Conversion to Muscular Endurance

No matter how intensive or comprehensive it is, strength training cannot result in adequate adaptation and have a positive training effect unless the specific physiological needs of the given sport are addressed. Most training specialists might agree with this statement, but in reality, strength training programs for sports and events in which endurance is either dominant or an important component are still inadequate. Olympic weightlifting and bodybuilding training methods still unduly influence these programs. Although 20 reps may result in what bodybuilders consider muscular endurance, such a training regimen is grossly inadequate for sports such as mid- and long-distance swimming, rowing, canoeing, boxing, wrestling, cross-country skiing, speedskating, and triathlon, in which aerobic endurance is dominant.

If a low-rep strength training program with submaximum (i.e., 70 percent of 1RM) or maximum loads (well over 80 percent) is employed, the energy supply, recovery, and physiological functioning of the organs and the neuromuscular system will adapt to such loading. Increased strength will result, but not muscular endurance. Such a program, therefore, will not result in optimal performance in endurance-dominant sports.

As already mentioned, high-load strength training activates fast-twitch muscle fibers. This is well known, accepted, and applied in strength training for sports in which speed and power are the dominant abilities. However, athletic activities of long duration require a different type of training. During longer-duration sports or events, the pace is often submaximal, and therefore the tension in the muscles is lower. As a result, the CNS recruits first those muscle fibers specialized and adapted to cope with long-lasting physiological functioning: the slow twitch and fast-twitch "A" muscle fibers. As a result of endurance training, the body is better able to use fat as fuel, sparing glycogen stores and disposing of and reusing lactic acid more efficiently. However, these physiological adaptations cannot be accomplished solely by performing the sport. Because the load in training remains the same, the body is not forced to adapt to a higher threshold stimulus. In other words, continuous rowing is not a sufficient stimulus for improving muscular endurance and sport performance. Strength training at low to moderate loads with high reps trains the slow-twitch and fast-twitch muscles to better respond to the dynamics of the sports. Because fatigue seems to occur in stages (Wilmore and Costill, 1988), when slow-twitch and fast-twitch fibers become exhausted, the fast and powerful fast-twitch "B" fibers are recruited to work. Organizing a training program with the intent of recruiting and maximizing the involvement of all three fibers is the best method of enhancing muscular endurance. Aerobic-dominant sports, therefore, should do the following:

- Use muscular endurance of long duration training methods that specifically address the adaptation of slow-twitch fibers, which are needed during long-duration sporting activities. The better they are trained, the longer they can produce the specific force in long-lasting events.

- Alternate muscular endurance of long duration with muscular endurance of short duration strength training methods so that fast-twitch A and fast-twitch B fibers are also recruited and, therefore, adapt to the specifics of long-duration activities.

- Use specific endurance training methods, such as long intervals (several reps of 10 to 30 minutes nonstop) and long-distance training to adapt the body to effectively use free fatty acids as a fuel and improve cardiovascular efficiency.

Endurance training also enhances the oxidative capacity of fast-twitch fibers, resulting in increased mitochondria and the oxidative enzymes. As a result, the athlete will rely more heavily on fat (free fatty acids) for ATP production (Wilmore and Costill, 1988). Under the previous training conditions, athletes are trained both in strength and specific endurance, according to the physiological profile of the sport.

A strength training program for endurance-dominant sports requires slightly higher loads than the resistance that must be overcome while competing, relatively low muscle tension, and a high number of reps that approach the duration of the event. This trains athletes to cope with the fatigue specific to the sport and to use simultaneous stimuli for both the cardiorespiratory and neuromuscular systems and thus match the needs for specific strength and endurance. The physiological requirements of such training will be very similar to those of competition. Fortunately, the neuromuscular system is capable of adapting to any type of training.

The importance of maximum strength for endurance-dominant sports increases in proportion to external resistance. For instance, 400-meter swimmers swim with a higher velocity than 800- to 1,500-meter swimmers. To create the higher velocity, 400-meter swimmers have to pull against the water resistance with greater force than 1,500-meter swimmers. Consequently, maximum strength is more important for 400-meter than for 1,500-meter swimmers. In both cases, maximum strength must be improved from year to year if athletes expect to cover the distance faster. Such improvement is possible only if swimmers improve their aerobic endurance and increase the force used to pull against the water resistance. Only this increased force will push the body through the water faster. The belief that maximum strength training will make swimmers slower because of the low velocity of training is a myth. Maximum strength training is the only way to adapt the neuromuscular system to pulling heavy loads, providing a strong foundation on which to enhance muscular endurance.

Muscular endurance is best increased through a strength training program that emphasizes a high number of reps performed at a steady pace. The selected exercises and the number of reps have to result in the desired adaptation to the physiological requirements of the sport or event. Athletes who do not apply adequate training methods during the conversion of maximum strength to muscular endurance cannot expect a positive transfer from training to the competitive environment. A bodybuilding or Olympic-weightlifting methodology, in which 20 reps are considered optimal, won't help athletes in a sport requiring over 200 nonstop strokes, such as swimming, rowing, and canoeing, or marathon running (with its 50,000 strides).

As in all sport-specific periodization models, the number of reps performed in the sport cannot suddenly appear in the athlete's training schedule. The increase in reps (at a specific load) must occur gradually. Load increases between 2.5 and 5 percent are optimal; any more of an increase can tremendously affect the number of reps performed.

For endurance sports, aerobic endurance and muscular endurance have to be trained at the same time. This can be done either by training each of them on separate days or, sometimes, combining them in the same training session. In the latter case, muscular endurance should be performed at the end of the session because the specific endurance work may often include technical training. Fatigue can limit combined workouts, and if the total work per day has to be decreased, muscular endurance is normally reduced. Athletes with proper technique and aerobic endurance will find that training muscular endurance separately is more beneficial. Following are the different types of muscular endurance training for different sports:

- *Muscular endurance dynamic, concentric-eccentric*, such as in any cyclic type of sports (rowing, swimming, cycling, cross-country skiing, canoeing, kayaking), but also for other sports, such as rugby, racket sports, and boxing.

- *Muscular endurance isometric*, such as in sailing and driving, in which the athlete may stay in a specific position (isometric contraction) for many minutes.

- *Muscular endurance mixed*, combining dynamic with isometric, such as in shooting and archery.

Because sports can range from requiring a few seconds to several hours of continuous physical activity, muscular endurance training has to address these differences. For best training efficiency, muscular endurance is divided into three parts: muscular endurance of short duration, muscular endurance of medium duration, and muscular endurance of long duration. After studying the following suggested training programs, coaches should feel free to adapt these programs to the specific needs of their athletes, their athletes' training backgrounds, and the physical environment of their sport.

Muscular Endurance of Short Duration Method

Sports with a duration of between 30 seconds and two minutes include certain events in track and field, swimming, canoeing, speedskating, and skiing. Other sports require intense activity of this duration regularly during a game or match, such as ice hockey, soccer, rugby, basketball, boxing, and wrestling. During such intense activity, athletes build up a high level of lactic acid, often more than 12 to 15 millimoles per liter, which shows that the lactic acid energy system is either dominant or an important component in the overall performance of the sport or event. Most of these sports require very strong anaerobic power as well as very good aerobic endurance.

One of the key objectives of training for endurance sports is to train athletes to tolerate fatigue; strength training should have the same goal. As the competitive phase approaches, strength training must be designed so that it challenges athletes' ability to tolerate a high buildup of lactic acid. Through training, the body adapts to tolerate the buildup of lactic acid by an increased expression of proteins responsible for the removal of lactate into and out of cells (Billat et al., 2003). This adaptation better prepares the athlete for the vigor of competition and the fatigue that ultimately affects performance.

Muscular endurance of short duration training is similar to the intensive interval training method used in circuit training in that athletes develop an oxygen debt. (This is typical for activities in which the anaerobic energy system prevails.) After 60 to 90 seconds of such activity, the heart rate can be as high as 200 beats per minute and blood lactic acid concentration can be between 12 and 15 millimoles per liter, or even higher. The energy sources for muscular endurance of short duration training are blood and muscle glucose and, in particular, the glycogen stored in the liver.

Program Design for Muscular Endurance of Short Duration Method

In muscular endurance of short duration (M-ES) training, as in circuit training, the reps are performed rhythmically and at a fast pace. The load is not very high, 50 to 60 percent of 1RM, but is performed at a high intensity, at or close to the rate in competition. For this reason, athletes should use the lowest number of exercises (three to six).

The number of reps can be set precisely, but as in interval training, it is more practical to decide the duration of each set (i.e., 30 to more than 60 seconds) and the speed of performance: fast but steady. If the number of exercises is low, the athlete can perform three to six sets or circuits. The speed of performance and the duration and number of sets have to be increased progressively over time from a lower level to that suggested in figure 11.5. To train athletes to tolerate lactic acid buildup, the rest interval must be short (60 to 90 seconds) so that the lactic acid accumulated during a set is not fully removed from blood. Table 11.9 lists the training parameters for muscular endurance of short duration training. Figure 11.5 is a sample six-week program for a national-class 100-meter fly swimmer.

No.	Exercise	Week 1	Week 2	Week 3	Week 4	Week 5	Week 6
1	Bent-over arm pulls; load 50%	2 × 30 sec.	2 × 30 sec.	2 × 45 sec.	2 × 30 sec.	2 × 45 sec.	3 × 45 sec.
2	Abdominal V-sits	2 × 20	2 × 25	2 × 30	2 × 25	2 × 30	2 × 35
3	Lay on back, arms above head, hold; medicine ball forward throws	1 × 25	2 × 25	2 × 30	2 × 25	2 × 30	2 × 30
4	Leg extensions; load 50%	2 × 30 sec.	2 × 30 sec.	2 × 45 sec.	2 × 30 sec.	2 × 45 sec.	2 × 45 sec.
5	Cable elbow extensions; load 60%	2 × 30 sec.	2 × 30 sec.	2 × 45 sec.	2 × 30 sec.	2 × 45 sec.	2 × 45 sec.

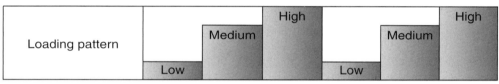

Figure 11.5 Suggested power-endurance training for a fly swimmer.

Table 11.9 Training Parameters for M-ES

Training parameters	Work
Load	50-60 percent
Number of exercises	3-6
Duration of activity	30-60 seconds
Number of sets per session	3-6
Rest interval	60-90 seconds
Speed of execution	Medium to fast
Frequency per week	2-3

Muscular Endurance of Medium and Long Duration Method

The development of muscular endurance is one of the main factors in improving performance for all sports in which performance time is greater than two minutes. A specific strength training program has to relate to the nonstop duration of activity for sports in which aerobic endurance is either dominant or an important component of the final performance.

Muscular endurance training is of major benefit for boxers, wrestlers, rowers, swimmers (400 to 1,500 meters), kayakers, canoeists (1,000 to 10,000 meters), road cyclists, cross-country skiers, and biathlon and triathlon runners. The incorporation of muscular endurance of medium duration training during the preparatory phase is also beneficial for some team sports, especially rugby, ice hockey, basketball, soccer, and Australian football.

Muscular endurance training can be performed following the principles of interval training of long duration. This training method can also be called "extensive interval training" because the term *extensive* implies a high-volume, long-duration type of activity. The main objective of training for muscular endurance is to increase the athlete's ability to cope with fatigue. Athletes improve anaerobic and aerobic endurance because muscular endurance training employs a high number of reps, often more than 100. In the early part of a nonstop set with many reps, energy is provided by the anaerobic system. This produces a buildup of lactic acid that creates physiological and psychological problems for athletes as they attempt to continue the activity. As athletes overcome these challenges and continue to work, energy is supplied by the aerobic system. Repetitive muscular endurance training results in a specific adaptation that improves cardiovascular regulation and aerobic metabolism.

Physiological adaptations promote better oxygen and energy supply and increase the removal of metabolic wastes. Repetitive muscular endurance training increases the amount of available glycogen stored in both muscles and liver. Thus, the specific benefit of muscular endurance training is an overall increase in physiological efficiency.

Because muscular endurance training employs such a relatively low load (around 30 to 50 percent of 1RM), the muscles improve their long-term contracting capability without any evident increase in muscle fiber diameter. Only a certain number of motor units are active at one time; the others are at rest and are activated only when and where the contracting fibers become fatigued. Improvement of maximum strength during that phase is also beneficial for sports in which muscular endurance represents an important training method. If the diameter of an individual muscle fiber has increased as a result of maximum strength, a lower number of motor units are required to perform a muscular endurance training task.

This type of strength reserve is critical and increases the muscle's capacity to produce work more effectively because fewer fibers are involved to overcome the resistance. Thus, maximum strength training should not be minimized. On the contrary, it should, within limits, be used for all the sports mentioned earlier. However, for sports of long duration, such as a marathon, or sports that require less than 30 percent of maximum strength, further increments of maximum strength have negligible, if any, benefits (Hartmann and Tünnemann, 1988).

Muscular endurance of medium duration (M-EM) and muscular endurance of long duration (M-EL) training have similar physiological bases. Muscular endurance of medium duration training is suggested for sports in which the duration of competition is between 2 and 10 minutes, whereas muscular endurance of long duration training is suggested for sports in which the duration is 10 minutes or longer. This distinction is necessary because muscular endurance of medium duration has a stronger anaerobic component, whereas muscular endurance of long duration is clearly aerobic. The program designs for each type of muscular endurance will be described separately because the load, duration of a set, and speed of execution are clearly different.

Program Design for Muscular Endurance of Medium Duration Method

This program can be designed either as circuit training or as interval training. The first option is suggested for sports in which more muscle groups must be trained (wrestling, boxing), whereas the second is advisable for sports in which one limb prevails (speedskating, canoeing). An example will be presented for each option.

The load for muscular endurance of medium duration training is 30 to 50 percent of 1RM (see table 11.10), performed progressively over a longer duration. As shown in tables 11.11 and 11.12, the duration and number of reps are increased progressively over a longer period. The duration of the conversion phase for muscular endurance must be 8 to 10 weeks. This length of time is necessary for physiological adaptation to such high training to occur. Throughout the muscular endurance of medium duration phase, the load, number of exercises, rest interval, and speed of execution remain constant. The number of reps, however, increases every second week (see table 11.11).

As shown in table 11.10, the rest interval between sets is short, so athletes have insufficient time to recover adequately. However, the program is designed precisely to expose athletes to high levels of fatigue constantly so they learn to cope with the pain and exhaustion of competition.

Table 11.11 shows a difference in the number of reps between the first four exercises and the last two. The latter exercises are considered a lower priority. The ability to perform more reps of these exercises requires a solid training background of several years. The load for a deadlift must be lower (30 to 40 percent of 1RM) and used carefully with beginners (long-term progression).

Table 11.10 Training Parameters for M-EM

Training parameters	Work
Load	30-50 percent
Number of exercises	4-8
Number of sets per session	2-4
Rest interval between sets	2 minutes
Rest interval between circuits	5 minutes
Speed of execution	Medium
Frequency per week	2-3

Table 11.11 Circuit Training for a Wrestler

Exercise	Number of weeks			
	2	2	2	2
Half squats	30	40	50	60
Arm curls	30	40	50	60
Leg curls	30	40	50	60
Bench presses	30	40	50	60
V-sits	15	20	25	30
Deadlifts	15	18	20	25

Circuit training designed for muscular endurance of either medium or long duration can use a barbell or any other piece of equipment. The advantage of using a barbell is that different limbs can be exercised without stopping to rest, as required in the circuit shown in table 11.12.

Table 11.12 M-EM Circuit for a Rower

Exercise	Number of weeks			
	3-4	3	3	2
Half squats	Take a load of 30-50 percent and progressively aim to perform 50-60 reps nonstop per exercise.	Perform two exercises nonstop, or 100 reps together; for instance, 50 half squats followed by 50 arm curls. Pair the remaining six exercises.	Perform four exercises nonstop, or 200 repetitions. After a rest interval, repeat the other four exercises in the same manner.	Perform all exercises nonstop: eight exercises × 50 repetitions = 400 repetitions nonstop.
Arm curls				
Bench presses				
Half squats				
Seated rows				
Toe raises				
Deadlifts				
V-sits				
Rest interval between exercises	1 minute	1-2 minutes between each group of two.	2 minutes between each group of four.	—
Rest interval between circuits	—	—	—	4-5 minutes

Note: A similar program can be developed for 400- to 1,500-meter swimming, middle-distance events in speedskating, kayaking, canoeing, and so on.

The circuit in table 11.12 includes eight exercises performed as follows. The athlete places a barbell of 40 percent of maximum strength on the shoulders and performs 50 half squats. After completing the last rep, the athlete sits on a bench and performs 40 arm curls. Then he lies on the bench and does 50 bench presses. The athlete then quickly places the barbell back on the shoulders and performs 50 half squats. He follows this with 50 vertical rowing actions. Again, he quickly places the barbell back on the shoulders and performs 60 toe raises followed by 50 deadlifts. Now he places the barbell on the floor and performs 50 V-sits for the abdominal muscles. The total number of reps performed in our hypothetical circuit is 400!

The advantage of this method is that the cardiorespiratory system is involved throughout the circuit because training alternates among different muscle groups. This develops muscular endurance and aerobic endurance, the two crucial abilities for any of the sports discussed in this chapter.

To further clarify the information in table 11.12, coaches should observe the following:

- The number of reps is progressively increased to reach 40 to 60 or even higher; two to four weeks may be needed to accomplish this.
- The number of exercises may vary depending on the needs of the sport.
- The same exercise can be repeated twice in the same circuit to emphasize the importance of that group of muscles in a given sport (half squats in our example).
- The number of exercises may not be the same for every limb. This decision should be based on the strengths and weaknesses of the athletes involved.

- Athletes should observe a steady speed throughout the circuit, even though they may have the urge to move faster and get the exercise over with.

- Coaches or trainers should set up all the equipment needed before training so the least amount of time is wasted changing from one exercise to another, especially in a gym setting. Barbell or dumbbell exercises that can be performed in a close space are a good choice in these settings.

- Athletes should perform two exercises nonstop in the second phase, four exercises in the third phase, and all of them in the last phase.

- The athlete may need six to eight minutes or longer to perform an eight-exercise circuit nonstop, depending on her classification. An even longer circuit can be designed for better improvement of muscular endurance of long duration.

- Because the physiological demands of muscular endurance of both medium and long duration are severe, this method should be applied only to athletes with a strong background in both strength and endurance training (national-class athletes and higher). For a less demanding circuit (for juniors), include only four to six exercises.

- Performing an even number of exercises is best because of the way they are performed— two, then four, then all of them together nonstop.

- As athletes adapt to performing the total number of exercises nonstop during the last phase, the coach can use a stopwatch to monitor improvement. As a result of adaptation, the time of performance should begin to decrease.

This type of muscular endurance of medium duration training should not be used for testing purposes or for comparing the achievements of two or more athletes. Because anthropometrics (size or length of limbs) differ from athlete to athlete, such comparisons are unfair, especially for tall athletes.

Figure 11.6 depicts a suggested muscular endurance of medium duration program for boxing. This program has to be performed nonstop, from the first to the last exercise, with a steady rhythm, but as fast as possible. The only exception is the jump half squat, in which the eccentric phase has to be performed to avoid deep knee compression. Also, for exercises 1 and 4 the athlete will need a partner(s) to continually feed him medicine balls, or throw the balls against a solid,

Exercise	Week 1	Week 2	Week 3	Week 4
1-arm medicine ball chest throw	45 seconds	45 seconds	1 minute	1 minute
Jump squats (50% of 1RM)	30 reps	30 reps	30 reps	30 reps
Between legs two-arm medicine ball forward throw, followed by a take-off, diagonally forward	1 minute	1 minute	1.5 minutes	1.5 minutes
1-arm medicine ball chest throw	45 seconds	45 seconds	1 minute	1 minute
Number of sets	2	2	3	3
Rest interval between sets	2	1	1	1

Note: Perform the exercises nonstop from exercise 1 to 4 for a complete set. To prolong the duration of a set, add another exercise, such as abdomen crunch. Professional boxers have to progressively use more numbers of sets (e.g., 5-8).

Figure 11.6 Suggested program for muscular endurance of medium duration for boxing

rebounding wall. The one-arm medicine ball throw has to imitate a boxing punch, performed horizontally forward with the other arm being used just as a support, to hold the ball in front of the chest. The weight of the ball can start (depending on the boxer's conditioning) at 6 to 8 pounds (2.7 to 3.6 kilograms). The weight should decrease every week by two pounds. During the last week or two, the ball should weigh 2 to 4 pounds (0.9 to 1.8 kilograms).

Program Design for Muscular Endurance of Long Duration Method

Sports of longer duration require a different kind of physiological training. In most of these sports, athletes apply force against a given resistance, for example, water in swimming, rowing, and canoeing; pedals in cycling (body weight applied as strength, especially uphill); ice in speed-skating; or snow and various terrains in cross-country skiing and biathlon.

The dominant energy system in these sports is aerobic endurance. Because improved performance is expected to come from increments in aerobic power, strength training must be designed to enhance this. To increase muscular endurance of long duration, therefore, the key training ingredient is a high number of reps performed nonstop. The other training parameters remain constant, as indicated in table 11.13.

Table 11.13 Training Parameters for M-EL

Training parameters	Work
Load	30-40 percent
Number of exercises	4-6
Number of sets per session	2-4
Rest interval	See table 11.12
Speed of execution	Medium
Frequency per week	2-3

Because one of the training goals of muscular endurance of long duration is to cope with fatigue, the rest interval does not allow full recovery. Only a very short rest is afforded as athletes change stations, usually two to five seconds.

Table 11.14 shows a typical training program for sports such as triathlon, marathon, kayaking and canoeing (10,000 meters and marathon), long-distance swimming, road cycling, and cross-country skiing. Note that the work is expressed in minutes rather than number of reps to facilitate monitoring the many minutes of steady work.

The first four exercises can be performed with any combination machine available in a fitness center or school gymnasium. The last two exercises must be performed using rubber cords, often called elastic cords, which are available in many sporting goods stores. To train long-distance kayakers or canoeists, the elastic cords must be anchored before training so that arm pulls or elbow extensions, typical motions for these two sports, can be performed from a seated position.

The number of sets per group of two, three, or all six exercises together, performed nonstop, must be determined based on the work tolerance and performance level of each athlete. The athlete must show a gradual rise in the number of reps performed per time limit per exercise before adding a great number of sets. Prematurely adding more sets can hamper the athlete's progress and lead to a state of overtraining.

Table 11.14 Training Program for M-EL for an Experienced Marathon Canoeist

Exercise	Number of weeks					
	2	2	2-3	2	2	2-3
Leg presses	Take a load of 30 percent and progressively perform 4 minutes of nonstop work for each exercise.	Perform the same work for 7 minutes nonstop for each exercise.	Perform 10 minutes of nonstop work for each exercise.	Perform two exercises nonstop, or 20 minutes of work. Repeat for exercises 3 and 4, and again for exercises 5 and 6.	Perform three exercises nonstop, or 30 minutes of work. Repeat for the other three exercises.	Perform all six exercises nonstop, or 60 minutes of work.
Arm pulls						
Bench presses						
Leg presses						
Arm pulls (cords)						
Elbow extensions (cords)						
RI between exercises	1-2 minutes	2 minutes	2 minutes	—	—	—
RI between circuits	—	—	—	2-4 minutes	3-4 minutes	5 minutes

Note: A similar concept of training can be applied to long-distance cross-country skiing, kayaking, marathon swimming, triathlon, and so on.

Muscular Endurance Isometric Method

A limited number of sports require athletes to use isometric contraction for long durations during the competition, such as sailing and motor sports (driving). During training and competition in sailing the athletes take a specific position, static in most cases, in which parts of the body are in long-duration isometric contraction. Seated on a side of the board, often holding a rope to maintain the mast(s) in the most wind-effective position, the athlete contracts parts of the body, such as the abdomen, legs, low back, and arms.

Program Design for Muscular Endurance Isometric Method

Unlike driving (motor sports), in which specific strength training is performed in the gym, the muscular endurance isometric training for sailing can be on-boat and off-boat, as the following example illustrates.

During training the athletes can use heavy vests to overload the upper body for the regattas to come. The program can follow the traditional progression by using a heavy vest, which overloads the athlete's body, thus creating an additional physiological challenge against the pull of gravity and the centrifugal force during turns. Heavy vests can have different weights, often carrying a load as heavy as 35 pounds (16 kilograms). The scope of training can be to progressively increase either the weight of the vest or the duration of using the vest.

Figure 11.7 suggests a progression for using a weighted vest for training in the boat. This is only a guideline, applicable according to the athlete's individual physical capabilities, needs, and training environment.

Training for sailing should include a preparatory phase regardless of whether the sailor lives in a climate that favors year-round training. Figure 11.8 illustrates a suggested strength training program for sailing, in which isometric training is dominant. Again, this is only a progression guideline; coaches should adapt it to fit the needs of their athletes, for both sailing and driving.

Weight of vest	10 kg	12 kg	15 kg
Duration	2 × 15 min.	3 × 15 min.	4 × 20 min.

Figure 11.7 Suggested progression for the in-boat use of heavy vests in sailing.

No.	Exercise	Week 1	Week 2	Week 3	Week 4	Week 5	Week 6	Rest interval
1	Arm pulls (min)	3 × 1 min.	3 × 2 min.	3 × 3 min.	2 × 4 min.	3 × 4 min.	4 × 4 min.	2-3 min.
2	Leg press	3 × 1	3 × 2	3 × 3	2 × 4	3 × 4	4 × 4	2-3 min.
3	Back extensions	3 × 15	3 × 20	2 × 25	2 × 25	3 × 25	4 × 30	1-2 min.
4	Leg curls; load 50%	2 × 30 sec.	2 × 45 sec.	2 × 1 min.	2 × 1.5 min.	2 × 2 min.	2 × 2 min.	2-3 min.
5	Bench press	3 × 1	3 × 2	3 × 3	2 × 4	3 × 4	4 × 4	2-3 min.
6	Leg extension	3 × 1	3 × 2	3 × 3	2 × 4	3 × 4	4 × 4	2-3 min.

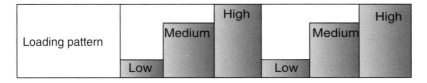

Loading pattern	Low	Medium	High	Low	Medium	High

Figure 11.8 Suggested isometric strength training program for sailing.

Muscular Endurance Using Mixed Contractions Methods

Muscular endurance using mixed contractions is very specific to certain sports, such as shooting and archery. The main scope of training for such sports is to expose athletes to mixed contraction training, such as concentric-isometric-eccentric, and as such, ready them for major competition. Consider pistol shooting, in which the pistol weighs 3 pounds (1.4 kilograms). During the competition the shooter lifts the pistol 50 times. Poorly trained athletes have a shaky arm, mostly toward the end of the competition, which is far from conducive to high shooting accuracy. Therefore, the scope of training in this sport is to prepare the athlete to have the capacity to lift the pistol at least as many times as during the competition, using weights higher than the weight of the pistol.

The technical action in pistol shooting is as follows: Lift the pistol from the side of the hips to shoulder level, hold it still for two to four seconds, shoot, and then lower the pistol to the starting position (hand on the side of the hips). A similar type of action is performed in archery, in which the concentric-isometric contraction against a resistance is performed while the string of the bow is stretched and held for very few seconds. The archer then releases the arrow and lowers the bow to prepare for a new attempt.

Phases 5 and 6: Competitive and Transition

Strength training is an important physiological contributor to overall athletic performance. The more explosive a skill is, the more important the role of maximum strength and power are; the longer the duration of an activity is, the more determinant the role of muscular endurance is. Superior performance levels cannot be achieved without the vital contribution of strength.

The benefits of strength to athletic performance are felt as long as the neuromuscular system maintains the cellular adaptations induced by training. When strength training stops, benefits decrease as the contractile properties of the muscles diminish. The consequence is detraining, defined as a visible decrease in the contribution of strength to athletic performance. During the competitive phase, athletes need sport-specific strength programs to avoid detraining.

Peaking, or performing at peak performance during the main competitions of the year, is also related to strength training. In several sports, especially power sports, peak performance is often achieved in the early part of the competitive phase. Coaches tend to overlook strength training at this time because specific technical and tactical training become dominant. Unfortunately, lack of strength training causes decreased performance as the season progresses. In the early part of the season, while strength benefits remain, performance is as expected. However, when the muscles' ability to contract powerfully diminishes, so does performance.

According to the theory of periodization of strength, gains in maximum strength during the maximum strength phase should be transformed into either muscular endurance or power during the conversion phase so athletes acquire the best possible sport-specific strength and are equipped with the physiological capabilities necessary for good performance during the competitive phase. To maintain good performance throughout the competitive phase, athletes must maintain this physiological base. This means that a coach must plan a sport-specific strength maintenance program throughout the competitive phase. Maximum strength is a crucial ingredient for sport-specific strength programs. Many sports require maintenance of some maximum strength during the competitive season, mostly using the maximum load method.

Gains in maximum strength decline faster if they resulted from processes dependent on the nervous system, such as the recruitment of large-motor units (Hartmann and Tünnemann, 1988). Often such gains result from power training without a strong maximum strength base. In many sports, the type of strength performed is event-specific power training. Maximum strength training using the maximum load method is often overlooked and gains are short-lived. When strength training is done mostly during the preparatory phase, strength gains deteriorate as the competitive phase progresses and approaches its peak.

Coaches should not question *whether* to prescribe strength maintenance training during the competitive phase, but rather *how* to do it. They must keep in mind the dominant ability of the sport and carefully consider what types of strength athletes should maintain. Most sports require some elements of maximum strength, power, and muscular endurance. The most important decision, therefore, is what *proportion* of each to maintain and how best to integrate them into training, *not* which of the three to maintain.

Power sport athletes must maintain both maximum strength and power. Because these abilities cannot substitute for each other, but rather are complementary, one should not be maintained at the expense of the other. For instance, throwers in track and field and linemen in American football must maintain maximum strength during the competitive phase, with a proportion between maximum strength and power of approximately 50–50. Most team sport athletes should maintain power and either power-endurance or muscular endurance, depending on the position they play. For endurance sports, however, the proportion among maximum strength, power, and muscular endurance depends on the duration of the event and on which energy system is dominant. For the majority of endurance sports, muscular endurance is the dominant component of strength.

The duration of the competitive phase is equally important in determining the proportion of different types of strength to maintain. The longer the competitive phase is, the more important it is to maintain some elements of maximum strength because this type of strength is an important component of both power and muscular endurance. Overlooking this fact will result in the detraining of maximum strength, which will affect both power and muscular endurance. Table 12.1 shows the proportions of different types of strength to be maintained during the competitive phase for various sports and positions.

The same training methods suggested in previous chapters should be applied during the maintenance phase. What differs during this phase is the volume of strength training compared to the technical, tactical, and other elements of physical training—not the training methodology.

The strength maintenance program should be subordinate to other types of training during the competitive phase. Athletes should use the lowest number of exercises (two or three, up to a maximum of four) to address the prime movers. This expends the least possible energy for maintenance of strength, leaving the majority of energy available for technical and tactical training.

The two or three strength training sessions per week during the competitive phase should be as short as possible. A good maintenance program can often be accomplished in 20 to 30 minutes of specific work. Obviously, the frequency of strength training sessions also depends on the competition schedule. If no competitions are scheduled on the weekend, a microcycle may have two (three maximum) strength training sessions. If a game or competition is planned on the weekend, one or at most two short strength training sessions can be planned, normally in the early part of the week.

The number of sets is usually low (one to four), depending on whether the athlete is training power or muscular endurance. For power and maximum strength, two to four sets are possible

Table 12.1 Strength Proportions for the Competitive Phase

Sport/event	MxS Concentric %	Eccentric %	P %	P-E %	M-E %
Athletics: Sprinting	20	—	60	20	—
Jumping	20	10	70	—	—
Throws	30	20	50	—	—
Baseball: Pitcher	40	—	40	20	—
Field players	20	—	70	10	—
Basketball	10	10	60	20	—
Biathlon	—	—	—	20	80
Boxing	20	—	20	30	30
Canoeing/Kayaking: 500 m	40	—	30	20	10
1,000 m	20	—	20	20	40
10,000 m	—	—	—	20	80
Cycling: Track 200	20	—	70	10	—
4,000-meter pursuit	10	—	30	20	40
Diving	—	10	90	—	—
Fencing	—	—	60	30	10
Field hockey	—	—	40	20	40
Figure skating	20	20	40	10	10
Football: Linemen	30	20	50	—	—
Linebackers	20	—	60	20	—
Running backs	20	—	60	20	—
Wide receivers	20	—	60	20	—
Defensive backs	20	—	60	20	—
Tailbacks	20	10	40	20	10
Football (Australian)	20	10	40	20	10
Ice hockey	10	—	50	30	10
Martial arts	—	—	60	30	10
Rowing	10	—	—	20	70
Rugby	20	—	40	30	10
Skiing: Alpine	20	20	30	30	—
Nordic	—	—	—	20	80
Soccer: Sweepers/goalie	20	10	60	10	—
Other positions	—	—	60	20	20
Speedskating: Sprinting	20	—	60	20	—
Distance	—	—	10	20	70
Swimming: Sprinting	20	—	50	20	10
Middle distance	10	—	10	20	60
Long distance	—	—	—	20	80
Tennis	—	—	60	30	10
Volleyball	15	5	50	20	10
Water polo	10	—	20	20	50
Wrestling	—	—	30	10	60

because the number of reps is usually low. For muscular endurance training, one or two sets are suggested because the number of reps is higher. During the competitive phase, the number of reps for muscular endurance of medium or long duration should not exceed 30 because these two components of muscular endurance are also developed during the technical, tactical, or conditioning program specific to the sport. The rest interval should be longer than usual so athletes can recover almost entirely during the break. The intent of the maintenance phase is to stabilize performance, not create fatigue.

The planning for each microcycle of a maintenance program depends on the type of strength sought. For power training, athletes should use exercises that enhance explosiveness by using resistance close to that encountered in competitions. Two types of resistance are suggested. *Increased load*, or a resistance slightly higher than in competition, enhances both specific maximum strength and power. Exercises should be specific to the prevailing skills of the particular sport. This type of exercise is suggested mostly for the early part of the competitive phase as a transition from maximum strength to power. *Decreased load*, or a resistance below that encountered in competition, enhances explosiveness and should prevail in the phase prior to the main competitions. Both loads increase the ability to recruit a high number of fast-twitch muscle fibers and improve synchronization of the muscles involved. If the competitive phase is longer than five months, athletes should dedicate 25 percent of the total work to the maintenance of maximum strength because the detraining of maximum strength will negatively affect overall muscular endurance capacity.

The maintenance of maximum strength is more elaborate because its effectiveness depends on the proportion between the types of contraction. Often a combination of concentric and eccentric contractions can be more effective than using only concentric contractions. A combination of 75 percent concentric, 15 percent eccentric, and 10 percent power seems most effective.

Variations of Loading Patterns for the Competitive Phase

Strength training is not a rigid process. On the contrary, programs should be flexible and adapted to the athlete's well-being and progress in training, the requirements of the sport, and the schedule of competitions or games. To illustrate this, the following sections present several practical examples of the dynamics in loading patterns for both individual and team sports during the competitive phase.

Individual Sports

Figure 12.1 shows a suggested strength training plan for athletes in the competitive phase of speed and power sports (sprinting, jumping, and throwing events in track and field; 50-meter swimming; the martial arts; fencing). For the first two or three days following competition, the objective of training is regeneration. Only two strength training sessions are planned, both later in the week, with the first being of low intensity. The only time strength training is challenging is during week 2. The third week is a peaking week, so only two strength training sessions are planned, the second being of low intensity. To ensure that the Wednesday session is of low load and low demand, the rest interval(s) between two or three sets of strength and power training should be long (four to five minutes) for full regeneration. This will avoid any residual fatigue before the upcoming competition.

Figure 12.2 addresses similar concerns for a situation in which competitions are planned two weeks apart. When designing such a plan, coaches should allow two or three days of regenerative, low-intensity training following the first competition. Training must again be of low intensity on the last two or three days before competition to facilitate peaking.

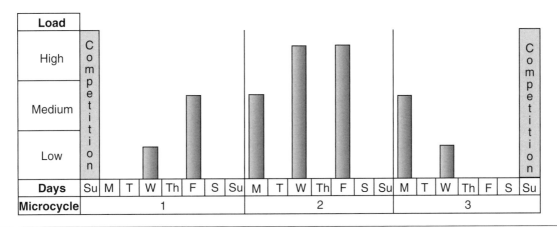

Figure 12.1 Suggested plan for strength training (and loading magnitude) for a speed- and power-dominant sport where competitions are planned three weeks apart.

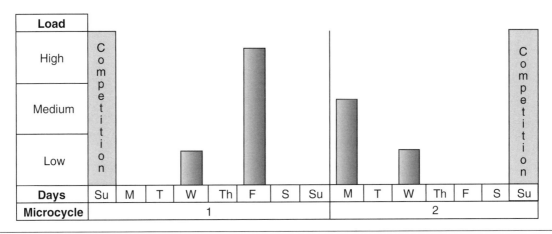

Figure 12.2 Proposed strength training schedule for a situation where competitions are planned two weeks apart.

Weekly competitions in individual sports are far from ideal simply because the more athletes compete, the less time they have for training. During periods of weekly competitions, especially when fatigue is high, most coaches look for training elements to cut, and unfortunately strength training is often the first to go.

For situations in which weekly competitions are the norm, figure 12.3 illustrates a strength training plan that can be altered to accommodate high levels of fatigue. Coaches should keep in mind, however, that planning too many training cycles with weekly competitions will have a predictable outcome: detraining with its ensuing loss of speed and power.

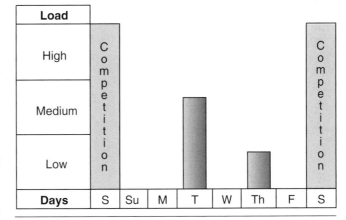

Figure 12.3 Possible scenario for strength training in which weekly competitions are the norm.

Team Sports

Without negating the importance of specific endurance, power is the dominant ability for most team sports. Consequently, to avoid detraining of power, a maintenance program must be planned throughout the competitive phase.

The examples presented in this section are for two competitive schedules: one and two games per week. They are valid for baseball, basketball, volleyball, American football, ice hockey, field hockey, Australian football, soccer, rugby, lacrosse, and water polo, in which specific endurance is an important component.

Despite other pressures on the team (the need for more technical or tactical training, placement in league standings), the coach must find the time and the athletes must find the energy for maintenance of power. The longer the competitive phase is, the more important it is to maintain power training.

Figure 12.4 suggests a plan for a cycle with a game scheduled every Saturday (it can be adjusted for any other day of the week). A strength training session of medium demand is proposed for Tuesday. If the athletes' level of fatigue is higher than expected, the overall demand can be reduced by using a low load.

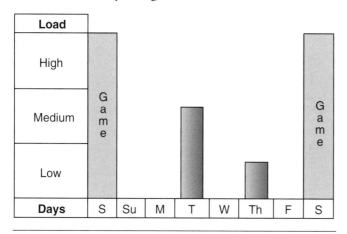

Figure 12.4 Suggested schedule for strength training for a team sport with a game every weekend.

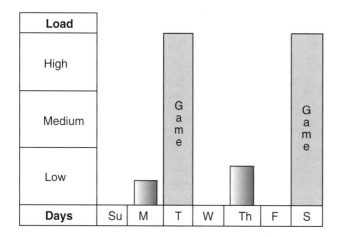

Figure 12.5 Suggested maintenance program for strength training for a team sport playing two games per week.

Even for team sports with two games per week, a maintenance program for strength training is still possible; however, it should be limited to one or two sets of three exercises at 70 percent of 1RM, or a maximum of 20 minutes (see figure 12.5).

The content of a training session must be related to the load used in training, the overall intensity or demand used in that session, and the proximity of the competition or game. The examples suggested here assume that strength training is performed following specific work on technique, tactics, and drills for speed and specific endurance. Consequently, because there is little time and energy to spare, strength training must be short and sport specific.

A heavy load or heavy demand strength training session lasts 20 to 30 minutes. Maximum strength or power, or combinations of the two, are trained. Athletes perform four or five exercises specifically for the prime movers with a load of 70 to 80 percent as fast and dynamically as possible. They perform five to eight reps in two to four sets with a rest interval of two to four minutes.

A medium load strength training session lasts 20 to 30 minutes. Maximum strength or power are trained. Athletes perform three or four exercises explosively using a load of 70 percent. They perform five to eight reps in two or three sets with a rest interval of two to three minutes.

A low-load strength training session lasts 15 minutes. Maximum strength or power are trained. Athletes perform two or three exercises explosively using a 60 to 70 percent load. They perform four to six reps over one or two sets with a rest interval of two to three minutes.

Strength training programs for athletes in some sports, such as linemen in American football, throwers in track and field, and heavyweight boxers and wrestlers, are quite different from the programs proposed earlier. The suggested program for such athletes lasts 60 to 75 minutes. The strength sought is 40 to 50 percent maximum strength and 50 to 60 percent power. Athletes perform four to six exercises as explosively as possible using a load of 70 to 90 percent. They perform five to eight reps over three to six sets with a rest interval of three to four minutes.

For athletes in team sports who perform many jumps during training and games (basketball, volleyball), plyometric training should be reduced to a minimum compared to the end of the preparatory phase. This will alleviate the strain on the athlete's legs throughout the season.

The strength maintenance program should end five to seven days before the most important competition of the year so that athletes can use all of their energies to achieve the best performance possible.

Peaking for Maximum Performance

The progressive decrease in the volume and intensity of all training activities during the competitive phase will facilitate the replenishment of energy stores and help athletes achieve supercompensation, relax mentally, and become motivated to attain their best performance on the date(s) planned for peak performance. During this time the focus shifts to recovery and regeneration with proper rest, nutrition, supplementation, and massage.

Peak performance can also be induced through the use of specific and novel training techniques. Considering their specific physiological benefits, these techniques are mostly suggested for speed and power sports: from team sports to the martial arts, and from racket sports to boxing and wrestling.

For maximum peak performance, the activities listed in figure 12.6 have to be applied in the suggested order. They are implemented in the precompetition days or hours to ensure maximum neuromuscular benefits prior to the major competition.

Tetanus training is a novel and sophisticated training and peaking technique discussed in greater depth in chapter 10. Briefly, the aim of tetanus training is to develop maximum tension in the muscle. This is relatively easy to achieve in a laboratory setting in which athletes are hooked up to electrodes and motor units are stimulated to maximally contract. A state of "fused" tetanus is achieved when all of the motor units within a muscle have been recruited and force plateaus. Maximum tension is difficult to achieve in a practical setting, however.

Training with heavy loads and implementing isometric contractions is a great technique for stimulating muscle and promoting maximum motor unit recruitment. Increased motor unit recruitment heightens an athlete's force development, which can then be applied to power training. Tetanus principles can also be used to heighten arousal in the weeks following competition and of course immediately prior to competition. This is achieved by the application of *posttetanic potentiation* and *postcontraction sensory discharge.*

The obvious training goal of every athlete is to reach maximum performance during the major competitions of the year. During the entire year of training, the great effort the athletes undergo for many months is directed toward one goal: achieve the highest performance possible during the day(s) of the main competition of the year. Of the techniques used to facilitate

Type of training	Taper/Unload	Tetanus training	Competition
Dynamics of volume	Decrease distance/duration by 30-50% Decrease the number of repetitions Increase rest interval to an almost full recovery Use psychological relaxation/physiotherapeutic techniques (e.g., massage) Use motivation/visualization techniques	Employ tetanic techniques Induce a prepeaking neuromuscular state	Posttetanic potentiation Increase the discharge rate of FT Maximum arousal of the neuromuscular system Increase the reactivity of the neuromuscular system
Dynamics of intensity	Decrease the number of drills for speed/power/agility		
Training benefits	Replenish energy stores Achieve supercompensation Relax mentally Increase confidence	Increase arousal Increase the recruitment of FT fibers Increase discharge rate of FT fibers	Achieve peak performance Maximum arousal Highest discharge rate of FT fibers

Figure 12.6 Suggested types of activities and their benefits to peak performance.

the best possible performance for a major competition, there is a big difference between the approach used by an individual and the approach used by team sports athletes. Most coaches use periodization of training, tapering, arousal, titanic force, and the physiological benefit of the posttetanus potentiation to help their athletes achieve peak performance. In the next sections we discuss how coaches can adapt these techniques to meet the unique needs of the athletes they are coaching.

Periodization Guidelines for Different Sports

Individual sports, team sports, racket sports, the martial arts, and artistic sports apply the periodization of training and the periodization of strength differently. Peak performance is directly influenced and facilitated by a well-organized periodization of training, in which the length of the preparatory phase is detrimental. Equally important, especially for speed and power sports, is the way periodization of strength is used to increase the athlete's physical potential. The following list of some periodization issues and how they affect peak performance is intended to invite coaches to reflect on their own periodization-planning techniques.

■ Individual sports (i.e., running, cycling, triathlon) tend to have a much longer preparatory phase than other sports because of such issues as planning competitions around climatic conditions.

■ Because team sports, the martial arts, and racket sports have either longer or more numerous competitive phases per year than individual sports, they follow a bi-, tri-, or multicycle periodization. The preparatory phase for these sports is comparatively shorter than that of individual sports.

- Sports with shorter preparatory phases tend to have a more superficial foundation of physical training. Coaches of these sports should try to lengthen the preparatory phase, especially the volume of training, or find imaginative ways to improve the quality of physical training.

- Athletes in individual sports have more days for general and specific training than their counterparts in other sports.

- Individual sports coaches tend to pay more attention to the benefits of physical training than coaches of other sports.

- The more important the technical and tactical training are in a given sport, the more coaches emphasize them. The end result can be quite predictable: neglecting the physical support necessary to achieve best performance.

- The achievement of peak performance at the time of major competitions depends on the effectiveness of the training during the preparatory phase.

- Periodization of strength is not well known or applied in many sports, especially some team sports. This might negatively affect peak performance.

- Maximum strength is either missing from training during the preparatory phase, or it is a formality in some sports (e.g., team sports, racket sports, the martial arts). A very short or superficial maximum strength phase will negatively affect athletes' ability to maximize power, speed, and agility or quickness.

- Athletes in individual sports, especially endurance-dominant sports, must reach peak performance only two or three times per year. Athletes in team sports, however, must play at peak performance throughout the competitive season. Coaches of team sports may consider using physiotherapy, nutrition, and supplements to improve their athletes' rate of recovery during the transition phase so it can be shortened to allow for a longer preparatory phase. This offers athletes more time for physical training, including strength training.

In the illustrations of planning periodization and training methods in chapter 7, a vertical bar was used to separate training phases. This may have implied that a certain type of training ends on the last day of one phase and a completely different type begins on the first day of the next. In reality, the transition between phases is not quite so abrupt. There is always an overlap, with a training method to be used in a given phase progressively introduced in the previous phase. Similarly, the method used in a previous phase is usually maintained for a short time in the next phase while progressively reducing its emphasis.

Each training phase has a dominant method(s) and another that may be progressively introduced. This allows for a more effective transition from one method to the next. For instance, the transition from maximum strength to power is performed progressively by introducing some elements of power training during the maximum strength phase and maintaining some maximum strength training during the conversion phase (figure 12.7).

A transition between two training methods or phases can take place over two microcycles. Figure 12.7 shows that as power is progressively introduced, maximum strength is progressively reduced. This is accomplished by creating different combinations between sets of maximum strength and power, as illustrated in table 12.2. For easier presentation, it is assumed that three strength training sessions of five sets per day are planned in each microcycle.

Another method of transitioning from the maximum strength phase to the conversion (power) phase is through the number of training sessions dedicated to each ability. Table 12.3 illustrates such an example. All three training sessions in microcycle 1 are dedicated to maximum strength; then maximum strength is decreased as power is increased until all three training sessions in microcycle 4 are dedicated to power.

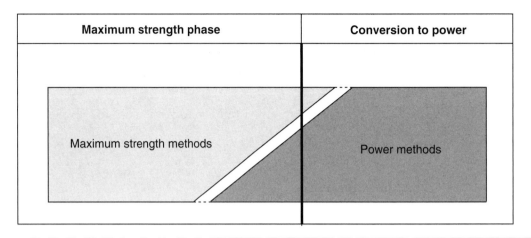

Figure 12.7 Maintaining strength in competitive phase.

Table 12.2 Progressive Transition From an MxS-Dominant Training Phase to Power

Training day		Microcycle 1			Microcycle 2		
		1	2	3	1	2	3
Sets	MxS	5	4	3	2	1	0
	Power	0	1	2	3	4	5

The transition from one type of training to another can be planned more elaborately, as illustrated in table 12.4. This chart shows the periodization of strength, the number of workouts per week, the duration of each phase in weeks, and the transition from one type of strength to another. In this case, the core strength for synchronized swimming, which is the strength of the hips, abdominal muscles, and low back, was emphasized or maintained throughout the yearly plan.

A well-organized coach will also structure a plan that shows how to use a certain type of training method and for how long. In doing so, the coach will plan the most appropriate methods for each training phase, showing the duration of each as well as which method is dominant.

Figure 12.8 illustrates how training methods can be planned. The example refers to hypothetical sports in which power is the dominant ability. As usual, the top of the chart shows the training phases of a mono-cycle, and below that is the periodization of strength. The bottom part of the chart lists several methods. Three types of symbols are used because in a given training phase, a certain method can have a higher priority than the others. The solid line indicates the method with the highest priority, the dashed line shows second priority, and the dotted line shows the third priority. For instance, during the anatomical adaptation phase, circuit training is the dominant training method. When the maximum strength phase begins, the maximum load method concentric prevails. The eccentric method is of secondary priority during some segments of the program.

In power training, only the ballistic method and plyometrics are presented. The dotted line shows that these methods are a third priority in some phases. Figure 12.8 is only a hypothetical example and does not show all available methods or all possibilities of how to use those that are presented.

Table 12.3 Progressive Transition From MxS to P

Microcycles		1	2	3	4
Training days	MxS	3	2	1	0
	P	0	1	2	3

Table 12.4 Transition to Different Types of Strength for Synchronized Swimming

Dates		Sep	Oct	Nov	Dec	Jan	Feb	Mar	Apr	May
Periodization	Competition		—		Provincial		Division			Natl. Champ
	Training phase	Preparatory			Competitive					
	Periodization of strength	AA core strength	MxS Maintenance of core strength		Conversion to Power M-E Maintenance of core strength				Cessation	
No. of workouts per week		3	3-4		4				2	
Duration in weeks		5	9		4	4	4	4	4	1
Type of strength		2AA 1 core	2-3 MxS 1 core		2 M-E 1P 1/2 MxS 1/2 core	2 M-E 1P 1/2 MxS 1/2 core	3 M-E 1 P	2 M-E 1 P	1 M-E 1 P	

Tapering for Peak Performance

Tapering, or unloading, refers to the strategies athletes use to facilitate supercompensation and, as a direct benefit, to reach peak performance. For an effective tapering, or unloading, coaches should consider the following:

- The tapering strategy should last one or two weeks.
- For speed or power sports the most fatiguing element of training (which for these sports is the volume of training) should be progressively reduced by 30 to 50 percent.
- For endurance-dominant sports the fatiguing element is intensity. As such, during the last two weeks before a major competition, athletes should progressively decrease the number of days, number of reps, and intensity of speed and power drills. However, endurance training can be maintained slightly above the intensity levels. Once the $\dot{V}O_2$max has reached high levels, less is needed to maintain its optimal capacity (Wilmore and Costill, 1988).
- For team sports, the strategy of lowering the volume and intensity of training is valid only for major tournaments, in which both the volume and intensity of training have to be reduced because their contribution to fatigue is almost the same.
- The direct benefit of a tapering strategy is the replenishment of energy stores. When glycogen is fully replenished, supercompensation is reached with all its physiological and psychological benefits.
- Peak performance is quite impossible without replenishing the energy stores.
- The reduction of intensity training (strength, power, maximum speed) will result in marked muscular strength via increased contractile mechanisms of the muscles, improved

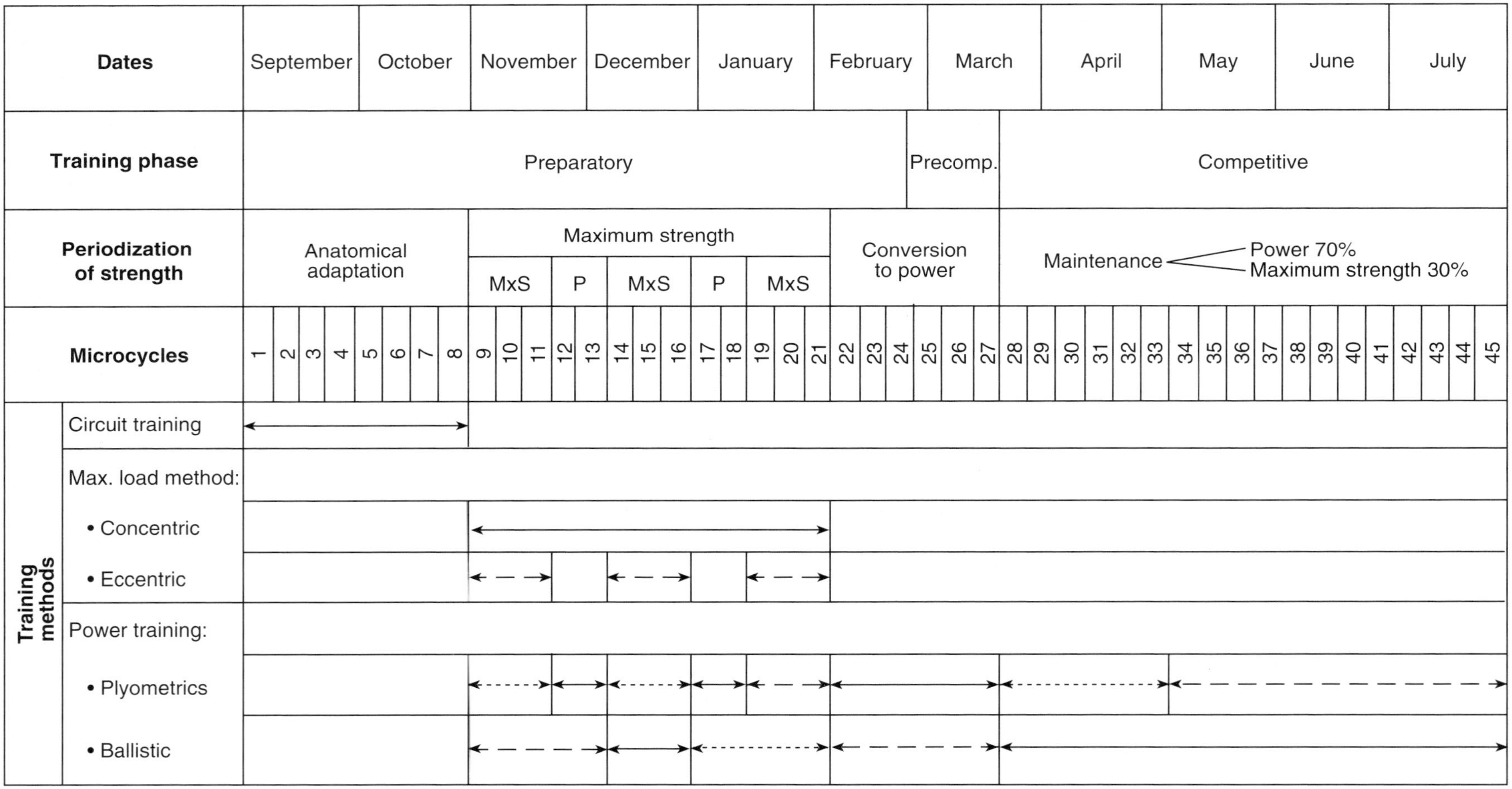

Figure 12.8 A hypothetical example of planning the training methods for a power-dominated sport.

Dates	September	October	November	December	January	February	March	April	May	June	July
Training phase	Preparatory						Precomp.	Competitive			
Periodization of strength	Anatomical adaptation		Maximum strength (MxS, P, MxS, P, MxS)				Conversion to power	Maintenance — Power 70% / Maximum strength 30%			
Microcycles	1 2 3 4 5 6 7 8		9 10 11 12 13 14 15 16 17 18 19 20 21			22 23 24 25 26 27	28	29 30 31 32 33 34 35 36 37 38 39 40 41 42 43 44 45			

Training methods

- Circuit training
- Max. load method:
  - Concentric
  - Eccentric
- Power training:
  - Plyometrics
  - Ballistic

fast-twitch muscle fiber recruitment, and an increased discharge rate of the fast-twitch fibers (Wilmore and Costill, 1988).

Improvement in muscular strength will directly and positively influence athletes' ability to perform skills with greater speed, quickness, power, and agility

Posttetanic Potentiation and Peaking

The greatest challenge faced by coaches and trainers is applying systematic laboratory settings to athletic training. Following intense isometric contractions or electrical stimulation causing a tetanus state, any further stimulation would elicit a maximal twitch force (Enoka, 2002). This maximal twitch force, or posttetanic potentiation, can be maintained for about 8 to 12 minutes before returning to control levels (Enoka, 2000). Posttetanic potentiation is smaller in the slow-twitch muscle fibers than it is in the fast-twitch fibers (O'Leary, Hope, and Sale, 1998), which explains the important application of posttetanic potentiation to speed and power sports. Furthermore, a warm muscle will elicit a higher posttetanic potentiation than a cold muscle will (Gossen, Allingham, and Sale, 2001).

Proper warm-up not only prevents injury but also increases the force-generating capability of the muscle. Through a process of adaptation, as the force-generating capacity of a muscle increases, so does the posttetanic potentiation. Preparation in peaking for a major competition can be accomplished by using the techniques in figure 12.6 to facilitate neuromuscular stimulation. Using these techniques prematurely, however, can result in early peaking followed by performance deterioration.

Peaking and Arousal

To peak for a competition, the athlete must be in a state of arousal. Arousal is a state of alertness that is mediated by the neuroendocrine system. Elevated levels of catecholamines, cortisol, and growth hormone, to name a few have been measured as a response to elevated arousal (Enoka, 2002).

Prior to major competitions, athletes are often in a state of anxiety, restlessness, and excitement. A controversial theory known as the inverted U hypothesis (Raglin, 1992) states that a moderate amount of arousal can maximize performance. Enoka (2002) speculated that changes in the contractility of muscle and coordination of the involved limbs caused by arousal increase strength production. Arousal appears more likely to contribute to increases in strength because some of the previously listed neuroendocrine factors positively affect the central nervous system. From a sport perspective, the athlete's physical and mental preparation should be optimal during the major competition. Because arousal is influenced by the performance of the central nervous system, short and intense exercises performed in the morning of the competition may well enhance an athlete's level of performance.

Postcontraction Sensory Discharge

Postcontraction sensory discharge is a physiological mechanism that can be applied on game day. Every athlete trains throughout the year to peak for a major competition. At that time the neuromuscular system is stimulated and ready for optimal performance. However, although training adaptations are no longer the focus, athletes can use certain methods to gain a neuromuscular edge on the day of competition. That edge is the essence of *postcontraction sensory discharge*. Brief and intense episodes of activity 15 to 20 minutes prior to the competition can heighten the neural response to subsequent movements that occur in sport (Enoka, 2002). For instance, highly trained sprinters often perform one or two sets of two to four reps of explosive plyometric exercises 5 to 10 minutes prior to the race. Such an activity increases the muscle spindle discharge (Enoka, 2002) and the subsequent neural drive to the prime movers. Short and intense activities lasting seconds will harness greater power output for the movement that follows.

In summary, peaking is truly an optimal state of arousal. As the athlete approaches the competitive phase, training volume must be reduced and intensity must take priority to facilitate peaking and optimal performance. Posttetanic potentiation can be used to heighten neuromuscular drive to the prime movers. On game day, following a proper warm-up, quick bursts of maximal contractions performed 10 minutes prior to the event can serve to increase the neural drive needed for maximal effort and optimal performance.

Strength Training During the Transition Phase

Following a lengthy period of hard work and stressful competitions, during which determination, motivation, and willpower are tested, athletes experience a high degree of physiological and psychological fatigue. Although muscular fatigue may disappear in a few days, fatigue of the central nervous system and the psyche (as observed in an athlete's behavior) can last much longer.

The more intensive the training is and the more competitions athletes are exposed to, the greater the fatigue will be. Any athlete would have difficulty beginning a new yearly training cycle under such conditions. Athletes must rest physically and psychologically before another season of training starts. When the new preparatory phase begins, they should be completely regenerated and ready to participate in training. In fact, following a successful transition phase, athletes should feel a strong desire to train again.

The transition phase, inappropriately called the off-season, represents a link between two yearly cycles. Its major objectives are psychological rest, relaxation, and biological regeneration, as well as to maintain an acceptable level of general physical training. This phase should last no longer than five weeks because athletes will detrain, visibly losing most of their fitness.

To maintain a decent level of fitness, athletes should train two or three times a week during the transition phase where at least one workout should be for strength training. Less effort is required to maintain 40 to 50 percent of the previous fitness level than to redevelop it from zero. An athlete who starts from zero after the transition phase has actually experienced a great deal of detraining. Detraining of strength has been documented since the 1960s. Hettinger (1966) found that muscles can lose up to 30 percent of their strength capacity in one week! A wealth of similar information exists in most exercise physiology and strength training books. Loss of muscle power refers to the reduction of fast-twitch muscle fibers' maximal shortening velocity. As a result of detraining, the myosin in the fast-twitch fibers becomes more like that in slow-twitch fibers (Wilmore and Costill, 1988).

During transition, athletes should perform compensation work to involve muscle groups that receive little attention throughout the preparatory and competitive phases. This means paying attention to the antagonist muscles and stabilizers. For example, following any informal physical training such as a pickup game or recreational play, 20 to 30 minutes can be dedicated to activating these two muscle groups. The program can be relaxed, with athletes working at their own pace for as long as they desire. The program need not be stressful. In fact, stress is undesirable during transition. Forget the formal program with its specific load, number of reps, and sets; for once, athletes should do as they please.

Fatigue, Muscle Soreness, and Recovery

Athletes are constantly exposed to various types of training loads, some of which exceed their tolerance thresholds. As a result, adaptation decreases, affecting overall performance. When athletes drive themselves beyond their physiological limits, they risk fatigue. The greater the fatigue, the greater the negative training aftereffects such as low rate of recovery, decreased coordination, and diminished power output. Fatigue from training can also increase if an athlete is undergoing other personal stresses.

The muscle fatigue and overreaching commonly associated with exercise-induced muscle damage are complex physiological and psychological phenomena. Fatigue can affect an athlete's force-generating capacity or result in the inability to maintain a required force. Although much research has been devoted to muscle fatigue, neither the exact sites nor the exact causes are well known. Coaches and instructors should become as informed as possible in this area so they can create better plans to avoid fatigue and overreaching in their athletes.

To improve performance, training loads must be high enough to stimulate adaptation. For adaptation to occur, training programs must intersperse work periods with rest and alternate various levels of intensity while avoiding large increments in training load. This practice creates a good work-to-rest balance; exposing athletes to loads beyond their capacity or underestimating the necessary rest will result in decreased ability to adapt to a new load. Failure to adapt triggers biochemical and neural reactions that take athletes from fatigue to chronic fatigue and ultimately to the undesirable state of overtraining.

Neuromuscular Fatigue

Although fatigue is assumed to originate in the muscles, the central nervous system (CNS) plays an important role because incentive, temperament, stress, and other psychological factors affect fatigue. Increasing evidence suggests that the CNS limits performance to a greater extent than once thought.

The CNS has two basic processes: *excitation* and *inhibition*. Excitation is a stimulating process for physical activity; inhibition is a restraining process. Throughout training, these two processes alternate. As a result of any stimulation, the CNS sends a nerve impulse to the working muscle, causing it to contract. The speed, power, and frequency of the nerve impulse depends directly on the state of the CNS.

Nerve impulses are most effective when (controlled) excitation prevails, resulting in a good performance. When fatigue inhibits the nerve cell, the muscle contraction is slower and weaker. Thus, the electrical activation of the CNS is responsible for the number of motor units recruited and the force of the contraction. Recruitment of motor units decreases as fatigue increases.

Nerve cell working capacity cannot be maintained for very long. Under the strain of training or competition, it decreases. If high intensity is maintained, the nerve cell will assume a state of inhibition to protect itself from external stimuli. Consequently, fatigue should be viewed as a self-protecting mechanism against damage to the contractile mechanism of the muscle. Furthermore, intense exercise leads to the development of acidosis, which is caused primarily by the buildup of lactic acid in the muscle cell. A high level of acidosis can affect the release of the calcium required for muscular contraction. In essence, an excitatory nerve impulse may reach the muscle membrane and be blocked by an inhibited calcium release membrane (Enoka and Stuart, 1992).

In speed and power sports, fatigue is visible to the experienced eye. Athletes react more slowly to explosive activities and show a slight coordination impairment and an increase in the duration of the contact phase in sprinting, bounding, rebounding, jumping, and plyometrics. In endurance events fatigue is generally expressed through the breakdown of technique and of course a gradual decrease in the average speed of movement. These activities rely on the activation of fast-twitch muscle fibers, which are more easily affected by fatigue than are slow-twitch fibers. Thus, even a slight inhibition of the CNS affects their recruitment. Coaches should watch for the symptoms of fatigue described here.

Skeletal muscle produces force by activating its motor units and regulating their firing frequency, which progressively increases to enhance force output. Fatigue that inhibits muscular activity can be neutralized to some extent by a modulating strategy of altering firing frequency. As a result, the muscle can maintain force more effectively under a certain state of fatigue. However, if the duration of sustained maximum contraction increases, the frequency of the motor units' firing decreases, signaling that inhibition will become more prominent (Bigland-Ritchie et al., 1983; Hennig and Lomo, 1987).

Marsden, Meadows, and Merton (1971) demonstrated that firing frequency at the end of a 30-second maximum voluntary contraction decreased by 80 percent compared to the frequency at the start of the contraction. Grimby (1992) reported similar findings: As contraction duration increased, the activation of large motor units decreased, lowering the firing rate below the threshold level. Any contraction beyond that level was possible through short bursts (phasical firing) but was not appropriate for a constant performance.

These findings should alarm those who promote the theory (especially in American football) that strength can be improved only by performing each set to exhaustion. The fact that the firing frequency decreases as a contraction progresses discredits this highly acclaimed method.

As a contraction progresses, fuel reserves become depleted, resulting in longer motor unit relaxation time and a lower frequency of muscle contraction. Fatigue is the suspected cause of such neuromuscular behavior. This should warn practitioners that short rest intervals (the standard one to two minutes) between two sets of maximum load are insufficient to relax and regenerate the neuromuscular system to produce high activation in subsequent sets.

When analyzing the functional capacity of the CNS during fatigue, coaches should consider the athletes' perceived fatigue and past physical capacity achieved in training. When physical capacity is above the level of fatigue experienced in testing or competition, it enhances motivation and, as a result, the capacity to overcome fatigue. Thus, the level of motivation must be related to past experience and the state of training.

Lactic Acid Accumulation

The buildup of lactic acid in the muscle decreases its ability to contract maximally (Fox, Bowes, and Foss, 1989). Any athletic movements requiring quickness or force of contraction must rely on the contraction of fast-twitch fibers. Because such actions are anaerobic, they rely on anaerobic types of fuel, resulting in increased production and the accumulation of lactic acid. During the performance of high-intensity (heavy-load) sets, fast-twitch fibers produce high levels of lactates, blocking any immediate excitation-stimulation coming from CNS. The next high-intensity set can be performed only after a longer rest period (see "Rest Interval" in chapter 5).

The biochemical exchanges during muscle contraction result in the liberation of hydrogen ions that in turn produce acidosis or the not yet clearly understood "lactate fatigue," which seems to determine the point of exhaustion (Sahlin, 1986). The more active a muscle is, the greater its hydrogen ion concentration is and thus the higher the level of blood acidosis is.

Increased acidosis also inhibits the binding capacity of calcium through the inactivation of troponin, a protein compound. Because troponin is an important contributor to muscle cell contraction, its inactivation may delay the onset of fatigue (Fabiato and Fabiato, 1978). The discomfort produced by acidosis can also be a limiting factor in psychological fatigue (Brooks and Fahey, 1985).

Adenosine Triphosphate, Creatine Phosphate, and Glycogen Depletion

Fatigue occurs when creatine phosphate (CP) in the working muscle is depleted, muscle glycogen is consumed, or the carbohydrate store is exhausted (Sahlin, 1986). The end result is obvious: The work performed by the muscle decreases. The possible reason is that in a glycogen-depleted muscle, adenosine triphosphate (ATP) is produced at a lower rate than it is consumed. Studies show that carbohydrates are essential to the ability of a muscle to maintain high force (Conlee, 1987) and that endurance capabilities during prolonged moderate to heavy physical activity are directly related to the amount of glycogen in the muscle prior to exercise. This indicates that fatigue occurs as a result of muscle glycogen depletion (Bergstrom et al., 1967).

For high-intensity activities of short duration, such as high-intensity sets, the immediate sources of energy for muscular contraction are ATP and CP. Total depletion of these stores in the muscle will certainly limit its ability to contract (Karlsson and Saltin, 1971).

With prolonged submaximum work such as muscular endurance of medium or long duration, glucose and fatty acids are used to produce energy. The availability of oxygen is critical in this type of strength training. When the supply of oxygen is limited, carbohydrates are oxidized instead of free fatty acids. Maximum free fatty acid oxidation is determined by the inflow of fatty acids to the working muscle and the aerobic training status of the athlete because aerobic training increases both the availability of oxygen and the power of free fatty acid oxidation (Sahlin, 1986). Lack of oxygen, lack of oxygen-carrying capacity, and inadequate blood flow all contribute to muscular fatigue (Bergstrom et al., 1967). This demonstrates the need for decent aerobic conditioning, even for speed and power sports.

Muscle Soreness

Muscle soreness after training can occur when athletes first start a strength training program, when they perform unfamiliar exercises that work muscles other than those they normally use, or any time they use heavy loads for a prolonged period. Beginners exposed to heavy loads without adequate adaptation will also experience muscle soreness.

Two basic mechanisms explain how exercise initiates damage: the disturbance of metabolic function and the mechanical disruption of the muscle cell. The metabolic mechanism of muscle damage is at work during prolonged submaximum work to exhaustion, which is typical of some bodybuilding methods. Direct loading of the muscle, especially during the eccentric contraction phase, may cause muscle damage, which may then be aggravated by metabolic changes. Disruption of the muscle cell membrane is one of the most noticeable types of damage (swollen mitochondria, lesion of the plasma membrane, distortion of myofibrillar components, sarcolemmal disruption, etc.) (Friden and Lieber, 1992).

Eccentric contraction produces greater muscle tension than concentric contraction does. Athletes who use the eccentric method without enough strength training background to tolerate it or without achieving connective tissue adaptation will suffer discomfort and muscle damage. Eccentric contraction produces more heat than concentric contraction does at the same workload. The increased temperatures can damage structural and functional components within the muscle cell (Armstrong, 1986; Ebbing and Clarkson, 1989).

Both mechanisms of muscle damage are related to muscle fibers that have been slightly stressed. Muscle fibers usually return quickly to their normal length without injury. If the stress is severe, however, the muscle becomes traumatized. Discomfort sets in during the first 24 to 48 hours following the exercise and is thus called *delayed-onset* muscle soreness. The sensation of dull, aching pain combined with tenderness and stiffness tends to diminish five to seven days after the initial workout.

Closely monitoring training will help prevent overtraining, fatigue, and injury.

The prevention of muscle soreness takes several forms, from training to medication. The most important preventive technique for a coach to consider is the principle of progressive increase of load in training. Furthermore, applying the concept of periodization of strength will help athletes avoid discomfort, muscle soreness, or other negative training outcomes.

An extensive overall warm-up will better prepare the body for work. Superficial warm-ups, on the other hand, can easily result in strain and pain. Stretching is also strongly recommended at the end of a training session. After extensive muscle contraction, typical of strength training, muscles are slightly shorter. It takes around two hours for them to return to resting length. Five to 10 minutes of stretching helps the muscles reach their resting length faster, which is optimal for biochemical exchanges at the muscle fiber level. Stretching also seems to ease muscle spasms.

Ingesting 1,000 milligrams of vitamin C per day may prevent or at least reduce muscle soreness. Similar benefits seem to result from taking vitamin E, along with sodium and potassium supplementation. Anti-inflammatory medication, such as Advil or aspirin, may help combat inflammation of muscle tissue. Proper diet also helps athletes recover from muscle soreness. Athletes exposed to heavy loads in strength training require more protein, carbohydrates, and supplements. Inadequate carbohydrates may delay recovery of the muscle from injury and soreness. Massage is conventionally believed to relieve muscle soreness as well. Coaches and athletes should keep in mind, however, that medication, diet, and massage provide only temporary relief. The best plan is to prevent muscle soreness in the first place. The best prevention strategy is a progression in the use of eccentric contraction, especially at the beginning of strength training, such as the following:

- Week 1: Use only concentric contraction.
- Week 2: Use 70 percent concentric and 30 percent eccentric contraction.
- Week 3: Use normal concentric–eccentric ratios.

Signs of Overtraining

Signs of overtraining are signals that athletes are adapting poorly, or not at all, to the training regimen. Overtraining doesn't usually settle in overnight; it is a slow process that occurs as a result of a prolonged training program that lacks sessions for recovery and regeneration. Without proper rest, relaxation, and recovery the athlete will coast into a state of chronic fatigue and poor motivation. Classic signs of overtraining include a higher than usual heart rate; irritability; trouble sleeping; loss of appetite; and of course fatigued, sore, and tight muscles.

At times, recovery from intense training programs can elicit many of the signs of overtraining. If these signs persist a few days following one or two intense bouts, it may be a sign of overreaching rather than overtraining. In other words, the athlete may be working at a level above her physiological comfort zone. With proper rest and recovery, the athlete will successfully overcome the fatigue and be ready for the next challenge. However, lack of proper recovery can quickly draw the athlete from a state of overreaching to a state of overtraining. Following are a few tools that can help the athlete and coach determine whether the athlete is entering a state of overtraining.

- **Record your heart rate.** An athlete or coach can record a daily morning heart rate to determine whether the athlete is working at the appropriate training level. A morning heart rate recording is best because the athlete is rested and not yet influenced by the stresses of the day. An increased resting heart rate over a two- or three-day period may be a sign of overtraining. If this occurs, the coach should alter the training program to a lower intensity level and keep a close eye on the heart rate response over 24 to 48 hours.

- **Keep a training log.** This simple concept often causes a lot of complaining among athletes. Athletes generally don't have a problem recording their loads or time in training, but they shy away from recording the intensity level of the session or level of fatigue. Every athlete trains and sacrifices to be the best. Admitting that a training session was too intense is not part of their nature and thus usually goes unrecorded. The coach should keep a close eye on the athlete and take the time to communicate the importance of not exceeding one's physical tolerability. The coach may need to keep a specific log book describing the physiological impact of the training lesson on the athlete. The log should include how the athlete felt immediately after a workout, after a few hours, and after a few days. Chronic muscle soreness and inflammation of the joints may be signs to decrease the amount and intensity of the training. If the response to training seems intolerable hours and days after training, the coach can try implementing a few recovery techniques following the workout. Stretching is a good way to decrease susceptibility to injury, and it is also a great way of relaxing the body at the end of the workout. Stretching is also an active way to remove some of the substances such as lactic acid and muscle debris that accumulate during training and could be impeding recovery. Partner-assisted stretches are an ideal way to fully stretch the muscles and relax while the workout partner or trainer does the work. Anecdotal evidence suggests that stretching decreases postworkout soreness and aids in recovery. If recovery techniques do not reduce or eliminate the signs of overtraining, however, the coach should alter the program.

Performing 5 to 10 minutes of light aerobic activity such as jogging or cycling is a great way to regenerate the body following a workout. Enjoying a nice sauna or hot shower for 5 to 10 minutes can also help muscles relax and heal following a strenuous workout. A contrast shower, which includes cycling between hot and cold water, is a great way of increasing blood flow from the skin to the organs and eliminating waste products from the body. Athletes should alter 30 to 60 seconds of hot water with 30 to 60 seconds of cold water for two or three sets. Of course this technique will take a little getting used to.

- **Use a handgrip dynamometer.** A handgrip dynamometer (a squeezing device held in the hand that records pressure) is a quick and effective way to objectively measure overtraining or daily fatigue. It can also serve as a good indicator of CNS fatigue. Before every workout, the athlete squeezes the dynamometer one hand at a time and records the score. If the score constantly decreases or is lower on a particular day, the athlete may be experiencing CNS fatigue and need to recover.

Coaches should remember that psychological stress may affect the athlete's response to training even though it is not a visible sign. Just because the program indicates a high-intensity training day does not mean that the coach or athlete cannot adjust the program to the athlete's current physical and emotional state. Sometimes less is more, and rest can, at times, have a stronger impact on adaptation than training has.

Recovery Techniques

Various techniques are available for recovery from fatigue. Understanding how to use these techniques during training is just as important as knowing how to train effectively. New loads or intensity levels are constantly implemented in athletic training programs, but the recovery methods used often do not keep pace. This can mean potential setbacks for athletes in peaking and regeneration following training. Approximately 50 percent of an athlete's final performance depends on the ability to recover. If recovery techniques are inadequate, adaptation may not be achieved.

No single factor affects recovery by itself; rather, the combination of these factors, all at varying degrees, contributes to the recovery process. Among the main factors to be considered are age, experience, gender, environment, cell replenishment, and emotional state.

Older athletes generally take longer to recover than younger athletes do. Better trained, more experienced athletes generally require less time to recuperate than less experienced athletes do because of their ability to adapt more quickly to a given training stimulus. Gender may affect the rate of recovery as a result of differences in the endocrine system. Female athletes tend to have a slower rate of recovery than male athletes do. Environmental factors such as time differences, altitude, and climate tend to affect the recovery process also, as does the replenishment of nutrients at the cellular level. The restoration of proteins, fats, carbohydrates, and ATP-CP within the working muscle cell is required for cellular metabolism, as well as for the production of energy (Fox et al., 1989; Jacobs et al., 1987). Finally, fear, indecisiveness, and lack of willpower tend to impede recovery.

The neuroendocrine response to training is an important component in recovery from strength training. As mentioned in chapter 6, after a strength training session the body is in a negative balance: Protein breakdown is greater than protein synthesis. Furthermore, the testosterone-to-cortisol ratio is lower, which places the body in a state of catabolism. Ingesting a protein mixture in the form of a protein shake immediately after high-intensity training can shift the body from a state of negative balance to a state of positive balance. The ingestion of protein increases testosterone levels, lowers cortisol levels, and kick starts the recovery and regeneration process.

Recovery is a slow process that corresponds directly with the training load employed. Similarly, the curve of recovery, which represents the body's ability to reach homeostasis, or its normal biological state, is not linear (see figure 13.1). In the first third of the recovery process, 70 percent of recovery occurs; in the next two thirds, 20 and 10 percent of recovery occurs, respectively.

The time interval for recovery depends on the energy system being taxed. Table 13.1 lists recommended recovery times for exhaustive strength training.

For greatest effectiveness, athletes should undertake recovery techniques during and following each training session (Fry, Morton, and Keast, 1991; Kuipers and Keizer, 1988). *Active recovery* is the rapid elimination of waste products (i.e., lactic acid) during moderate aerobic recovery exercise. During the first 10 minutes of continuous light jogging, 62 percent of lactic acid is removed. An additional 26 percent is removed in the next 10 minutes of jogging. Thus, maintaining an active recovery period for 10 to 20 minutes after strength training seems advantageous (Bonen and Belcastro, 1977; Fox et al., 1989).

Complete rest, or *passive rest*, is perhaps the one necessity that all athletes have in common. To function at full capacity, most athletes require about 10 hours of sleep a day, a portion of which is usually gotten in the form of naps. Athletes should also have regular sleeping habits and be in bed no later than 11:00 p.m. Relaxation techniques prior to bedtime will put the athlete's mind in a more restful state (Gauron, 1984).

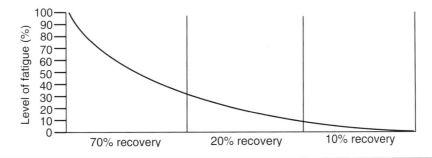

Figure 13.1 The dynamics of a recovery curve divided into three phases.

Table 13.1 Recovery Times After Exhaustive Strength Training

Recovery process	Recovery time
Restoration of ATP/CP	3-5 minutes
Restoration of muscle glycogen: After prolonged exercise After intermittent exercise (such as strength training)	24-48 hours 24 hours
Removal of lactic acid from muscle and blood	1-2 hours
Restoration of vitamins and enzymes	24 hours
Recovery from overly taxing strength training (both metabolic and CNS to reach overcompensation)	2-3 days
Repayment of the alactacid oxygen debt	5 minutes
Repayment of the lactacid oxygen debt	30-60 minutes

Adapted, by permission, from E. Fox, 1989, *Physiological basis of physical education and athletics* (New York: McGraw Hill), 56.

Massage, the systematic manipulation of soft body tissues for therapeutic purposes, is often the treatment of choice for most athletes (Cinique, 1989; Yessis, 1990). To achieve the best results from massage therapy, athletes are urged to use a certified specialist. The physiological effects of a massage are the result of mechanical intrusion, sensory stimulation, or both.

The mechanical effects of massage include the relief of muscle fatigue and the reduction of excessive swelling. Massage can be especially beneficial when treating certain types of inflammation. Massage also stretches muscle adhesion. The mechanical pressure and stretching of tissue aids in mobilizing muscle adhesion for removal by the circulatory system. Massage also increases blood circulation. Squeezing relaxed muscles empties veins in the direction of the applied pressure. This stimulates the small capillaries to open and increases blood flow in the massaged area. At rest, approximately 4 percent of capillaries are open; this can be increased to 35 percent through massage (Bergeron, 1982). The end result is the increased availability of "fresh" blood to the massaged area, allowing greater interchange of substances between capillaries and tissue cells.

Lymphatic circulation also increases as a result of massage. Massage assists circulation in the veins and the return of fluid (lymph) from the tissues. Unlike veins, which have one-way valves, lymphatic vessels have no valves so lymph can move in any direction, depending on external pressure. Gravity and muscle pumping (including breathing activities) are the primary movers of lymph. Massage is the most effective external means of moving extravascular fluid into the lymph vessels and through these vessels into the circulatory system. This might be described as a cleaning-out action.

The sensory effects of massage are primarily reflexive in nature and are not fully understood. Massage may relieve pain and tenderness by slowly increasing the sensory input to the CNS. This necessitates massaging gradually into the painful area. Light stroking of the skin results in temporary dilation of capillaries. The stronger the stroking is, the greater and more prolonged the dilation will be. Massage has only a local effect on metabolism that is due primarily to increased circulation throughout the massaged area. The breakdown of waste products and their absorption into the circulatory system may be increased up to 2.5 times above resting levels.

Massage also relieves muscle spasm. Light stroking of an involuntary muscle contraction such as a muscle spasm may bring about relaxation through reflex mechanisms. Muscle spasms should first be stroked lightly in a direction parallel to the muscle fibers. If this fails, firm pressure should be applied to the muscle belly with both hands. If this also fails, deep thumb pressure into the muscle belly may help. In all cases, only gentle stretching of the muscle in spasm is recommended. Firm or deep pressure or sudden, violent stretching may increase the severity of the spasm.

Heat therapy in the form of steam baths, saunas, and heat packs can have a relaxing or regenerating effect. Although heat packs primarily heat the skin and not the underlying tissues, this modality is still useful. If applied long enough (at least 20 minutes), heat can be an effective way of increasing the circulation around the muscle. The only drawback is that the skin may become too hot before any muscle tissue has been heated. The best uses of heat may be to help athletes relax and to heat surface rather than deep muscle tissue.

Cold therapy such as ice, ice baths, ice whirlpools, and cold packs for 10 to 15 minutes may have important physiological benefits for recovery from fatigue. Rubbing ice on an excessively strained muscle may reduce swelling. In conjunction with heat, it may induce expansion (heat) or contraction (cold) of the damaged muscle tissue. Perhaps the best time to use ice is immediately following an intense training session in which microtearing of the muscle tissue is likely.

Before discussing *diet and dietary supplementation*, a few words regarding caloric intake are in order. Ideally, athletes should maintain an energy balance each day; that is, their daily energy expenditure should roughly match their energy intake. Athletes can judge rather easily whether their diet is adequate in calories. If they are losing weight while on a rigorous workout schedule, they probably are not consuming enough calories.

Even if they consume a "well-balanced" diet, athletes should not shy away from taking vitamin and mineral supplements. No matter how well balanced a diet may be, it usually cannot replenish all the vitamins and minerals used during a training session or competition. Athletes typically experience a deficiency in all vitamins except vitamin A (Yessis, 1990). During periods of heavy training, supplements should be as much a part of the training table as any other nutrient.

According to Fahey (1991), diet may play a part in muscle tissue recovery. Aside from the obvious need for protein (in particular, animal protein), carbohydrates are also required. Recovery from muscle injury has been shown to be delayed when muscle carbohydrate stores are inadequate. Thus, from the standpoints of energy expenditure and recovery, athletes must pay strict attention to diet.

In planning a supplement program, coaches and athletes should consider each period of training throughout the yearly plan and adjust the supplements accordingly. For example, during the transition phase, the need for large doses of vitamins, particularly vitamins B_6, B_{12}, and C and certain minerals will be much less because of the decreased intensity and volume of training. Planning for vitamin and mineral supplements can be relatively easy by putting them in chart form with columns representing specific phases during the yearly training plan.

According to Clark (1985) and Yessis (1990), mealtime can affect the rate of recovery. These authors believe that athletes should develop an eating pattern in which their daily intake is divided into at least four small meals a day, rather than three large meals. They reason that foods are better assimilated and digested with such a pattern. They recommend that about 20 to 25 percent of the daily intake be consumed in the early morning meal, 15 to 20 percent in a second breakfast, 30 to 35 percent in the midday meal, and 20 to 25 percent in the evening meal. Athletes should allow no more than five hours to pass between meals and no more than 12 hours between the evening meal and breakfast.

Clark (1985) and Yessis (1990) also believe that athletes should not eat immediately before a training session because a full stomach raises the diaphragm, forcing the cardiovascular and respiratory systems to work harder. Athletes should also avoid eating right after training because few gastric juices are secreted during that time. Instead, athletes should consume only fluids that contain carbohydrates and mineral supplements directly after training. The posttraining meal can follow 20 to 30 minutes later. Carbohydrates as well as foods rich in potassium are vital to normal muscle function (Clark, 1985; Fox, 1984).

Psychological recovery refers to factors such as motivation and willpower, which can be affected by stress from both physical and psychological stimuli. How fast the body reacts to various forms of external and internal stimuli greatly affects athletic performance. The more focused athletes are, the better they react to various training stimuli and the greater their working capacity is. Lifestyle almost always has an effect on an athlete's rate of recovery. Poor relationships with a significant other, siblings, parents, teammates, and coaches can have a negative impact on the recovery process. A sport psychologist can be helpful to an athlete who is experiencing deep emotional problems that affect motivation and willpower.

Relaxation techniques can greatly improve an athlete's ability to focus. If the brain is relaxed, all other parts of the body assume the same state (Gauron, 1984). Perhaps the best time to employ such methods would be just before retiring for the evening. A warm bath or shower before bed might help induce a more relaxed state.

Recovery from short-term overtraining should start with the interruption of training for three to five days. Following this rest period, the athlete should resume training by alternating each training session with a day off. If overtraining is severe and the athlete needs more recovery time, for every week of training missed, roughly two weeks will be required to attain the previous level of conditioning (Terjung and Hood, 1986). Repair of damaged muscle tissue falls under the category of short-term overtraining, requiring at least five days, whereas the regeneration of muscle tissue takes up to 20 days (Ebbing and Clarkson, 1989).

Recovery from muscle damage during the early part of the injury (approximately two to four hours postinjury) or the acute phase is best treated with ice, elevation, compression, and active or complete rest (depending on the extent of damage). After three days of this treatment, the coach should introduce other modalities such as massage. Alternation of hot and cold temperatures can also be an effective way of loosening the stiffness associated with exercise-induced muscle damage (Arnheim, 1989; Prentice, 1990).

Bibliography

Aagard, P., Simonsen, E.B., Anderson, J.L., Magnusson, S.P., Halkaer-Kristensen, K. 1994. Moment and power generation during maximal knee extensions performed at low and high speeds. *European Journal of Applied Physiology, 89*: 2249–2257.

Abbruzzese, G., Morena, M., Spadavecchia, L., and Schieppati, M. 1994. Response of arm flexor muscles to magnetic and electrical brain stimulation during shortening and lengthening tasks in man. *Journal of Physiology London, 481*: 499–507.

Abernethy, P.J., Thayer, R., and Taylor, A.W. 1990. Acute and chronic responses of skeletal muscle to endurance and sprint exercise. A review. *Sports Medicine, 10* (6): 365–389.

Adams, T.M., Worlay, D., and Throgmartin, D. 1987. The effects of selected plyometric and weight training on muscular leg power. *Track and Field Quarterly Review, 87*: 45–47.

Appell, H.J. 1990. Muscular atrophy following immobilization: A review. *Sports Medicine, 10* (1): 42–58.

Armstrong, R.B. 1986. Muscle damage and endurance events. *Sports Medicine, 3*: 370–381.

Armstrong, R.B., Warren, G.L., and Warren, J.A. 1991. Mechanics of exercise induced muscle fiber injury. *Sports Medicine, 12* (3): 184–207.

Arnheim, D. 1989. *Modern principles of athletic training.* St. Louis, MO: Times Mirror/Mosby College.

Ashton-Miller, J.A., Wojtys, E.M., Huston, L.J., and Fry-Welch, D. 2001. Can proprioception be improved by exercise? *Knee. Surg. Sports Traumatol. Arthrosc, 9* (3): 128–136.

Asmussen, E., and Mazin, B. 1978. A central nervous system component in local muscular fatigue. *European Journal of Applied Physiology, 38*: 9–15.

Åstrand, P.O., and Rodahl, K. 1985. *Textbook of work physiology.* New York: McGraw-Hill.

Atha, J. 1984. Strengthening muscle. *Exercise and Sport Sciences Reviews, 9*: 1–73.

Augustsson, J., Thomee, R., Hornstedt, P., Lindblom, J., Karlsson, J., and Grimby, G. 2003. Effect of pre-exhaust exercise on lower extremity muscle activation during a leg press exercise. *Journal of Strength and Conditioning Research, 17* (2): 411–416.

Baroga, L. 1978. Contemporary tendencies in the methodology of strength development. *Educatie Fizica Si Sport, 6*: 22–36.

Behm, D., and Sale, D.G. 1993. Intended rather than actual movement velocity determines velocity specific training response. *Journal of Applied Physiology, 74*: 359–368.

Bergeron, G. 1982. Therapeutic massage. *Canadian Athletic Therapist Association Journal*, Summer: 15–17.

Bergstrom, J., Hermansen, L., Hultman, E., and Saltin, B. 1967. Diet, muscle glycogen and physical performance. *Acta Physiologica Scandinavica, 71*: 140–150.

Bigland-Ritchie, B., Johansson, R., Lippold, O.C.J., and Woods, J.J. 1983. Contractile speed and EMG changes during fatigue of sustained maximal voluntary contractions. *Journal of Neurophysiology, 50* (1): 313–324.

Billat, V.L., Sirvent, P., Py, G., Koralsztein, J.P., and Mercier, J. 2003. The concept of maximal lactate steady state: A bridge between biochemistry, physiology and sport science. *Sports Medicine, 33* (6): 407-426.

Bompa, T. 1965a. Periodization of strength. *Sports Review, 1*: 26–31.

Bompa, T. 1965b. Periodization of strength for power sports. International Conference on Advancements in Sports Training, Moscow. November 22–23.

Bompa, T. 1977. Characteristics of strength training for rowing. International Seminar on Training in Rowing, Stockholm. October 27–28.

Bompa, T. 1988. *Periodization of strength for bodybuilding.* Toronto: York University.

Bompa, T. 1993a. *Periodization of strength: The new wave in strength training.* Toronto: Veritas.

Bompa, T. 1993b. *Power training for sport: Plyometrics for maximum power development.* Oakville-New York-London: Mosaic Press/Coaching Association of Canada.

Bompa, T. 1999. *Periodization: Theory and methodology of training.* 4th ed. Champaign, IL: Human Kinetics.

Bompa, T., and Cornacchia, L. 1998. *Serious strength training.* Champaign, IL: Human Kinetics.

Bompa T., Hebbelinck, M., and Van Gheluwe, B. 1978. A biomechanical analysis of the rowing stroke employing two different oar grips. The XXI World Congress in Sports Medicine, Brasilia, Brazil.

Bompa, T.O. (2005). Treinando atletas de deporto colectivo. San Paulo, Brazil. Phorte Editora.

Bonen, A. 2001. The expression of lactate transporters (MCT1 and MCT4) in heart and muscle. *European Journal of Applied Physiology, 86* (1): 6–11.

Bonen, A., and Belcastro, A.N. 1976. Comparison of self-selected recovery methods on lactic acid removal rates. *Medicine and Science in Sports and Exercise, 8* (3): 176–178.

Bonen, A., and Belcastro, A. 1977. A physiological rationale for active recovery exercise. *Canadian Journal of Applied Sports Sciences, 2*: 63–64.

Borsheim, E., Cree, M.G., Tipton, K.D., Elliott, T.A., Aarsland, A., and Wolfe, R.R. 2004. Effect of carbohydrate intake on net muscle protein synthesis during recovery from resistance exercise. *Journal of Applied Physiology, 96* (2): 674–678.

Bosco, C., and Komi, P.V. 1980. Influence of countermovement amplitude in potentiation of muscular performance. Biomechanics VII Proceedings (pp. 129–135). Baltimore: University Park Press.

Brooks, G.A., Brauner, K.T., and Cassens, R.G. 1973. Glycogen synthesis and metabolism of lactic acid after exercise. *American Journal of Physiology, 224*: 1162–1166.

Brooks, G.A., and Fahey, T. 1985. *Exercise physiology: Human bioenergetics and its application.* New York: Wiley.

Brooks, G.A, Fahey, T.D., and White, T.P. 1996. *Exercise physiology: Human bioenergetics and its applications.* 2nd ed., Mountainview, CA: Mayfield.

Bührle, M. 1985. *Grundlagen des Maximal-und Schnellkraft trainings.* Schorndorf: Hofmann Verlag.

Bührle, M., and Schmidtbleicher, D. 1981. Komponenten der Maximal-und Schnellkraft-Versuch einer Neus-truk-turierung auf der Basis empirischer Ergenbnisse. *Sportwissenschaft, 11*: 11–27.

Burke, R., Costill, D., and Fink, W. 1977. Characteristics of skeletal muscle in competitive cyclists. *Medicine and Science in Sports and Exercise, 9*: 109–112.

Burkes, L.M., Collier, G.R., and Hargreaves, M. 1998. Glycemic index—A new tool in sport nutrition? *International Journal of Sport Nutrition, 8* (4): 401–415.

Caraffa, A., Cerulli, G., Projetti, M., Aisa, G., and Rizzo, A. 1996. Prevention of anterior cruciate ligament injuries in soccer. A prospective controlled study of proprioceptive training. *Knee Surgery, Sports Traumatology, Arthroscopy, 4* (1), 19–21.

Carroll, T.J., Riek, S., and Carson, R.G. 2001. Neural adaptations to resistance training: Implications for movement control. *Sports Medicine, 31* (12): 829–840.

Cinique, C. 1989. Massage for cyclists: The winning touch? *The Physician and Sportsmedicine, 17* (10): 167–170.

Clark, N. 1985. Recovering from exhaustive workouts. *National Strength and Conditioning Journal,* January: 36–37.

Compton, D., Hill, P.M., and Sinclair, J.D. 1973. Weight-lifters' blackout. *Lancet II:* 1234–1237.

Conlee, R.K. 1987. Muscle glycogen and exercise endurance: A twenty-year perspective. *Exercise and Sport Sciences Reviews,* 15: 1–28.

Coombes, J.S., and Hamilton, K.L. 2000. The effectiveness of commercially available sports drinks. *Sports Medicine, 29* (3): 181–209.

Costill, D., Coyle, E.F., Find, W.F., Lesmes, G.R., and Witzmann, F.A. 1979. Adaptations in skeletal muscle following strength training. *Journal of Applied Physiology, 46*: 96–99.

Costill, D., Daniels, J., Evans, W., Fink, W., Krahenbuhl, G., and Saltin, B. 1976. Skeletal muscle enzymes and fibre composition in male and female track athletes. *Journal of Applied Physiology, 40*: 149–154.

Councilman, J.E. 1968. *The science of swimming.* Englewood Cliffs, NJ: Prentice Hall.

Coyle, E.F. 1999. Physiological determinants of endurance exercise performance. *Journal of Science and Medicine in Sport, 2* (3): 181–189.

Coyle, E.F., Feiring, D.C., Rotkis, T.C., Cote, R.W., Roby, F.B., Lee, W., and Wilmore, J.H. 1991. Specificity of power improvements through slow and fast isokinetic training. *Journal of Applied Physiology: Respiratory Environment Exercise Physiology*, *51* (6): 1437–1442.

David, R.M., Welsh, R.S., De Volve, K.L., and Alderson, N.A. 1999. *International Journal of Sports Medicine*, *20* (5): 309–314.

Davis, J., Jackson, D.A., Broadwell, M.S., Queary, J.L., and Lambert, C.L. 1997. Carbohydrate drinks delay fatigue during intermittent, high-intensity cycling in active men and women. *International Journal of Sports Nutrition*, *7* (4): 261–273.

De Luca, C.J., LeFever, R.S., McCue, M.P., and Xenakis, A.P. 1982. Behaviour of human motor units in different muscles during linearly varying contractions. *Journal of Physiology London*, *329*: 113–128.

Dons, B., Bollerup, K., Bonde-Petersen, F., and Hancke, S. 1979. The effects of weight lifting exercise related to muscle fibre composition and muscle cross-sectional area in humans. *European Journal of Applied Physiology*, *40*: 95–106.

Dorado, C., Sanchis-Moysi, J., and Calbet, J.A., 2004. Effects of recovery mode on performance, O_2 uptake, and O_2 deficit during high-intensity intermittent exercise. *Canadian Journal of Applied Physiology*, *29* (3): 227–244.

Dudley, G.A., and Fleck, S.J. 1987. Strength and endurance training: Are they mutually exclusive? *Sports Medicine*, *4*: 79–85.

Ebbing, C., and Clarkson, P. 1989. Exercise-induced muscle damage and adaptation. *Sports Medicine*, *7*: 207–234.

Edgerton, R.V. 1976. Neuromuscular adaptation to power and endurance work. *Canadian Journal of Applied Sports Sciences*, *1*: 49–58.

Enoka, R. 1996. Eccentric contractions require unique activation strategies by the nervous system. *Journal of Applied Physiology*, *81* (6): 2339–2346.

Enoka, R.M. 2002. *Neuromechanics of human movement.* 3rd ed. Champaign IL: Human Kinetics.

Enoka, R.M., and Stuart, D.G. 1992. Neurobiology of muscle fatigue. *Journal of Applied Physiology:* 72 (5):1631–1638.

Enoka, R.M. Neuromechanical basis of Kinesiology (2nd ed). Human Kinetics, Champaign IL, 1994.

Evans, W.J. 1987. Exercise-induced skeletal muscle damage. *The Physician and Sports Medicine*, *15* (1): 89–100.

Evertsen, F., Medbo, J.I., Jebens, E.P., and Gjovaag, T.F. 1999. Effect of training on the activity of five muscle enzymes studied on elite cross-country skiers. *Acta Physiologica Scandinavica*, *167* (3): 247–257.

Fabiato, A., and Fabiato, F. 1978. The effect of pH on myofilaments and the sarcoplasmic reticulum of skinned cells from cardiac and skeletal muscle. *Journal of Physiology*, *276*: 233–255.

Fahey, D. 1991. How to cope with muscle soreness. Power Research.

Fitts, R.H., and Widrick, J.J. 1996. Muscle mechanics: Adaptations with exercise-training. *Exercise Sports Science Review*, *24*: 427–473.

Fleck, S.J., and Kraemer, W.J. 1996. *Periodization breakthrough.* New York: Advanced Research Press.

Florescu, C., Dumitrescu, T., and Predescu, A. 1969. *The methodology of developing the motor abilities.* Bucharest: CNEFS.

Fox, E.L. 1984. *Sports physiology.* New York: CBS College.

Fox, E.L., Bowes, R.W., and Foss, M.L. 1989. *The physiological basis of physical education and athletics.* Dubuque, IA: Brown.

Frank, C.B. 1996. Ligament injuries: Pathophysiology and healing. In J.E. Zachazewski, D.J. Magee, and W.S. Wilson (eds), *Athletic injuries and rehabilitation* (pp. 9–26). Philadelphia: Saunders.

Friden, J., and Lieber, R.L. 1992. Structural and mechanical basis of exercise-induced muscle injury. *Medicine In Science and Sports Exercise*, *24*: 521–530.

Fry, R.W., Morton, R., and Keast, D. 1991. Overtraining in athletics. *Sports Medicine*, *2* (1): 32–65.

Gauron, E.F. 1984. *Mental training for peak performance.* New York: Sports Science Associates.

Gibala, M.J., MacDougall, J.D., Tarnopolsky, M.A., Stauber, W.T., and Elorriaga, A. 1995. Changes in human skeletal muscle ultrastructure and force production after acute resistance exercise. *Journal of Applied Physiology*, *78* (2): 702–708.

Goldberg, A.L., Etlinger, J.D., Goldspink, D.F., and Jablecki, C. 1975. Mechanism of work-induced hypertrophy of skeletal muscle. *Medicine and Science in Sports and Exercise*, *7*: 185–198.

Gollhofer, A., Fujitsuka, P.A., Miyashita, N., and Yashita, M. 1987. Fatigue during stretch-shortening cycle exercises: Changes in neuro-muscular activation patterns of human skeletal muscle. *Journal of Sports Medicine, 8*: 30–47.

Gollnick, P., Armstrong, R., Saubert, C., Piehl, K., and Saltin, B. 1972. Enzyme activity and fibre composition in skeletal muscle of untrained and trained men. *Journal of Applied Physiology, 33* (3): 312–319.

Gordon, F. 1967. Anatomical and biochemical adaptations of muscle to different exercises. *Journal of the American Medical Association, 201*: 755–758.

Gossen, R.E., Allingham, K., and Sale, D.G. 2001. Effect of temperature on post-tetanic potentiation in human dorsiflexor muscles. *Canadian Journal of Physiology and Pharmacology, 79*: 49–58.

Graham, T.E. 2001. Caffeine and exercise: Metabolism, endurance and performance. *Sports Medicine, 31* (11): 785–807.

Gregory, L.W. 1981. Some observations on strength training and assessment. *Journal of Sports Medicine, 21*: 130–137.

Grimby, G. 1992. Strength and power in sport. In Komi, P.V. (ed.), *Strength and power in sport.* Oxford, UK: Blackwell Scientific.

Grosser, M., and Neumeier, A. 1986. *Tecnicas de entrenamiento (Training techniques).* Barcelona: Martinez Roca.

Hainaut, K., and Duchatteau, J. 1989. Muscle fatigue: Effects of training and disuse. *Muscle & Nerve, 12*: 660–669.

Häkkinen, K. 1986. Training and detraining adaptations in electromyography. Muscle fibre and force production characteristics of human leg extensor muscle with special reference to prolonged heavy resistance and explosive-type strength training. *Studies in Sport, Physical Education and Health, 20.* Jyväskylä, Finland: University of Jyväskylä.

Häkkinen, K. 1989. Neuromuscular and hormonal adaptations during strength and power training. *Journal of Sports Medicine and Physical Fitness, 29* (1): 9–26.

Häkkinen, K. 1991. Personal communications on maximum strength development for sports. Madrid.

Häkkinen, K., and Komi, P. 1983. Electromyographic changes during strength training and detraining. *Medicine and Science in Sports and Exercise, 15*: 455–460.

Harre, D. (Ed.). 1982. *Trainingslehre.* Berlin: Sportverlag.

Hartmann, J., and Tünnemann, H. 1988. *Fitness and strength training.* Berlin: Sportverlag.

Hay, J.G. 1993. *The biomechanics of sports techniques.* Englewood Cliffs, NJ: Prentice Hall.

Hellebrand, F., and Houtz, S. 1956. Mechanism of muscle training in man: Experimental demonstration of the overload principle. *Physical Therapy Review, 36*: 371–383.

Hennig, R., and Lomo, T. 1987. Gradation of force output in normal fast and slow muscle of the rat. *Acta Physiologica Scandinavica, 130*: 133–142.

Hettinger, T. 1966. *Isometric muscle training.* Stuttgart: Georg Thieme Verlag.

Hettinger, T., and Müler, E. 1953. Muskelleistung and muskel training. *Arbeitsphysiologie, 15*: 111–126.

Hickson, R.C., Dvorak, B.A., Corostiaga, T.T., and Foster, C. 1988. Strength training and performance in endurance-trained subjects. *Medicine and Science in Sports and Exercise, 20* (2) (Suppl.): 586.

Hoff, J., Gran, A., and Helgerud, J. 2002. Maximal strength training improves aerobic endurance performance. *Scandinavian Journal of Medicine Science and Sport, 12* (5): 288–295.

Hortobagyi, T., Hill, J., Houmard, A., Fraser, D., Lambert, J., and Israel, G. 1996. Adaptive responses to muscle lengthening and shortening in humans. *Journal of Applied Physiology, 80* (3): 765–772.

Houmard, J.A. 1991. Impact of reduced training on performance in endurance athletes. *Sports Medicine, 12* (6): 380–393.

Howard, J.D., Ritchie, M.R., Gater, D.A., Gater, D.R., and Enoka, R.M. 1985. Determining factors of strength: Physiological foundations. *National Strength and Conditioning Journal, 7* (6): 16–21.

Israel, S. 1972. *The acute syndrome of detraining.* Berlin: GDR National Olympic Committee 2: 30–35.

Jackson, C.G., Dickinson, A.L., and Ringel, S.P. 1990. Skeletal muscle fiber area alterations in two opposing modes of resistance-exercise training in the same individual. *European Journal of Applied Physiology and Occupational Physiology, 61* (1–2): 37–41.

Jacobs, I., Esbornsson, M., Sylven, C., Holm, I., and Jansson, E. 1987. Sprint training effects on muscle myoglobin, enzymes, fibre types, and blood lactate. *Medicine and Science in Sports and Exercise, 19* (4): 368–374.

Kanehisa, J., and Miyashita, M. 1983. Effect of isometric and isokinetic muscle training on static strength and dynamic power. *European Journal of Applied Physiology, 50*: 365–371.

Karlsson, J., and Saltin, B. 1971. Diet, muscle glycogen and endurance performance. *Journal of Applied Physiology*, *31* (2): 203–206.

Komi, P., Rusko, H., Vos, J., and Vihko, V. 1977. Anaerobic performance capacity in athletes. *Acta Physiologica Scandinavica*, *100*: 107–114.

Komi, P.V., and Bosco, C. 1978. Utilization of stored elastic energy in leg extensor muscles by men and women. *Medicine and Science in Sport and Exercise*, *10* (4): 261–265.

Komi, P.V., and Buskirk, E.R. 1972. Effect of eccentric and concentric muscle conditioning on tension and electrical activity of human muscle. *Ergonomics*, *15* (4): 417–434.

Kugler, A., Kruger-Franke, M., Reininger, S., Trouillier, H.H., and Rosemeyer, B. 1996. Muscular imbalance and shoulder pain in volleyball attackers. *British Journal of Sports Medicine*, *30* (3): 256–259.

Kuipers, H., and Keizer, H.A. 1988. Overtraining in elite athletes: Review and directions for the future. *Sports Medicine*, *6*: 79–92.

Lange, L. 1919. *Über functionelle anpassung.* Berlin: Springer Verlag.

Latash, M.L. 1998. *Neurophysiological basis of movement.* Champaign IL: Human Kinetics.

Laubach, L.L. 1976. Comparative muscle strength of men and women: A review of the literature. *Aviation, Space, and Environmental Medicine*, *47*: 534–542.

Lephart, S.M., Ferris, C.M., Riemann, B.L., Myers, J.B., and Fu, F.H. 2002. Gender differences in strength and lower extremity kinematics during landing. *Clinical Orthopedic*, *402*: 162–169.

Logan, G.A. 1960. *Differential applications of resistance and resulting strength measured at varying degrees of knee flexion.* Doctoral dissertation, USC, Los Angeles, CA.

MacDougall, J.D., Gibala, M.J., Tarnopolsky, M.A., MacDonald, J.R., Interisano, S.A., and Yarasheski, K.E. 1995. The time course for elevated muscle protein synthesis following heavy resistance exercise. *Canadian Journal of Applied Physiology*, *20* (4): 480–486.

MacDougall, J.D., Sale, D., Jacobs, I., Garner, S., Moroz, D., and Dittmer, D. 1987. Concurrent strength and endurance training do not impede gains in $\dot{V}O_2$max. *Medicine and Science in Sports and Exercise*, *19* (2): 588.

MacDougall, J.D., Sale, D.G., Elder, G., and Sutton, J.R. 1976. Ultrastructural properties of human skeletal muscle following heavy resistance training and immobilization. *Medicine and Science in Sports and Exercise*, *8* (1): 72.

MacDougall, J.D., Sale, D.G., Moroz, J.R., Elder, G.C.B., Sutton, J.R., and Howald, H. 1979. Mitochondrial volume density in human skeletal muscle following heavy resistance training. *Medicine and Science in Sports and Exercise*, *11* (2): 264–266.

MacDougall, J.D., Tuxen, D., Sale, D.G., Moroz, J.R., and Sutton, J.R. 1985. Arterial blood pressure response to heavy resistance exercise. *Journal of Applied Physiology*, *58* (3): 785–790.

MacDougall, J.D., Ward, G.R., Sale, D.G., and Sutton, J.R. 1977. Biochemical adaptation of human skeletal muscle to heavy resistance training and immobilization. *Journal of Applied Physiology*, *43* (4): 700–703.

Marsden, C., Meadows, J.F., and Merton, P.A. 1971. Isolated single motor units in human muscle and their rate of discharge during maximal voluntary effort. *Journal of Physiology* (London) 217: 12P–13P.

Mathews, D.K., and Fox, E.L. 1976. *The physiological basis of physical education and athletics.* Philadelphia: Saunders.

Matsuda, J.J., Zernicke, R.F., Vailn, A.C., Pedrinin, V.A., Pedrini-Mille, A., and Maynard, J.A. 1986. Structural and mechanical adaptation of immature bone to strenuous exercises. *Journal of Applied Physiology*, *60* (6): 2028–2034.

Maughan, R.J., Goodburn, R., Griffin, J., Irani, M., Kirwan, J.P., Leiper, J.B., MacLaren, D.P., McLatchie, G., Tsintsas, K., and Williams, C. 1993. Fluid replacement in sport and exercise—A consensus statement. *British Journal of Sports Medicine*, *27* (1): 34–35.

McDonagh, M.J.N., and Davies, C.T.M. 1984. Adaptive response of mammalian skeletal muscle to exercise with high loads. *European Journal of Applied Physiology*, *52*: 139–155.

McLester, J.R. 1997. Muscle contraction and fatigue. The role of adenosine 5-diphosphate and inorganic phosphate. *Sports Medicine*, *23* (5): 287–305.

Micheli, L.J. 1988. Strength training in the youth athletes. In E.W. Brown and C.E. Branta (eds.), *Competitive sports for children and youth* (pp. 99–105). Champaign, IL: Human Kinetics.

Morgan, R.E., and Adamson, G.T. 1959. *Circuit weight training.* London: G. Bell and Sons.

Moritani, T. 1992. Time course of adaptations during strength and power training. In P.V. Komi (ed.), *Strength and power in sport* (pp. 266–278). Champaign, IL: Human Kinetics.

Nelson, A.G., Arnall, D.A., Loy, S.F., Silvester, L.J., and Conlee, R.K. 1990. Consequences of combining strength and endurance training regimens. *Physical Therapy, 70* (5): 287–294.

O'Leary, D.D., Hope, K., and Sale, D.G. 1998. Influence of gender on post-tetanic potentiation in human dorsiflexors. *Canadian Journal of Physiology and Pharmacology, 76*: 772–779.

Ozolin, N.G. 1971. *Athlete's training system for competition.* Moscow: Phyzkultura i sports.

Piehl, K. 1974. Time course for refilling of glycogen stores in human muscle fibres following exercise-induced glycogen depletion. *Acta Physiologica Scandinavica, 90*: 297–302.

Pincivero, D.M., Lephart, S.M., and Karunakara, R.G. 1997. Effects of rest interval on isokinetic strength and functional performance after short-term high intensity training. *British Journal of Sports Medicine, 31* (3): 229-34.

Powers, S.K., Lawler, J., Dodd, S., Tulley, R., Landry, G., and Wheeler, K. 1990. Fluid replacement drinks during high intensity exercise: Effects on minimizing exercise-induced disturbances in homeostasis. *European Journal of Applied Physiology Occupational Physiology, 60* (1): 54–60.

Prentice, W.J. 1990. *Rehabilitation techniques in sports medicine.* Toronto: Times Mirror/Mosby College.

Raglin, J.S. 1992. Anxiety and sport performance. *Exercise Sports Science Review, 20*: 243–274.

Ralston, H.J., Rolissan, M.J., Inman, F.J., Close, J.R., and Feinstein, B. 1949. Dynamic feature of human isolated voluntary muscle in isometric and free contraction. *Journal of Applied Physiology, 1*: 526–533.

Sahlin, K. 1986. Metabolic changes limiting muscular performance. *Biochemistry of Exercise, 16*: 86–98.

Sale, D. 1986. Neural adaptation in strength and power training. In L. Jones, L.N. McCartney, and A. McConias (eds.), *Human muscle power* (pp. 289–304). Champaign, IL: Human Kinetics.

Sale, D.G., MacDougall, J.D., Jakobs, I., and Garner, S. 1990. Interaction between concurrent strength and endurance training. *Journal of Applied Physiology, 68* (1): 260–270.

Sale, D. (1992). Neural adaptations to strength training. In P.V. Komi (ed), *Strength and power in sport.* (pp. 249–265). Oxford: Blackwell Scientific.

Schmidtbleicher, D. 1984. *Sportliches Krafttraining.* Berlin: Jung, Haltong, und Bewegung bie Menchen.

Schmidtbleicher, D. 1992. Training for power events. In P.V. Komi (ed.), *Strength and power in sport* (pp. 381–395). Oxford, UK: Blackwell Scientific.

Scholich, M. 1992. *Circuit training for all sports.* Edited by P. Klavora. Toronto: Sports Books.

Soderman, K., Wener, S., Pietila, T., Engstrom. B., and Alfredson, H. 2000. Balance board training: Prevention of traumatic injuries of the lower extremities in female soccer players? A perspective randomized intervention study. *Knee Surgery, Sports Traumatology, Arthroscopy, 8* (6): 356–363.

Staron, R.S., Hagerman, F.C., and Hikida, R.S. 1981. The effects of detraining on an elite power lifter. *Journal of Neurological Sciences, 51*: 247–257.

Stone, M.H., and O'Bryant, H.S. 1984. *Weight training: A scientific approach.* Minneapolis, MN: Burgess.

Terjung, R.L., and Hood, D.A. 1986. Biochemical adaptations in skeletal muscle induced by exercise training. Cited in D.K. Layman (ed.), *Nutrition and aerobic exercise* (pp. 8–27). Washington, DC: American Chemical Society.

Tesch, P. 1980. Muscle fatigue in man. *Acta Physiologica Scandinavica Supplementum, 480*: 3–40.

Tesch, P., Sjödon, B., Thorstensson, A., and Karlsson, J. 1978. Muscle fatigue and its relation to lactate accumulation and LDH activity in man. *Acta Physiologica Scandinavica, 103*: 413–420.

Tesch, P.A., and Karlsson, J. 1985. Muscle fibre types and size in trained and untrained muscles of elite athletes. *Journal of Applied Physiology, 59*: 1716–1720.

Tesch, P.A., Dudley, G.A., Duvoisin, M.R., Hather, M., and Harris, R.T. 1990. Force and EMG signal patterns during repeated bouts of concentric or eccentric muscle actions. *Acta Physiologica Scandinavica, 138*: 263–271.

Thacker, S.B., Stroup, D.F., Branche, C.M., Gilchrist, J., Goodman, R.A., and Proter Kelling, E. 2003. Prevention of knee injuries in sports. A systematic review of literature. *Journal of Sports Medicine and Physical Fitness, 43* (2): 165–179.

Thorstensson, A. 1977. Observations on strength training and detraining. *Acta Physiologica Scandinavica, 100*: 491–493.

Thorstensson, A., Larsson, L., Tesch, P., and Karlsson, J. 1977. Muscle strength and fibre composition in athletes and sedentary men. *Medicine and Science in Sports and Exercise, 9*: 26–30.

Tipton, K.D., and Wolfe, R.R. 2004. Protein and amino acid for athletes. *Journal of Sports Science, 22* (1): 65–79.

Van Cutsem, M., Duchateau, J., and Hainaut, K. 1998. Changes in single motor unit behaviour contribute to the increase in contraction speed after dynamic training in humans. *Journal of Physiology, 513*: 295–305.

Verkhoshanski, Y. 1969. Perspectives in the improvement of speed-strength preparation of jumpers. *Yessis Review of Soviet Physical Education and Sports, 4* (2): 28–29.

Verhoshansky, Y.V. 1997. The path to a scientific theory and methodology of sports training. Teoriya i Practika Fizicheskoi Kultury.

Wade, A.J., Broadhead, M.W., Cady, E.B., Llewelyn, M.E., Tong, H.N., and Newham, D.J. 2000. Influence of muscle temperature during fatiguing work with the first dorsal interosseous muscle in man: A 31P-NMR spectroscopy study. *European Journal of Applied Physiology, 81*(3): 203–209.

Wathen, D. 1994. Agonist-antagonist ratios for slow concentric isokinetic movements. In T.R. Baechle (ed.), *Essentials of strength training and conditioning*. Champaign, IL: Human Kinetics.

Welsh, R.S., Davis, J.M., Burke, J.R., and Williams, H.G. 2002. Carbohydrates and physical/mental performance during intermittent exercise to fatigue. *Medicine In Science Sports and Exercise, 34* (4): 723–731.

Wester, J.U., Jespersen, S.M., Nielsen, K.D., and Neumann L. 1996. Wobble board training after partial sprains of the lateral ligaments of the ankle: A prospective randomized study. *Journal of Orthopaedic & Sports Physical Therapy, 23* (5): 332–336.

Wigernaes, I., Hostmark, A.T., Stromme, S.B., Kierulf, P., and Birkeland, K. 2001. Active recovery and post-exercise while blood cell count, free fatty acids and hormones in endurance athletes. *European Journal of Applied Physiology, 84* (4): 358–366.

Willems, T., Witvrouw, E., Verstuyft, J., Vaes, P., and Clercq, D. D. 2002. Proprioception and muscle strength in subjects with a history of ankle sprains and chronic instability. *Journal of Athletic Training, 37* (4): 487–493.

Wilmore, J.H., and Costill, D.L. 1988. Training for sport and activity. In *The physiological basis of the conditioning process*. Dubuque, IA: Brown.

Wilmore J.H., Parr, R.B., Girandola, R.N., Ward, P., Vodak, P.A., Barstow, T.J., Pipes, T.V., Romero, G.T., and Leslie, P. 1978. Physiological alterations consequent to circuit weight training. *Medicine and Science in Sports and Exercise, 10*: 79–84.

Wilson, G., Newton, R., Murphy, A., and Humphries, B. 1993. The optimal load for the development of dynamic athletic performance. *Medicine Science Sports and Exercise, 25* (11): 1279–1286.

Wojitys, E.M., Huston, L J., Schock, H.J., Boylan, J.P., and Ashton-Miller, J.A. 2003. Gender differences in muscular protection of the knee in torsion in size-matched athletes. *The Journal of Bone and Joint Surgery America, 85-A* (5): 782–789.

Woo, S.L.-Y., An, K.-N., Arnoczky, S.P., Wayne, J.S., Fithian, D.C., and Myers, B.S. (1994). Anatomy, biology and biomechanics of tendon, ligament, and meniscus. In S.R. Simon (ed.), *Orthopaedic basic science* (pp.45–87). Park Ridge, IL: American Academy of Orthopaedic Surgeons.

Wright, J.E. 1980. Anabolic steroids and athletics. In R.S. Hutton and D.I. Miller (eds.), *Exercise and sport sciences reviews*: 149–202.

Yessis, M. 1990. *Soviet training methods*. New York: Barnes & Noble.

Zanon, S. 1977. Consideration for determining some parametric values of the relations between maximum isometric relative strength and elastic relative strength for planning and controlling the long jumper's conditioning training. *Athletic Coach, 11* (4): 14–20.

Zeller, B.L., McCrory, J.L., Kibler, W.B., and Uhl, T.L. 2003. Differences in kinematics and electromyographical activity between men and women during the single-legged squat. *American Journal of Sports Medicine, 31* (3): 449–456.

Zijdewind, I., and Kernell, D. 2001. Bilateral interactions during contractions of intrinsic hand muscles. *Journal of Neurophysiology, 85* (5): 1907–1913.

Index

Note: The italicized *f* and *t* following page numbers refer to figures and tables, respectively.

About the Authors

Tudor Bompa is recognized worldwide as the foremost expert on periodization training. He developed the concept of "periodization of strength" in Romania in 1963 as he helped the eastern bloc countries rise to dominance in the athletic world. Since then, periodization training has become a standard method for conditioning champion athletes. Bompa has proven his system time and again, using it to train many world-class athletes, including 11 Olympic medalists.

A professor emeritus at York University in Toronto, Bompa has authored several books on physical conditioning, including *Serious Strength Training, Periodization: Theory and Methodology of Training, Total Training for Young Champions, Training the Team Sports Athletes,* and *Power Training for Sport: Plyometrics for Maximum Power Development,* as well as numerous articles on the subject. His work has been translated into 18 languages, including Chinese, Russian, French, Spanish, and Italian, and he has made presentations on training theories, planning, and periodization in more than 35 countries. His publications, conferences, and ideas are highly regarded and enthusiastically sought after by many top professional athletes and training specialists.

Bompa currently offers a certification program in training, planning, and periodization called the Tudor Bompa Training System. The program is designed for personal trainers, instructors, coaches, athletes, and educators. For more information visit www.tudorbompa.com or e-mail tudor.bompa@sympatico.ca.

Bompa lives in Sharon, Ontario, Canada.

Michael Carrera is a health and lifestyle expert, published author, and international presenter who currently serves as vice president of exercise planning and development for Truestar Health, a revolutionary Web-based health and fitness site. A specialist in the field of periodization and fitness planning, Carrera is responsible for designing a unique, phase-based circuit training system for the Truestar for Women Nutrition & Fitness Centers.

As a leading exercise expert, Carrera has developed and implemented corporate wellness programs and health management strategies for many large North American companies. He holds a masters degree in exercise science and a specialized honors degree in kinesiology and health science. Nationally certified as a professional fitness and lifestyle consultant (PFLC), he also holds a certificate in fitness assessment and exercise counseling. For more information about Carrera, visit www.planbhealth.com

Carrera resides in Toronto, Ontario, Canada, with his wife, Sandra, and their son.

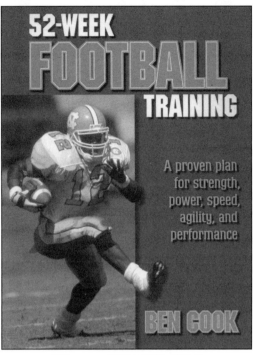

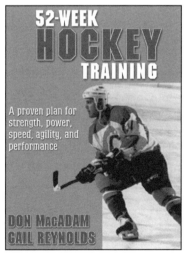